Youth and the Law: New Approaches to Criminal Justice and Child Protection

SECOND EDITION

Laurence M. Olivo, Ralph Cotter, and Rebecca Bromwich

2007
Emond Montgomery Publications Ltd.
Toronto, Canada

Emond Montgomery Publications Limited
60 Shaftesbury Avenue
Toronto ON M4T 1A3
http://www.emp.ca

Printed in Canada.

We acknowledge the financial support of the Government of Canada through the Book Publishing Industry Development Program (BPIDP) for our publishing activities.

Statistics Canada information is used with the permission of Statistics Canada. Users are forbidden to copy this material and/or redisseminate the data, in an original or modified form, for commercial purposes, without the expressed permission of Statistics Canada. Information on the availability of the wide range of data from Statistics Canada can be obtained from Statistics Canada's Regional Offices, its World Wide Web site at http://www.statcan.ca, and its toll-free access number 1-800-263-1136.

The events and characters depicted in this book are fictitious. Any similarity to actual persons, living or dead, is purely coincidental.

Acquisitions editor: Jennifer McPhee
Marketing manager: Christine Davidson
Copy editor: Anita Levin
Supervising editor: Jim Lyons, WordsWorth Communications
Production editor: Cindy Fujimoto, WordsWorth Communications
Proofreader: Nancy Ennis, WordsWorth Communications
Text designer and typesetter: Tara Wells, WordsWorth Communications
Indexer: Paula Pike, WordsWorth Communications
Cover designer: John Vegter

Library and Archives Canada Cataloguing in Publication

Olivo, Laurence M., 1946-
    Youth and the law : new approaches to criminal justice and child protection / Laurence M. Olivo, Ralph Cotter and Rebecca Bromwich. — 2nd ed.

ISBN 978-1-55239-210-2

    1. Juvenile justice, Administration of—Canada—Textbooks.   2. Juvenile delinquency—Canada—Textbooks.   I. Cotter, Ralph, 1964-   II. Bromwich, Rebecca   III. Title.

KE9445.O55 2007   364.360971   C2006-906607-8
KF9780.ZA2.N374

To Joyce, as always
— L.M.O.

To Wendy, Emily, and Abigail
— R.C.

For Helaina and Andromeda
— R.B.

Contents

Preface ix

About the Authors xi

PART I

The Roots of Youth Criminality: Patterns, Motivations, and Prevention

CHAPTER 1
Youth Crime: Perceptions and Realities 3

Introduction 3

The Social Meaning of "Youth" 4

Historical Perceptions of Youth Crime 6

Contemporary Perceptions of Youth Crime 6

Emerging Factors in Contemporary
    Perceptions of Youth Crime 8

The Reality of Youth Crime: Collecting and
    Analyzing Crime Data 9

Police Perceptions 20

Conclusions: Is Youth Crime on the Increase? 20

Chapter Summary 21

Key Terms 22

Notes 23

Exercises and Review 24

CHAPTER 2
Youth Crime: Patterns and Causes 29

What Types of Crime Do Youth Commit? 29

Theories of Youth Crime 34

Causes of Youth Crime 36

Chapter Summary 43

Key Terms 43

Notes 43

Exercises and Review 45

CHAPTER 3
Prevention and Rehabilitation Programs to Control Youth Crime: What Works? 51

Some Concepts Underlying Prevention and
    Rehabilitation Approaches 52

Prevention and Rehabilitation Programs:
    What Works and What Does Not 53

Does Anything Work? 61

Chapter Summary 63

Key Terms 63

Notes 64

Exercises and Review 65

PART II

Legislative Approaches: Outside the Justice System

CHAPTER 4
The Child and Family Services Act 73

Introduction 74

Purposes of the CFSA 74

Delivery of Services 75

Consensual Services 75

Duty to Report Abuse or Neglect 76

Child Protection Proceedings 78

Abuse or Neglect Offences 80

Detention of Adolescents 81

Rights of Children in a Residential, Detention,
    or Custody Facility 82

Children Suffering from a Mental Disorder 83

The Economic Issue 84

Chapter Summary 85

Key Terms 85

Notes 85

Exercises and Review 86

CHAPTER 5
Youth and Provincial Offences 91

Introduction 91

Regulations Everywhere 92

Intent Standards 92

The Provincial Offences Act 93

Other Provincial Legislation 96

Chapter Summary 98

Key Terms 98

Notes 98

Exercises and Review 99

PART III
Legislative Approaches:
Inside the Justice System

CHAPTER 6
Early Initiatives: The Juvenile Delinquents Act
and the Young Offenders Act 103

Introduction 103

Background to the Juvenile Delinquents Act 104

The Juvenile Delinquents Act 105

Criticisms of the Juvenile Delinquents Act 106

Legislative Reform: Passage of the Young
    Offenders Act 107

Purposes of the Young Offenders Act 108

Criticisms of the Young Offenders Act 109

Criticisms of the Youth Criminal Justice Act 110

Chapter Summary 111

Key Terms 111

Notes 111

Exercises and Review 113

CHAPTER 7
The Youth Criminal Justice Act:
Principles and Structure 119

Introduction 119

Principles and Objectives of the Youth Criminal
    Justice Act 120

Structure of the Youth Criminal Justice Act 121

Chapter Summary 128

Key Terms 128

Notes 128

Exercises and Review 129

CHAPTER 8
Police Procedures and the Youthful Suspect:
Extrajudicial Measures, Charging, Arrest,
and Interviewing 133

Introduction 134

Police and the Young Suspect: First Contacts 134

The Admissibility of Youth Statements 141

Searches and Charter Rights at the Time
    of Arrest 143

Questioning Upon and After Arrest 143

Chapter Summary 151

Key Terms 152

Notes 152

Exercises and Review 153

CHAPTER 9
The Pre-Trial Period 157

Guidelines for Pre-Trial Detention 158

The Show-Cause Hearing 161

Judicial Interim Release 162

Pre-Trial Detention in Practice Under the YCJA . . . 163

Chapter Summary 164

Key Terms 164

Notes 165

Exercises and Review 165

CHAPTER 10
The Trial of a Young Accused 169

Jurisdiction of the Youth Court 169

No Transfer to Adult Court 170

The Youthful Accused's Right to Counsel 170

Youth Justice Committees and Conferences 172

Diversion to Extrajudicial Measures
    and Sanctions 173

Pleas in Youth Justice Court 174

Preliminary Motions 174

Youth Court Trial Process 175

Appeals 176

Chapter Summary 176

Key Terms 176

Notes 176

Exercises and Review 177

CHAPTER 11
Sentencing 179

Introduction 179

Purpose and Principles of Sentencing 180

Limits on Custodial Sentences 182

Pre-Sentence Reports 183

Victim Impact Statements 184

Sentences in Youth Justice Court 184

The Imposition of Adult Sentences 187

Over-Age Transfer 191

Reintegration into the Community 191

Termination of a Youth Sentence 192

YCJA Sentencing Principles as Applied So Far:
   A Critical Assessment 192

Chapter Summary 193

Key Terms 193

Notes 194

Exercises and Review 195

PART IV

**Emerging Trends in the Youth
Criminal Justice System**

CHAPTER 12
**Restorative Justice and the
Young Offender** 201

Introduction 201

Restorative Justice and the Young Offender 202

Restorative Justice and the YCJA 203

Restorative Justice: A Form of ADR 204

Interest-Based Mediation 204

Sentencing Circles 205

Family Group Conferencing 205

Criticisms of Restorative Justice/ADR 206

Restorative Justice Under the YCJA:
   A Critical Assessment 206

Chapter Summary 208

Key Terms 208

Notes 208

Exercises and Review 209

CHAPTER 13
**Emerging Issues and Youth Crime:
Changing Social Realities and
Public Perceptions** 213

Introduction 213

Gangs and Guns 214

Changing Gender Roles 215

Economic Globalization 218

Technological Changes 218

Demographic Patterns 220

International Tensions 220

Chapter Summary 221

Key Terms 222

Notes 222

Exercises and Review 224

APPENDIX
Youth Criminal Justice Act 227

GLOSSARY 277

INDEX 281

Preface

The first edition of this book was published in 2001, shortly before the *Youth Criminal Justice Act* (YCJA) came into force. Since then, a great deal has changed. The drafters of the Act insisted that the new legislation would address issues of overincarceration and ensure that serious violent and repeat offenders would be held accountable. Did the YCJA actually do what its drafters said it would? At the time the first edition of this book was written, we, like the drafters, could only guess how the Act would actually work. We now know a good deal more about the YCJA's strengths and weaknesses, and we know much more about how the Act works in practice. In spite of the placating political rhetoric that ushered in the YCJA, the public remains concerned about youth violence and crime. While it could be argued that the YCJA has reduced the court's use of incarceration at both the pre-trial and sentencing stages, the use of "alternative to custody" and "diversion" programs varies across jurisdictions, and is limited primarily to major urban centres, because these programs depend on the availability of local community services. This new edition considers these issues as well as other criticisms raised against aspects of the implementation of the YCJA. We also assess procedural and policy changes that have occurred since the Act came into force.

Law and public policy are constantly changing. This edition aims to provide a realistic account of their current state. The book builds on the strengths of the original text while incorporating insights and examples that have been gained from real cases and several years of experience with the YCJA. Emond Montgomery Publications once again has consulted with key players in the youth justice and child protection system to ensure the accuracy of the second edition.

We have sought to meet the high standards set by the first edition, and we encourage readers to explore and consider the future direction of youth justice in Canada.

Laurence M. Olivo
Ralph Cotter
Rebecca Bromwich

About the Authors

Laurence M. Olivo, BA, LLB, MA, lawyer, educator, and writer with many years of university and college teaching experience, researched and wrote part I, and developed the book's format for chapter content and exercises.

Ralph Cotter, BaSc. (Hons.), LLM, has 10 years of experience as a probation officer and is now a provincial prosecutor with the Ontario Ministry of the Attorney General. He teaches Youth in Conflict with the Law at Conestoga College, and provided an insider's understanding of the youth criminal justice system and valuable consultation with respect to pre-trial, trial, and sentencing procedures.

Rebecca Bromwich, BA (Hons.), LLB, LLM, practising lawyer, lecturer at the University of Western Ontario Faculty of Law, and professor at Fanshawe College, provided a legal academic and practitioner's perspective in updating and developing this new edition.

PART I

The Roots of Youth Criminality: Patterns, Motivations, and Prevention

CHAPTER 1

Youth Crime: Perceptions and Realities

■ CHAPTER OBJECTIVES

After completing this chapter, you should be able to:

- Understand social and historical factors that contributed to the creation of adolescence as an age category.

- Understand that youth crime has both emerging and longstanding dimensions.

- Critically assess media portrayals of youth crime and understand sources and reasons for public anxiety about youth crime.

- Understand how the uniform crime report system and the self-report studies system work.

- Identify the strengths and weaknesses of each report system.

- Conduct an elementary analysis of uniform crime report statistics to identify apparent trends and patterns of youth crime and limitations in the data that require qualifications of any conclusions drawn.

Introduction

For a variety of reasons, adding the adjective "youth" to any media report of a violent incident introduces an extra measure of shock value into bad news. Just as we are appalled and saddened to hear that a victim of violence was "a mere child," we are disturbed to read that a violent act was committed by a young person.

As former youths, and perhaps as parents of youths, our expectations of how the young should behave are coloured by personal and family experience. Whether we view youth as vulnerable and innocent or as threatening and troublesome, or some combination of both, accounts of youthful involvement in violence confirm or challenge our personal beliefs. And the further we grow from our own younger selves, the less we remember about what it is like to be a young person in an adult world. Much fear is rooted in misunderstanding, and as we struggle to understand youth, or "today's youth," it is easy to become concerned about reports of their apparently increasing propensity for criminal behaviour.

Are offences by young people really on the rise? As compared with which period(s) in time? And what about violent offences as a subgroup—has there been any significant change in the rate of youth violence? It is perhaps telling that these questions are the source of continued debate, or that something as apparently straightforward as the crime rate escapes reliable measure.

If we hope to effectively measure the success of legislation, programs, and procedures designed to punish, control, or prevent youth criminality, or to improve the lives of youth generally, we must grapple with these unresolved questions. We must accept the limitations of the data available to us, rationally consider the extent to which forces such as the media distort that already fragile data, and come to our own informed conclusions. It is only after we have completed this process that we can make a credible assessment of current initiatives and offer suggestions for how they might be improved.

The Social Meaning of "Youth"

Before we can understand perceptions and realities of youth crime, we need to appreciate the transitional phase between childhood and adulthood that we describe as youth or adolescence. Before the 18th century, in Western civilization, the concept of childhood was thought of very differently from the way we think about it today. The idea of the teenage years as a transitional stage from childhood to adulthood was simply beyond contemplation. In fact, "adolescence" was not a term in general use, outside scientific writing, until the beginning of the 20th century.[1] Children entered the adult world abruptly, and at a much earlier age than they do today. The assumption of adult status began for some aspects of life as early as age 6 or 7. With the exception of the children of the very wealthy, young children were often apprenticed, sent out to work, or otherwise expected to be economically productive. Most children were confirmed as full-status members of their religion, were generally integrated into society alongside adults, and participated fully in social life. In effect, they were treated as small-sized adults. Their participation might differ in some respects from that of full-sized adults, but the differences in participation were often based on experience, size, and strength rather than on some notion of mental development and maturity. Thus, an 8-year-old apprenticed to a blacksmith might not be expected to shape ironwork on an anvil, but that would be because he had not learned the skill and because he was not strong enough, not because he was a child. An examination of European cultural history indicates that children dressed like adults and participated with adults in marriage, sex, games, religious life, social events, work, and life in general. There is no evidence before the 18th century that children were segregated from the rest of the population once they were past infancy.

The fact that children were thought of as the same as adults, only smaller, meant that they received the same treatment—including equal treatment before the law. Young offenders, like old ones, were presumed to know the difference between right and wrong, and if they chose illegal behaviour, they suffered the same consequences as older offenders. Thus, a 10-year-old thief might suffer the same punishment as a 30-year-old thief. Because there was virtually no meaningful distinction between wrongdoers on the basis of age, there was no legal concept of "juvenile delinquent" or "young offender" requiring differential treatment. Nor was there a perception of young people being particularly violent or threatening as a group. People before the 18th century would have been puzzled by the discussions and fears about "youth crime" that preoccupy newspaper editorial writers and politicians today.

Beginning in the 18th century, however, several changes in cultural outlook and social and economic organization resulted in the removal of the young from the adult sphere and the creation or construction of an age-based social category that we call adolescents or teenagers. These changes did not happen with reference to all children equally; white children of members of the upper classes were afforded the protected status of childhood long before the young of the less fortunate.

First, through the writings of thinkers of the **Enlightenment**, an appreciation developed in the 18th century that children go through a psychosocial developmental process over time in which they mature physically, intellectually, and emotionally into young adults. Childhood requires that a person be nurtured and protected well beyond infancy, and that he or she be generally treated as a child for a much longer period than had been customary. In this view, a 7-year-old was an immature, developing child, not a fully mature, though small, adult.

Second, the construction and segregation of an age category consisting of adolescents arose as a result of institutional changes brought about by the Industrial Revolution at the end of the 18th century.[2] As one commentator put it, "The adolescent was invented at the same time as the steam engine."[3] For the first time, a group of persons in a particular age group were seen to have specific attributes that set them off from both small children and older adults. One cause of this change was a growing professional middle class engaging in complicated occupations that took a long time to master. Before mastering a profession, it was necessary to master a cluster of skills. To do this effectively, the professional classes made use of schools—particularly boarding schools—to aid in the transition to trained professional and, incidentally, full adult status. In England, for example, the elite public schools (actually private boarding schools) took on the job of training and **socializing** children of the middle and upper classes, keeping them segregated from adults and young children, and in the process created an age category for privileged children—adolescence.

Working-class children were also segregated, but for different reasons. As a result of the Industrial Revolution at the end of the 18th century, increased mechanization of industry led to labour surpluses and falling wages, which brought about unionization of the labour force and pressure to limit the use of cheap child and female labour. At the same time, the development of the idea of childhood as a "special" period gave rise to humanitarian efforts to protect children from the harshness and dangers of the factory system. The combined efforts of humanitarians and workers' organizations gave rise to legislation controlling and eliminating child labour. One of the effects of the elimination of child labour in factories was the creation of a large number of unemployed children in urban areas. In very little time, this group, segregated by age and deprived of a useful social role, was identified

Enlightenment
an intellectual movement characterized by rationalism and scientific inquiry as the basis for understanding the world

socialization
process whereby one learns the norms, values, and culture of the society or social group

as a class of thieves and petty criminals and as an urban social problem. Modern society now had its first juvenile delinquents—mostly males and mostly committing property offences. The creation of a class of delinquents was blunted somewhat in the middle of the 19th century by the gradual growth of the movement for free, public education. Thus, by the 1870s in Europe and North America, working-class children found themselves removed from a world where they were integrated with adults and segregated, supervised, and socialized into being good citizens in schools. While free public education was seen as a way of spreading knowledge and skills in a society of free individuals, it was also seen as a way of disciplining and controlling the large number of "street urchins" in the cities and limiting the crime they were believed to cause.[4]

Historical Perceptions of Youth Crime

While problems with youth crime are often seen as urgent contemporary crises, youth's offending behaviour has a recorded history in Canada that goes back to the 19th century. Like European cities, Canadian cities experienced industrialization and similar problems with unemployed young males meeting economic needs by committing property crimes. Initially, because Canada was primarily an agricultural country, the problem did not appear to be as severe as it was in more industrialized countries. But it became more so as Canada become a dumping ground for the orphans and street youth of Britain's cities, starting in the 1860s and continuing into the 1920s. Between 75,000 to 90,000 children were "exported" to Canada in this period, largely as part of a humanitarian effort to save destitute children by placing them on Canadian farms. However, these children were perceived by many in Canada as a source of the spreading of criminal values and criminality generally, because of their previous history and because they were thought to be of "inferior stock," a characteristic they were perceived to share with the children of poor, non-British immigrants.[5]

Contemporary Perceptions of Youth Crime

An examination of contemporary perceptions of youth crime reveals concerns that would have been familiar and worrisome to previous generations. It also reveals some new issues and concerns.

There is no question that people are concerned about crime in general and youth crime in particular. Opinion polls consistently reveal that the public is very concerned with crime, particularly violent crime. A large part of this concern and anxiety is focused on youth crime. Statistically, most of us are never the victims of youth crime, so our perceptions of youth crime often come from somewhere other than our own experience. For most of us the primary source of information is the media. Newspaper, television, and radio reports feature a constant stream of stories about violence in schools, swarmings, home invasions, robberies, assaults, and addictions to crack and other drugs. Accompanying these accounts are the comments of editorial writers, politicians, police officials, social workers, and other commentators. The alleged increase in youth crime is attributed to, for example, too much leisure time, working mothers, the collapse of "family values," widespread drug use, heavy metal and rap music, violence on television, and a host of other phenomena.

But is there more youth crime than previously? Are the types of crimes more vicious and serious than they used to be? Are youth gangs on the increase? Is the fabric of society under more stress as a result of youth crime? Consider these newspaper reports:

- Student shoots teacher in the leg.

- Another outbreak of street gang fighting has reawakened citizens to the extent of the problems that these young people present.

This kind of reporting probably sounds familiar to you. However, the shooting incident referred to occurred in 1901, on the day Queen Victoria died. It was reported on the front page of the *Toronto Globe*, although, thanks to Queen Victoria's demise, it got less space than it otherwise might have. The gang fighting incident was reported in the Toronto *Globe and Mail* in 1949.[6] It involved a gang called the "Junction Boys," whose activities included car theft, breaking and entering, liquor offences, street brawling, and inciting riots in neighbourhoods outside their own district. This behaviour was attributed to broken homes and "declining moral standards."[7] Note that this was before violent television shows, rap or heavy metal music, and crack.

Clearly, the past was not as peaceful and untroubled as we like to think, and youth crime is not new. An examination of newspaper coverage of youth behaviour from the 1950s to the early 1980s in the United Kingdom reveals similar arguments and concerns to today's. In fact, content analysis of news reports back beyond the 1950s to the Victorian era of the late 19th century reveals how unchanged are the concerns about youth crime. Some common themes emerge:

- There is a golden age, usually about 20 years previously, when young people were better behaved, the police were able to act more effectively, parents had better control over their children, family values were respected, and courts could hand out appropriate punishments.

- Current youth crime is getting worse.

- Stiffer punishments for young offenders are needed to control youth crime.[8]

Canadian studies on crime perceptions show similar results. Media reports on youth tend to exaggerate and sensationalize, often presenting atypical situations as representative of youth in general.[9] The result is a picture of youth that is distorted and misleading. This picture, in turn, affects people's perceptions. A Canadian Sentencing Commission study in the early 1990s determined that most people derived their information and views about youth from the media, in which violent crime (both in actual news reports and in drama and entertainment) was vastly over-represented. It is not surprising that the study found that the public consistently overestimated the amount of crime, the amount of violent crime, and the **recidivism** rates and underestimated the maximum penalties for offences and the actual punishments handed out to offenders.[10] A more recent study of public perceptions of youth crime by Canadian researchers Doob, Sprott, Marinos, and Varma suggest that there has been little change in public perceptions in the last 10 years—Canadians

recidivism
phenomenon of a prisoner re-offending and being sent back to prison for subsequent offences

still tend to overestimate crime rates, violent crime rates, and youth crime rates and to underestimate the severity of sentences imposed for youth crime.[11]

Emerging Factors in Contemporary Perceptions of Youth Crime

Globalization, technological changes, shifting immigration patterns, perceptions about gangs, guns, changing gender roles, and international tensions are emerging factors contributing to anti-youth sentiment on the part of the public in Canada, and so is a perception that youth crime is more of a growing problem than statistical data imply.

Globalization is increasing public perception that adolescents are prone to criminal behaviour. The development of global television news networks has led to increased coverage of violent crime, especially youth crime. We are now much more aware of incidents of violent crime by youth than we previously were. These reports make us feel closer to such crimes, fostering in the viewing public a sense that it is us, or people close to us, who have been the victim of such crimes, when really the incidents have often taken place far away and affected no one we know. Advertising campaigns orchestrated by multinational companies that specifically target youth also play a significant role in encouraging a negative attitude toward youth in the general public. Youth subcultures in First World nations have global dimensions, identifying more with, and appearing more "like," each other than their forebears in any particular place. To aging adults, these young people can seem both dangerous and disappointing.

Technological change is also playing an important role in changing the nature of youth crime. Telecommunications technology and particularly the advent of the Internet have made new kinds of crime possible worldwide. There is a technological "generation gap," and youth tend to be far more computer literate than their parents. On chat rooms, via Internet "blog" sites, and by email, people communicate with each other instantaneously around the globe. The Internet has allowed for the international organization of much activity, including criminal activity, as evidenced by the proliferation of hate group and child pornography websites. It appears that adolescents, because they are often more computer literate than older people, have become disproportionately involved in new kinds of criminal activity, such as hacking, harassment via Internet sites, the development of computer viruses, and identity theft. The Internet has also become a tool used in less innovative youth crime, such as bullying and harassment.

Low birth rates and high proportions of visible minority immigrants have, in the past few decades, changed the face of First World nations, especially among the young. Visible minority populations and populations of Aboriginal people are increasing dramatically relative to those of white people of European descent. At the same time, Canada's white European population, and particularly the "baby boom" generation, is aging. We now have a large population of young people who are visibly culturally and racially different from many adults in Canadian society. Commentators have suggested that racism and **xenophobia**, meaning a fear of strangers or the unknown, may be lurking behind today's public perceptions that we are facing a crisis of ever-increasing youth crime.

xenophobia
fear of strangers or the unknown, especially cultural and racial elements that are considered alien

Many members of the Canadian public believe that adolescent girls have become more criminally active and more prone to violent behaviour than girls were in the past. Available statistics, as is discussed elsewhere in this chapter, do not, on the whole, support this perception. What our society expects of, and accepts from, women and girls in terms of behaviour has changed markedly over the past 30 years or so. Feminist activism and legal change have altered the role of women in society. Women today are, for the most part, educated in the same manner as men and, more often than not, work outside the home. Canadian adolescent girls have come to expect equal treatment in education and under the law, and in many cases their interpersonal interactions have changed. It has become acceptable for girls and women to be more assertive. These changes can confuse and surprise the elderly and conflict with expectations of behaviour that some new Canadians bring from their own cultures of origin.

Perhaps the most significant difference between contemporary perceptions of youth crime and those of the past has to do with international politics. While the late 20th century saw the emergence of global tourism and relaxed international travel, our confidence in our safety at home and abroad has now been undermined. Repeated and systematic terrorist attacks have marred the early 21st century, most significantly those on September 11, 2001 in New York City, but also those that followed in London, England and Madrid, Spain. These attacks led to America's "war on terror" and public xenophobia about potential terrorists, particularly those perceived to be Islamic. Although no al-Qaida attacks have taken place in Canada at the time of writing, 17 individuals who were allegedly conspiring to attack targets in Ontario were arrested in June 2006. It is likely that these terrorism arrests will exacerbate public fears about alien, hostile youth living among us and increase public perceptions that youth violence in Canada is on the rise.

Emerging public perceptions and realities about youth crime will be discussed in more detail in chapter 13.

The Reality of Youth Crime: Collecting and Analyzing Crime Data

How does the perception of youth crime generated by the media actually square with the reality as revealed by official statistics and other forms of investigation? The media, politicians, and lobbyists on youth issues all resort to statistics at one time or another. As objective analysts, you need to know what kind of information is out there, how it is collected, what it shows, and what its limitations are. It is also important to know that we do not have data on every aspect of youth delinquency. We have little statistical information on lesser and symbolic forms of youth deviance. For example, we do not have data on the effect of aggressively negative rock or rap music (though we have lots of speculation). Nor do we collect crime data on the basis of race in Canada, though many writers suspect patterns exist on this basis.

In Canada, the courts and the police keep statistical records on crime in general and youth crime in particular. Since 1962, criminal incidents have been tallied by a system of **uniform crime reports**, originally developed in the United States and designed to provide comparable and consistent crime statistics. Police record two categories of crime: those detected by the police themselves and those reported to

uniform crime reports system for classifying reported incidents by type of crime, based on crime detected by police and reported by public; used by virtually all law enforcement agencies in Canada and the United States, it permits comparisons among jurisdictions and comparisons of data in any specific year with data from previous or subsequent years

them by victims and members of the public. Only about 10 percent of recorded crimes are detected by the police; the rest are reported to them by the public. Dependence on the public leads to selective reporting and statistical distortions in a variety of ways. The most obvious distortion is underreporting. Many illegal acts are never reported—victimization surveys consistently show that those surveyed know of illegal acts that were not reported. The reasons for non-reporting vary: the offence might seem trivial; the act may not be seen as illegal; the victim may not trust the police or believe the police will be effective; or the victim fears the perpetrator, or knows the perpetrator and would rather deal with the matter informally. Similarly, the police may note an incident and deem it too trivial to justify an arrest or charge; they may find it more useful to deal with the problem informally or, depending on the circumstances, not proceed with a charge if the complainant does not want to. Statistics on crimes detected by the police may also be distorted by policy decisions about whom or what to police. For example, a "war on drugs" is likely to feature many more charges for drug offences than would otherwise occur.

Official statistics almost always underestimate the volume of crime, so that it is difficult to speak accurately of the extent of youth crime. Nor is it easy to accurately attribute increases or decreases in recorded youth crime as real rather than apparent. Increased efficiency may lead to more charges while the actual rate of occurrence remains unchanged. Also, public willingness to report crime may artificially increase the crime rate. One study has demonstrated that "rising youth crime" is the result of a self-fulfilling prophecy: if people believe youth crime is on the rise, there is a greater likelihood of increased reporting.[12] Even policy decisions may change the incident rate. The decisions of some school boards to have a "zero-tolerance" policy on violence in the schools may lead to charges for relatively trivial assaults on school premises that previously would have been handled informally or internally.

An examination of the uniform crime report statistics, including the data set out in figures 1.1 and 1.2 and in tables 1.1 to 1.4, reveals some interesting trends and patterns:

- Data from both Canada and the United States indicate that the arrest rate rises through adolescence, peaks at age 19, and then falls off in the 20s. Those in their teens seem to commit mostly property crimes, while the extent of violent crime rises among those in their 20s.

- Male and female youth have very different patterns of offending behaviour. Over 80 percent of arrested youth are males; the rate is even higher for violent crimes. The data are similar for all industrialized countries. Although the evidence shows that offending behaviour in both males and females is related to having been a victim of violence or abuse, the correlation is stronger for girls; where female youth commit violent offences, it is particularly likely they have been victims of violence in the past.[13]

- The number of charges laid against youth has fallen over time. In 1994, 119,625 *Criminal Code* charges were laid. In 1998, there were 106,984, a drop of 21 percent. However, since 2000, there have been increases in the numbers arrested; in 2003, there was an increase of 5 percent over the previous year. But formal charges actually declined 15 percent in 2003, because the number of arrested accused who were not formally charged

Figure 1.1   Youth Crime Rate

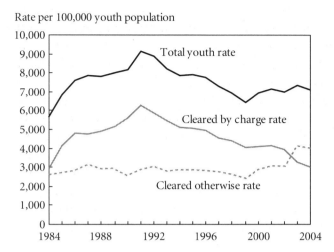

Rate per 100,000 youth population

Source: Adapted from Statistics Canada, "Crime Statistics in Canada, 2004" (July 21, 2005), vol. 25, no. 5 *Juristat* 13, catalogue no. 85-002.

Figure 1.2   Youth Violent Crime

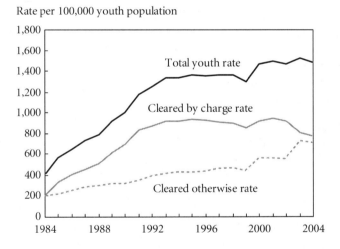

Rate per 100,000 youth population

Source: Adapted from Statistics Canada, "Crime Statistics in Canada, 2004" (July 21, 2005), vol. 25, no. 5 *Juristat* 13, catalogue no. 85-002.

and diverted out of the court system increased by 30 percent over the previous year. Note that starting in 2003, the *Youth Criminal Justice Act*[14] may have caused increased police reporting of those arrested while charges decreased, because the police are encouraged under the Act to clear charges by means other than formal charges and court proceedings in appropriate cases; in addition, even if charges are laid, the Crown may opt to divert a young offender out of the court system prior to a conviction being registered.[15]

In 2004, police data show that the number of youth formally charged dropped by 6 percent over the previous year, and those otherwise cleared or diverted from the system prior to being charged decreased by 2 percent, for an overall decrease in the youth crime rate of 4 percent. So, while the youth crime rate had been declining through the 1990s, and appeared to increase in the 2000–2003 period, it appears to be declining again, continuing the long-term trend toward a general decline in youth crime (see figure 1.1). The decline in the number of youths formally charged is probably due in part to the provisions in the Act that encourage the use of other alternatives to clear charges, although the police may also be reporting more arrests that do not lead to formal charges. An incident is "cleared otherwise than by charging" if the police have identified an accused and there is sufficient evidence to lay a charge in connection with the incident but the accused is not charged and is processed by other means—for example, by diversion to community programs or through formal police cautions.[16]

- The rate of arrest for females remained constant at about 24,000 per year from 1994 to 1998, so the decline in arrests in this period can be attributed to fewer males being charged. However, the number of young women charged with violent crimes has increased since 1998. This may be partly attributed to zero tolerance of violence of any kind by numerous school boards.

- In 2004, the youth *violent* crime rate decreased by 3.4 percent. For the previous decade it had remained relatively stable. Youths otherwise cleared on violent crime without formal charges declined by 1 percent (see figure 1.2). Despite the press about youth gang shootings and the perception of increased youth violence, the youth homicide rate dropped by 30 percent and the robbery rate by 4.8 percent.[17]

- The youth property crime rate decreased steadily from 2001 to 2005, from 1,811.3 to 1,045.1 per 100,000 youth population, a drop of 57 percent over the period (see table 1.2). This reduction in the number of charges laid may reflect the police decision to clear arrests by diverting the accused out of the system rather than by charging them. It also may reflect the decreasing number of youth in the age cohorts most likely to commit offences.

- The vast majority of youth offences concern crimes against property, not crimes of violence. At the beginning of the period from 2001 to 2005, there were over 50 percent more charges related to property offences than there were for violent offences. The charge rates for both types of offences dropped over the period, but the decline was greater for property offences, with violent offences declining at a slower rate. At the end of the period, there were only 25 percent more charges for property offences than there were for violent offences. The slower rate of decline for violent offences may be due to increases in certain types of violent offences, and because arrests for crimes of violence generally may be less likely to be diverted out of the system.

- Canada's violent crime rate for both youth and adults has generally declined since 1990, after increasing throughout most of the previous three decades. The higher rates prior to 1990 probably reflect the presence of "baby boomers" occupying the youth and young adult age cohorts most likely to be involved in crime. The decline after 1990 probably has more to do with smaller numbers of young people in the relevant age cohorts than with an outbreak of pacifism. In the period from 2001 to 2005, the adult violent

Table 1.1   Adults Charged by Type of Offence, per 100,000 Population

	2001	2002	2003	2004	2005
All incidents	**2,255.4**	**2,208.3**	**2,164.3**	**2,174.6**	**2,084.8**
Criminal Code offences					
(excluding traffic offences)	1,676.5	1,645.1	1,643.6	1,644.0	1,580.2
Crimes of violence	516.5	498.8	480.7	468.0	462.6
Homicide	1.8	1.8	1.8	2.0	1.9
Attempted murder	2.3	2.1	2.1	2.1	2.0
Assaults (level 1 to 3)[a]	411.7	397.8	382.9	373.2	368.1
Sexual assault	32.5	31.1	28.4	27.4	26.4
Other sexual offences	2.7	2.7	2.5	2.5	2.2
Robbery	29.3	28.4	28.5	28.7	28.8
Other crimes of violence[b]	36.2	35.0	34.4	32.0	33.1
Property crimes	521.7	506.6	514.1	514.2	481.5
Breaking and entering	86.0	81.1	81.3	79.5	70.1
Motor vehicle theft	36.1	34.1	35.0	32.1	27.1
Theft over $5,000	8.8	8.2	7.9	6.7	6.7
Theft $5,000 and under	233.4	223.5	227.7	229.4	215.1
Possession of stolen goods	64.6	74.0	76.7	81.1	79.3
Frauds	92.8	85.6	85.6	85.4	83.2
Other *Criminal Code* offences	638.3	639.7	648.8	661.9	636.1
Criminal Code offences					
(traffic offences)	348.2	335.5	325.4	313.5	294.6
Impaired driving	288.7	275.5	264.9	253.5	236.8
Other *Criminal Code* traffic					
offences[c]	59.5	60.0	60.5	60.0	57.8
Federal statutes	230.7	227.6	195.3	217.1	210.0
Drugs	202.5	198.9	171.9	186.8	181.7
Other federal statutes	28.3	28.7	23.4	30.4	28.3

[a] "Assault level 1" is the first level of assault. It constitutes the intentional application of force without consent, the attempt or threat to apply force to another person, or openly wearing a weapon (or an imitation) while accosting or impeding another person.

[b] Includes unlawfully causing bodily harm, discharging firearms with intent, abductions, assaults against police officers, assaults against other peace or public officers, and other assaults.

[c] Includes dangerous operation of motor vehicle, boat, vessel or aircraft; dangerous operation of motor vehicle, boat, vessel or aircraft causing bodily harm or death; driving motor vehicle while prohibited; and failure to stop or remain.

Source: Adapted from Statistics Canada website http://www40.statcan.ca/l01/cst01/legal14c.htm, December 4, 2006.

offence charge rate dropped by approximately 11 percent. But the homicide rate remained steady at 1.8 per 100,000 population for most of the period, increasing to 2.0 in 2004, and dropping back to 1.9 percent in 2005 (see table 1.1). Charges for violent crimes among youth also showed a steady decline between 2001 and 2005, dropping by 18 percent. However, there were increases in charge rates in two areas: homicide charge rates increased between 2001 and 2005 by almost 50 percent, going up from 1.3 to 2.5 per 100,000 youth population (see table 1.2). Within the period, the rate rose from 2001 to 2003, dropped slightly in 2004, and rose again in 2005. These statistical spikes may be related to episodes of gang violence in urban areas, particularly Toronto. Also as noted in table 1.2, "other crimes of violence" (which include abductions, unlawful discharges of firearms, and assaults against peace officers) rose by 5 percent from 2001 to 2005. The rate dropped slightly in 2002 and 2003, only to rise again in 2004 and 2005. Given the short time period, it is too early to say whether or not there is a long-term increase in the charge rate for these offences. Note also that some percentage increases may not point to trends of real significance. A 2 percent increase in one year in a category of crime with a very low rate compared with other categories, such as homicide, does not necessarily indicate a significant crime problem.

- Available data from Toronto covering the 10-year period from 1988 to 1998 provide a look at violent crime in more detail.[18] Notably, reported violent crime by females in the city rose by 127 percent in this period. Meanwhile, the rate for serious assault remained stable but the robbery rate increased, making it the most common violent crime committed by young people. However, murder is, and has been, a rare crime among young offenders—during the 1988–1998 period the average was 51 murders per year by young offenders for all of Canada. As noted in the preceding paragraph, there is a slight upward trend, but it is not clear that the trend is statistically significant.

- Most crimes of violence committed by young people are directed against other young people. Assaults by youth on adults are relatively unusual. Only 2 percent of victims of violent crimes by young offenders in 1998 were 55 or older. Attacks on strangers are also relatively rare. In 60 percent of assaults by youth, the offender and the victim knew each other.

- In addition to *Criminal Code* offences, a number of charges arise from provincial liquor legislation and regulations and from other federal statutes, principally the *Narcotics Control Act* and the *Food and Drug Act*. In 1998, 117,036 youths were charged with some kind of offence. Of these, 10,000, or 8.5 percent, were charged under federal statutes on matters largely related to substance abuse. Of these charges, 25 percent involved females.[19] The rate for charges, particularly related to possession of cannabis, has fallen dramatically since 2000, reflecting police reluctance to use resources on possession charges in the face of a series of appellate court decisions on possession offences.

- The media, particularly in the 1990s, presented youth crime as being on the increase and an image of convicted youth getting a mere slap on the wrist under the *Young Offenders Act* (YOA). Since April 2003, the *Youth Criminal*

Table 1.2 Youths Charged by Type of Offence, per 100,000 Population

	2001	2002	2003	2004	2005
All incidents	**4,655.8**	**4,490.1**	**3,690.4**	**3,499.0**	**3,297.9**
Criminal Code offences					
(excluding traffic offences)	4,117.5	3,917.0	3,275.1	3,041.2	2,864.2
Crimes of violence	947.0	919.0	805.7	779.1	782.4
Homicide	1.3	1.7	2.2	1.7	2.5
Attempted murder	2.8	2.3	2.6	1.9	1.8
Assaults (level 1 to 3)[a]	681.7	669.9	569.8	552.5	549.0
Sexual assault	65.2	64.3	57.4	53.6	48.2
Other sexual offences	6.4	6.2	5.1	5.0	5.6
Robbery	145.4	130.7	125.6	119.8	128.5
Other crimes of violence[b]	44.3	44.0	43.0	44.6	46.7
Property crimes	1,811.3	1,713.8	1,348.1	1,181.2	1,045.1
Breaking and entering	484.0	449.6	433.1	383.5	316.9
Motor vehicle theft	246.6	219.7	191.5	169.0	127.4
Theft over $5,000	11.9	11.6	9.3	7.0	8.3
Theft $5,000 and under	768.0	739.0	468.7	387.3	372.9
Possession of stolen goods	222.4	225.7	190.8	186.7	175.9
Frauds	78.4	68.2	54.6	47.7	43.6
Other *Criminal Code* offences	1,359.2	1,284.1	1,121.3	1,080.9	1,036.7
Criminal Code offences					
(traffic offences)	0.0	0.0	0.0	0.0	0.0
Impaired driving	0.0	0.0	0.0	0.0	0.0
Other *Criminal Code*					
traffic offences[c]	0.0	0.0	0.0	0.0	0.0
Federal statutes	538.3	573.1	415.3	457.8	433.7
Drugs	343.1	337.8	210.0	233.0	221.2
Other federal statutes	195.3	235.3	205.3	224.8	212.5

[a] "Assault level 1" is the first level of assault. It constitutes the intentional application of force without consent, the attempt or threat to apply force to another person, or openly wearing a weapon (or an imitation) while accosting or impeding another person.

[b] Includes unlawfully causing bodily harm, discharging firearms with intent, abductions, assaults against police officers, assaults against other peace, or public officers and other assaults.

[c] Includes dangerous operation of motor vehicle, boat, vessel or aircraft; dangerous operation of motor vehicle, boat, vessel or aircraft causing bodily harm or death; driving motor vehicle while prohibited; and failure to stop or remain.

Source: Adapted from Statistics Canada website http://www40.statcan.ca/l01/cst01/legal14b.htm, December 4, 2006.

Justice Act has been in effect, replacing the YOA. While we are still in the early days of this new legislation, media criticism and calls by politicians to "toughen" the way we deal with young offenders are again emerging. In addition to the increase in clearing incidents other than by charging youth, as discussed above, the *Youth Criminal Justice Act* appears to have caused some changes in disposition following conviction. As can be seen from figure 1.1, the provisions in the YCJA that are designed to divert out of the criminal justice system many of those apprehended for less serious offences appear to be working, because the diversion rate rose noticeably in 2003, the first year that the Act was in force. It is also fairly clear that where charges were laid, the courts relied on custodial sentences with or without fines in less than 30 percent of the cases. Probation and community service continue to be used in the majority of cases, as was the case under the YOA.

To compensate for distortions or inadequacy in uniform crime report statistics, other data-collection methods have been developed. The best-known and most frequently used of these other methods is **self-report studies**. Respondents, often adolescents, usually in a school setting, use a questionnaire or are interviewed on a range of activities that are offences for which they could be charged, whether or not those offences were reported or detected. The self-report methodology is important because

- it provides information on how many times a person has engaged in deviant or illegal acts, and

- it records the acts of those who have not been categorized as delinquents as well as the acts of those who have, thereby permitting comparisons between the two.

Self-reporting, therefore, provides a way of determining how representative those reported as delinquent are of youth generally. This is important because official statistics only record a small proportion of actual offenders and may overrepresent or underrepresent some types of offenders, reflecting police biases or discretionary practices in laying charges: visible minority or poor youth may be overrepresented while white middle-class youth and females generally may be underrepresented among those charged.

Self-reporting has been criticized as containing its own biases and built-in inaccuracies:

- Respondents on an interview or questionnaire may be reluctant to accurately report incidents that might land them in legal difficulties, particularly if the incident involves serious crime.

- Respondents may omit through oversight or faulty memory some of the incidents they have been involved in.

- Respondents may brag about, exaggerate, or invent incidents.

Some criminologists have taken steps to insert validity checks on self-report data—for example, following a survey with lie detector tests or verifying data by interviewing a respondent's friends. But as survey polls have generally demonstrated, if a sample is representative of the general population it purports to provide information about, it is usually reasonably accurate. Self-report data, when tested against

self-report studies
method of data gathering that relies on self-administered surveys or questionnaires given to a target group in order to obtain a group profile of the identified behaviours in which the researcher is interested

Table 1.3   Total Persons Charged by Type of Offence

	2001	2002	2003	2004	2005
All incidents	**2,482.2**	**2,422.7**	**2,306.8**	**2,297.4**	**2,196.5**
Criminal Code offences					
(excluding traffic offences)	1,907.2	1,858.7	1,795.9	1,773.5	1,698.4
Crimes of violence	557.2	538.3	511.0	496.8	492.1
Homicide	1.7	1.8	1.8	2.0	2.0
Attempted murder	2.4	2.1	2.2	2.1	2.0
Assaults (level 1 to 3)[a]	437.2	423.4	400.4	389.8	384.7
Sexual assault	35.6	34.2	31.1	29.9	28.4
Other sexual offences	3.1	3.0	2.8	2.8	2.6
Robbery	40.3	38.0	37.6	37.1	38.0
Other crimes of violence[b]	37.0	35.8	35.2	33.2	34.3
Property crimes	643.5	620.0	592.0	576.0	533.4
Breaking and entering	123.6	115.8	114.1	107.7	92.9
Motor vehicle theft	56.0	51.6	49.6	44.7	36.4
Theft over $5,000	9.1	8.6	8.0	6.7	6.8
Theft $5,000 and under	283.9	272.0	250.2	244.0	229.6
Possession of stolen goods	79.5	88.2	87.4	90.9	88.2
Frauds	91.5	84.0	82.7	81.9	79.5
Other *Criminal Code* offences	706.4	700.3	692.9	700.7	673.0
Criminal Code offences					
(traffic offences)	315.3	303.9	295.0	284.4	267.4
Impaired driving	261.4	249.6	240.1	230.0	215.0
Other *Criminal Code* traffic					
offences[c]	53.9	54.4	54.9	54.4	52.5
Federal statutes	259.8	260.1	215.9	239.4	230.6
Drugs	215.7	212.0	175.5	191.0	185.4
Other federal statutes	44.0	48.2	40.4	48.4	45.3

[a] "Assault level 1" is the first level of assault. It constitutes the intentional application of force without consent, the attempt or threat to apply force to another person, or openly wearing a weapon (or an imitation) while accosting or impeding another person.

[b] Includes unlawfully causing bodily harm, discharging firearms with intent, abductions, assaults against police officers, assaults against other peace or public officers, and other assaults.

[c] Includes dangerous operation of motor vehicle, boat, vessel or aircraft; dangerous operation of motor vehicle, boat, vessel or aircraft causing bodily harm or death; driving motor vehicle while prohibited; and failure to stop or remain.

Source: Adapted from Statistics Canada website http://www40.statcan.ca/l01/cst01/legal14a.htm, December 4, 2006.

external validity checks, have generally proven to be accurate guides to all but the most serious delinquency.[20]

The general findings from self-reporting can be summarized as follows:

- Delinquent behaviour is more common than the official statistics indicate.

- Delinquency crosses ethnic and social class lines. It is not restricted to poor youth or to ethnic or racial minorities.

- A majority of respondents revealed participation in delinquent behaviour for which charges could be laid, although most of the identified behaviours of "unofficial" delinquents were relatively minor and trivial—for example, trivial shoplifting (a candy bar) or alcohol consumption.

- More serious delinquency is relatively rare. Most who report serious illegal acts are likely to be identified as "official" delinquents and show up in crime report statistics.

- There are some differences between those who are involved in trivial delinquency and those who are involved in more serious incidents—serious delinquents are predominantly older, male, and working-class adolescents.

- Female adolescents engage in fewer delinquent acts than males, but commit the same sorts of offences, usually minor property crimes. Females self-report lower levels of all types of criminal offending.[21] Self-reporting data do not support the idea that females commit mainly **status offences** or prostitution.

status offences
offences associated with a personal characteristic such as age or gender

- Self-reporting does not reveal greater involvement in delinquency among working-class youth than among middle-class youth. This is at variance with uniform crime report statistics, which record a higher delinquency rate among working-class youth. This difference could support the thesis that class is not a significant indicator of delinquency, but it could also support the thesis that working-class youth are charged more often and watched more closely by the police, reflecting a societal bias. What is more likely is that the two measurement methods are recording different things. Self-report surveys target students in attendance at high school. This means that adolescents who skip class or drop out are underrepresented in the survey sample. It is likely that the class skippers and dropouts are more likely to be involved in serious delinquency, so this type of delinquency is underreported on the self-report surveys. Self-report surveys also do not explicitly ask about hardcore delinquency and this too contributes to underreporting of serious delinquency. In effect, self-reporting may mask collective, gang-related delinquency, serious delinquency generally, and the impact of other factors such as race or social class.

victimization surveys
crime surveys based on incidents of crime (either reported to police or unreported) as described by self-identified victims

Finally, crime may also be measured by reference to **victimization surveys**, which are based on reports by victims who have suffered from crime. These reports provide less useful information about offender characteristics because, in many crimes, the victim knows little about the offender and may not even encounter him or her—for example, in the case of break-ins. Victimization surveys are, however, useful in that they show, perhaps surprisingly, that the profiles of victims are quite similar to those of offenders—that is, victims are disproportionately young, male, and working class. Despite perceptions that other, more seemingly vulnerable groups

Table 1.4   Total Youth Court Cases, by Decision

	1999	2000	2001	2002	2003
Total offences	**87,600**	**87,617**	**85,640**	**84,592**	**70,465**
Total *Criminal Code*	71,305	70,957	69,030	68,209	57,880
Crimes against the person	22,432	22,674	22,510	22,462	20,416
Homicide	51	38	31	44	42
Attempted murder	46	46	47	43	54
Robbery	3,032	2,714	2,789	2,932	2,500
Sexual assault	1,126	1,146	1,103	1,115	1,095
Other sexual offences	527	615	595	566	535
Major assaults	4,748	4,791	4,948	4,935	4,744
Common assaults	9,019	9,229	8,708	8,968	8,010
Uttering threats	3,150	3,360	3,636	3,244	2,821
Criminal harassment	262	240	202	208	205
Other crimes against persons	471	495	451	407	410
Property crimes	35,518	34,694	33,086	32,465	25,663
Theft	13,667	13,611	13,103	12,913	9,172
Break and enter	9,088	8,223	7,522	7,415	6,632
Fraud	1,730	1,653	1,578	1,411	1,176
Mischief	3,994	4,213	4,128	4,247	3,258
Possession of stolen goods	6,583	6,452	6,243	6,039	4,915
Other property crimes	456	542	512	440	510
Administration of justice	7,551	7,917	7,698	7,790	6,784
Other *Criminal Code* offences	4,566	4,506	4,525	4,267	3,896
Criminal Code traffic	1,238	1,166	1,211	1,225	1,121
Impaired driving	800	697	669	658	585
Other *Criminal Code* traffic	438	469	542	567	536
Other federal statutes	16,295	16,660	16,610	16,383	12,585
Drug possession	3,107	3,773	4,058	4,137	2,413
Drug trafficking	1,849	1,994	2,000	1,770	1,518
Youth Criminal Justice Act/ Young Offenders Act	11,217	10,766	10,414	10,325	7,692
Residual federal statutes	122	127	138	151	962

Source: Adapted from Statistics Canada website http://www40.statcan.ca/l01/cst01/legal25a.htm, December 4, 2006.

(women, the elderly) are at particular risk for victimization, these surveys have shown that youth are at comparatively high risk for victimization, and that crimes against youth are often underreported, due in part to reduced access to police or to victimization by important (and intimidating) adults in the youthful victims' lives.

Police Perceptions

The perceptions of police personnel with respect to crime rates are especially important for two reasons. First, police in regular contact with delinquent youth might be expected to have a much more accurate perception of variations in the rate of crime than do the rest of us. Second, as the initiators of charges against youth, police are the people most likely to translate perceptions of growing violent and non-violent crime into formal charges.

A 1997 study conducted for the solicitor general of Canada[22] indicated that, over the three years preceding the study, a relatively modest 54 percent of police personnel had perceived an increase in youth violence. It is important to remember that police were reporting their own *perceptions*, based anecdotally on personal experience. When asked about the nature of the increase, police reported increases in

- hate and bias crime (16 percent),
- gang violence (38.7 percent),
- crime by youth under age 12 (39.4 percent), and
- crime by young women (66.7).

Police also reported a change in the *quality* of violent crime, noting that youth crime had become more violent/intense and that youth were more likely to use a weapon in the commission of a crime.

The same study assessed officers' perceptions of the justice system's responses to youth crime. While most officers believed that responses to crime were meaningful for minor non-violent and violent offences, officers were more critical of responses to more serious offences and were quite critical of responses to repeat offences. Nevertheless, police officers were not categorically in favour of custodial sentences for serious crime—only 46.7 and 45.3 percent, respectively, believed that a custodial sentence was needed for repeat serious property offences and repeat serious violent offences.

This study suggests that, although police do perceive a slight increase in youth crime, their perceptions are much closer to reality than those of the general public. It also suggests that, while they may be frustrated by a perceived high rate of recidivism, police are not particularly supportive of longer custodial sentences as a means of crime control.

Conclusions: Is Youth Crime on the Increase?

Because uniform crime reports underreport the actual volume of youth crime, and because of distortions in the statistics arising from policy and legislative changes, societal biases about who should be charged, and changing enforcement patterns, it is difficult to accurately determine whether youth crime is on the increase and whether the behaviour of young people is on some kind of downward slide.

For example, the uniform crime report statistics all indicate an increase in violent crimes among youth, but the statistics do not explain the cause—are youth more violent, or is greater sensitivity to violence causing people to pursue complaints they otherwise would not have pursued? Many school boards have adopted a "zero-tolerance" policy about violence in schools. This may well lead to more charges in situations that previously would have been handled internally or informally; it may also lead to more charges in incidents where the violence is minor, if not trivial. In addition, because policing generally is reactive to public pressure rather than proactive, concerns about violence may lead to more vigorous policing on this issue than was previously the case. Court and police statistics could only be presumed to be a valid representation of change over time if attitudes of the public and the police toward laying charges remained unchanged over time. Clearly, public attitudes, public policy, and police activity do change over time. These changes make it more difficult to determine whether more offences are being committed or whether the increase is due to more charges being laid.

Other information-gathering techniques can provide data that can give insight into the official crime statistics, though these other techniques have some problems of their own. Self-reporting, while it tracks minor infractions relatively well, underreports serious offences. It also tends to miss the activities of those who are not in school and who are more likely to be involved in serious delinquency.

Despite problems with the data-gathering techniques in use today, the information available from them gives us a reasonably accurate view of youth crime generally. Media reports on youth crime, on the other hand, do not provide a basis for accurate generalizations about criminal behaviour of young people today or in the past. The media have been pushing panic buttons on the subject of youth crime since the Victorian era. Therefore, it is probable that the problem of youth crime is less a cause for alarm than the media image and public perception suggest.

Chapter Summary

This chapter examined some common perceptions about youth crime and certain realities as revealed by statistical and other data on youth crime. Until the end of the 18th century, there was no concept of adolescence as an age category with unique qualities; youth crime was not understood as a unique problem. A child simply became a small-sized adult, did so at a relatively early age, taking on adult responsibilities, and generally became part of the adult world. This began to change toward the end of the 18th century with the emergence of the idea that children take a long time to mature into adults and that adolescence is a transitional stage to adulthood. In addition, the Industrial Revolution brought about changes in society that resulted in the creation of adolescence as a distinct age category. Middle-class and upper-class youth were segregated in schools to train them for adulthood. Working-class youth found themselves excluded from the workforce, deprived of a useful social role, and transformed into an urban social problem, becoming the first juvenile delinquents.

The problem of youth crime is not new. It was a matter of public concern 100 years ago, just as it is now. It was perceived by the media at the turn of the 20th century, and thus by the public, in much the same way as it is perceived now. Persistent media themes have been that youth crime is getting worse, that it is more violent, that more punishment is needed to control it, and that things were better 20 years ago. Because the public gets its information from the media, these media perceptions become the public's perceptions.

The reality of youth crime is measured by uniform crime reports, which provide official statistics of crime, and by self-report studies, which provide information about delinquent behaviour that is missed by the official statistics. The data collected by the two methods complement each other in providing us with a more accurate picture of the reality of youth crime. Each method, however, has limitations that result in distortion of the data and prevents us from having a perfectly accurate picture of the reality of youth crime. Notwithstanding these limitations, the picture of youth crime that emerges is quite different from that described in the media. Youth crime rates do not change a great deal over time, and youth crime is probably not increasing, although probably more exists than is revealed by crime statistics. Youth crimes generally are property offences, rather than crimes of violence, and are generally directed toward other youths rather than adults. Serious crimes of violence are probably not increasing, and the most serious—murder—has been and continues to be relatively rare.

Although the problem of youth crime is not itself new, emerging factors are shifting the nature of some offences as well as public perceptions of youth criminality. Globalization, technological changes, shifting immigration patterns, changing gender roles, and international politics are emerging factors contributing to anti-youth sentiment on the part of the public in Canada and to a perception that youth crime is more of a growing problem than statistics would indicate.

Even with the emergence of new varieties of crime and despite media reports to the contrary, the reality of youth crime appears to be less a cause for alarm than public perceptions suggest.

KEY TERMS

Enlightenment

socialization

recidivism

xenophobia

uniform crime reports

self-report studies

status offences

victimization surveys

NOTES

1. J. Kett, "Adolescence and Youth in Nineteenth Century America," in T. Rabb and R. Bothberg, eds., *The Family in History* (New York: Harper and Row, 1971).

2. For a detailed discussion of the creation of an adolescent youth category in modern society, see F. Musgrove, *Youth and the Social Order* (London: Routledge & Kegan Paul, 1964).

3. Ibid., at 33.

4. W.G. West, *Young Offenders and the State: A Canadian Perspective on Juvenile Delinquency* (Toronto: Butterworths, 1984), 26-27.

5. Ibid., at 28-29; and J. Tanner, *Teenage Troubles: Youth and Deviance in Canada* (Scarborough, ON: Nelson, 1996), 18-23.

6. Referred to in an article by *The Globe and Mail* columnist Colin Vaughan on June 8, 1992, quoted in Tanner, supra note 5, at 1-2.

7. Tanner, supra note 5, at 1-2.

8. Ibid., at 3. The study referred to is G. Pearson, *Hooligan* (London: Macmillan, 1983).

9. Tanner, supra note 5, at 6.

10. Ibid., at 7-8, quoting R. Corrado and A. Mackwart, "The Evolution and Implementation of a New Era of Juvenile Justice in Canada," in R. Corrado et al., eds., *Juvenile Justice in Canada: A Theoretical and Analytical Assessment* (Vancouver: Butterworths, 1992).

11. A.N. Doob, J.B. Sprott, V. Marinos, and K.N. Varma, *An Exploration of Ontario Residents' Views on Crime and the Criminal Justice System* (Toronto: Centre of Criminology, University of Toronto, 1998).

12. Ibid., at 38, citing R. Merton, *Social Theory and Social Structure* (New York: Free Press, 1968).

13. See R. Fitzgerald, "An Examination of Sex Differences in Delinquency," *Crime and Justice Research Paper Series*, Canadian Centre for Justice Statistics, catalogue no. 85-561-MIE—No. 001.

14. *Youth Criminal Justice Act*, SC 2002, c. 1.

15. Statistics Canada, "Crime Statistics, 2003," *The Daily*, July 28, 2004.

16. Statistics Canada, "Crime Statistics in Canada, 2004" (July 21, 2005), vol. 25, no. 5 *Juristat* 12-13, catalogue no. 85-002.

17. Ibid., at 13.

18. Cited in "Fear and the Tracking of Violent Youth," *The Globe and Mail*, January 17, 2000, A12.

19. Statistics Canada, "Youths and Adults Charged in Criminal Incidents, Criminal Code and Federal Statutes, by Sex," 1999, matrices 2198 and 2199.

20. Tanner, supra note 5, at 49.

21. See Fitzgerald, supra note 13.

22. T. Caputo and K. Kelly, *Police Perceptions of Current Responses to Youth Crime* (Ottawa: Solicitor General, 1997).

EXERCISES AND REVIEW
Review Questions

1. How was childhood thought of before the 18th century?

2. What factors caused the creation of adolescence as a particular age category?

3. How do the media generally describe youth crime?

4. What do the media say causes youth crime? Have media messages changed much over time?

5. How are data collected for uniform crime reports?

6. How are data collected for self-report studies?

7. What are the strengths of the uniform crime report system? What are its weaknesses?

8. What are the strengths of the self-report studies system? What are its weaknesses?

9. At what age does the arrest rate peak for young people?

10. Is it true that older people are often the victims of young offenders?

11. Is it true that a stranger is likely to be the victim of a violent attack by a young person?

12. "Youth courts just give young offenders a slap on the wrist and then let them out to wreak more havoc." Do the statistics support this proposition?

13. Discuss ways in which recent changes in international politics, technology, and global economics affect both people's perceptions of, and realities in relation to, youth crime.

Discussion Questions

1. Using an Internet search engine, do a search for "youth crime" and conduct a review of the first 10 Web postings retrieved that deal with youth for a specified period. Analyze the articles in terms of whether the article is concerned with, alludes to, mentions, or cites the following:

   a. gang activity

   b. race or ethnicity

   c. poverty

    d. other economic circumstances

    e. social values

    f. adequacy of the law

    g. need for stricter punishment

    h. violence

    i. positive or negative views about youth

2. Discuss what is meant by the observation that "adolescence was created at the same time as the steam engine."

3. Using the data in statistical tables 1.1 to 1.4, indicate what the data tell you about

    a. whether youth crime is increasing or decreasing

    b. whether crimes of violence by youth are increasing or decreasing

    c. whether there are more crimes of violence than there are crimes against property by youth

    d. whether crime among young females is increasing or decreasing

    e. whether the proportion of violent crimes that can be classed as serious violent crime is rising or falling for youth

4. Based on the data available from the uniform crime reports and from self-report studies as described in this chapter:

    a. What is the picture of contemporary youth crime that emerges from the data?

    b. How does the picture of youth crime drawn from the data in (a) differ from the picture of youth crime that appears in the media?

CHAPTER 2

Youth Crime: Patterns and Causes

■ CHAPTER OBJECTIVES

After completing this chapter, you should be able to:

- Understand shifts in general trends and patterns of delinquency since the 1950s.

- Identify certain principal types of crimes that young people commit.

- Explain how hate crime differs from other kinds of youth crime.

- Understand and explain, in general terms, conflict theory, functionalist theory, and symbolic interactionist theory.

- Understand what is meant by the "social psychology of crime."

- Understand why racial or ethnic minorities may engage in delinquent activity in different ways from youth who are members of the dominant mainstream.

- Identify and explain connections between economic disadvantage or unemployment and youth crime.

- Explain, in general terms, how one's school experience might contribute to delinquency.

What Types of Crime Do Youth Commit?

In chapter 1, we examined issues relating to the frequency and extent of youth crime and, in the course of doing so, we made some observations about what sorts of crimes are commonly committed by young people. We now examine this issue in more detail.

Record keeping, as we noted earlier, has been uneven and has not always provided an accurate picture of youth crime. However, some generalizations can be made from records we have. Until 1950, youth crime was characterized by what some commentators refer to as "old-fashioned delinquency."[1] Such offending largely consisted of working-class males committing petty offences, with fairly steady rates of conviction. The 1950s saw the beginnings of a statistical rise in the rate of youth crime with some changes. Increased gang activity and increased substance abuse, particularly with respect to illegal drugs, began in the 1960s. The 1960s also brought offences associated with political action. Some argue that the crimes committed were increasingly more violent and more serious, but this may be a distortion of the evidence based on improved reporting and data gathering by police and other state officials, and may be caused by an increase in the youth population overall as a result of the "baby boom" between 1946 and 1965. It is still arguable that, aside from drug offences and a general erosion of civility, youth crime is still largely "old-fashioned delinquency" where primarily male offenders are apprehended for mostly petty offences and middle-class and female offenders are largely diverted out of the criminal justice system to be dealt with in other ways.

If we take a closer look at the actual offences committed, a pattern does emerge, with certain types of offences characteristic of youth crime. It also becomes clear that even though certain types of crime are committed by both adults and youths, youth criminal involvement may be motivated by factors that differ from typically adult motivations. These factors can include recklessness, retaliation, thrill seeking, and street life. As we will see in later chapters, this difference in motivation may explain why traditional crime-reduction strategies such as deterrence and custodial sentences seem less effective for youthful offenders.

VANDALISM

Statistics generally describe vandalism as "mischief to private property"[2] and "public mischief."[3] Broadly speaking, vandalism involves destruction of, or damage to, property. It is often committed by young children and, like shoplifting, may provide an entry point or "gateway" to youth crime. Because damage to property necessarily requires some violence, vandalism is sometimes viewed as a crime of violence and is often equated, at least publicly, with violence against persons. Many acts of vandalism are directed against schools and private residences, which may indicate that these locations are not chosen randomly but are targeted for reasons of retaliation or to vent anger.

While many acts of vandalism, particularly minor ones, go unreported, there is some evidence to indicate that vandalism is more widespread than the uniform crime reports indicate. A survey of 1,222 students in Ontario indicated that 89 percent of those surveyed of high school age had committed an act of vandalism in the preceding year.[4]

Because it is seen as a gateway to more serious youth crime, at least one jurisdiction has taken a novel approach to vandalism by youth. On May 1, 2006, London, Ontario's city council passed an unprecedented bylaw that puts the city on the vanguard of regulating the conduct of youth in Canada. It is now illegal for persons under the age of 18 to purchase spray paint or permanent markers in the city. The extent to which this extreme approach is effective in preventing vandalism, or whether it has the effect of alienating youth and so leading to an increase in youth crime, remains to be seen. The impact of this law is likely to have important ramifications for the rest of Canada.

While most vandalism is committed by small groups of youth, occasionally crowd vandalism erupts, often following a major public event such as a loss by a local sports team. While this kind of vandalism appears to be worrisome, it is neither new nor a growing phenomenon. Episodes of mob action featuring property destruction have occurred in all societies since the first cities arose about 5,000 years ago, and, typically, the participants have not been senior citizens.

One form of vandalism that needs to be considered separately is arson. Many arsonists are very young and under the age covered by young offender legislation. Arson may be a component of vandalism, or it may result from a fire set for monetary gain, though this is more characteristic of adult arson. Of particular interest and concern is fire setting by youths who seem to be fascinated by the act itself. This kind of arson is often perceived to indicate some degree of mental illness or disturbance.

As noted in the preceding chapter, as technology changes, we need to be aware that crime is changing with it. Vandalism is no exception. We can now include in vandalism computer "hacking," where a young person who is a proficient computer user can breach database security systems and destroy information or badly damage it by introducing a computer virus into a data system. The proliferation of computer anti-virus programs is testimony to the extent of this kind of vandalism. While very little research has been done on who becomes a computer hacker or why, anecdotal evidence suggests that hacking is typically a crime of young, middle-class males with the education and financial resources to engage in this kind of crime.

BREAK AND ENTER

Breaking into private premises is closely related to vandalism. It is usually thought of as an adult offence involving theft from the premises broken into, but there is increasing statistical evidence to show growing youth involvement. Uniform crime report statistics from 1995 and thereafter roughly consistently show that 40 percent of all break and enters were committed by young offenders.[5]

One aspect of property offences that has generally been ignored is the relationship between street youth and crimes against property. Starting in the 1980s throughout Europe and North America, a growing number of homeless youth have become increasingly detached from the rest of society and resemble the "street urchins"— homeless, unemployed youths, often in loosely organized gangs—that people from the Victorian era worried about 150 years ago. Like street youth of an earlier period, many of these young people survive by stealing. Though there are not a lot of data, some studies in Canada indicate that reported property crimes in a given city are committed by a relatively small number of street youth criminals.[6]

MOTOR VEHICLE THEFT

Car theft is and has long been a common offence committed by the young. While adult car theft is often for gain, and frequently forms part of a sophisticated and complex operation, car theft by the young, like vandalism, often occurs for other reasons. In fact, the *Criminal Code* has long included the offence commonly known as "joyriding"[7] in which, typically, a car is stolen and driven around and then abandoned. However, it appears that the rate at which car theft is committed has been falling. Between 2001 and 2005, the car theft rate dropped by about 50 percent.

SUBSTANCE ABUSE

Youth substance abuse is often presented as a relatively recent and growing problem. Historically, however, substance abuse has always been a problem. Ever since humans learned to distill alcohol from vegetable products, young people have had to learn to come to terms with alcohol. With legal consumption restrictions, the likelihood of reports of drinking offences by young people increases. Tobacco has long presented similar problems. However, added to the ever-present problem of alcohol and tobacco has been the problem of non-prescription drugs, which involves both the crimes of possession and, for some, trafficking. The non-medical use of drugs became common in the late 1960s, with fluctuations in use since. Crime statistics do not give a reliable indication of the extent of the problem and most commentators prefer the data obtained from self-report surveys. These indicate a decline in drug and alcohol use, generally, during the 1980s with the beginnings of an increase in the 1990s, particularly on the part of girls. The cause of the recent increase is not entirely clear, but it may stem from the "baby boom echo"—a population surge among those who were entering adolescence in the 1990s.

CRIMES OF VIOLENCE

As noted in chapter 1, crimes of violence dropped by 18 percent between 2001 and 2005 (see table 1.2). This decrease was consistent with Canada's 10 percent drop in violent crime over the preceding decade.[8] While there were increases in violent crime during certain years over this period, these increases may reflect changes in policy about laying charges for crimes of violence—for example, with respect to "zero-tolerance" policies of some school boards. It may also reflect periodic "spikes" in violence due to fights among gang members in major urban centres. Interestingly, the increase in violent crimes all but evaporates if all minor assaults are removed from the data. Serious violence by youth is still a relatively rare event, as is murder.

Despite the relatively stable rate of violent crime in Canada, many people feel there has been an increase in the rate of violent crime committed by young women and girls. Police statistics concerning female offending suggest that, although involvement in recorded crime by females has increased in recent years, the increase has mainly occurred in less serious assaults and in victimless crimes such as offences against the administration of justice, such as probation breaches and failing to appear in court. As shown in figure 2.1, females continue to be a small minority of young offenders charged by police.[9] While crimes of violence are still an overwhelmingly male phenomenon, as discussed in chapter 1, the male violent crime rate has declined in recent years while the female rate appears to have remained about the same; this translates into a relative increase in the rate of crimes committed by young females as compared to males.

Whether or not it is on the increase, female youth crime poses unique problems for the Canadian justice and corrections systems, which are tailored primarily to accommodate male offenders. Rehabilitation programs, for example, are generally designed based on research about what treatments are most effective in controlling *male* violence. Custody facilities are generally not set up for handling inmates of both sexes.

Some of the recent concern about gang activity has focused on the involvement of young women in gangs. One view is that girls use gang subculture to build

Figure 2.1 Rate of Police Charges per 100,000 Males and Females Aged 12-17 years, 2001

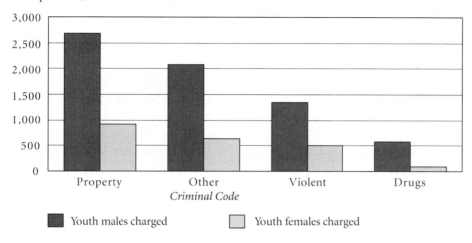

Rate per 100,000 males and females

Note: "Other *Criminal Code*" includes offences such as bail violations, mischief, offensive weapons, and disturbing the peace.

Data source: Statistics Canada, Uniform Crime Reporting Survey, 2001.

Source: Adapted from Statistics Canada, *An Examination of Sex Differences in Delinquency*, catalogue no. 85-561-MIE, no. 1, at 13, June 19, 2003.

themselves a social group to overcome the effects of isolation, and that female gang involvement is more tentative and of shorter duration than that of males. Young women are less likely to "graduate" from delinquency to become adult criminals. There also appears to be little evidence to support the existence of gangs of young women who are as violent or as aggressive as their male counterparts.[10] We will discuss offending by female young offenders in more detail in chapter 13.

Historically, females have always been largely absent from crime statistics and from studies of delinquency. It has often been assumed that young females do not engage in delinquent acts, but, as noted above with respect to the violent crime rate, this is not the case. Young women, like young men, also commit minor property offences, such as shoplifting, with greater frequency than the uniform crime report data indicate, and with greater frequency than their male counterparts. This is also the case for prostitution. Females were more often charged as "runaways" under the *Juvenile Delinquents Act*, which is discussed elsewhere in this book, reflecting a greater familial protectiveness, or perhaps a more proprietary attitude towards young women.

GANGS AND GUN VIOLENCE

Adolescents are strongly peer-focused and tend to organize themselves into groups. Sometimes these groups become involved in criminal activity with varying degrees of organization. When they do so, they are often referred to as "gangs." Gang violence is not a new phenomenon. However, some commentators believe that this style of violence has moved into the mainstream youth culture.

Recent high-profile cases of gun violence have given rise to a great deal of public concern about the increase in the use of guns and the proliferation of youth gangs in Canada. Much of this concern resulted from media reports about incidents in Toronto. Gun violence and gang activity has been blamed on the availability of guns, an alleged cultural celebration of guns and violence, rap and heavy metal music, violence in entertainment such as television and movies, video games, and war toys. It is very difficult to say with certainty what social, cultural, or other factors might cause increases in gang activity and gun violence.

Reliable information about youth gangs in Canada is relatively scarce. However, where empirical data are available, it does not support the proposition that gun violence and gang activity are dramatically on the rise in Canada. As discussed in chapter 13 and in chapter 1, far from showing such an increase, the most recent data show that Canada's rates of violent crime and youth crime have in fact fallen. Nonetheless, there is a sense among urban police officers, as well as expressions of concern in media reports, that there is an increase in gang activity on the part of teenagers. Gangs and guns will be explored more in chapter 13.

Theories of Youth Crime

There are almost as many theories and explanations about why young people commit offences as there are people studying and thinking about the matter. However, most of them fall into one of three broad theories that explain how societies work: conflict theory, functionalist theory, and symbolic interactionist theory.

conflict theory approach to how societies work that emphasizes conflict, power relations, differences among groups, and social change resulting from group conflict

Conflict theory seeks to understand social relationships by identifying social groups that are engaged in conflict and by studying that conflict. The focus of social inquiry is on conflict, power differences among social groups, and social change. Society is presumed to be composed of various groups in conflict with one another, with each group seeking to improve its position at the expense of another group. The goals, norms, and values of one group often clash with those of other groups. The theory holds that if one group can dominate the society, there will be social peace and stability, though the dominant group, which has benefited, will need to use force or the threat of force to contain those groups that lack power.

functionalist theory approach to how societies work that emphasizes the way various parts of society function and interact to produce social harmony or equilibrium

Functionalist theory sees society as composed of coherent social systems where all the system parts work harmoniously and contribute to the well-being of society. When social systems are working well, they are stable or in equilibrium. When they do not work well, there is strain between the society's goals and values and an individual's ability to achieve those goals and internalize those values. Social systems that make up society are seen to evolve and change slowly, as does the society of which they are a part. Functionalist theory emphasizes order rather than social change. Functionalists tend to focus on social systems and structures such as the family and educational and religious institutions, usually examining how they help maintain social stability.[11]

Both conflict and functionalist theories agree that shared values are required for society to function. Conflict theorists see this as the result of coercion where some groups force their values on others and on the society's institutions. On the one hand, conflict theorists studying youth crime see crime as an expression of resistance to the imposition of "mainstream" social values, often by relatively powerless working-class or minority youth. Functionalist theorists, on the other hand, see youth crime resulting from some youth imperfectly learning the society's value system due to dysfunctional families, mental illness, poverty, inadequate schools, or poor neighbourhoods. Conflict and functionalist assumptions about the causes of delinquency can be compared when set out side by side, as they are below (see box).

Symbolic interactionist theory takes a different approach from functionalist and conflict theories. This theory does not begin with a preconceived model of society; rather it focuses on individual interaction, often in small groups, assuming that an analysis of why people behave as they do can only be understood in the context of interactions with others, individually or in groups. Symbolic interactionists often conduct **ethnographic studies** where they closely observe and describe behaviours without using preconceived hypotheses concerning the meaning of human behaviour. Symbolic interactionists find that individuals consciously read the symbolic meaning of interactions with others and pursue various behavioural strategies to reach meaningful goals. This is a fluid situation in which individuals can redefine their identities and change their behavioural courses as a result of how they consciously interpret different interactions and experiences.

symbolic interactionist theory
approach that holds that individual behaviour is influenced through people's interaction with others and that self-image is constructed by a conscious reading of the symbolic meaning of these social interactions

ethnographic studies
studies that arise from a research approach originally used to describe the social interactions of tribal groups using a variety of observational techniques

Comparison of Conflict and Functionalist Assumptions About the Causes of Delinquency

Conflict assumptions	Functionalist assumptions
Delinquent and non-delinquent behaviour arises from people acting in ways that suit their social class and power position in society. Delinquency is a reaction to the life conditions of a person's social class.	All societies have agreed-upon norms, values, customs, and rules that most people internalize and adopt. Delinquency arises because some people absorb norms and values that lead to delinquent behaviour.
Youth crime is concentrated in lower classes because the ruling class sees only acts that come out of lower-class life as delinquent.	Youth crime is more common among lower classes because institutions that socialize people, such as the family, schools, peer groups, and neighbourhoods are not effective or are dysfunctional.
The lower classes are more likely to be arrested and labelled delinquents because the ruling class controls those who manage law enforcement agencies.	The lower classes are more likely to be arrested because they commit more delinquencies.
Delinquency varies from society to society depending on the political and economic structures of the society.	Delinquency is a constant feature in all societies.
Socialist societies should have much lower rates of youth crime because the less-intensive class conflict should reduce the forces leading to, and the functions of, delinquency.	Capitalist and socialist societies that are industrialized and bureaucratized should have the same levels of youth crime.

Source: Modification of comparative theoretical list from W. Chambliss, "Functional and Conflict Theories of Crime," in W. Chambliss and M. Mankoff, *Whose Law? What Order?* (Wiley: New York, 1976), reproduced in G. West, *Young Offenders and the State* (Toronto: Butterworths, 1984), 38-39.

The symbolic interactionist approach reveals motivation and gives crucial information about what causes different people to commit delinquent acts, but it has been criticized for not being useful for drawing general conclusions about behaviour, because, logically, there is no certainty that there are shared reasons for committing delinquent acts where individual reaction to the social context is deemed to be so important. As well, focusing on the delinquent actor alone does not necessarily tell us all we need to know about behaviour. We also need to look at the actions and perceptions of all the actors involved—police, teachers, parents, and other community members. Also, given the focus on the individual, symbolic interactionists may fail to take into account the extent to which socioeconomic factors such as race, ethnicity, family status, education, and employment records affect what individuals do, or are likely to do.

A subtheory of symbolic interactionism that has attracted recent attention studies crime from the perspective of social learning, and gives new emphasis to the importance of considering variable individual psychology within the moderating environment of a shared social context.[12] This theory, sometimes described as the social psychological approach, admits that criminal behaviour is difficult to predict at a societal level, but endorses the risk–needs system for assessing individual risk for recidivism or dangerous behaviour.

labelling theory
a subtheory of symbolic interactionism that suggests that individuals will "live up to" stereotypical labels—for example, "juvenile delinquent"—ascribed to them by others

Another subtheory of symbolic interactionism is **labelling theory**, which holds that socially deviant behaviour is determined by the social response to it. Labelling theorists suggest that individuals will "live up to" stereotypical labels—for example, "juvenile delinquent"—ascribed to them by others. A child who is labelled a juvenile delinquent will, in response to being labelled that way, behave as society expects juvenile delinquents to behave, and the child will come to believe that he or she is truly deserving of the label.

These three critical approaches—conflict, functionalist, and symbolic interactionist—are important because they underlie many theories that explain the causes of youth crime. But they are also important because they make different assumptions about social organization and social interaction. You might assume that if the theories rest on contradictory assumptions, one or more must be wrong. While unquestioned assumptions can lead to a researcher misinterpreting data, the different theoretical approaches can be used to answer different questions. You might benefit from thinking of the theories as tools. You would not use a hammer to do the job that a screwdriver does. Similarly, you might use functionalist theory to explore the way in which dysfunctional families, poor schools, and low income contribute to the creation of delinquent behaviour. Or, if you are examining the behaviour of gangs of marginalized poor or visible minority youth, a conflict model may explain much of the motivation for gang behaviour as a response to a lack of power and a lack of social mobility. Finally, a symbolic interactionist approach may give you more insight into individual motivations and into how individual behaviour might change over time.

Causes of Youth Crime

We can now turn to specific research findings and theories about the causes of youth crime.

RACIAL MINORITIES AND YOUTH CRIME

Many commentators—some explicitly, some more subtly—have suggested that people who belong to ethnic minorities and recent immigrants cause more crime than other groups because of conflict between their own culture and the dominant culture.[13] This conflict is perceived to be caused in three different ways. One purported cause, part of functionalist theory, is that some minorities subscribe to norms and values that encourage criminality, or that are more tolerant of it. The second cause is a form of resistance to the norms of the dominant culture. Many of the conflict theory studies of youth gangs have documented resistance to dominant norms as a contributor to gang formation and delinquency. The third cause is perceived to arise from the difficulty minorities have in adapting to dominant societal norms and successfully participating in societal institutions, resulting in frustration that produces attempts to achieve socially approved goals (for example, having a comfortable lifestyle) by resorting to criminal gang activity. A number of functionalist theories focus on problems that minority and immigrant youth have in adapting to the dominant society. Ethnicity and race are not so obvious as factors in youth crime when observing individuals, but they become more evident when individuals of the same **ascribed ethnicity** form subcultural groups. Because minority members acting in groups, including gangs, are easiest to study, many of the assumptions and findings about minorities and youth crime have come from observations of gangs, many of them American. Some of the earliest studies of youth subcultures in the 1920s and 1930s examined gangs that were ethnically based.[14] When we consider that uniform crime report statistics do not give the racial or ethnic backgrounds of young offenders as individuals, we do not have all that much information from which to draw conclusions about race and youth crime, except as a result of ethnographic studies of minority group gangs.

Canadian studies indicate that different minorities at different times have been perceived to have been associated with criminal activity. In the 1930s, the Irish immigrants had the highest crime rate among adults. However, since then, youth whose parents were born in Canada have supplanted them, leaving young immigrants relatively uninvolved in criminal activity. More recently, "black crime" has begun to become an issue in larger cities, but much of this reflects "the black occupancy of American mythology as being a crime prone racial/ethnic group" rather than an empirical reality. The equivalent racial stereotype in Canada would be native Canadians, including Métis.[15] But statements about ethnicity and crime remain largely speculative. Most of the data about crime rates referred to above concerned adults. There have been relatively few studies concerning ethnicity and youth crime, but those studies that have been done in Canada indicate, as American studies do, that the important link is not race or ethnicity and youth crime, but social class and youth crime. Most of the studies that have anything to say on this have been ethnographic studies of groups of minority youth, some in gangs, and some in looser groups of youth whose lives centre on the street or neighbourhood. Generally, the studies found that it was not ethnicity but socioeconomic deprivation, particularly a lack of employment and/or education, that made it difficult for individuals to successfully integrate into the **host society** and diverted minority youth into marginal groups, some of which were involved in crime. It is telling that many of the minority youth involved in delinquency studied in the past, mainly the

ascribed ethnicity
characteristics assigned to ethnic group members by the host society, whether or not the ethnic group members actually possess these characteristics

host society
society to which ethnic migrants come and to which they must adapt in some way

sons of European immigrants in the 1920s and 1930s, ceased to be a part of the minority youth crime picture as their minority groups **acculturated** or **assimilated** to the ways of the host society.

One Canadian study illustrates the link between ethnicity, acculturation, and assimilation difficulties and resistance to host society expectations. A group of black students in a Toronto high school, all relatively recent arrivals from various islands in the West Indies, were the subject of a study that explicitly examined the impact of race or minority status on the formation of a cultural subgroup in a Toronto high school. The study demonstrated that when the minority cultural practices and the experience of the boys clashed with the white authority structure of the school and its demands on the students, race-based resistance was a result. The resistance helped to preserve the self-respect of the group members in the face of denigration of their culture, but it also contributed to further marginalization as the group members were deflected by their experiences from accepting school norms and doing well academically, which in turn made it more likely that group members would end up in low-paying, unskilled jobs.[16]

The Toronto study focused on a group, not a gang. But groups of minority youth that evolve into gangs have been studied extensively in the United States. The findings suggest that racial and ethnic minority youth, particularly visible minority youth, may be part of a socially and economically deprived urban underclass. With few opportunities for employment, group members often turn to gang delinquency as a means of maintaining respect, self-esteem, and economic opportunity. For example, studies of Mexican-Americans in southern California show a persistence of minority youth subcultural groups and gangs going back to the late 1940s. Historically, these groups were not gangs structured to engage in youth crime. They started as informal groups of young males in low-paying jobs who joined together for sports and entertainment activities. In the 1950s, as the barriers to integration and opportunities for these youth became more extensive, the informal street groups began to turn explicitly to criminal activity and more conscious forms of resistance to host society institutions. For **barrio** youth, gangs offered a sense of identity and community for Mexican youth who had to sort out the conflicting demands of their parents' Mexican culture and the host society's culture. Those most involved in gangs were those least connected to schools, adult-sponsored youth activities, and religious institutions, and whose family ties were weak because of adult unemployment, poverty, and inadequate housing. The gang provided a community alternative for these youth—entertainment, criminal activity, alcohol, drugs, and fighting. The gang community emphasized loyalty to family, friends, and neighbours, and rejected educational achievement and regular employment—often because good jobs were not available.[17]

ECONOMIC DEPRIVATION

As indicated in the discussion of youth crime and ethnicity, socioeconomic deprivation and poverty generally are strongly associated with delinquency, although a careful look at the data indicates that it is not simply being poor that is linked to delinquency as much as some of the things that at times go along with being poor. Certainly, "official delinquency" as reported in the uniform crime report statistics and court records supports the hypothesis that most of those involved are working

---

acculturation
process whereby migrants to a society learn its ways of doing things but do not necessarily give up their ethnic identity

assimilation
process whereby migrants to a society learn its ways of doing things and give up or cease to be seen as having a separate ethnic identity

barrio
Spanish word for "neighbourhood"; used in English to describe a Hispanic neighbourhood or district

class. But remember that self-report surveys demonstrate that petty youth crime is evenly spread across the class system, and that many studies show that the police are less likely to charge a middle-class youth than a poor one.

It would therefore be a mistake to assume simply that poverty leads to delinquency. In a US study by Mercer Sullivan, youth cliques from three poor communities were studied—one black, one Hispanic, and one traditional working-class white. There were certain similarities for the three groups—for example, patterns of early involvement in petty delinquency for younger members of the groups were similar for all three groups. But there were also some differences. One difference explained the slightly lower crime rate for the white group. In this neighbourhood, factory jobs were available through neighbourhood contacts and through word of mouth. For the other two groups, employment prospects were much bleaker. The result was that older members of the white subgroup were able to meet their needs through legitimate employment and their delinquent behaviour tailed off. For the other two groups, with bleaker job prospects, delinquency and group criminal activity continued longer, became more serious, and was more likely to be used to meet economic needs. A secondary purpose of continued youth crime was to symbolically reject a mainstream culture with many barriers to entry.[18]

Sullivan's findings mirror the findings in studies of British youth gangs, with the difference that British gang members studied did not differ racially from the host society. But the same poverty, coupled with the lack of meaningful employment opportunities, appears to be a root cause of the maintenance of gang activity and delinquency.

Where there are few economic opportunities, not all economically disadvantaged youth will continue on to more serious youth crime. Gordon West, in a Canadian study in the 1960s, found that there was a further requirement—access to adult criminal networks. If access to adult criminals was present, economically disadvantaged young males were more likely to continue on in crime, although relatively few of these young males went on to become serious, adult professional criminals. Many seemed to outgrow both gang and criminal activity. They settled down, married, had children, and moved into low-wage, unskilled, and unsatisfying work.[19]

West's findings in the 1960s may have to be modified today. His subjects were mostly young thieves. Today, the drug trade provides higher returns, less risk, and more economic opportunity for poor youth, whether they are members of minority groups or not. The apparent revival of gangs in the United States and, to some extent, in Canada may well be linked to the drug trade, with some observers claiming that gangs are starting to operate in the same way as legitimate businesses. It is likely in these circumstances that more poor young males may be recruited to gangs dealing in the drug trade, and stay involved longer than was previously the case because it is perceived to be economically worthwhile to continue the involvement.[20]

YOUTH UNEMPLOYMENT

The effect of employment, or the lack of it, on delinquency has long been noted and has been referred to earlier in this chapter. Unemployment for the past 20 years in all market-oriented, advanced industrial nations has been steadily increasing. Deindustrialization has led to the permanent loss of relatively high-paying, low-skilled

structural unemployment
persistent and permanent unemployment in a job market that is contracting and thus not providing enough work for the working population

factory jobs that previously were available to working-class youth who had limited school experience and restricted employment opportunities. This has been accompanied by the growth of the service sector, which contains what some economists refer to as "Macjobs"—jobs that are unskilled, part-time, and poor paying. There is also growing evidence of **structural unemployment** with a permanent unemployed or underemployed underclass, whose lives are increasingly likely to be characterized by poverty and homelessness. Labour statistics indicate that young people entering the job market have borne the brunt of this type of unemployment, and this is especially so for those with limited education. In some places, notably Britain in the 1980s, this led to a new form of delinquency in the form of street riots among unemployed youth. Conflict theorists argued that this may be part of a politically conscious form of resistance. Both Marxist and traditional conflict theorists may take it a step further, with Marxists seeing this as the first steps in a more politically coherent form of rebellion, while traditionalists see it as the first steps toward a breakdown of public order. There seems, however, to be little evidence that delinquent youth have become politicized to act in this way.

It has often been assumed that as unemployment worsens, more young people turn to crime. This certainly seems to be a rational assumption, but what may be happening is that we have assumed that unemployed youth will turn to crime and are, therefore, a threat to society. Labelling theorists argue that we have labelled them as delinquent, and they have acted accordingly. Tanner cites two studies, one by Box and Hale in Britain[21] and one by O'Grady in Newfoundland,[22] that suggest that the judiciary share this public perception that unemployed youth are threatening and a danger to public order, and have acted accordingly by imposing prison terms where they might not have otherwise done so, and by imposing longer than usual prison terms. This harsh reaction to a perceived problem does not appear to be justified by actual crime trends. Both O'Grady and Box and Hale found that the rate of violent property crime most feared did not rise significantly with increased rates of unemployment, suggesting that judges, like the rest of us, can fall prey to stereotyping and labelling, producing a response that is out of proportion to the threat.[23]

There are some studies that suggest that unemployment and lack of money are not as directly linked to youth crime as we assume. More important as a cause of youth crime are idleness and boredom, according to self-report surveys. Those with time on their hands, particularly when combined with the recklessness that comes with immaturity, are simply more likely to get into trouble. One study goes further, suggesting that post–high school employment, or the lack of it, is not a crucial explanatory factor, at least for violent crime. Instead, the biggest predictor of continued crime is marital status—those who remain single or who are divorced or separated report higher frequencies of violent crime. However, one study by Tanner indicates that there is a positive relationship between work and delinquency. His study of Canadian high school seniors indicated that those who were employed part-time during high school were slightly more likely to be involved in delinquent acts, including drug and alcohol abuse. A careful examination of the data reveals that higher rates of deviance were related to contact with others engaged in deviance, and that this "meeting of minds" tended to occur in the workplace. Caution should be observed here, Tanner says, because the deviance engaged in was not particularly serious, and other factors such as the degree of parental control exercised may have more of an effect on the extent of involvement in delinquency.[24]

Lastly, there is the chicken-and-egg question of whether delinquency in adolescence actually contributes to unemployment in adults. Delinquent behaviour precedes full-time adult employment, and may well influence later employment. Extensive and serious delinquency is more likely to correlate with future unemployment and longer involvement in the delinquent subculture than is the case for those whose delinquencies are less serious and end at an earlier age. However, there are probably other factors at work. Tanner suggests that those engaged in delinquent behaviour for longer acquire deviant friends and join deviant networks, and have greater opportunities to engage in criminal activity. Having parents who are engaged in criminal activity also increases the likelihood of conventional unemployment, but it also increases the likelihood of "employment" in criminal activity, which in itself serves as a barrier to conventional employment.[25]

FAMILY AND UPBRINGING AS A FACTOR IN DELINQUENCY

As noted above, having criminals for parents is one way to increase the likelihood that children will be delinquents and go on to adult crime. But how else does family interaction affect delinquency? It is often assumed that coming from a "broken home" is closely associated with delinquency. But coming from a family where the parents have separated is not closely associated with delinquency unless the separation involved family breakdown and disruption. There are other features of family life that have also been found to correlate with children involved in official delinquency. Low parental supervision and control, low family cohesiveness, high parental conflict, infrequent family recreation, large family size, high family criminality, and low social class all seem to be associated with delinquent behaviour. However, if the parents did not engage in criminality, were in stable relationships, and had higher than average intelligence, the other factors, such as infrequent family recreation, family conflict, and family size, did not have much effect on rates of delinquency.[26]

Whether related to poor parenting or not—and the correlation is very much in debate—behaviour problems in early childhood have been proven to be somewhat predictive of later delinquency.[27] The etiology (causation) of such problems is varied and complex: some, such as fetal alcohol syndrome/fetal alcohol effects (FAS/FAE) and autism/autistic spectrum disorder, are almost certainly **organically based**. The cause of others, such as attention deficit hyperactivity disorder (ADHD) and some kinds of learning disabilities, is currently a matter of debate. And others, like aggressiveness, or social withdrawal due to shyness, may simply be a matter of individual personality.

organically based
symptoms or behaviours that flow from a disease, defect, or disability of the physical body

How parents, teachers, and other adults react to child behaviour problems may also be a factor in later criminal behaviour. According to researchers Anthony Doob and Jane Sprott, the self-esteem of aggressive children is often overestimated—while aggressive youngsters may appear to be assertive and blustering, when studied more closely, these children feel "bad, sad and rejected"[28] by their peers, teachers, and parents. These findings suggest that criminal prosecution, and the additional condemnation that it implies, is the *worst* response that can be made with respect to these youth.

Regardless of the cause of problem behaviour, the correlation with later delinquency is strong enough to inspire calls for crime prevention strategies aimed at subjects as young as "prenatal to age six."[29]

URBAN LIFE AS A CAUSE OF YOUTH CRIME

It has long been assumed that urban life is associated with youth crime. An examination by Gordon West of Ontario government data from 1981 indicates, however, that the overall crime rate was slightly higher in rural areas than in urban areas, although certain of the more serious crimes such as robbery and large thefts were more common in urban areas. Urban crime rates vary tremendously by neighbourhood. The police, acting on the basis of complaints and also on stereotypical assumptions, deploy more officers in working-class and minority neighbourhoods than they do in middle-class areas, which contributes to a higher arrest rate. One study found that arrests in working-class neighbourhoods in Montreal were double those in middle-class neighbourhoods, though self-report surveys of delinquency indicated that the number of crimes self-reported were almost equal.[30]

EFFECT OF SCHOOLS ON DELINQUENCY

anomie
state of "normlessness" where an individual who has failed to learn the norms and values of society and thus to adapt to society is likely to become a social outsider, living on the margins of society

control theory
theory that focuses on different social and environmental factors that shape human behaviour in society

Most studies of the causes of delinquency assign an important role to schools. Functionalist-**anomie** theories, **control theories**, and conflict theories all see school experience as a crucial factor in delinquency. Functionalists see school failure by working-class boys, caused by their inability to adapt to middle-class school norms and values, as a cause of their rejection of mainstream values and acceptance of delinquent status. Conflict theorists say much the same thing, focusing on resistance to preserve cultural integrity by marginalized working-class youth. Control theory emphasizes elements leading to school success as creating a positive response to mainstream social integration.

There is clear evidence that those with middle-class origins who experience school failure and diminished economic opportunities experience as much delinquency as those with lower-class origins and low academic expectations and economic opportunities. Those with middle-class and working-class origins who are successful in school have much lower rates of delinquency. Certainly, there is a lot of evidence that students in less rigorous academic programs and students who are failing are less committed to schools and school values, and plan to leave as soon as possible.

A negative school experience has long been seen as a factor that can lead to more serious delinquency. However, there are some data that suggest that dropping out results in lower rates of delinquency, perhaps because the strain of dealing with a negative school experience is removed, particularly if the youth who drops out finds employment.[31] But do some schools actually cause delinquency? In a study of a homogenous working-class youth population in the east end of London, England, researchers found varying rates of delinquency. While social background, class, treatment by police, and other factors did not account for the variation, the school they attended was strongly associated with the presence or absence of serious delinquency. Other studies have shown the same trends.[32] A closer examination of the data reveals that schools that "produce" higher delinquency rates are larger than other schools; have a higher staff turnover; have larger classes; are conservative, authoritarian, and non-progressive in their teaching methodology; and do not involve the students in the school's organization or operation. Teachers were also more resistant to granting older students some adult autonomy—for example, by permitting smoking in designated smoking areas. Schools that were more progressive and allowed students more autonomy produced fewer delinquents than their more authoritarian counterparts.

Chapter Summary

This chapter identified the principal types of crime that young people commit and examined various explanations for the causes of youth crime. General trends and patterns in youth crime since the 1950s were discussed, in addition to some of the explanations for increases, decreases, and changes in types of crime committed. Several types of crime that are typically committed by young offenders were identified: vandalism, break and enter, motor vehicle theft, substance abuse, and crimes of violence. Special attention was paid to the crimes of young female offenders, which differ in some respect from those of males.

The chapter then examined theories and explanations of the causes of youth crime. It began with a general discussion of conflict, functionalist, and symbolic interactionist theories because these are the principal theoretical approaches to explaining youth crime. While the theories make different assumptions about human nature, and about how youth crime is caused, you were encouraged to look at the theories as tools for explaining different aspects of youth crime, with an appreciation that one approach may be more effective than others in explaining certain aspects of youth crime. With this theoretical context in mind, we then turned to factors that may influence youth crime, including racial or ethnic minority status, economic deprivation, unemployment, family relationships, and urban–rural residence. The chapter also explored the notion that delinquents do not share a single subculture and that three subcultures have been identified in relation to delinquency. The subcultures were described and analyzed in terms of how group members engage in or avoid delinquent behaviour. Lastly, the chapter explored how school experience may contribute to delinquent behaviour, with attention paid to those aspects of schools that may contribute to or lessen student delinquency.

KEY TERMS

conflict theory	acculturation
functionalist theory	assimilation
symbolic interactionist theory	barrio
ethnographic studies	structural unemployment
labelling theory	organically based
ascribed ethnicity	anomie
host society	control theory

NOTES

1. D. Carrigan, *Juvenile Delinquency in Canada: A History* (Concord, ON: Irwin Publishing, 1998), 153.

2. *Criminal Code*, RSC 1985, c. C-46, as amended, s. 430.

3. Ibid., s. 140.

4. Louise Biron and Danielle Gauvreau, *Portrait of Youth Crime* (Ottawa: Secretary of State, 1984), cited in Carrigan, supra note 1, at 172.

5. Carrigan, supra note 1, at 175.

6. J. Hagan and B. McCarthy, "Streetlife and Delinquency" (December 1992), vol. 43, no. 4 *British Journal of Sociology* 533-61; B. McCarthy and J. Hagan, "Homelessness: A Crimogenic Situation?" (Autumn 1991), 4 *British Journal of Criminology* 393-410.

7. *Criminal Code*, supra note 2, s. 335.

8. Statistics Canada, "Crime Statistics in Canada 2004" (2004), vol. 25, no. 5 *Juristat* 12-13, catalogue no. 85-002-XPE.

9. See, for example, P. Carrington and S. Moyer, "A Statistical Profile of Female Young Offenders," Department of Justice Canada Technical Report, 1998, http://www.justice.gc.ca/en/ps/rs/rep/1998/tr98-4a.html.

10. Anne Campbell, *The Girls in the Gang* (New York: Blackwell, 1984). This is an American study of female gangs in New York City.

11. For a more detailed introduction to these two theories and some of their key social theorists, see G. Johnson and K. Bauer, *Sociology and Canadian Society*, 2nd ed. (Toronto: Emond Montgomery, 2004), 4-5, and chapter 1, generally.

12. D.A. Andrews and J. Bonta, *The Psychology of Criminal Conduct*, 2nd ed. (Cincinnati, OH: Anderson, 1998).

13. For example, see C. Shaw and H. McKay, *Juvenile Delinquency and Urban Areas* (Chicago: University of Chicago Press, 1942).

14. F.M. Thrasher, *The Gang* (Chicago: University of Chicago Press, 1927) and W. Whyte, *Street Corner Society*, 2nd ed. (Chicago: University of Chicago Press, 1955).

15. W. West, *Young Offenders and the State* (Toronto: Butterworths, 1984), 66-67.

16. P. Solomon, *Black Resistance in High School: Forging a Separatist Culture* (Albany, NY: State University of New York Press, 1992), referred to in J. Tanner, *Teenage Troubles: Youth and Deviance in Canada* (Scarborough, ON: Nelson, 1996), 116-19.

17. Tanner, supra note 16, at 140-43.

18. M. Sullivan, *Getting Paid* (Ithaca, NY: Cornell University Press, 1989), referred to in Tanner, supra note 16, at 138-39.

19. G. West, "The Short Term Careers of Serious Thieves" (1978), vol. 20, no. 2 *Canadian Journal of Criminology* 169-90.

20. F. Padilla, *The Gang as an American Enterprise* (New Brunswick, NJ: Rutgers University Press, 1992).

21. S. Box and C. Hale, "Economic Crisis and the Rising Prisoner Population in England and Wales" (1982), 17 *Crime and Social Justice* 20-25.

22. W. O'Grady, "Crime, Violence and Victimization: A Newfoundland Case," in R. Silverman et al., eds., *Crime in Canadian Society* (Toronto: Butterworths, 1991).

23. Tanner, supra note 16, at 126-30.

24. Ibid., at 156-59.

25. Ibid.

26. West, supra note 15, at 70.

27. I. Theilheimer with files from M. Angus, "Communities and Families Working to Prevent Youth Crime: A Snowball's Chance?" (March 1996), *Transition* [Vanier Institute of the Family, Canada].

28. A. Doob and J. Sprott, "Bad, Sad, and Rejected: The Lives of Aggressive Children" (2000), vol. 42, no. 2 *Canadian Journal of Criminology* 123-33.

29. D. McNally in Theilheimer, supra note 27, at 3.

30. West, supra note 15, at 68-70.

31. Tanner, supra note 16, at 152.

32. M.J. Power et al., "Neighbourhood, School and Juveniles Before the Court" (1972), 12 *British Journal of Criminology* 111-32; see also West, supra note 15, at 152-53.

EXERCISES AND REVIEW

Review Questions

1. What is "old-fashioned delinquency"?

2. How has delinquency changed from what it was in the 1950s?

3. Describe the profile of the type or types of young person who is likely to commit vandalism.

4. Are young offenders likely to steal a car for the purpose of shipping it overseas for sale abroad? Why or why not?

5. How do hate crimes differ from other crimes of violence?

6. How are patterns of criminal behaviour of young females different from those of young males? How are they similar?

7. In what ways do race or ethnicity influence whether an individual may become involved in delinquency?

8. In what ways might being poor make a person more likely to be charged with a criminal offence?

9. What factors appear to be important in predicting whether economically disadvantaged youth do or do not get involved in youth crime?

10. What is the likely relationship between structural unemployment and youth crime?

11. If the number of unemployed increases, and the number of persons convicted and sentenced to prison for robbery and other violent property offences increases, but the number of persons charged with these offences per 100,000 population does *not* change, what might explain the increased imprisonment rate?

12. In what ways can family interaction positively and negatively affect youth crime?

13. How might youth criminality be prevented when it's caused by

    a. organically based behaviour problems?

    b. behaviour problems related to family dysfunction?

    c. behaviour problems related to personality traits, such as aggressiveness?

14. How does youth employment (such as part-time, after-school employment) affect the rate of criminality?

15. What types of schools might contribute to delinquency?

Discussion Questions

1. Delinquency circa 1950 is sometimes referred to as the "old-fashioned delinquency," with the implication that delinquency now is very different from the way it was before. In fact, delinquency has not changed since 1950—the same kinds of kids are doing the same kinds of things. Discuss the extent to which this statement is or is not accurate.

2. The involvement of racial or ethnic minority youth in criminal activity does not really have much to do with race or ethnicity. Discuss.

3. Choose four factors that are most closely associated with causing someone to turn to youth crime. Explain why these factors are important and how they influence behaviour.

CHAPTER 3

Prevention and Rehabilitation Programs to Control Youth Crime: What Works?

■ CHAPTER OBJECTIVES

After completing this chapter, you should be able to:

- Distinguish between prevention and rehabilitation programs in their application to adolescents convicted of offences.

- Be aware of some of the factors that make it difficult to assess the effectiveness of rehabilitation and prevention programs.

- Assess the effectiveness of institutionalization and incarceration generally as criminal deterrents and whether they are more useful in deterring some offenders than others.

- Explain why, and in what circumstances, it might be better to do nothing with an offender than to treat him or her or resort to preventive programs.

- Explain the rationale behind diversion and recognize the circumstances where diversion is likely to be effective.

- Assess the effectiveness of community policing in controlling youth crime.

- Identify the types of schools that would likely prevent criminal offending by youths and explain what might contribute to their effectiveness.

- Identify and explain parenting characteristics that might prevent youths from committing criminal offences.

- Explain what early intervention is and how it might prevent or reduce criminal offences committed by youths.

- Explain why the justice system might be generally more effective in preventing youth crime than we usually assume it is.

Some Concepts Underlying Prevention and Rehabilitation Approaches

incarceration
imprisonment

In chapter 2 we examined factors that were associated with youth crime. In this chapter we examine what researchers have discovered about what does and does not work in preventing or rehabilitating youth who become involved in criminal behaviour. In reading about various techniques, you will note that some programs, like **incarceration**, therapy, or probation, are designed to treat the problem after it occurs; others, such as early childhood intervention programs, are designed to prevent the problem from occurring.

It is always difficult to assess whether a particular program works at all, let alone whether it works well, because there are many factors or variables that contribute to criminal behaviour. Thus it is difficult to tell whether changes to some of those factors brought about by a rehabilitation or prevention program are the cause in the decline in delinquency in a sample population or whether it would have happened anyway if nothing had been done. If an increase in delinquency results, the question becomes whether the program has actually made matters worse.

classical theory of crime
older theory that assumes that individuals make rational choices about committing crimes and can be deterred from crime by severe punishment, which inflicts a cost that a rational person would choose to avoid

environmental theory of crime
theory of crime that assumes that factors in an individual's environment make it more or less likely that the individual will become involved in crime

The kinds of programs and approaches that have been used have changed over the past three centuries and, in some cases, over a span of two or three decades. In the late 18th and early 19th centuries in Canada, most people believed in the **classical theory of crime**, in which the individual has free will and is responsible for his or her actions. A person was seen to make conscious, rational, and deliberate choices, and was expected to foresee and accept the consequences. Accordingly, transgressors were held accountable for their actions, and corrective programs focused on harsh punishments that would deter potential lawbreakers, who would see that the costs of law breaking outweigh the gains. In the late 19th century through most of the 20th century, as the rates of personal violence in society declined, an **environmental theory of crime** developed where crime was not seen simply to be the product of rational decision making, but was caused by external and environmental factors that were largely beyond the individual's control. Crime control under this model focused on controlling or eliminating those environmental factors, such as poverty, bad parenting, and child neglect, that were associated with criminal behaviour. Here there was less emphasis on punishment and more emphasis on rehabilitation and social improvement.

Starting in the last two decades of the 20th century, most commentators believe that we have been moving back toward a classical view of crime, where more severe punishments and retribution generally are seen by the public and the media to be more effective in controlling juvenile crime. There is much research to suggest that public reactions to crime are cyclical—moving back and forth from strict punishment to rehabilitation. This cyclical pattern has been reflected in our law. The *Juvenile Delinquents Act*, first passed in 1908, focused on rehabilitation of the child; the *Young Offenders Act* (YOA), passed in the 1980s, paid more attention to punishment than its predecessor had. The *Youth Criminal Justice Act* (YCJA) maintains much of its predecessor's emphasis on punishment for many young offenders, but does attempt some innovations with respect to rehabilitation, particularly through the use of pre- and post-charge diversion measures.

Prevention and Rehabilitation Programs: What Works and What Does Not

INSTITUTIONALIZATION/INCARCERATION AND THE PRINCIPLE OF FORMAL DETERRENCE

A prison term, particularly a long one, is usually justified by its proponents on the ground of deterrence. Incarceration is designed to deter the offender and, by example, to deter others who might be contemplating doing what the offender has done. Imprisonment also has another effect—it incapacitates an offender. Obviously, an offender who is locked up is not free to commit more offences.

Imprisonment of young offenders may also include attempts at rehabilitation through prison-based programs. Although the short duration of some sentences under the YOA was criticized as impairing opportunities for custody-based programs, there is some evidence that *properly designed* rehabilitative efforts in the corrections system are modestly successful in reducing recidivism.[1]

A number of commentators have observed that under the YOA, imprisonment was resorted to increasingly and inappropriately. Some have characterized this as an overreaction by the courts to relatively minor offences, particularly offences against the administration of justice, such as charges for failing to appear in court. At the same time, the maximum YOA sentence for very serious crimes such as aggravated assault and murder was criticized as insufficient, given the gravity of the offence. Other commentators, particularly in the mainstream media, criticized the YOA as too lenient as a result.

Does imprisonment of young offenders prevent crime? In the short term, the answer is yes for that particular person; a jailed offender is an incapacitated offender. But is the offender deterred as a result of being imprisoned or being threatened with imprisonment? Is a "boot camp" more effective than other types of institutions? Would less restrictive and less expensive responses to youth crime work as well, or better?

One way of getting some answers about the usefulness of imprisonment is to examine the results of **cohort studies**. One such study examined a cohort of 10,000 males in Philadelphia, born in 1945, who lived in the city from ages 10 to 18. Of those studied, some 6 percent committed 52 percent of all of the offences recorded in that period. So, if every first offender was locked up until he reached the age of majority, two-thirds of all of these offences would not have been committed. However, the other 48 percent who did not commit further offences after the first offence would also be locked up when it was not necessary to do this to deter them. They simply committed no further offences, without having been incarcerated.

cohort study
study in which the researcher follows a large number of people, or cohort, linked together by some characteristic such as age, profession, or gender to identify and track patterns particular to that cohort

There are a number of studies that show, particularly for the adolescent involved in a less serious offence and who is not strongly committed to an offender subculture, that the first contact with the police and the courts is enough to divert the young person from further acts of delinquency.[2] In this case, leniency or inaction seems as effective as incarceration, and deterrence is either unnecessary or is achieved simply by the contact with police.

There have been some suggestions that young offenders can be deterred from further serious crime by subjecting them to a "scared straight" program—frightening them by having them tour a maximum security prison and talk to inmates who are serving long sentences. This approach was used in Rahway, New Jersey in 1979. A documentary on this method of deterrence noted that 16 of 17 persistent young offenders had given up their offending ways and had stayed out of trouble for at least three years. A further 9,000 took part in this program, and of these, 90 percent stayed out of trouble after the experience. The New Jersey experiment was copied in other US jurisdictions.

The young offenders were exposed to the most negative aspects of imprisonment, including the unpleasant physical conditions, the threats of violence, and the noise, both by seeing the prison first-hand and by talking to inmates. This program was based on the assumption from classical crime theory that offenders will rationally assess their options and thus choose to give up their criminal activities because the costs of continuing them is too high.[3]

Notwithstanding the claim that this is an inexpensive and effective means of preventing juvenile crime, later studies have cast some doubt on the results. James Finckenauer evaluated this program and found that offenders' encounters with prisoners did not alter their perception of the realities of prison as a form of punishment. Nor did he find that exposure to life in a maximum-security prison reduced the delinquency of those who participated in the program. In fact, in comparing a group of participants with a control group of non-participants, he found that those who participated in the New Jersey program actually committed further offences at a much higher rate (41.3 percent) than was the case for the control group (11.4 percent), which was in every respect similar, except that its members did not take part in the program.[4] Subsequent followup studies by others have not shown such dramatic results, but they have demonstrated that this type of deterrent program does not conclusively reduce further criminal activity.[5] While the shock from seeing the effects of severe punishment may have had some initial effect, the impact seemed to have faded relatively quickly.

There has not been extensive use of "scared straight" programs in Canada; however, there have been some proponents of short jail terms or "shock incarceration" for youth convicted of relatively minor offences, with the objective of scaring these offenders out of further involvement in crime. The effectiveness of this approach has been questioned, and in their 1999 meta-analysis of the effectiveness of corrections programs, Canadian researchers Craig Dowden and D.A. Andrews found that shock incarceration was actually associated with an *increased* recidivism rate compared with other treatment approaches.[6]

Another popular approach to deterring youth crime has been to send offenders to boot camp. This approach was increasingly popular in the 1990s. Boot camps are military-style prisons, often in rural areas, requiring physical work and involving strict discipline. The idea behind boot camps is that offenders will benefit from a highly structured program with military-style discipline. This kind of program, emphasizing discipline and obedience to superiors, is designed to deter offenders from further delinquency. American studies of boot camps indicate that boot camp environments actually foster more aggression on the part of both inmates and guards than one finds in a more traditional prison setting.[7] There is also no reliable evidence of a lower recidivism rate following discharge from boot camps.

In the face of this research, in 1995, the Ontario government announced its intention to establish a "strict discipline" boot camp–styled program with a military structure for young offenders in custody. In 1997, Project Turnaround opened its doors near Barrie, Ontario. The camp was intended to be a pilot project after which other facilities were to be modelled. Its operation was contracted to a private, for-profit organization, Encourage Youth Inc. The facility was to hold 12 young offenders, ages 16 and 17, with a history of difficult and defiant behaviour. However, after several offenders escaped, the program was limited to offenders without serious medical or mental disorders, or a history of homicide, arson, or sex offences. The new requirements also stipulated that offenders must be serving sentences of more than four months but less than six months. Despite it's annual operating budget of $2.3 million, the program was not a success. It was marred by escapes, was underused, and was very expensive to operate. Project Turnaround officially closed on January 31, 2004. The government of the day cited the expense of the project as the reason for its termination, but the failure of the project to reduce recidivism rates, combined with a change in attitudes toward custody as a sentencing option ushered in by the YCJA, also likely contributed to its demise.

Having considered the foregoing deterrence-based approaches to youth crime, we have learned that measuring the effectiveness of deterrence is problematic. We can measure recidivism rates, but we can never be sure whether calculated deterrence in the form of incarceration, threats of it, or exposure to the conditions that characterize incarceration represent a significant motivation for youths who abandon delinquency after an initial experience. According to legal researcher Nicholas Bala, traits characteristic of adolescence (and particularly of those prone to offending)—immaturity, lack of foresight and judgment, and recklessness—make this group much less susceptible to deterrence than their more calculating adult counterparts.[8] And, having learned in the previous chapter that youth who develop close connections with criminal networks (as often occurs in custody) are at a substantially increased risk for offending, our current trend toward increased institutionalization of young offenders deserves critical scrutiny. This rethinking of custody is evident, as we will see, in the preamble and principles provisions of the new YCJA.

PROBATION

With the inception of the YOA, probation became the most common sentence faced by young offenders, particularly for a first offence. Probation remains a very common sentence under the YCJA and is discussed in more detail in chapter 11. Probation has been criticized as being a "mere slap on the wrist" and as being ineffective, given the heavy case loads of probation officers. Since the YCJA came into force, probation has been imposed in serious offences and on chronic offenders. This approach is supported by the research, which shows that probation works well with younger offenders and with those offenders who commit property offences. It is also a relatively inexpensive program to run and appears reasonably effective as a prevention tool. Its prevention function probably does not arise from substantial counselling and advice from probation officers. Most probation officers have heavy caseloads and lack the time to do that kind of work. However, they can perform an important function of broker or case manager in referring the young offender to various community-based programs that attempt to address the underlying reasons for the offending behaviour. Additionally, probation officers prepare pre-sentence reports, in which probation officers gather useful information about the offender that allows them to assess with a fair degree of accuracy whether the offender is likely to re-offend. In addition, probation serves as a warning, with the proviso that a breach of probation by getting into trouble again may result in a return to court and possible termination of probation, with the offender serving custodial time for the original offence. Also, probation officers are sometimes able to positively intervene in the life of some probationers. While it is not always successful, court-ordered probation is relatively inexpensive and flexible enough to provide some preventive response for the less serious offenders.[9]

However, anecdotally, police and probation officers question to what extent probation can be an effective means of addressing youthful offending when inadequate resources are provided. Some probation officers are concerned that they do not have the equipment, such as handcuffs, pepper spray, or access to holding rooms, that would allow them to incapacitate an offender on an arrest for breach of probation until police officers arrive. Others do not believe such tools would properly reflect a probation officer's role, which they would define less as one of enforcement than one of social work. Disagreement about the proper role and appropriate resources to allocate probation officers will continue to have an impact on the effectiveness of probation as a sentence.

COMMUNITY ACTION PROGRAMS

Diversion

Police and prosecutors have always had discretion whether to arrest or prosecute. This discretion is affected by legislation other than the YCJA. Even though police have discretion whether to arrest under the *Criminal Code*, they are also governed by the *Police Services Act*, which sets out when police must make an arrest. Police officers can face neglect of duty charges for failing to arrest in some circumstances. Even so, middle-class male offenders and females have traditionally benefited from prosecutorial discretion that results in **diversion** from the justice system, with reliance on non-legal methods to deal with some offenders.

diversion
formal or informal process whereby offenders are diverted out of the justice system to have their transgression dealt with in other ways

In the 1970s and 1980s, diversion began to be developed as a formal alternative to the justice system with the introduction of the YOA and its alternative measures program. This program only operated at the post-charge stage and was at the discretion of the prosecutor. The notion of alternative measures was incorporated and expanded in the YCJA. As is discussed in chapter 12, these informal alternatives to the court process are now called "extrajudicial sanctions" and are offered by the Crown after a charge has been laid. The YCJA also allows for the use of "extrajudicial measures," whereby police can divert adolescents from the formal justice system before a charge is laid. Extrajudicial sanctions are a way of treating an offence more seriously; where a charge has been laid, the accused can be brought back to court if he or she does not complete the alternative program. The availability of these programs varies from province to province.

Diversion has historically depended on the availability of outside agencies—particularly youth agencies, many staffed by volunteers—to provide diversion options. Under the YCJA, this continues to be the case. However, early indications are that provincial governments, most notably Ontario and Quebec, are beginning to direct more money into these programs, which may result in more counselling, academic assistance, job placement, group activities, family mediation, referrals to group homes, and victim–offender reconciliation. It is difficult to assess the effectiveness of diversion programs because they vary tremendously in quality from jurisdiction to jurisdiction. Because the ability to divert successfully depends on their awareness of available programs, law enforcement and justice system personnel have a duty to investigate the range and quality of diversion options available in their communities, and to promote the development of new programs where opportunities are limited.

Although there is little information available about the degree of success of various forms of diversion, many commentators have suggested that diversion activities that foster, build, or rebuild connections between youth and "positive" societal influences—family, school, church, community, and so on—are the most likely to succeed. Many delinquency studies have suggested that alienation from positive community influences promotes criminal behaviour and increases youth affiliation with criminal subcultures.

Some basic diversion programs (such as job placement or community service) may work simply by counteracting boredom and decreasing the offender's unsupervised time—two factors that correlate with increased criminal activity. More sophisticated programs are aimed specifically at building skills that foster reconnection. An approach called "multisystemic therapy" (MST), which requires community-based daily or weekly work, is aimed at modifying problem behaviour in the environment where it occurs (typically between family members and in school). Alan Leschied, the university professor who developed this program, emphasizes the importance of environmental continuity for most youths, noting that "to not only effectively understand but to treat anti-social youth it is necessary to maintain them in their natural ecology."[10] Leschied also endorses the use of "cognitive behavioral" based interventions, which offer the best results because they assist offenders to identify and address the underlying thinking errors that are behind their criminal behavior.

In the case of first-time and minor delinquency, diversion apparently works well, but this may be because it is most appropriate for less serious offenders who are ready to leave criminal behaviour behind anyway. In a study of one program that featured goal setting and counselling, there appeared to be a 72 percent success rate. The failures seemed to represent those involved in more serious crime with fewer outside influences that would discourage further crime. Diversion is discussed in more detail in chapter 12.

Community Policing

Does more aggressive community policing prevent delinquency? Many North American cities have developed community policing that is designed to make the police a more visible presence by patrolling on foot, getting to know people in the neighbourhood, using neighbourhood police substations, and involving the police in community ventures and activities. It is important to note, however, that funding shortages can seriously limit a police force's ability to provide community policing. It is likely that this kind of policing leads to more juvenile arrests, and it probably reduces street crime in the short run. But there is some evidence that those who persist in crime, including street youth, simply move on to somewhere else. When aggressive policing clears those people the police think likely to commit offences from an area—such as the tourist district in New York's Times Square, or the Yonge Street strip in Toronto—the crime rate in those areas certainly goes down, at least initially. But critics charge that the problem does not go away because the factors giving rise to it have not gone away. Only the location has changed—it is swept somewhere else—and all the police have done is create a **Potemkin village**.

One community action plan that has been advertised as effective in controlling crime is the area project approach. Area projects were first used in Chicago and ran from the 1930s to the early 1960s. Areas of high crime were identified and explained in terms of the neighbourhood being socially disorganized. If the disorganization was eliminated, it was argued, the crime rate would fall. The way to do this was through community action and involvement, and the community assumption of responsibility for crime prevention. "Assistance was provided to help neighbourhoods organize self-help groups that provided recreational programs for neighbourhood youth, counselling … and the assignment of youth workers, independent of the courts and police, to work with street gangs and advocate for youth in trouble with the law."[11] The Chicago venture, though much praised, was never carefully studied. However, other projects based on the Chicago project have been assessed, and they have not been deemed to be very successful. They do not seem to reduce rates of delinquency, and they are very expensive to maintain. Tanner, among others, notes that we know what factors correlate highly with crime—few employment prospects, poor education, disrupted families, ineffective parenting, and contact with criminal networks. Providing counselling, recreation centres, and assigning youth workers, Tanner argues, does not really address the factors that are closely related to delinquency.[12]

Potemkin village place that has a superficial facade that looks pleasant and prosperous but that hides an ugly and unpleasant reality; named after Catherine the Great's prime minister, who erected fake villages along a route Catherine travelled so that she would not have to look at the misery in which her peasants actually lived

Schools

Classical crime theory and the general public see schools and schooling as preventing delinquency. The traditional theory is that schools, in general, inculcate good manners, good morals, and good behaviour. Education is also the route to eventual adult employment, and, as the concerned Victorians would have acknowledged, it took unemployed youth off the street and kept them out of trouble—at least for part of the day—courtesy of mandatory attendance requirements.

Although most people regard schools as preventing crime, there is a good deal of research, much of it done in Canada, that indicates that some things that happen in schools may reinforce delinquency. Gordon West argues that "compulsory schooling effectively cuts adolescents off from participating in the social and economic life of the community: it reduces their commitments and attachments which … in turn makes delinquency more likely."[13] This is particularly so for working-class youth who have not been academically successful. The usually middle-class values espoused by school authorities and the insistence by school staff on maintaining order, authority, and control directly confront many potentially criminal students, who tend to be more autonomous than other adolescents and who seek adult autonomy and status. This confrontation may lead to, and often does lead to, criminal acts in school and outside of it. To some extent, then, we can say that schools are capable of producing crime rather than preventing it. As noted in the previous chapter, however, some schools do not produce offenders, at least at quite the same rate.[14] A British study noted that several schools that drew on the same working-class London neighbourhood had different rates of crime. The school with the lowest delinquency rate was smaller than the others, had a more committed staff with less staff turnover, had smaller classes, was progressive in its approach to teaching, and involved students in helping maintain school order. Teachers were seen as more willing to accommodate older adolescent demands for some autonomy. Of these factors, teacher attitude toward students was seen to be especially important, as was collaboration and cooperation among teachers and between the principal and teachers. The authors of this study noted that this type of school produced about 50 percent fewer offenders than other schools in the district that were more authoritarian, traditional, and coercive.

Beyond the traditionally cited crime-control aspects of schooling (such as the inculcation of good manners and respect for authority), some schools have sought to introduce special programming designed to achieve various goals directly or indirectly related to crime control. For example, schools have for many years invited law enforcement officers to participate as guest speakers, in an effort to dispel student mistrust of police and to educate students about the role of police in society. In a small number of high schools in Toronto, police officers work out of substations located right at the high schools. Students can report problems directly to these officers. Given the statistics that suggest that crime against youth is underreported, these kinds of programs seem well intentioned and can be better classed as anti-victimization programs rather than as crime prevention programs. Programs aimed at "streetproofing" children or at encouraging the reporting of child abuse fall into the same category; however, these efforts have sometimes been criticized as unnecessarily frightening, or even as tending to increase false reports of victimization. Additionally, police officers report that speaking in high schools tends to be more effective at the elementary level than at the high school level because elementary students tend to be more receptive to their message.

A more recent trend in school-based programs involves teaching conflict avoidance, conflict management, or anger-management skills. These programs are aimed both at potential victims and at the bullies themselves, and tend to emphasize assertiveness and communication skills as an antidote to violence. The effectiveness of these programs has not yet been established, and it is difficult to imagine how success in this context could be measured.

Some critics argue that recent reports of incidents of school violence and the "zero tolerance" aggression policies that these reports have engendered have impaired the ability of schools to make a contribution to prevention and rehabilitation. Schools that are too ready to request police involvement in handling minor acts of violence have been accused of shirking responsibility. In a government round table discussion held during the development of the YCJA, one commentator, a youth street worker, charged:

> A lot of the education system in the city of Toronto tends to abandon these kids I end up working with. I find one of the greatest problems right now is the lack of responsibility by the [school] boards when it comes to dealing with youth who are showing signs of becoming involved in criminal activity or not following the right path. There is a lot of overcriminalization in the school yard.[15]

PARENTING

It has long been noted that there is a strong relationship between dysfunctional families and delinquency. A review of research reports on the relationship between problem families and delinquency notes the following:

- Families where there is no serious conflict between spouses are associated with lower rates of delinquency.

- Single-parent families are associated with higher rates of delinquency although the single-parent aspect is not necessarily the cause; rather, it is the stresses that are often associated with this kind of family, such as family instability, economic deprivation, and reduction in parental supervision, that are most closely associated with delinquency.

- Involvement in criminal behaviour by parents or by other children in the family is strongly associated with delinquency.

- Parental supervision and parental affection shown toward children during childhood appear to be the two most important positive family factors that deter later adult criminal behaviour.[16]

From the perspective of prevention and rehabilitation, influencing parenting practices is a problematic proposition. Parenting is a deeply personal and private activity, and many parents are resistant to interference from outside influences. Where there is a clear deficiency—for example, where a child protection agency has obtained custody of a child—parents may be required to accept counselling and training as a prerequisite to regaining the right to parent their child. But the vast majority of parenting problems are much subtler, and attempts to influence parents have for the most part been limited to public education campaigns, which have covered a wide range of topics (typically health and safety related), such as those warning of the effects of prenatal consumption of alcohol or promoting the health advantages of breastfeeding. Other campaigns encourage reading to children or preparing videos of them for identification in the case of future abduction. Finally, both Canadian and US agencies have recently sponsored general parenting "resource" programs based on the developmental importance of the very early childhood years.

EARLY INTERVENTION

There have been a number of studies that suggest that children who are likely to become offenders can be identified at a relatively early age. In one study in 1994, a team of researchers in Montreal studied a group of students in the public school system who had been identified as disruptive. These students were tracked for a 10-year period: nearly half were chronically aggressive, and over half had fallen behind in school by at least one grade. The study concluded that early intervention was warranted, even before children reached school age. Counselling parents to be effective parents, working with children on anger management and academic problems, and providing other therapy were all seen as a way of deflecting children from paths that lead to criminal behaviour. Working on parenting skills, in particular, appears to be very productive in reducing the aggressiveness of children. However, the study did not indicate whether the children studied went on to a criminal lifestyle, nor did it indicate how serious their crimes were or how embedded in criminal subculture these children became. It is also worth noting that early intervention and remediation is often done one-on-one and is expensive. You may wonder whether governments are prepared to make the necessary expenditure to pursue this preventive strategy.[17]

Does Anything Work?

In reading this chapter, you will have seen that various studies looking at particular factors do not suggest any "magic bullet" that will prevent crime in all cases. Partly, this is because there is not one criminal subculture but several, and different things may work for one type of youth that may not work for another. Another reason may be that, while we can associate certain factors and behaviours with crime, we do not always understand why and how these factors may cause crime.

In the first chapter we made the observation that youth crime is not new. It has been a feature of life in industrialized societies since the late 18th century. Various techniques, both punitive and rehabilitative, have been tried in an attempt to reduce or eliminate delinquency, but levels of youth crime do not seem to change all that much, despite what the media may say and the public think. Will anything work to prevent youth crime?

In 1974, Robert Martinson wrote a paper[18] in which he evaluated the effectiveness of an array of treatment and prevention programs designed to rehabilitate offenders. He concluded that nothing worked very well. It did not seem to matter whether offenders were sentenced to prison or put on probation. Nor did it matter how long offenders were imprisoned, or what kind of prison-based programs they participated in; nor did it matter whether they were in group-based or community-based programs. Regardless of the program, the recidivism rates remained stable. Martinson's analysis has often been used to justify abandonment of rehabilitation in favour of classical deterrence. If attempts to rehabilitate do not work, then we can at least jail offenders and, by doing so, incapacitate them.

More recent commentators suggest that Martinson's analysis is oversimplified. In reviewing Martinson's study, Thomas Bernard comes to the conclusion that the justice system is more effective with rehabilitation than it appears to be. Bernard says that we often start our examination of preventive measures by looking at what everyone agrees are the system's failures—the incorrigibles who have been imprisoned. We then track them through their careers. We start with a warning to the young teen. The teen is then apprehended again, but this time he or she is charged. The teen is then diverted out of the system before trial. Apprehended again, the youth is tried, and this time gets a custodial sentence. If we look back into what went wrong that resulted in this young person becoming a criminal, we see that the youth was initially treated leniently. Some would then argue that if the youth had been treated more punitively earlier, all the later trouble would not have occurred.

What this analysis does not see, Bernard argues, is the youth who interpreted leniency by the police, probation officers, and the courts as an opportunity to get out of the pattern of delinquency. If we remember that there is strong statistical evidence that most juvenile crimes, particularly serious ones, are committed by a relatively small number of offenders, we can see that most youth do not advance beyond petty offences, and leave crime behind them at a relatively early age. Bernard calculates that in the United States, 18 out of 100 apprehended youth end up on probation or in prison. But the other 82 do not. A success rate of 82 percent, he argues, represents success, not failure.

At the same time, Bernard and those who agree with him do not think that all of the responses to juvenile crime are equally effective.[19] In particular, programs like the "scared straight" program and purely punitive institutionalization do not appear to be effective if we look at the recidivism rates. These studies conclude, remarkably, that for minor property offences and trifling "violence" (such as some schoolyard scuffles), the less rehabilitation or prevention used, the better. Offenders involved in these kinds of offences will often leave crime behind them relatively early of their own accord.

Also, probation is often effective, simply because, as we noted earlier, probation officers have a great deal of information about offenders and can often predict trouble before it happens. The probation officer can also "breach" the probationer if the offender does not obey the conditions attached to the probation order. Furthermore, attaching conditions to an order, particularly one requiring participation in a community rehabilitation program, is often reasonably effective, especially when compared with the prospect of imprisonment. However, for probation with conditions to be effective, offenders must be screened. Generally, property offenders—even chronic property offenders—can be shown to benefit from probation with conditions. Prison is appropriate only for those who are the most violent, or who are the most embedded in a criminal subculture.

In fact, according to research by Andrews, Zinger, Hoge, Bonta, Gendreau, and Cullen, overreliance on incarceration is one of the worst possible policy mistakes a state can make. Because imprisonment provides inevitable opportunities for youth to make connections with the criminal subculture, weakens community ties, and affects employment prospects, imprisonment itself can be said to increase the recidivism risk for first-time offenders. Because of this effect, Andrews and his colleagues are concerned with the recent Canadian trend toward imposing short prison sentences, as opposed to choosing other dispositions, for relatively minor offences.

Most modern corrections research supports the theory that, in order to be effective, approaches to youth criminal behaviour must be highly responsive to the recidivism *risk* and the criminogenic (crime-causing) *needs* of individual offenders. Rehabilitation programs that begin with an assessment of risk and need, and that tailor responses to these, have been proven to be considerably more successful than their traditional counterparts. Addressing broader needs of adolescents, such as testing for learning disabilities, may also be helpful. For example, a generally well-behaved teenager who participates in setting up a bathroom stink bomb and is contrite when caught by a teacher may be found to be at very low risk of recidivism. The principle of matching the intensity of response to the level of risk suggests that a warning by school personnel would probably be a sufficient deterrent for this offender. In contrast, a youth with a history of academic problems at school and who is caught, for the third time, setting fires in wastebaskets in the teachers' staff room may be found to have a level of recidivism risk and a list of **criminogenic needs** (academic problems, antisocial attitudes, self-control problems)

criminogenic needs unmet needs of an offender—for example, the need for help in controlling anger or in reducing substance abuse—that promote the commission of further crimes to warrant calling police for the laying of a charge, which might, upon conviction, attract a probation sentence with a counselling component.

Where the principles of risk and need inform prevention and rehabilitation choices, even much-maligned custody dispositions can be shown to reduce recidivism. In the 1999 article, "What Works in Young Offender Treatment: A Meta-Analysis," Canadian researchers Dowden and Andrews found that "the introduction of human service within a justice context is associated with strong reductions in the reoffending levels of young offenders" as long as the rehabilitative services provided are designed to address properly identified levels of risk and criminogenic needs. Offenders in programs that met the appropriateness criteria in this study had recidivism rates of 35 percent, while the offenders in the control group who received no rehabilitative service, or inappropriate service, had a recidivism rate of 65 percent.[20] These findings suggest that, instead of throwing up our collective hands in the face of stable or growing crime rates, we would do well to continue to invest resources in the development and delivery of programs such as MST and cognitive behavioral based programs that meet the criteria associated with success.

Chapter Summary

In this chapter we examined some of the kinds of prevention and rehabilitation programs that currently exist and attempted to assess their effectiveness in controlling youth crime. The evaluation began with a review of imprisonment and custodial programs, including "scared straight" programs and boot camps. Probation was then examined, along with various community action programs, such as diversion, community policing, and school structures. Finally, effective parenting and early intervention programs were explored. In evaluating and assessing all of these prevention and rehabilitation programs, an attempt was made to identify the circumstances and type of offenders for whom some programs are likely to be effective or ineffective. The Martinson "nothing works" theory was examined, as was newer research that confirms the moderate effectiveness of matching response intensity and type to offender risk of recidivism and criminogenic needs.

KEY TERMS

incarceration

classical theory of crime

environmental theory of crime

cohort study

diversion

Potemkin village

criminogenic needs

NOTES

1. C. Dowden and D.A. Andrews, "What Works in Young Offender Treatment: A Meta-Analysis" (1999), vol. 11, no. 2 *Forum on Corrections Research* 21.

2. See J. Tanner, *Teenage Troubles: Youth and Deviance in Canada* (Scarborough, ON: Nelson, 1996), 222-25.

3. Ibid., at 216-18.

4. J. Finckenauer, *Scared Straight and the Panacea Phenomenon* (Englewood Cliffs, NJ: Prentice Hall, 1982).

5. Tanner, supra note 2.

6. Dowden and Andrews, supra note 1, at 23.

7. Tanner, supra note 2, at 218.

8. N. Bala, *Young Offenders Law* (Toronto: Irwin Law, 1997), 3.

9. Tanner, supra note 2, at 225; M. Jacobs, *Screwing the System and Making It Work* (Chicago: University of Chicago Press, 1990).

10. A.W. Leschied, "Implementing Alternatives to Custody in Addressing Youth Crime: Applications of the Multisystemic Therapy Approach in Canada," article for a presentation made at *Beyond Prisons*, an international symposium hosted by Corrections Canada, CIDA, and Queen's University in Kingston, Ontario, March 1998, at 4.

11. Tanner, supra note 2, at 222.

12. Ibid.

13. G. West, *Young Offenders and the State* (Toronto: Butterworths, 1984), 169; see, generally, 143-79 for a detailed discussion of the research on the effects of schools on adolescents in general and on offenders in particular.

14. Ibid., at 152.

15. E. Duarte, youth street worker, in evidence presented at a June 3, 1996 round table of the Standing Committee on Justice and Legal Affairs, House of Commons, 35th Parliament, 2nd session.

16. Ministry of the Solicitor General of Canada, *Programs Branch User Report*, no. 1985-06, 171-75, cited in D. Carrigan, *Juvenile Delinquency in Canada* (Concord, ON: Irwin Publishing, 1998), at 284-86.

17. Ibid., at 304-6.

18. R. Martinson, "What Works? Questions and Answers About Prison Reform" (Spring 1974), 35 *The Public Interest* 22-54; see also Tanner, supra note 2, at 219-21.

19. Tanner, supra note 2, at 222-27, citing R. Lundman, *Prevention and Control of Juvenile Delinquency*, 2nd ed. (New York: Oxford University Press, 1992).

20. Dowden and Andrews, supra note 1, at 21.

EXERCISES AND REVIEW
Review Questions

1. What is the difference between a rehabilitation and a prevention program?

2. How has the attitude toward offenders over time affected the types of programs developed to control youth crime?

3. Explain the extent to which the following programs are effective or ineffective in treating or preventing youth crime:

   a. purely punitive imprisonment

   b. "scared straight" programs

   c. custody-based rehabilitation programs

   d. probation

4. Explain what conclusions about imprisonment can be drawn from the Philadelphia age-cohort study.

5. What is the basis for saying that, for some offences, the best rehabilitation and prevention is to do nothing?

6. Explain why probation may effectively prevent further recidivism in some circumstances.

7. Suggest circumstances in which probation would be effective, as well as circumstances where it would not be effective.

8. Explain what is meant by "criminogenic needs." Can you come up with a list of such needs?

9. Describe the profile of the kind of family that is most likely to encourage criminal behaviour.

10. Describe the profile of the kind of family that is least likely to encourage criminal behaviour.

Research Exercise

This chapter introduced community diversion (as an alternative to charge/conviction) and prevention programs designed to reduce youth crime, but did not describe the specifics of these programs, because their availability varies from community to community.

In your particular community, research the availability of diversion and prevention programs, and answer the following questions:

1. Are there any formal diversion or "extrajudicial measures" community programs in your community?

    a. List and describe them.

    b. How and when do youth typically get referred to these programs?

    c. What is the typical profile of youths referred to this type of program? Are they first-time or repeat offenders? What kinds of offences do they typically commit? How old are they?

    d. How are local diversion programs funded? How did they start?

2. Are there any crime prevention programs directed at youth or children in your community?

    a. List and describe them.

    b. How are these programs delivered—for example, through schools or community centres, or by referral?

    c. Who are the typical recipients of these programs? Are they youth identified as being "at risk" or youth in general? What age groups are targeted by these programs?

    d. How are these programs funded, and how did they get started?

3. Do you believe your community is well served when it comes to diversion and prevention programs? Why or why not?

4. Can you come up with any ideas for programs that might benefit your community?

    a. List and describe each of these programs.

    b. How might the program(s) you describe be started? How might it or they be funded or staffed?

Discussion Questions

1. Identify the type of program that might deflect the following individuals from continuing their criminal behaviour; explain why the program would likely be successful in doing this.

    a. Albert is a 13-year-old shoplifter. This is the second time he has been charged. The first time he was placed on probation. He lives at home with his parents, both of whom work; the family is stable and earns a middle-class family income, but the parents do not spend a lot of time with Albert or his 7-year-old brother, who is in school-age day care after school. Neither child is notably disruptive in school, and both are in the middle of the pack academically.

b. Bella, a 16-year-old girl, assaulted her mother. She has no previous record, has done well in school, and is not known to have behavioural problems. Her mother is a single parent, and the assault followed the mother's attempt to prevent Bella from going out on a school night at 11 p.m. to hang out with her friends.

c. Charles, age 17, is charged with car theft. This is his fourth offence since he was 15. He comes from a two-parent family, but his parents are barely talking to him, and his father, on learning of the charges, locked Charles out of the house and has told him to live somewhere else. Both parents are clear that they have had enough of his behaviour and do not want him in the house.

d. Dan, age 14, is charged with selling amphetamines. He has no previous record and comes from a stable family, although his father has a lengthy criminal record. Dan has a history of drug use, is disruptive at school, and is doing poorly academically.

e. Edward, age 17, is charged with robbery. He has a police contact record going back to age 12 that includes sexual assault, other assaults, and various thefts. His last charge, which was for theft, resulted in three months' imprisonment. His academic record is quite good, but he is disruptive in school. A number of his friends have equally lengthy criminal histories.

2. Schools are just as likely to encourage and foster criminal behaviour as discourage it. Discuss this statement, explaining why it is or is not accurate.

3. "Early intervention with a kindergarten kid to prevent criminal behaviour later is a lot of hooey. All the kid needs is a smack on the behind. The early interventionist stuff is just a lot of bleeding heart nonsense." Can early intervention work, and in what circumstances?

4. Does anything work? List what you think are the "top five" programs that are most likely to be successful with most young offenders.

PART II

Legislative Approaches: Outside the Justice System

CHAPTER 4

The Child and Family Services Act

■ CHAPTER OBJECTIVES

After completing this chapter, you should be able to:

- Summarize the paramount purpose of the *Child and Family Services Act* (CFSA).

- Describe the mandate of children's aid societies with respect to the delivery of consensual/non-residential services.

- List several examples of "services" provided to children and families under the CFSA.

- List the signs or criteria that, if observed in relation to a child, could trigger a duty to report that the child might be at risk of abuse or neglect.

- Describe the process for taking a child suspected to be in need of protection into the care of a children's aid society pending proceedings.

- Explain the method set out by the CFSA for dealing with a child under the age of 12 who is suspected of having committed an act that is a crime under the *Criminal Code*.

- Describe the criteria that must be met before a child can be committed to secure care for a mental disorder.

- Describe the rights of a child in detention or protective custody.

Before turning to a detailed examination of Canada's youth criminal justice system, it is useful to first place that system within the broader context of laws affecting youth in Canada. For the purpose of this text, we will restrict our examination of youth law to a review of selected statutes that directly address the circumstances of children and youth.

Although there are many statutes (such as the Ontario *Family Law Act*,[1] and other provincial equivalents) that have a considerable effect on the lives of children and adolescents, the *Child and Family Services Act*[2] (CFSA), the *Provincial Offences Act*,[3] and the *Education Act*[4] deal with youth as individuals in their own right, separate from the family unit, and govern their interactions with the state. In regulating these interactions, and interactions between youth and the rest of society, these statutes (to varying extents and for different purposes) acknowledge the differences between children and adolescents, and adults; and they convey, both explicitly and implicitly, community and state expectations with respect to the role of youth in society, and the responsibility of other members of society with respect to youth. By taking the time to review this general legislative context, we will be better prepared to understand the subcontext of the youth criminal justice system.

Introduction

The *Child and Family Services Act* is the most important child protection legislation in Ontario. Each province in Canada has similar legislation, and much of it originated near the beginning of the 20th century. Around that time, there was a lot of overlap between the federal *Juvenile Delinquency Act* (JDA) and provincial child protection legislation. Both forms of legislation professed to seek the "best interests" of children in society. Societal attitudes to situations in which youths find themselves in conflict with the law have since shifted somewhat, from an explicitly rehabilitation-oriented approach to a punitive/rehabilitative approach. Still, protection (and to a lesser extent rehabilitation) remains an important societal value, especially with respect to children under the age of 12. Ontario's *Child and Family Services Act* is available online at http://www.e-laws.gov.on.ca.

Purposes of the CFSA

The "paramount purpose" of the CFSA is "to promote the best interests, protection and well being of children" (s. 1). The expression of a paramount purpose is new; before a 1999 amendment, the legislation provided a list of purposes, including one emphasizing minimal interference with the family unit. In the wake of concerns that the legislation was being interpreted too conservatively in situations where children at risk were concerned, s. 1 was redrafted to set the first purpose apart, and to accord it primary importance.

The other purposes of the Act, which must be interpreted such that they are "consistent with the best interests, protection and well being of children," are:

1. To recognize that while parents may need help in caring for their children, that help should give support to the autonomy and integrity of the family unit and, wherever possible, be provided on the basis of mutual consent.

2. To recognize that the least disruptive course of action that is available and is appropriate in a particular case to help a child should be considered.

3. To recognize that children's services should be provided in a manner that

    a. respects children's needs for continuity of care and for stable family relationships, and

    b. takes into account physical and mental developmental differences among children.

4. To recognize that, wherever possible, services to children and their families should be provided in a manner that respects cultural, religious, and regional differences.

5. To recognize that status Indian and other native people should be entitled to provide, wherever possible, their own child and family services, and that all services to Indian and native children and families should be provided in a manner that recognizes their culture, heritage, and traditions and the concept of the extended family.

Purposes (1) and (2) communicate the high value that the legislation places on the "autonomy and integrity of the family unit," and require that child protection approaches that are minimally disruptive to that unit be given due consideration. Ideally, these approaches will involve parental participation and will be provided on a consensual basis. It is useful to note, however, that the same set of amendments that strengthened the Act's primary purpose diluted these pro-family purposes, removing a direction in favour of "the least restrictive" course of protective action.

The remainder of the purposes section of the Act is dedicated to ensuring that any services provided are sensitive to the family's background. Services should take the child's physical and mental development into account. Services should respect the particular family's "cultural, religious and regional differences." This is evidenced by specialized child and family service agencies operating in Ontario, such as the Catholic Children's Aid Society and the Jewish Child and Family Services agency. Each agency provides services that are mandated within this Act in a culturally specific manner. Finally, purpose 5 is dedicated to the recognition of the uniqueness of the native community and family structure.

Delivery of Services

The legislation administers its protective mandate by empowering various authorities to intervene where suspected child abuse or neglect has taken place.

Part I of the CFSA deals with the services that can be provided to children and families under the Act. Within that part, s. 15(2) authorizes the designation of a children's aid society. The functions of a children's aid society ("a society") are to

> 15(3)(a) investigate allegations or evidence that children who are under the age of sixteen years or are in the society's care or under its supervision may be in need of protection;
>
> (b) protect, where necessary, children who are under the age of sixteen years or are in the society's care or under its supervision;
>
> (c) provide guidance, counseling and other services to families for protecting children or for the prevention of circumstances requiring the protection of children;
>
> (d) provide care for children assigned or committed to its care under this Act;
>
> (e) supervise children assigned to its supervision under this Act;
>
> (f) place children for adoption under Part VII; and
>
> (g) perform any other duties given to it by this or any other Act.

Consensual Services

Child protection workers and police officers are often portrayed by the media as causing the breakup of families wherever there is suspected child abuse. While this (though overly simplified) may be the case in the most serious situations, it certainly does not represent the majority of cases. In most circumstances, a call is made to the authorities about a potential abuse or neglect situation. A social worker and/or police officer goes to the home within 24 hours of the call and assesses the household. Often, a **consensual services** proposal is established between the service provider and child and/or family to create a plan to improve the situation.

As expressed in its principles, the CFSA attempts to provide services to families in a consensual manner. Part II of the Act contains the provisions dealing with voluntary access to services. This section applies to families who are willing and who often request the temporary assistance of the children's aid society where the family environment has become too difficult for parents to handle on their own.

In general, a service provider must obtain a child's consent before administering a service if the child is over 16 years of age.[5] Where the child is younger than 16 and **residential service** is sought, consent must be obtained from the child's parent. Consent need not be obtained, however, if the child is in the custody of the Children's Aid Society (CAS). Although consent from the child for residential service is not required, s. 27(6) ensures that the child's wishes are taken into account.

For counselling services that do not require a residential placement, consent must be obtained directly from children over the age of 12. Section 28 specifies that "no other person's consent is required." This provision is intended to enable the child to provide full disclosure to the social worker without the fear that the child's parents will have knowledge of the meetings. However, for children under 16 years of age, the section encourages the social worker to discuss parental involvement "at the earliest appropriate opportunity."

Duty to Report Abuse or Neglect

In cases of abuse and **neglect**, the child's life may be in danger. Troubled parents, dealing with problems of their own, may not recognize that their child is being harmed, even while physical or verbal abuse escalates to the point where it may become more obvious to people outside the home. The child may exhibit marked changes in behaviour, or may show up at school with unusual bruises on his or her body. Teachers may begin to take notice and become suspicious. Or, police may be called to the home in response to a reported disturbance, or at the request of neighbours who suspect that young children are wandering unsupervised, or being left at home, while the parents are out.

The CFSA requires that perceived child abuse or neglect be treated not as a private family problem, but rather as society's problem. As such, certain provisions of the Act require the public in general, and people who work with children in particular, to report suspected abuse or neglect. As of the recent passage of the latest set of amendments to the CFSA, the reportable signs and symptoms of abuse or neglect have been codified in detail. The **duty to report** provisions now read as follows (in part):

72(1) Despite the provisions of any other Act, if a person, including a person who performs professional or official duties with respect to children, has reasonable grounds to suspect one of the following, the person shall forthwith report the suspicion and the information on which it is based to a society:

1. The child has suffered physical harm, inflicted by the person having charge of the child or caused by or resulting from that person's,

> i. failure to adequately care for, provide for, supervise or protect the child, or
>
> ii. pattern of neglect in caring for, providing for, supervising or protecting the child.

2. There is a risk that the child is likely to suffer physical harm inflicted by the person having charge of the child or caused by or resulting from that person's,

> i. failure to adequately care for, provide for, supervise or protect the child, or
>
> ii. pattern of neglect in caring for, providing for, supervising or protecting the child.

3. The child has been sexually molested or sexually exploited, by the person having charge of the child or by another person where the person having charge of the child knows or should know of the possibility of sexual molestation or sexual exploitation and fails to protect the child.

4. There is a risk that the child is likely to be sexually molested or sexually exploited as described in paragraph 3.

5. The child requires medical treatment to cure, prevent or alleviate physical harm or suffering and the child's parent or the person having charge of the child does not provide, or refuses or is unavailable or unable to consent to, the treatment.

6. The child has suffered emotional harm, demonstrated by serious,

> i. anxiety,
>
> ii. depression,
>
> iii. withdrawal,
>
> iv. self-destructive or aggressive behaviour, or
>
> v. delayed development,

and there are reasonable grounds to believe that the emotional harm suffered by the child results from the actions, failure to act or pattern of neglect on the part of the child's parent or the person having charge of the child.

7. The child has suffered emotional harm of the kind described in subparagraph i, ii, iii, iv or v of paragraph 6 and the child's parent or the person having charge of the child does not provide, or refuses or is unavailable or unable to consent to, services or treatment to remedy or alleviate the harm.

8. There is a risk that the child is likely to suffer emotional harm of the kind described in subparagraph i, ii, iii, iv or v of paragraph 6 resulting from the actions, failure to act or pattern of neglect on the part of the child's parent or the person having charge of the child.

9. There is a risk that the child is likely to suffer emotional harm of the kind described in subparagraph i, ii, iii, iv or v of paragraph 6 and that the child's parent or the person having charge of the child does not provide, or refuses or is unavailable or unable to consent to, services or treatment to prevent the harm.

10. The child suffers from a mental, emotional or developmental condition that, if not remedied, could seriously impair the child's development and the child's parent or the person having charge of the child does not provide, or refuses or is unavailable or unable to consent to, treatment to remedy or alleviate the condition.

11. The child has been abandoned, the child's parent has died or is unavailable to exercise his or her custodial rights over the child and has not

made adequate provision for the child's care and custody, or the child is in a residential placement and the parent refuses or is unable or unwilling to resume the child's care and custody.

12. The child is less than 12 years old and has killed or seriously injured another person or caused serious damage to another person's property, services or treatment are necessary to prevent a recurrence and the child's parent or the person having charge of the child does not provide, or refuses or is unavailable or unable to consent to, those services or treatment.

13. The child is less than 12 years old and has on more than one occasion injured another person or caused loss or damage to another person's property, with the encouragement of the person having charge of the child or because of that person's failure or inability to supervise the child adequately.

Section 72 also provides that the duty to report does not end with the initial report, but is ongoing, and applies to later-observed signs or incidents (s. 72(2)); and that the duty must be discharged personally, and may not be delegated to another person or agency.

While the duty to report extends to the public at large, certain classes of people, typically those who work with children, are subject to closer scrutiny with respect to s. 72, because their failure to report signs of abuse or neglect observed in the course of their professional duties constitutes an offence under s. 72(4). The professionals subject to a fine under this section are listed below. In the case of lawyers, this duty can be superseded by the lawyer's duty to keep confidential disclosures made by his or her clients.

72(5) Subsection (4) applies to every person who performs professional or official duties with respect to children including,

(a) a health care professional, including a physician, nurse, dentist, pharmacist and psychologist;

(b) a teacher, school principal, social worker, family counsellor, operator or employee of a day nursery and youth and recreation worker;

(b.1) a religious official, including a priest, a rabbi and a member of the clergy;

(b.2) a mediator and an arbitrator;

(c) a peace officer and a coroner;

(d) a solicitor; and

(e) a service provider and an employee of a service provider.

Child Protection Proceedings

Upon receiving a report that a child is at risk (or upon making that determination itself), a society may apply to the court, under s. 40(1), for a determination that the child is in need of protection. The grounds for finding a **child in need of protection** (set out in s. 37(2)) are the same as the grounds that trigger the duty to report.

Generally, the bringing of child protection proceedings includes the apprehension of the child. Section 40 enables a justice of the peace to "issue a warrant authorizing a child protection worker to bring a child to a place of safety" if the justice of the peace is satisfied, on reasonable and probable grounds, that "the child is in need of protection; and a less-restrictive course of action is not available or

child in need of protection
legal definition/ determination, based on an established set of criteria and evidence, that forms the basis of a protective order

will not protect the child adequately." In emergency situations, apprehension may take place without a warrant.

For the purposes of the child apprehension provisions, a peace officer (under s. 40(13)) has the powers of a child protection worker. Or, if a child protection worker initiates the apprehension, a police officer may be called in to assist under s. 40(8). If necessary, the child protection worker or police officer may use force to enter the premises in which a child is being held,[6] and may temporarily detain the child in a "place of open temporary detention," which is defined in the young offender sections in part IV of the Act. In such cases, police officers may enter the premises without a warrant.

The apprehension of a child in preparation for child protection proceedings may also take place in circumstances where there are no signs of abuse or neglect, but where a child under 12 years of age is suspected of having committed an act that would attract criminal liability if committed by a person aged 12 or older. As we will learn in later chapters, the youth criminal justice legislation applies to children ages 12 to 18, but it has been traditionally accepted that child welfare legislation is more appropriate for children outside of that age jurisdiction. A peace officer who suspects that a child under 12 years of age has committed an act that, if proven, would otherwise constitute an offence, may apprehend that child without a warrant, and on doing so

> 42(1)(a) shall return the child to the child's parent or other person having charge of the child as soon as practicable; or
>
> (b) where it is not possible to return the child to the parent or other person within a reasonable time, shall take the child to a place of safety to be detained there until the child can be returned to the parent or other person.

If the police officer has reasonable grounds to believe that returning the child to the parent may put the child at risk, the police officer can take the child to a place of safety instead. A group home made available by child welfare authorities or perhaps even the home of a relative could constitute a place of safety.

Children who are apprehended for the reasons above are placed in detention pending a child protection hearing. There are provisions to ensure a quick resolution. Section 46 guarantees that, within five days of detention, a plan is to be established—either court proceedings are commenced, the child is returned to his or her home, or a temporary care arrangement is made.

Section 47 deals with the child protection hearing. Regardless of the child's age at the time of the hearing, a child protection hearing will proceed if the child was under 16 years of age at the time of apprehension or the commencement of the proceedings. At the hearing, the judge will decide whether the child is in need of protection. If the child is not in need of protection, he or she will be returned home.

If the child is found to be in need of protection, the court will make one of four orders, as provided by s. 57:

1. a supervision order can be made whereby the child is returned home, subject to the society's supervision for 3 to 12 months.

2. The child can be made a **ward** of the society. In this case, the child is kept away from home and placed in the society's care and custody for a period not exceeding 12 months.

ward/wardship
traditional legal term that implies both clienthood as we understand it today and a fiduciary/protective relationship

3. In the most serious cases, the child can be named a ward of the Crown. Here, the child is placed in the custody of the society until the child attains the age of 18 or marries, or a successful application to terminate the wardship is brought under s. 64 (by the child himself or herself, by the society, by a parent or guardian, by a foster parent, or, in the case of a First Nations child, by a community or band representative).

4. Consecutive orders of society wardship and supervision may be made whereby the child is made a society ward for a specified period and then returned home under supervision for a combined period not exceeding 12 months.

When making one of these orders, the judge must consider the written plan for the child's care that has been prepared by the society. The required features of this plan are set out in s. 56. In considering the plan and the proposed order, the judge must prefer "less-disruptive" care alternatives, including placement in the child's community with extended family, a neighbour, or a member of the child's band or First Nations community;[7] but, in choosing these alternatives, the court must be convinced that the choice is adequate for the protection of the child. If the court determines that the child would not be put at risk, his or her parents may be given access to him or her under s. 58.

Abuse or Neglect Offences

A person who neglects a child or subjects a child to physical or sexual abuse can be found guilty of an offence under s. 85(2). (Such a person also, obviously, faces the risk of a charge under the *Criminal Code.*) "Abuse" for the purpose of the CFSA offence is defined in s. 79 as "a state or condition of being physically harmed, sexually molested or sexually exploited,"[8] and "neglect" is broadly defined to include lack of supervision; failure to treat a mental, emotional, or developmental condition; and allowing a child to loiter late at night. (If a child is found in a public place between midnight and 6 a.m. unaccompanied by a parent or designated adult, under s. 79(6), a police officer may, without a warrant, apprehend the child. One example of this would be a child left outside a bingo hall or casino. In all of the above circumstances, police could lay a charge against parents under s. 85(2). Parents convicted under this section may face a fine of up to $2,000 or a prison term of up to two years. Note, however, that such a charge would not give rise to a criminal record.

Charges may also be initiated against a person who interferes with a supervision or wardship order. Furthermore, it is an offence to interfere with an application order or a police officer's attempt to apprehend a child. The legislation also provides for restraining orders against abusers and potential abusers, and for civil proceedings (for damages or other compensation) brought by the Children's Lawyer where such proceedings would be in the child's best interests.

Another offence set out in the CFSA relates to the existence of a curfew of midnight for youth under 16 years of age in Ontario. Section 79(5) of the Act provides that the person responsible for the youth shall not permit him or her to loiter in a public place without parental accompaniment between the hours of midnight and six in the morning. While not currently evenly enforced throughout the province, this provision is nonetheless *enforceable* provincewide and can give rise to liability on the part of parents or guardians of youth to a fine up to $1,000.

Detention of Adolescents

Under the Canadian constitution, while the federal government has jurisdiction over criminal law, the provinces have jurisdiction over property and civil rights. The designation of a certain act or omission as a crime falls within the federal criminal law jurisdiction. Incarceration, however, is not primarily a matter of criminal law but is rather essentially a matter of civil rights. The provincial government, therefore, has the authority to create legislation for custodial facilities. As a result of this provincial jurisdiction over custodial facilities, there is considerable variation among provinces in the nature of facilities constructed and programs in place, depending upon differing provincial agendas. In Ontario, detention of adolescents falls under part IV of the CFSA, which deals with young offenders in Ontario.

The YCJA, in keeping with its goal of reducing over-reliance on custody for adolescents, provides, when s. 3 (in the Declaration of Principle) and s. 83 are read together, that the primary goal of any custodial facility should be rehabilitation of the adolescents held there. This means that programming should be instituted to seek to rehabilitate the youth in custody rather than simply punish or incapacitate them.

Further, adolescents are to be detained apart from adults. The *Young Offenders Act* (s. 7(2)) required that where detention was required, young persons (ages 12 to 18) were to be, with certain exceptions, detained separately from adults. This requirement continues under the YCJA, which provides in s. 84 that, where practicable, young persons should be held separately from adults. Allowing for exceptions to this general rule at all is controversial. The YCJA incorporates reference to the United Nations Convention on the Rights of the Child (CRC) in its preamble as an interpretive aid, and that convention prohibits detention of persons under the age of 18 with adults (at article 37(c)). The CRC admits no exception to this prohibition. By even theoretically allowing for such exceptions, Canada has been criticized internationally. Thus, detaining adolescents separately from adults is a high priority.

There are limited circumstances under which a provincial director (usually the minister responsible for the relevant service or his or her designate) can place or transfer a young person to an adult facility. Sections 76(1)(b) and (c) of the YCJA allow for placement of a young person in an adult facility when he or she has been subjected to an adult sentence (a sentence that could be imposed on an adult). Sections 89 to 93 govern placement of a young person with adults when he or she has been subjected to a youth sentence, and s. 30(3) allows for pre-trial detention of adolescents with adults in certain circumstances. In particular, s. 92 allows for the transfer of an individual charged and sentenced under the YCJA to an adult facility once he or she attains the age of 18 in order to prevent the other adolescents in the youth facility from being held with an adult. Additionally, the YCJA does not preclude the holding of young persons with adults where other facilities are unavailable. For example, in remote areas, and particularly for female offenders, there may be no youth facility nearby.

If a young person is not satisfied with the provincial director's decision with regard to the level of custody, he or she has the right to apply for a review. A review may be held on the following grounds: the provincial director's placement or transfer of a young person to a maximum-security place of custody; the particular place in which the young person is held or to which he or she is transferred; the provincial director's refusal to grant a temporary release to the young person; and where a young person is transferred from open custody to closed custody. Following a review, the Custody Review Board is authorized to make the appropriate recommendations to the provincial director. However, there is no provision guaranteeing that a provincial director must follow the board's recommendations.

As is the case with adults in correctional facilities, there have been instances of escape from youth custody facilities. Section 98 authorizes a police officer to apprehend a youth with or without a warrant if he or she has "left the place without the consent of the person in charge." A police officer who "on reasonable and probable grounds" believes that the young person is on any premises may enter the premises by force, if necessary, to apprehend the young person.

Rights of Children in a Residential, Detention, or Custody Facility

Children in residential placements (including foster homes), detention, or custody facilities have restrictions placed on their liberty. They are entitled to protection of their rights under s. 7 of the *Canadian Charter of Rights and Freedoms*,[9] which protects life, liberty, and security of the person and enjoins the state from subjecting them to cruel or unusual punishment. They are also protected, at least in theory, by the provisions of the United Nations Convention on the Rights of the Child, discussed above. Canada is a signatory to this convention and has incorporated it into the preamble of the YCJA, making it an important aid to interpreting Canadian youth justice and other laws affecting youth. Adolescents are also guaranteed special rights under the CFSA and under the guiding principles for custody and supervision set out in part V, s. 83, of the YCJA. Section 100 of the CFSA restricts service providers from locking children up in facilities other than secure custody or secure temporary detention facilities. Furthermore, service providers and foster parents are prohibited from inflicting corporal punishment (spanking or other physical punishment) on children within the facility.[10]

A child in care has the right to visit regularly with family members, to receive private visits from his or her solicitor or a child's advocate, and to send and receive mail.[11] Inferentially, this protection should extend to include email; a child in care should be able to send and receive text messages on cell phones and communicate via email with an expectation of privacy. A child who is a Crown ward, however, does not have the right to visit his or her parents unless an access order is in place, and recent amendments to the rules with respect to access to Crown wards have been passed to ensure that this access be dependent on whether it is beneficial to the child. Section 104 guarantees that a child in care has reasonable privacy and access to personal belongings. Furthermore, a child has the freedom to practise his or her religion and to receive religious instruction.

Children have the right to a comprehensive plan of care while in custody, and to good, basic care (balanced meals, appropriate clothing, medical care, and so on). Furthermore, children have the right to be heard in decisions affecting their lives while in custody. Parents of children in care retain the right to direct their children's religious and educational upbringing and to provide consent to medical treatment.[12] These parental rights, however, are not accorded to parents whose children are society or Crown wards. In these situations, such rights are held by the society.

Complaint and review procedures are in place for children who have been deprived of one or more of their rights. The child, his or her parent, or another person representing the child is entitled to complain to the service provider. If the complainant is not satisfied with the result, he or she is entitled to a review by a person appointed by the minister. The person appointed to review complaints cannot work for the service provider.

Children Suffering from a Mental Disorder

A minority of children who commit offences suffer from a mental disorder, and their violent acts can sometimes be attributed to that disorder. As such, they do not require sentencing in the regular system, but rather specialized treatment. Thus, the CFSA contains provisions to regulate the use of **secure treatment programs** for children in this context.

secure treatment program
program designed to treat mentally ill children that incorporates restrictions on their liberty, either to ensure completion of the program or for the protection of the public

Section 113 of the CFSA authorizes the minister to establish or approve "programs for the treatment of children with mental disorders, in which continuous restrictions are imposed on the liberty of the children." These facilities may be locked. A child may be committed to a secure treatment program following an application to the court under s. 114. If the child is less than 16 years old, an application may be made by the child's parent, a person who is caring for the child with a parent's consent, or the society that has custody of the child with the child's consent. If the child is 16 years or older, an application may be made by the child, the child's parent with the child's consent, the society that has custody of the child with the child's consent, or a physician.

An order committing a child to a secure treatment program greatly limits the child's liberty. Therefore, provisions are in place to ensure that the child's rights are restricted as minimally as possible. Where an application is made and the child has no legal representation, the court shall "as soon as practicable and in any event before the hearing of the application, direct that legal representation be provided for the child."[13] Generally, the child is entitled to be present at the hearing. However, the court may prohibit the child's attendance where it would cause him or her emotional harm or where he or she, after obtaining legal advice, consents to being absent throughout the hearing.

As a result of the severity of a secure treatment program, there are strict requirements, set out in s. 117, that must be met before secure treatment will be ordered:

1. The child must have a mental disorder.

2. The child must have recently caused or attempted to cause bodily harm to himself or herself or to another person.

3. The child, within 12 months before the application, must have caused or attempted to cause serious bodily harm on a second occasion or attempted to murder another person.

4. The treatment program would be effective at changing the child's violent behaviour.

5. The appropriate treatment is available for the child at the particular secure treatment facility.

6. There is not a less restrictive method of treatment available that would be appropriate for the child.

Unless all of these requirements are met, the court will not order that the child be placed in a secure treatment facility.

There are restrictions on the period of time that a child can be kept in a secure treatment facility. Generally, the child cannot be kept longer than 180 days.

Police officers play an important role in carrying out the secure treatment provisions. A police officer is authorized by s. 125 to take a child to a secure treatment facility after the court orders that the child be detained. Furthermore, if a child leaves a secure treatment facility without consent, a police officer may apprehend the child without a warrant and return him or her to the facility.

A child may be placed in isolation from the other children in the facility for one hour. The use of secure isolation, however, should be reserved for the most serious situations. The child may be placed in secure isolation if the service provider believes that the child will, in the immediate future, cause serious property damage or bodily harm to another person and that no less restrictive method would be effective at preventing it. The child may be kept in isolation for longer than one hour with approval from the person in charge of the facility. However, a child cannot be kept in isolation for more than 8 hours within a 24-hour period or more than 24 hours within a 7-day period.

Intrusive measures are a controversial issue in the context of secure treatment programs. "Intrusive measures" may include "mechanical means of controlling behaviour" and "aversive stimulation techniques." The intended effects of intrusive measures are to control the behaviour of children who are acting inappropriately. In every facility, a review team is established to review and approve or reject the use of intrusive measures. The CFSA attempts to ensure that the review team is somewhat independent of the facility and includes a medical practitioner.[14]

The Economic Issue

The most recent set of amendments to the CFSA have been characterized as evidence of a dramatic shift of ideology in favour of state protection of children. The grounds for finding a child in need of protection, and the corresponding factors triggering a duty to report abuse or neglect, have been broadened, and the legislation's presumption in favour of less intrusive/home-based treatment has been limited in many contexts. Although the degree to which these changes will increase the number of children taken into protective custody remains to be seen, we can predict that reporting will increase, and that more children will be apprehended.

Unfortunately, the changes in the legislation have not been matched by a sufficient increase in government funding for child protection agencies. Without the necessary funds to back these changes, it is difficult to see how the already strained child protection system will be able to maintain, let alone improve, the execution of its protective mandate.

Chapter Summary

The *Child and Family Services Act* is designed to allow the state to protect children at risk of abuse or neglect. The legislation creates a duty to report suspected abuse or neglect, and covers consensual services for children who need not be taken into protective custody, as well as the apprehension and care of children who do require custodial care. The legislation also governs the establishment and administration of open and secure custody facilities for young offenders, and the committal of children suffering from serious mental disorders.

KEY TERMS

consensual services

residential services

neglect

duty to report

child in need of protection

ward/wardship

secure treatment program

NOTES

1. *Family Law Act*, RSO 1990, c. F.3.

2. *Child and Family Services Act* (CFSA), RSO 1990, c. C11, as amended by SO 1992, c. 32; SO 1993, c. 27; SO 1994, c. 27; SO 1996, c. 2; SO 1999, c. 2, ss. 1-35; SO 1999, c. 6, s. 6; SO 1999, c. 12, sched. E, s. 1, and sched. G, s. 16.

3. *Provincial Offences Act*, RSO 1990, c. P.33.

4. *Education Act*, RSO 1990, c. E.2.

5. CFSA, s. 27.

6. CFSA, s. 40(6).

7. CFSA, ss. 57(3), (4), and (5).

8. CFSA, s. 79(1).

9. *Canadian Charter of Rights and Freedoms*, part I of the *Constitution Act, 1982*, RSC 1985, app. II, no. 44.

10. CFSA, s. 101.

11. CFSA, s. 103.

12. CFSA, s. 106.

13. CFSA, s. 114(6).

14. CFSA, s. 129.

EXERCISES AND REVIEW

Review Questions

1. What is the age jurisdiction of the *Child and Family Services Act*?

2. Which agencies administer the protective services mandated by the CFSA?

3. Why does the CFSA (and not the *Criminal Code* or the *Youth Criminal Justice Act*) govern the detention of convicted young offenders?

4. What typically happens under the CFSA if a child under the age of 12 is suspected of having committed a serious crime?

5. When a child has been made a ward of the Crown, can the parents visit with the child?

6. Where might a child live once child protection proceedings have been commenced?

7. What happens to a child in protective custody once he or she reaches his or her 18th birthday?

8. How long can a child remain a ward of a children's aid society?

9. A 5-year-old child is made a ward of the Crown; there is no expectation that she will ever be able to return to her parents. Where or with whom might she be living at age 6? What if the child were 15 at the time she was made a ward—where do you think she would she be living at age 16?

10. Why does the CFSA state a preference for a "consensual" basis for the delivery of non-custodial services?

Discussion Questions

1. Review the three scenarios below. Has the duty to report under s. 72 been triggered? Discuss or defend your answer.

   a. A gym teacher notices that, while many of the 6-year-olds in her grade 1 class have bruises and scrapes on their legs and elbows, one little boy in particular routinely has bruises of various colours on his upper arms and shoulders. He behaves normally, seems cheerful, and interacts well with teachers and the other children.

   b. An architect who works at home notices that the two children who live next door, ages 7 and 9, arrive home from school around 4:00 in the afternoon. Their mother does not get home from work until about 5:30, and no other adult appears to be in the home between 4:00 and 5:30. Most of the time the children watch TV indoors or roughhouse in the backyard. They usually seem fine, but yesterday the younger one sat crying on his back porch for nearly 20 minutes.

c. An elementary school principal has been having problems with the mother of one of the students. The mother refuses to send her daughter to school on the days that compulsory standardized tests are conducted. Last year, when half the grade 2 class contracted head lice, this mother refused to administer the scalp treatment the school required as a condition of re-admission. This year, another parent reported that this mother lied about her daughter's vaccination status on the registration form; the child is, in fact, not vaccinated against measles, mumps, and rubella. The principal feels that this mother is irresponsible and is not acting in her child's best interests.

2. Where a child under the age of 12 commits an act that would be a crime under the criminal law, the CFSA empowers a peace officer to temporarily detain that child for the purpose of determining whether he or she might be a "child in need of protection." What, if anything, does this method of dealing with underage criminality imply about families, or about child behaviour? Do you see any problems with this mechanism? If so, can you suggest an alternative mechanism?

3. Recent amendments to the CFSA have expanded the criteria for finding a child in need of protection, but spokespeople for the child protection system in Ontario claim that the system has been and continues to be in a state of economic crisis. What is the likely fallout from this situation? What are the implications, if any, for policing and law enforcement?

CHAPTER 5

Youth and Provincial Offences

■ CHAPTER OBJECTIVES

After completing this chapter, you should be able to:

- Describe the difference between *mens rea*, strict liability offences, and absolute liability offences.

- Explain the significance of the cases *R v. Sault Ste. Marie* and *R v. Wholesale Travelgroup Inc.*

- Understand that, like adults, youth may be charged with offences outside the *Criminal Code*.

- List a few provincial statutes that create offences with which youth may be charged.

- Review the general purpose and structure of the *Provincial Offences Act*.

- Describe the age jurisdiction of part VI of the *Provincial Offences Act*.

- Detail special procedures for dealing with youth that are created by part VI of the *Provincial Offences Act*.

- Compare sentences applicable to youth found guilty of a provincial offence with those applicable to adult offenders.

- Explain where the procedures required for the administration of legislation such as the *Education Act* can be found.

Introduction

Not all offences in Canada are listed in the federal *Criminal Code.*[1] The Code is a product of the federal government's authority over criminal matters. Each province, however, has the authority to impose penalties for offences committed contrary to any provincial statute. Many provincial statutes contain penalties for quasi-criminal offences or provincial offences. Municipalities, exercising powers delegated to them by the provinces, can also create regulatory offences. These offences are generally less serious in nature than crimes listed in the Code and, theoretically, do not "stigmatize" the accused upon conviction. That is, provincial offences are acts that are prohibited because they represent conduct that is disorderly or undesirable for logistical reasons, but are not generally condemned as immoral. However, the penalties for violating provincial statutes can be serious; several provincial statutes set out penalty sections that allow provincial courts under the *Provincial Offences Act* (POA) to impose significant financial penalties.

Each province has its own overarching statute that regulates the processing of provincial offences. In Ontario[2] and Newfoundland and Labrador, the regulatory statute is called the *Provincial Offences Act* (POA); in Nova Scotia and Prince Edward Island, the *Summary Proceedings Act*; in Alberta and New Brunswick, the *Provincial Offences Procedures Act*; in Manitoba, the *Summary Convictions Act*; in Quebec, the *Code of Penal Procedures*; in Saskatchewan, the *Summary Offences and Procedures Act*; in British Columbia, the *Offences Act*; in Northwest Territories, Yukon, and Nunavut, the *Summary Convictions Procedures Act*. These provincial statutes create the jurisdictional framework that allows provincial courts to operate. These laws supplement the various provincial statutes that set out provincial offences.

Regulations Everywhere

Our lives are legally regulated in a myriad of ways. The Supreme Court of Canada stated in *R v. Wholesale Travel Group Inc.*,[3] a case where the accused corporation was charged with several counts of false or misleading advertisement under the federal *Competition Act*:

> It is difficult to think of any aspect of our lives that is not regulated for our bene-fit and for the protection of society. From cradle to grave, we are protected by regulations; they apply to doctors attending our entry into the world and to the morticians present at our departure. Every day from waking to sleeping, we profit from regulatory measures which we often take for granted.

The Supreme Court confirmed what was previously noted by the Law Reform Commission of Canada in 1980—that federal and provincial regulations are per-vasive in nature. This point is further borne out when one compares the number of offences listed in the *Criminal Code* to the number of regulatory offences enacted on a continual basis. For example, when the Law Reform Commission made its comments, there were approximately 700 *Criminal Code* offences but more than 40,000 federal and provincial regulatory offences in existence at that time.

Intent Standards

To commit a criminal offence in violation of the *Criminal Code*, a person has to not only do the prohibited thing (*actus reus*) but also mean to do so, or have a guilty mind (*mens rea*). This is not always the case for provincial offences. In the land-mark Supreme Court of Canada case of *R v. City of Sault Ste. Marie*,[4] a municipality was charged with discharging refuse into public waterways. The City of Sault Ste. Marie hired Cherokee Disposal to dispose of the city's waste, and the city con-structed a disposal site 20 feet from a stream. When Cherokee Disposal filled the site with waste, it caused seepage into the nearby water. The city was charged under

s. 32(1) of the *Ontario Water Resources Act*. The issue before the court was the intent standard for the offence. The court ordered a new trial on the basis that the offence for which the city was charged should not have been treated by the trial judge as one for which there was no defence on the basis of a lack of intent. The city was therefore given a chance to defend itself where it had not been permitted to do so before. The court described three different intent standards for different sorts of offences: *mens rea* offences, strict liability offences, and absolute liability offences.

Regulatory offences, unlike criminal offences, are generally offences of strict liability. The court in *Sault Ste. Marie* described this type of offence as:

> Offences in which there is no necessity for the prosecution to prove the existence of *mens rea*; the doing of the prohibited act *prima facie* imports the offence, leaving it open to the accused to avoid liability by proving that he took all reasonable care.

This definition describes the defence of due diligence. If an accused committed the act, that person is considered guilty of the regulatory offence unless that person shows that he or she conducted himself or herself in a prudent and reasonable manner. The question to be asked is whether the accused exercised the expected standard of care required of a reasonable person in similar circumstances. If the accused acted reasonably under this test, there can be no finding of guilt.

While the intent standard for most regulatory offences is one of strict liability, there also exists a category of regulatory offences for which due diligence is no defence. These are absolute liability offences. To support a finding of guilt for the committal of such a regulatory offence, the prosecution need only prove that the accused committed the prohibited act. The Supreme Court, in *Sault Ste. Marie*, confirmed the constitutionality of absolute liability offences but also made clear that they are not the norm. The court stated that, unless specifically stated in the legislation, there is a presumption of a regulatory offence being one of strict liability.

The Provincial Offences Act

The enactment of the Ontario POA in 1979 represented a major change in the way offences created under provincial statutes were being treated. It was one of the most sweeping legislative reforms of the procedures governing the prosecution of offences since the enactment of the original *Criminal Code* in 1892.[5] The POA was the first attempt by the Ontario legislature to draft comprehensive **procedural provisions** to govern the prosecution of offences it has created by statute.

procedural provision
provision that prescribes procedures or rules that govern how justice will be administered rather than regulating a substantive matter

The purpose of the POA is to replace the summary conviction procedure for the prosecution of provincial offences with a new system of procedure. This new procedure is meant to reflect the distinction between provincial offences (created by provincial statutes) and criminal offences (created by the *Criminal Code*).[6] It was also designed to provide a fair and efficient method for the trial of the numerous cases that are handled by the provincial offences court.

All offences created by provincial legislation are regulatory. Examples include offences under the *Highway Traffic Act*[7] and the *Liquor Licence Act*.[8] An "offence" under the POA is defined as "an offence under an Act of the legislature or under a regulation or by-law made under the authority of an Act of the legislature." In summary, the POA, unlike the *Criminal Code*, does not primarily create offences. Instead, it regulates the prosecution of offences contained in various other provincial statutes.

The POA is divided into eight distinct parts with the first three parts setting out the processing options for the different types of offences. Part I regulates proceedings in respect of offences commenced by a **certificate of offence**. These are less formal than proceedings commenced by a part III **information**. The maximum fine under part I is $500 and there is no provision for imprisonment. Accuseds charged under part I have five options:

1. to plead not guilty and set a trial,

2. to dispute the charge without appearing in court,

3. to plead guilty with "**representations**,"

4. to plead guilty in writing, or

5. to be deemed not to dispute the charge where none of these options are exercised within 15 days of service of the offence notice.

Part II of the POA applies to proceedings in respect of parking infractions that are commenced by a **certificate of parking infraction**.

Part III of the POA deals with proceedings in respect of offences that may be commenced by the laying of an information and the issuing of a summons. These are relatively more serious charges (but generally not as serious as a criminal offence). There is a broad range of sentencing options for part III offences, including imprisonment, probation, and restitution. Part IV of the POA governs trials and sentencing. Fines represent the primary disposition imposed under the POA. The maximum fine is $5,000 unless stated otherwise (such as in part I). Part V outlines some general provisions.

Part VI, which is the most important part for the purposes of this text, deals with the treatment of young persons under the POA. This part reflects the principle that provincial offences should be treated fundamentally differently from criminal offences. The POA has jurisdiction over all provincial offences, including those committed by young people. A "young person" under s. 93 of the POA is defined as a person between the ages of 12 and 15. This jurisdictional distinction is often confusing because the federal *Youth Criminal Justice Act* exerts its jurisdiction over all young persons between the ages of 12 and 17 that contravene the *Criminal Code*. The key point to remember is that it is the type of offence (criminal or provincial offence), and not the age of the accused, that dictates which act applies.

Part VII deals with appeals, and part VIII pertains to arrest, bail, and search warrants. There is no general power of arrest under the POA. A person can be arrested for a provincial offence only if the statute that creates the offence specifically authorizes an arrest.

PART VI: YOUNG PERSONS AND THE ONTARIO PROVINCIAL OFFENCES ACT

Provincial offences are typically recognized as a category of conduct fundamentally different from criminal offences. Thus, a young person who commits a provincial offence will not face prosecution under federal criminal justice legislation. The

certificate of offence
unsworn, formulaic document (that is, following a set form and requiring set content) for the commencement of certain (less serious) types of proceedings

information
statement sworn, typically before a justice of the peace, for the purpose of laying a more serious charge

representations
in this context, evidence provided by the offender that is intended to excuse or mitigate guilt, and thus support a lighter penalty

certificate of parking infraction
parking "ticket" or "tag"

authority for police to arrest for provincial offences is found in each provincial act being enforced. Age generally becomes a factor only after police officers charge someone.

Generally, a young person cannot be arrested for a provincial offence without a warrant. Section 106, however, enables a police officer to arrest a young person without a warrant in two situations. First, where there are "reasonable and probable grounds to believe it is necessary in the public interest" to establish the identity of the young person, an arrest may be made without a warrant. Second, if the purpose of the arrest is to prevent the continuation or repetition of an offence that seriously endangers the young person or the person or property of another and there is not time to obtain a warrant, a valid arrest without a warrant may be made.

Similarly, a police officer is required to release a young person from custody after arrest unconditionally or upon the service of a summons.[9] This is qualified in two situations: (1) where the police officer has reasonable and probable grounds to believe that it is necessary in the public interest to detain the young person in order to establish his or her identity;[10] or (2) to prevent the continuation or repetition of an offence that seriously endangers the young person or the person or property of another.[11]

Where the investigating police officer believes that it is necessary to continue to detain a young person after arrest, he or she is required to deliver the young person to the officer in charge.[12] If the officer in charge does not release the young person, he or she is required to notify, as soon as possible, the young person's parents in accordance with s. 107(4). Section 107(6) requires that, where a detention order is made, the young person is not to be detained in a place where adults are also detained. A justice of the peace, however, has the discretion to order otherwise where it is not safe for the young person or other young persons to have the young person in question detained in a place of temporary detention or where there is no temporary detention facility available within a reasonable distance.

Section 95 provides that a young person cannot be issued an offence notice under part I. Therefore a young person who contravenes a provincial offence must be given a summons to attend court. While there are provisions under part I to issue a certificate of offence and a summons, it is accepted practice to proceed by way of part III information and summons.

Section 98(1) requires a young person to be present in court during his or her trial. There are, however, exceptions as well as the court's discretion under s. 98(2) to excuse the young person from attending court. In extreme cases, where a young person is required to attend court and fails to do so, the court may issue a warrant for his or her arrest.[13]

Like the federal youth criminal justice legislation, the POA recognizes the importance of protecting the identity of young persons involved in proceedings. Section 99(1) stipulates that the identity of a young person may not be published in connection with an offence or alleged offence. Any person who breaches this provision has committed an offence punishable by a maximum fine of $10,000.[14] This represents one of the few instances in which the POA has created an offence within the Act.

Section 97 outlines the sentencing options applicable to a young person who is guilty of committing a provincial offence. In a proceeding commenced by a certificate of offence, the court may enter a conviction under s. 97(1)(a) and impose a maximum fine of $300 or suspend the passing of sentence and place the young person on probation. Where a young person is placed on probation under s. 97(1)(a)(ii), the regular provisions respecting probation apply. However, the maximum term of probation is 90 days instead of two years, which is the maximum term for adults.[15] The court also has the option of imposing an absolute discharge in accordance with s. 97(1)(b). Unlike under the federal youth criminal justice legislation, there are no conditional discharges available under the POA.

Section 101 exemplifies the differential treatment of provincial offences and federal criminal offences. The section expressly limits the sentences available for proceedings commenced by way of information. A young person may not be imprisoned except upon conviction for a breach of probation under s. 75 and, if imprisoned, the maximum penalty is 30 days. Section 103 requires the place of incarceration to be an "open facility" as defined by the federal youth criminal justice legislation. Alternatively, the young person may be fined up to $1,000 under s. 101(1)(b) of the POA.

Where a young person is convicted of an offence prosecuted by way of an information, the court may impose a fine not exceeding $1,000 (s. 101(2)(a)(i)) or it may suspend the passing of a sentence and place the young person on probation (s. 101(1)(a)(ii)). The maximum period of probation is one year as opposed to the two-year limit available for adults (s. 101(3)). An absolute discharge may also be imposed by the court (s. 101(2)(b)).

Other Provincial Legislation

As discussed above, the POA is a provincial statute that regulates the imposition of penalties on people (including young persons) who commit provincial offences. Most provincial offences are not established by the POA but rather by numerous other provincial statutes. The *Education Act*[16] (EA), the *Highway Traffic Act* (HTA) and the *Liquor Licence Act* (LLA) create some of the provincial offences of which young persons are often accused.

EDUCATION ACT

The purpose of this statute is to govern the operation of schools and the delivery of educational programs. The EA, and specifically part II of the EA, is discussed here in an effort to elaborate on the interplay between the POA and other provincial statutes.

Part II of the EA contains provisions that deal with the mandatory requirement of children's attendance in schools. Section 21(1) sets out the general rule requiring all children to attend school between the ages of 6 and 16 years. Children within these ages are excused from school only if the EA expressly excludes their attendance for one of the reasons listed in s. 21(2). These reasons include satisfactory instruction at home, sickness or other unavoidable cause, insufficient transportation, suspension or expulsion, and holy days. Section 21(5) places a positive duty on the parent or guardian of the child to enroll the child in school.

Section 30 of the EA creates offences with respect to a child's non-attendance at school. A parent whose child is absent from school for a reason other than those listed in s. 21(2) may be found guilty of a provincial offence and, on conviction, is liable to a fine of not more than $200.[17] Similarly, a person who employs a child between the ages of 6 and 16 during school hours may be found guilty of an offence and, on conviction, is liable to a fine not exceeding $200. These provisions are examples of where a provincial statute creates provincial offences. Although the maximum fines are specified, the EA is silent on the trial procedures. These are left to part IV of the POA.

Section 30(5) of the EA exemplifies the interplay between an offence created by a provincial statute and part VI of the POA (the part dealing with young people). This section creates an offence for children of school years who have failed to attend school without a legal excuse. It states:

> 30(5) A child who is required by law to attend school and who refuses to attend or who is habitually absent from school is guilty of an offence and on conviction is liable to the penalties under Part VI of the *Provincial Offences Act*.

The authority of police officers established by the EA is applicable here to arrest a child, a parent, or an employer who has committed an offence under the EA. Following arrest, the subsequent provisions apply as well.

Truancy remains an ongoing issue for young people, their families, and school officials. Youth are regularly placed on POA probation orders as a result of failure to attend school. This in itself is not problematic as long as the young person complies with the probation order. Unfortunately, young persons often do not. As a result, they may face a s. 75 POA "breach of probation" charge. This creates problems for the court when it comes to sentencing. The YCJA makes it clear that a young person cannot be given custody on a first conviction of breach of probation on a YCJA-based probation order. However, as noted previously, because the breach is a violation of a POA order, sentencing for it falls under the jurisdiction of the POA, and therefore the court can and often does impose a period of open custody.

HIGHWAY TRAFFIC ACT

Each province has legislation governing the conduct of motor vehicle traffic. These statutes are similar to Ontario's *Highway Traffic Act* (HTA). This Act sets out the regulatory offences related to operation of motor vehicles, including the age re-strictions. Young persons who drive before the age of 16 often find themselves charged with "driving without a valid driver's licence" or "being in possession of an altered driver's licence." The date of birth is often altered, purporting the youths to be older than they actually are (that is, 19 years or older so they can legally buy alcohol). As with the *Education Act*, young people who are convicted of these offences often find themselves with a probation order under the jurisdiction of the POA. The results of breaching such an order are described above.

In many cases, young people who commit driving offences are also charged with a criminal offence. For example, a young person who takes a vehicle without permission may be charged with "taking a motor vehicle or vessel without consent" under s. 335(1) of the *Criminal Code*. If the young person flees from police, he or she may be charged with "failing to stop the vehicle" under s. 249.1(1).

In addition, the Ontario Ministry of Transportation can generate a driver's licence number for a person under the age of 16 who is charged with certain driving offences. If the offence includes a point reduction, the points will come off the young person's licence if they obtain one upon turning the age of 16.

THE LIQUOR LICENCE ACT

Just as each province has an equivalent law to the HTA, each province has an equivalent law to the *Liquor Licence Act*. While there are many offences created as a result of the regulation of the sale and consumption of liquor, the most pertinent for young people is the legal drinking age. Young persons who consume liquor underage are in violation of the LLA. When convicted of underage alcohol possession or consumption, sentences can range from fines to probation.

Chapter Summary

Not all offences with which youth may be charged are listed in the *Criminal Code*. Youth, like adults, are subject to being charged with provincial offences—offences created by the provincial legislatures under numerous and varied pieces of legislation, such as the *Education Act*, the *Highway Traffic Act*, and the *Liquor Licence Act*. In the absence of conflicting or specific provisions contained in these acts, the procedure to be followed in prosecuting provincial offences is set out in an administrative statute, the *Provincial Offences Act*. This Act, like the federal youth criminal justice legislation, creates special procedures for dealing with young people, including notice of detention to parents, restrictions on place of detention, protection of suspect/offender identity, and reduced penalties on conviction.

KEY TERMS

procedural provision

certificate of offence

information

representations

certificate of parking infraction

NOTES

1. *Criminal Code*, RSC 1985, c. C-46.

2. *Provincial Offences Act* (POA), RSO 1990, c. P.33.

3. *R v. Wholesale Travel Group Inc.*, [1991] 3 SCR 154.

4. *R v. City of Sault Ste. Marie*, [1978] 2 SCR 1299.

5. Douglas W. Drinkwalter and Douglas J. Ewart, *Ontario Provincial Offences Procedure* (Toronto: Carswell, 1980), iii. For a detailed examination of the POA and enforcement procedures of provincial offences under various Ontario statutes, see Ugo Capy and Erin MacCarthy, *Provincial Offences* (Toronto: Emond Montgomery, 2000).

6. POA, s. 2(1).

7. *Highway Traffic Act*, RSO 1990, c. H.8.

8. *Liquor Licence Act*, RSO 1990, c. L.19.

9. POA, s. 107(2).

10. POA, s. 107(2)(a).

11. POA, s. 107(2)(b).

12. POA, s. 107(3).

13. POA, s. 98(4).

14. POA, s. 99(2).

15. POA, s. 97(2).

16. *Education Act* (EA), RSO 1990, c. E.2.

17. EA, s. 30(1).

EXERCISES AND REVIEW

Review Questions

1. What part of the POA deals specifically with youthful offenders?

2. What part of the POA contains the list of provincial offences?

3. Can a youth be arrested on suspicion of having committed a provincial offence? If so, under what circumstances?

4. List the sentences available to a judge when a youth is found guilty of a provincial offence.

5. Where will a youth given a custodial sentence under the POA be sent to serve his or her time?

6. What do you think happens when a child under the age of 12 is found committing what would be considered a provincial offence?

Discussion Questions

1. Part VI of the POA, which governs the legislation's application to youth, defines "young person" as a person between the ages of 12 and 16 years. As we will see in the following chapters, the federal youth criminal justice statute's age jurisdiction extends to age 18. Why do you think the Ontario legislature has maintained a more limited age jurisdiction for provincial offences? Do you have an opinion about the appropriate age of adult criminal or quasi-criminal responsibility? Defend your view.

2. Thinking back to the discussion of patterns of youth criminality discussed in chapter 2, under which provincial statutes do you think youth are most often charged? Make a list.

PART III

Legislative Approaches: Inside the Justice System

CHAPTER 6

Early Initiatives: The Juvenile Delinquents Act and the Young Offenders Act

■ CHAPTER OBJECTIVES

After completing this chapter, you should be able to:

- Describe the classical theory of criminology.
- Describe positivist theory as it relates to youth criminal behaviour.
- Explain the principle of *parens patriae*.
- Describe the primary purpose(s) of the *Juvenile Delinquents Act*.
- List the primary criticisms made of the *Juvenile Delinquents Act*.
- Explain what is meant by "due process" and a "rights-based" approach to youth justice.
- Describe the philosophic compromise that was intended to be achieved by the *Young Offenders Act*.
- Describe the primary purpose of the *Young Offenders Act*.
- List the primary criticisms made of the *Young Offenders Act*.
- Describe how the *Youth Criminal Justice Act* differs from its predecessors.
- List the primary criticisms to date of the *Youth Criminal Justice Act*.

Introduction

The *Juvenile Delinquents Act* (JDA)[1] was the guiding legislation for youth criminal justice for three-quarters of a century, from 1908 until the implementation of the *Young Offenders Act* (YOA)[2] in 1984. The *Young Offenders Act* enjoyed a shorter tenure and was repealed by the *Youth Criminal Justice Act* (YCJA) in 2003. Each legislative regime has been a creature of its time and a response, in part, to criticisms and the strengths of its precursor. To thoroughly understand the current legislation and its political and social context, it is useful to learn about the philosophies behind its predecessors, and to understand the criticisms that led to their replacement.

Background to the Juvenile Delinquents Act

In the 19th century, before the implementation of the JDA, criminology was dominated by the "classical" school of thought. This philosophy was premised on the assumption that people are rational beings who are capable of comprehending all consequences of their actions. The punishment for any deviation from the "norm" was proportionate to the seriousness of the offence committed. Thus, classical criminologists placed an emphasis on clear and precise laws, process, and dispositions, with few protections for the accused.[3]

As discussed in chapter 1, prior to the 19th century, western society did not view children and youth as different from adults. Classical criminologists shared this understanding. Like adults, children and youth were perceived by classical theorists to appreciate the consequences of their actions and were faced with a predictable punitive response to their criminal behaviour. Reformatories and industrial schools were established for children and youth who committed offences.

By the end of the 19th century, there was growing dissatisfaction with the classical approach to criminology. A social movement led primarily by social workers and church workers mobilized in response to a perceived increase in juvenile crime rates and poor treatment of children in reformatories and industrial schools. These reformers sought to decrease the use of institutionalization, favouring a home environment approach instead.[4] If parents were unable to control their child's behaviour, probation officers and social service workers could be called on to provide support and encouragement in the child's home. In this way, the state could manifest its control over the delinquent child within his or her family.

positivist school of thought
behavioural/ criminological theory that places an emphasis on rehabilitation and that attributes criminal behaviour, at least in part, to the influence of social problems on the individual

In criminology, the period between the late 19th century through the middle of the 20th century was dominated by the **positivist school of thought**. Unlike the dominant assumption of rationality inherent in the classical approach, the positivist paradigm emphasized the effect of social ills as a cause of crime. This new theory characterized crime prevention as a responsibility of society as a whole and sought to prevent crime by promoting the welfare of the population. As a result, the new criminology shifted the emphasis away from a punitive response toward a rehabilitative response to criminality. Unlike classical thinkers, positivists believed that crime was caused, not by a deliberate act, but by forces, such as societal and/or parental failure, that were out of the individual's control. Much like a patient suffering from a medical illness, the criminal should be "treated" and reintegrated into society. This scientific approach to youth criminality set the stage for the implementation of the JDA, which has been described as

> a product of a diverse social reform movement dedicated to "saving" or "rescuing" children from what were perceived to be undesirable and harmful aspects of life in the increasingly urbanised and industrialised society of the nineteenth and early twentieth centuries.[5]

The Juvenile Delinquents Act

The positivist approach was highly influential in the drafting of the JDA. Through this legislation, the drafters sought to integrate a welfare approach based on the best interests of children, and a framework to address "delinquency" or misbehaviour. Children were not to be perceived as "criminal," but rather "sick," or at least afflicted with a "condition." Section 2(2) read:

> Where a child is adjudged to have committed a delinquency he shall be dealt with, not as an offender, but as one in a condition of delinquency and therefore requiring help and guidance and proper supervision.

Because of its welfare focus, the youth justice system created by the JDA was closely tied to social services. Lines between redress for adolescent offending and provision of social services for youth in need were blurred. The court's role was similar to that of a parent, intervening in the place of parents who were not able to effectively guide the child into adulthood. Section 38 stipulated that

> the care and custody and discipline of a juvenile delinquent shall approximate as nearly as may be that which should be given by his parents, and that as far as practicable every juvenile delinquent shall be treated, not as a criminal, but as a misdirected and misguided child.

This system was modelled after the ***parens patriae*** approach that dominated the English Chancery Court.

Parens patriae, loosely translatable as "state as parent," is a legal doctrine or concept that emphasizes state protection of the property and lives of vulnerable persons. The doctrine implies a connection between flawed care and control (that is, usually "poor" parenting) and juvenile criminality. Reitsma-Street noted:

> [I]f young persons committed crimes, it was evidence that a different combination of care and control by the family group or a state representative was needed to promote the young person's best interests.[6]

Hence, the same theorists who advocated at the end of the 19th century for *An Act for the Prevention of Cruelty to and Better Protection of Children*[7] in Ontario lobbied hard for the welfare-oriented JDA. The common purpose of both pieces of legislation was to protect "misdirected" young persons from their own "evil tendencies" and from becoming criminals, and to save them from willful neglect and the prospect of "idle, dissolute, immoral lives."[8] Even at the turn of the 20th century, there was an understanding that children's need for protection from corrupting tendencies was best achieved through early intervention: the age jurisdiction of the JDA extended from ages 7 to 17 years.

The court's structure under the JDA was procedurally informal. The purpose of this informality was to allow for ample flexibility in the design of rehabilitation programs suited to individual needs. Judges had almost infinite discretion to impose any disposition for an indeterminate length of time. The legislation specified little if any procedural rights for the alleged delinquent child. The court processes were "informal and speedy, not subject to the discipline of public scrutiny in the courts or in the press, judicial appeal, or **due process** procedures. Discretion and informality were promoted, despite the potential for coercive action."[9] Children had no

parens patriae
legal doctrine based on a concept of the state as parent/protector in relation to its citizens

due process
the administration of justice through the courts in accordance with established rules and principles, especially to enforce and protect private rights

explicit right to legal representation, and appeals were extremely limited. The court took a paternalistic stance, with the assumption that it knew what was in the child's best interest. The positivist philosophy underlying the JDA remained unchallenged for the first half of the 20th century.

Criticisms of the Juvenile Delinquents Act

In the mid-20th century, many groups who had been excluded or oppressed by systems of power lobbied successfully for expansion of human and legal rights to address these disadvantages. Women, racial minorities, and, not least, youth made remarkable gains toward recognition of their rights under law. This "rights revolution" and other sociopolitical influences of the late 1960s inspired an increase in critical writing on youth justice. Bolton et al. noted that the proliferation of research in this field stemmed from the "institutionalization of criminology as a science."[10] The new research reflected a growing dissatisfaction with the JDA's paternalistic approach to youth criminality. Competing theories began to cast doubt on the effectiveness of rehabilitation for juvenile delinquents. Furthermore, in response to the limited rights afforded to children under the JDA, many critics advocated due process in the administration of youth justice.

There were four major influences that led to proposals to reform the JDA.[11] First, empirically based theories called for deinstitutionalization. Second, many scholars pushed for due process rights for children. Third, there was empirical consensus that rehabilitation had not been effective at preventing recidivism. Fourth, community-based programs known as "diversion" were a growing alternative to incarceration.

Symbolic interactionism, the first of the critical theories, questioned the notion that criminality was a disease. As discussed in chapter 2, its central argument was that individuals are shaped, not only by their biological predisposition, but also by their interaction with their environment. In this way, individuals are constantly changing to adapt to the world around them. In the context of a juvenile justice system, symbolic interactionists feared that a paternalistic approach would instill resentment and anger in adolescents in conflict with the law. This, in turn, could manifest into criminal behaviour in adulthood.

Symbolic interactionists put forward two main arguments against the JDA. Their first argument related to the social influence on individual development. Here, they argued that placing delinquent children with other delinquent children would do nothing to decrease recidivism. Instead, the negative experience would transpire into further criminal behaviour. To counter this potential, symbolic interactionists argued that it would be more appropriate to integrate these children with "normal" children and adults who could provide a more positive influence in their lives.

The second symbolic interactionist argument, known as labelling theory, also discussed in chapter 2, held that an otherwise "normal" child is transformed into a criminal as a result of the label that society places on him or her. When the community places a label such as "juvenile delinquent" on an impressionable child, that child acts in a way that is expected of him or her. Furthermore, the child's own self-image deteriorates and he or she truly believes that he or she is "bad." These subtheorists of symbolic interactionism attempt to minimize the stigmatizing effect of labelling by doing away with the "juvenile delinquent" label.

Developmental psychologists formed a second group of theorists critical of the positivist approach to the JDA. They focused on the age jurisdiction appropriate for a youth criminal justice system. Their theory was premised on the idea that as children progress through the different developmental stages, they develop a more comprehensive "sense of justice."[12] Thus, developmental psychologists advocated for a differential criminal justice response for youth at different stages of development.

In addition to the socioscientific theories, advocates for due process pushed for reform to the JDA. By the late 1960s, social workers and lawyers became increasingly uneasy about the vast discretion given to judges who sit in the juvenile courts. They argued that children should be accorded, at minimum, the same legal rights as adults. In the light of children's lack of sophistication and experience with the court system, many even advocated for *additional* rights.

Due process, or a rights framework, regards young people as persons, entitled to a minimum number of social goods because they are individuals and citizens.[13] Unlike the paternalistic approach of the JDA, a rights approach requires that criminal justice officials justify their imposition on and control over an alleged delinquent. A shift toward children's rights is accompanied by a shift toward increased accountability in recognition of society's rights as well. When there is justification for intervention, the state should impose the least restrictive means in balancing the interests of the individual criminal and society's need for protection. Emphasis should be placed on diversion programs and community-based alternatives to incarceration.

Supreme Court decisions in the United States set the stage for due process advocacy in Canada. Although a similar line of cases did not follow in Canada, a due process movement developed that sought reform through legislation.

Legislative Reform: Passage of the Young Offenders Act

The journey from criticism of the JDA to enactment of the YOA was a particularly long road. In response to criticism levelled at the JDA, the federal government, in 1965, appointed a committee of the Department of Justice to research the problem of juvenile delinquency and offer its recommendations for legislative reform. The result was a lengthy report[14] that led to a draft bill[15] to replace the JDA. This was followed, in 1970, with Bill C-192,[16] which died after second reading. As a result of this bill's failure, a solicitor general's committee was established to evaluate the proposed reforms. This eventually led to Bill C-61,[17] which came into force as the *Young Offenders Act* in 1984.

Bolton et al.[18] point to three important developments that contributed to successful reform in the late 1970s and early 1980s. First, empirical studies demonstrated that rehabilitative techniques consistent with the *parens patriae* system had been ineffective in preventing recidivism. Second, academics and professionals increasingly emphasized the potential of diversion programs, and these were proliferating. As discussed in chapter 3, "diversion" encompasses anything from community absorption plans to police screening, pre-trial diversion, and alternatives in sentencing.[19] Third, Canadians were becoming more conservative and this was reflected in their exaggerated perceptions of juvenile involvement in crime. The new legislation was a way in which the government could demonstrate its response to the public's various concerns.

To some extent, the resulting legislation incorporated a shift backward to the classicist approach to juvenile justice that existed before the implementation of the JDA. This corresponded with a shift from a purely rehabilitative response to a more punitive response to juvenile crime. In part because the custody implications of this more punitive response seemed inappropriate for younger children, and in part as a measure to draw a clearer distinction between the justice and social services systems (which are uneasy bedfellows from a constitutional and funding point of view), the age jurisdiction under the new legislation was narrowed to 12 to 17 years inclusive.

Purposes of the Young Offenders Act

In breaking from a *parens patriae* approach, the YOA incorporated a rights-based framework. Although it sought to balance the rights of the child with the rights of society, the child's rights were intended to be paramount; and, though to a lesser extent than under the JDA, "protection of young people and promotion of their best interests [were] still part of the philosophy of the YOA."[20]

According to early critics, the YOA was primed for conflict from its inception because it attempted to compromise two disparate philosophies:

> [W]hile many reformers wished to de-institutionalize the juvenile justice system and to introduce community-based treatment programs, others wanted to make youth more accountable and to introduce more protections for society from juvenile crime.[21]

This uneasy compromise was reflected in an internally contradictory declaration of principle (s. 3). The following subsections demonstrate some of its apparent inconsistencies:

> 3(c.1) the protection of society, which is *a* primary objective of the criminal law applicable to youth, is best served by rehabilitation, wherever possible, of young persons who commit offences, and rehabilitation is best achieved by addressing the needs and circumstances of a young person that are relevant to the young person's offending behaviour; ...
>
> (d) where it is not inconsistent with the protection of society, taking no measures or taking measures other than judicial proceedings under this Act should be considered for dealing with young persons who have committed offences; ...
>
> (f) in the application of this Act, the rights and freedoms of young persons include a right to the least possible interference with freedom that is consistent with the protection of society, having regard to the needs of young persons and the interests of their families. [Emphasis added.]

These inconsistencies left the legislation incapable, according to some, of providing coherent philosophic guidance. This lack of guidance, in turn, set the stage for abuses of judicial discretion: having reference to the above-noted principles, it is not difficult to see how a judge might interpret the YOA in a way that suits his or her own values. A judge who is biased toward "protecting society" might impose a lengthy custodial sentence (called a "disposition" under the YOA) in the name of "rehabilitation." In contrast, a judge with a bias toward "minimal intrusion" in a child's life might rely on s. 3(f) to justify no custody at all for a similar conviction. Despite this effect, however, in *R v. T.(V.)*,[22] the Supreme Court of Canada affirmed s. 3's reflection of "the complex nature of youthful criminality and the inadequacy of a single-minded approach in dealing with young offenders."[23]

Criticisms of the Young Offenders Act

Ironically, the YOA was widely accepted by all major political parties, academics, criminal justice officials, and the public at its inception in 1984. But since then, and until its repeal, it attracted continual calls for reform from two major schools of opposition.

On the one hand, the "punitive response" critics argued that young offenders were getting away with overly lenient sentences. The "rehabilitation" critics, on the other hand, argued that the legislation did not go far enough in providing for meaningful rehabilitation. The latter critics called for a return to legislation more similar to the JDA.

The punitive response critics argued that crime had increased since the enactment of the YOA. (As discussed in chapter 1, this perception probably stemmed in part from higher levels of reporting and charging.) In response, these critics sought reform calling for tougher, longer sentences and provisions making it easier to have a young offender transferred to adult court. However, many "get tough" advocates failed to acknowledge that, under the YOA, there was actually a substantial increase in custodial dispositions (though typically for shorter durations than those ordered under the JDA),[24] and the prevailing criminological research demonstrated that a more punitive approach to youth criminality would not likely act as an effective deterrent.[25]

The rehabilitation critics, on the other hand, argued that since enactment of the YOA, the rehabilitation ideal had been forgotten. Many mental health professionals expressed concern about the legislation's original requirement under s. 22 of consent on the part of those young offenders who are "detained for treatment." This prevented many youths from obtaining necessary treatment because a majority would not provide consent. Bala, however, argued that "the real obstacle to the provision of rehabilitative services to young offenders [was] not s. 22, but rather the reluctance of provincial governments to provide adequate resources."[26]

Other criticisms of the YOA were directed at what was perceived as its "overboard" response to calls for due process rights for youth. Many reformers, recognizing the great expense of our criminal justice system, fought to eliminate the YOA's guarantee of a lawyer at the state's expense. Many also believed that the standard for police questioning was too high because it often led to the exclusion of important evidence in circumstances where the youthful accused was most likely guilty. These critics argued that judges should have been given the discretion to admit statements in circumstances of a good faith effort on the part of police personnel to comply with the statute.[27]

Finally, considerable debate developed over the provisions dealing with access to information about the young offender. In its original form, the YOA restricted any public access to information about the individual young offender. Many reformers argued that this denied the public the ability to ensure protection from offenders who were released. In response, amendments were made in 1986 to allow for greater access to information about the identity of young suspects and offenders in special circumstances.

Despite this and numerous other amendments in the late 1980s and early 1990s, pressure to reconsider the entire system led to reform discussions and formal hearings/presentations as early as 1996. But the new *Youth Criminal Justice Act* followed a passage into law as rocky as its predecessor—a first attempt to pass it, in 1998–1999, was unsuccessful. A second attempt, in March 1999, was similarly unsuccessful. When Parliament adjourned in June of that year, the Bill died on the order paper, but was reintroduced as Bill C-3. Prior to its third reading, an election was called and the Bill again died on the order paper. For a third time, in February 2001, the YCJA was reintroduced as Bill C-7. After lengthy debate, on February 4, 2002 the House of Commons did pass Bill C-7, the *Youth Criminal Justice Act*, in its current form.

Criticisms of the Youth Criminal Justice Act

The YCJA came into force on April 1, 2003, and so has been in existence for only a short period of time. So far, it has not met with the public outcry that the YOA attracted toward the end of its existence. However, as noted above, while the YOA went on to become, in media reports, arguably the most publicly disparaged piece of legislation of its time, it was almost unanimously welcomed when passed in 1984. It is therefore difficult to predict how well accepted the YCJA will be.

The YCJA is already the object of some criticism from several sources, including law enforcement officers, politicians, Crown prosecutors, and the bench. Some characterize the legislation as excessively lenient. Drafted and enacted by Canada's Liberal party under Jean Chrétien, the Act has not found favour with the Conservative government elected in January 2006. New Prime Minister Steven Harper campaigned for harsher sentences for adolescent offenders. As discussed in chapters 8 and 9, some law enforcement officers and Crown prosecutors have expressed a great deal of frustration with the new Act's strong policy preference against custody, especially in the pre-trial period. Conversely, others criticize the Act as too harsh. As is discussed in more detail in chapter 11, adult sentencing has been a particularly controversial aspect of the new regime. Many critics, including academic writers and recently the Ontario Court of Appeal, have stated that the reverse onus provisions for adolescents as young as 14 years of age charged with certain serious offences are unduly harsh and unconstitutional. "Reverse onus" means that the youth, and not the Crown, bears the burden of proving to the court that an adult sentence would *not* be appropriate in their circumstances. From another perspective, others have expressed concern about the high level of discretion accorded police officers and other justice system actors by the increased emphasis on diversion from the formal court process and on parental involvement. There is concern that certain youth, particularly if they are from visible minority backgrounds or are otherwise marginalized by poverty or family problems, will receive unequal treatment. Others have simply complained that the new Act is too lengthy and complex in its drafting.

Despite these criticisms, as is discussed elsewhere throughout this book, it is evident that certain crucial goals of the drafters of the YCJA are being met. As is discussed in chapter 12, more adolescents are being diverted from the formal justice system, to be dealt with informally in the community. Community agencies are increasing their level of involvement with at-risk youth and adolescent offenders. As is discussed in chapter 11, perhaps most important, fewer adolescents are being sentenced to terms in custody and custodial youth facilities are closing as a result. How effective and popular the YCJA will ultimately be remains to be seen, but early indications are positive.

Chapter Summary

Before the turn of the 20th century, youth criminals were treated in much the same way as were adult criminals. The emergence of the positivist theory of criminology at the turn of the 20th century informed the passage of a statute—the *Juvenile Delinquents Act*—that adopted a radically different approach to youth crime, one that emphasized protection, rehabilitation, and *parens patriae* values. Concerns about recidivism, labelling, and a lack of due process for youth led, 78 years later, to the introduction of a new statute, the *Young Offenders Act*. That statute sought to achieve a balance between protection of the legal rights of youth offenders through the introduction of due process principles, and increased accountability on the part of youths for the crimes they committed. However, perceived philosophical inconsistencies plagued the new legislation, and it attracted criticism from both the crime-control and protective-rehabilitative camps. Despite several rounds of reform, the legislation was repealed in 2002 by the *Youth Criminal Justice Act*. The YCJA is an attempt to address the criticisms of the YOA and to improve upon Canadian youth justice, as will be discussed in the following chapters.

KEY TERMS

positivist school of thought

parens patriae

due process

NOTES

1. *Juvenile Delinquents Act*, RSC 1970, c. J-3.

2. *Young Offenders Act*, RSC 1985, c. Y-1.

3. J. Bolton et al., "The *Young Offenders Act*: Principles and Policy—The First Decade in Review" (1993), 38 *McGill Law Journal* 939, at 945.

4. J.S. Leon, "The Development of Canadian Juvenile Justice: A Background for Reform" (1977), 15 *Osgoode Hall Law Journal* 71, at 81.

5. Ibid., at 72.

6. M. Reitsma-Street, "More Control Than Care: A Critique of Historical and Contemporary Laws for Delinquency and Neglect of Children in Ontario" (1989), 3 *Canadian Journal of Women and the Law* 511, at 512.

7. *An Act for the Prevention of Cruelty to and Better Protection of Children*, SO, 56 Vict., 1893, c. 45.

8. Reitsma-Street, supra note 6, at 514-15.

9. Ibid., at 515.

10. Bolton et al., supra note 3, at 949.

11. Ibid.

12. Ibid., at 955.

13. Reitsma-Street, supra note 6, at 517.

14. Department of Justice, *Report of the Department of Justice Committee on Juvenile Delinquency* (Ottawa: Queen's Printer, 1965).

15. Department of the Solicitor General, *First Discussion Draft: An Act Respecting Children and Young Persons* (Ottawa: Queen's Printer, 1967).

16. Bill C-192, *An Act Respecting Young Offenders and to Repeal the Juvenile Delinquents Act*, 3d Sess., 28th Parl., 1970.

17. Bill C-61, *Young Offenders Act*, 1st Sess., 32d Parl., 1981.

18. Bolton et al., supra note 3, at 967.

19. Law Reform Commission of Canada, *Diversion*, Working Paper no. 7 (Ottawa: Queen's Printer, 1975), 1.

20. Reitsma-Street, supra note 6, at 519.

21. Bolton et al., supra note 3, at 973.

22. *R v. T.(V.)*, [1992] 1 SCR 749.

23. Ibid.

24. N. Bala, "What's Wrong with YOA Bashing? What's Wrong with the YOA? Recognizing the Limits of the Law" (1994), 36 *Canadian Journal of Criminology* 247, at 248.

25. A. Leschied and L. Vark, *Assessing Outcomes of Special Need Young Offenders* (London, ON: Family Court Clinic, 1989).

26. Bala, supra note 24.

27. Ibid., at 258.

EXERCISES AND REVIEW

True or False?

____ 1. During the period in which criminology was dominated by the "classical" school of thought, reform schools and industrial schools were established for youth who committed offences.

____ 2. The welfare of children and youth was the guiding philosophy of the *Juvenile Delinquents Act*.

____ 3. The court structure under the JDA was procedurally formal.

____ 4. Labelling theorists believe that the "juvenile delinquent" label effectively categorizes youth who commit crimes, allowing social service workers to provide the necessary help.

____ 5. Diversion programs were an important development in the implementation of the *Young Offenders Act*.

Multiple Choice

Circle the best answer.

1. The following is not a major development that led to proposals to reform the JDA:

    a. empirically based theories called for deinstitutionalization of youth in society

    b. advocates pushed for due process rights for children

    c. thousands of youth organized a rally in Ottawa to pressure the government to make changes

    d. studies showed that rehabilitation had not been effective

2. In the 1960s, advocates for due process believed that

    a. children did not have enough rights under the JDA

    b. judges did not have enough discretion in the juvenile courts

    c. children were as sophisticated as adults in their interactions with the court system

    d. youths who commit crimes should not be accountable to society for their actions

3. Researcher Nicholas Bala points out the following as an inaccurate argument by the "punitive response" critics of the YOA:

    a. crime had decreased since the inception of the YOA

    b. an increased number of young females have committed crimes

    c. there has been a decrease in the use of custodial dispositions for criminal youths under the YOA

    d. rehabilitation is more appropriate than incarceration for youths who commit crimes

Review Questions

1. What statute governed crimes committed by youth *before* the passage of the JDA?

2. Define "due process."

3. Is there a message about the view of parental competence inherent in the principle of *parens patriae*?

4. Before the advent of positivist theory, what cause or causes were attributed to criminal acts?

5. Would a high rate of recidivism after rehabilitation support or contradict the positivist theory of criminal behaviour?

6. What rehabilitation strategy(ies) might a symbolic interactionist recommend for problem youth? What would be some potential challenges associated with implementing these strategies?

7. What did researcher Nicholas Bala identify as the primary obstacle to successful rehabilitation of delinquent youth? Do you agree?

8. List the four major influences that led to the passage of the *Young Offenders Act.*

9. Did the rate of custody dispositions increase or decrease under the YOA? What about the duration of individual custody dispositions?

10. What was the age jurisdiction under the YOA? Why do you think the minimum age increased? Provide at least three possible reasons.

11. Given the timing of the passage of the YOA, why might the principle of due process have been given such a significant priority?

12. The YOA was criticized for providing excessive judicial discretion with regard to sentencing ("dispositions"). What might be some positive aspects of the availability of judicial discretion?

Discussion Questions

1. In her award-winning book *The Nurture Assumption* (New York: Free Press, 1998), researcher Judith Rich Harris challenges the widely accepted notion that parenting is a determining influence on children's personalities and behaviour, including children's tendencies to engage in criminal activity. Do you think parents play a significant role (either positive or negative) in influencing rates of youth crime? How do your beliefs on this issue inform your opinion of laws, like the JDA, that adopt a *parens patriae* or paternalistic approach to youth delinquency?

2. Positivist theory, viewed simplistically, suggests that youths who engage in criminal activity are "afflicted" rather than "bad." In chapter 1, you read a statistic that more than 50 percent of youths have engaged in illegal behaviour. Were all of these youths "afflicted" at the time of the reported behaviour? What are the pitfalls of equating criminality with mental (or social) illness?

3. According to researcher Nicholas Bala, the most significant obstacle to rehabilitation of troubled youth is government reluctance to allocate sufficient resources to the necessary programs. If you were a member of an interest group charged with promoting the development and funding of youth rehabilitation programs, what economic arguments would you make to justify your request for increased government funding?

CHAPTER 7

The Youth Criminal Justice Act: Principles and Structure

■ CHAPTER OBJECTIVES

After completing this chapter, you should be able to:

- State the principal goal of Canada's youth criminal justice system.
- Explain the legal effect of a declaration of principle such as the one contained in s. 3 of the *Youth Criminal Justice Act* (YCJA).
- Summarize the declaration of principle as expressed in s. 3 of the YCJA.
- Note three differences between the YCJA and its predecessor, the *Young Offenders Act* (YOA).
- Identify one provision in the YCJA that provides for the application of judicial discretion.
- Understand the overall structure of the YCJA.
- Define "extrajudicial measures" for the purpose of the YCJA.
- Identify the age jurisdiction of the YCJA.
- Identify the part of the YCJA that deals with pre-trial detention.
- Identify the part of the YCJA that deals with publication and records.

Introduction

The goal of this chapter is to provide an overview of the principles and structure of the *Youth Criminal Justice Act* (YCJA). While the principles that inform the interpretation of all provisions of the YCJA will be discussed in detail in this chapter, the provisions of other sections of the Act are merely introduced and will be covered in detail in subsequent chapters.

For ease of reference, the full text of the *Youth Criminal Justice Act* appears in an appendix to this book.

Principles and Objectives of the Youth Criminal Justice Act

Unlike its predecessor, the *Young Offenders Act* (YOA), the YCJA begins with a **preamble**. Traditionally, a preamble serves as a guide to legislative intention, providing information about the values of the legislators and the objectives sought to be achieved by the legislation. In interpreting a legislative provision, judges are required to look first to the words of the provision itself to discern its meaning, but where those words leave room for ambiguity or their application to a particular situation remains in doubt, judges may look to a preamble for helpful clues about the intent of the creators of the legislation.

The preamble to the YCJA gives us some indication of a shift in emphasis: "[the YCJA] reserves its most serious intervention for the most serious crimes and reduces the over-reliance on incarceration for non-violent young persons." This statement epitomizes the essential philosophy of the YCJA and its practical effect; namely, the reduction in the use of incarceration for young people in general, and non-violent young people in particular.

The balance of the preamble echoes many concepts of its predecessors, including "societal protection" and "effective rehabilitation." The concept of "accountability" through "meaningful consequences" receives particular new emphasis. This reflects widespread criticism that, historically, youth criminal justice legislation did not go far enough to ensure that young persons who committed offences were held accountable for their actions.

Section 3 of the YCJA contains a declaration of principle that is intended to provide direction to professionals within the youth criminal justice system. As a numbered section, this declaration of principle, while similar in tenor to the preamble, is directly and specifically binding upon decision makers (in contrast to a preamble, which is more of an aid to interpretation). The s. 3 declaration is somewhat altered from that of its predecessor. Nonetheless, many of the principles are similar.

The drafters of the YCJA sought to remedy the lack of "**statutory prioritization**" by identifying, in s. 3(1), four primary principles:

1. the long-term protection of the public;

2. a system separate from the adult system with special rehabilitative, procedural, and timeliness emphases;

3. culturally sensitive sentencing that promotes respect and reparations "within the limits of fair and proportionate accountability"; and

4. "special considerations" applicable to young persons, including full civil rights, sensitivity to victims, and support for parental involvement.

Each principle is followed by a list of subprinciples, such as rehabilitation, **reparation**, meaningful consequences, enhanced procedural rights, timely intervention, and notice to victims and parents. These subprinciples are designed to support the primary principles.

Although the drafters intended to clarify their message, it seems the considerable judicial discretion that has existed in the past will continue. Judges with differing personal values, for example, may view the means to the end differently. One judge may see rehabilitation of the youth as the best way to protect society, while another judge may see tougher sentencing as the answer. Further, young persons in conflict with the law require specialized treatment that reflects their individual histories and backgrounds. Judicial discretion, as a result, is entirely appropriate to meet these individual needs.

The declaration of principle specifies, at s. 3(1)(b), that the criminal justice system for youth must be separate from that of adults. This principle recognizes the reduced level of maturity and greater dependency of young persons, which in turn justifies the need for measures that ensure "proportionate accountability" for harm done.

Another significant difference from the previous system is a shift in emphasis toward the recognition of victims' rights. Whereas the YOA's declaration of principle made no mention of victims' rights, the YCJA dedicates two subsections to the issue. Police should take note of this, because administering interactions between victims and the court, and victims and the offenders themselves, is a sensitive matter that often requires the involvement of police personnel.

Finally, as in the YOA, the YCJA includes a section requiring that the "Act ... be **liberally construed** in order to ensure that young persons are dealt with in accordance with the principles" set out in s. 3.

Structure of the Youth Criminal Justice Act

PART 1: EXTRAJUDICIAL MEASURES

Part 1 of the YCJA authorizes the use of "**extrajudicial measures**" with respect to youth who commit offences. Section 4(d) states that these measures are appropriately used if "they are adequate to hold a young person accountable for his or her offending behaviour." The term "extrajudicial measures" refers to any alternative measures to traditional court proceedings. They include pre-charge diversion, including the administration of police or Crown "**cautions**" and referrals to community mental health facilities, as well as more onerous "**sanctions**," which consist of a type of extrajudicial sentence (usually attendance at a community program or performance of community service). Section 6 requires the police to consider, before laying a criminal charge, the following options: (1) taking no action, (2) warning the young person, and/or (3) referring the young person to a community-based program. These measures are discussed in greater detail in chapter 8, "Police Procedures and the Youthful Suspect."

PART 2: ORGANIZATION OF THE YOUTH CRIMINAL JUSTICE SYSTEM

Section 13(1) authorizes the establishment of provincial courts and judges with specific jurisdiction over YCJA proceedings. These courts, designated as youth courts, have exclusive jurisdiction over youths in conflict with the law under the YCJA. Section 14 states that "a youth justice court has exclusive jurisdiction in respect of any offence alleged to have been committed by a person while he or she was a young person."

liberal construction
principle of statutory interpretation that requires judges to interpret legislation broadly (liberally) to promote the accomplishment of a general statutory objective

extrajudicial measures
in effect, a sort of sentence or remedy imposed under the YCJA, within strict guidelines, by police or Crown personnel, without a finding of guilt or resort to the court system

caution
formal warning, delivered by police or Crown personnel, under the extrajudicial measures section of the YCJA

sanction
in the YCJA context, an extrajudicial measure that goes beyond a caution to impose compliance with a rehabilitative or community service program

Age Jurisdiction

A "young person" is defined in s. 2 as any person who is between the ages of 12 and 17 or who, in the absence of evidence, appears to be within those ages.

Children under 12 years of age fall outside the jurisdiction of the YCJA and were not faced with prosecution under the YOA either. Certain "punitive response" advocates would have liked to see this minimum age lowered. Also, many conservative reformers lobbied to lower the upper limit of youth jurisdiction age to 16. Apparently, neither of these positions held enough sway to change the age jurisdiction of the YCJA, although there is more flexibility in the new legislation with respect to the availability of adult sentences for serious crimes, at least for older adolescents.

Age jurisdiction issues will be discussed further in chapter 10, "The Trial of a Young Accused."

Trial by Judge and Jury

Under the YOA as it was originally drafted, all offences were treated as summary offences for the purpose of procedure. Under the YCJA, there is no provision stating that all offences shall be treated as summary conviction offences. It is therefore presumed that the same provisions dealing with summary conviction and indictable offences under the *Criminal Code* apply to offences under the YCJA. This means that, for certain indictable offences, youths in conflict with the law are, like adults, entitled to a trial by jury. For summary conviction offences, the youth is tried by a judge only and does not have the right to a trial by jury.

PART 3: JUDICIAL MEASURES

The first provision (s. 23) in this part allows the attorney general to establish a "program of pre-charge screening" that sets out circumstances in which the consent of the attorney general must be obtained for prosecutions in the jurisdiction to which the program applies. Where such a program is established in a jurisdiction, police officers will need to abide by its rules when considering a charge against a young person.

The Right to Counsel in the Youth Court Process

Youth in conflict with the law have the right to consult counsel (s. 25). This right arises early, even in the absence of a charge, including "before and during any consideration of whether, instead of starting proceedings against the young person under this Act, to use an extrajudicial sanction to deal with the young person" (s. 25(1)).

The right to counsel includes, as is the case with adults, the right to be informed of that right without delay and the opportunity to exercise the right. In that sense, the right to counsel implies both an information and implementational component. The legislation also includes special "enhancements" of the right in the youth context, including special notice provisions (including mention of the right to counsel in notices to parents in s. 26 and elsewhere) and a court's power to order that a youth be represented by counsel independent of counsel for the parents.

The right to counsel will be discussed more fully in chapters 8 through 10.

Parental Involvement in the Youth Court Process

Parental involvement in a youth's case is a particular concern, especially because many parents pay for their child's legal costs. Most parents can be very helpful to their children in such a crisis. However, parents who are angry with or embarrassed by their child may put pressure on their child and their child's lawyer to plead guilty as a form of punishment and to get on with the process. They may take such initiatives on their own in contrast to their child's wishes and even best interests. For this reason, s. 25(8) empowers a youth court judge to order legal representation independent of the child's parents.

Like its predecessor, the YCJA contains provisions dealing with parental notice of a child's arrest. Section 26(1) requires that an officer in charge must, as soon as possible, give notice to parents of their child's arrest "stating the place of detention and the reason for the arrest." Furthermore, s. 27(1) authorizes a youth court to order a parent's presence "if in its opinion the presence of the parent is necessary or in the best interests of the young person." Section 27(4) enables a court to hold a parent in contempt if he or she fails to appear following an order. Unlike adults, young people also have the right to contact and consult with their parents or with a responsible adult before being questioned by police. That right is in addition to their right to consult counsel before providing a statement to police.

Detention of a Young Person Before Sentencing

For many youths charged with committing an offence, pre-sentencing detention is the first time they have been placed in a facility outside their community. The experience can be extremely traumatic and intrusive in their lives—they are separated from their friends, families, and schools. For these reasons, there are numerous restrictions on the use of pre-sentencing detention, which are discussed more fully in chapter 9, "The Pre-Trial Period."

Medical and Psychological Reports

Section 34 of the YCJA empowers a youth court judge to order a psychological assessment of a young person by a "qualified person." The purposes for which an assessment may be ordered are listed in s. 34(2) and include the need to make a decision with respect to pre-trial release, the imposition of an adult sentence, and the making or review of a youth sentence. In certain appropriate cases, a youth may (under s. 34(4)) be remanded in custody for a period not exceeding 30 days for a psychological assessment, but there is a general presumption against remand for this purpose.

The final medical and/or psychological report must be given to the youth, his or her attending parents, the youth's counsel, the prosecutors, and any non-attending parent of the young person who has an active interest in the proceedings. Pursuant to s. 34(10), disclosure of the final report may be withheld from the young person, his or her parents, or a private prosecutor, if it could impede the young person's rehabilitation, or physically or mentally endanger another person. This is qualified, however, where "the interests of justice make disclosure essential" (s. 34(11)).

Referral to Child Welfare Agency

Section 35 of the YCJA allows the youth court, "[i]n addition to any order that it is authorized to make," to refer a young person to a "child welfare agency for assessment to determine whether the young person is in need of child welfare services." This option was not included in the previous legislation and was drafted in response to critics who believed that judges, for lack of a suitable alternative, were sending some young persons into custody to get them out of difficult living circumstances or in the hope that they would be helped by rehabilitative programs. The inappropriateness of this approach is condemned in s. 29(1):

> 29(1) A youth justice court judge or a justice shall not detain a young person in custody prior to being sentenced as a substitute for appropriate child protection, mental health or other social measures.

However, unless appropriate child welfare funding is available to support such referrals, the benefit of the common sense and good intentions behind the provision will be limited by scarce resources.

PART 4: SENTENCING

disposition
word used in place of "sentence" under the YOA; the YCJA has reverted to the more traditional word "sentence"

Provisions relating to sentencing (rather than the euphemistic term "**disposition**" under the YOA) and the administration of youth custody and supervision are covered by 72 of the YCJA's 200 provisions. Section 42 alone, which sets out the range of sentences available to a youth court judge, is more than 2,500 words long. The complexity of these provisions attests to the complexity of the subject in general, which, of all of the aspects of the youth justice system, has been the most consistently controversial.

Canada has been criticized for having one of the highest youth-custody sentence rates in the world. A major criticism of the YOA was that it provided little guidance to judges regarding the appropriate sentence for particular crimes. Although the YOA contained general principles intended to set the tone for the entire Act, the principles themselves were seemingly contradictory and not easily reconcilable. Judges maintained vast discretion to order sentences reflective of their own values. Some judges, for example, were rehabilitation-oriented while others were punitive-oriented. As a result, and as a result of regional differences in the availability of programs, sentences for similar crimes varied widely across and even within provinces.

Unlike under the YOA, the YCJA has a guiding provision, s. 38, which establishes the purpose(s) of sentencing in the youth court system. It is intended to guide judges in their decisions:

> 38(1) The purpose of sentencing ... is to hold a young person accountable for an offence through the imposition of just sanctions that have meaningful consequences for the young person and that promote his or her rehabilitation and reintegration into society, thereby contributing to the long-term protection of the public.

Section 38(2) outlines sentencing principles:

> 38(2) ... (a) the sentence must not result in a punishment that is greater than the punishment that would be appropriate for an adult who has been convicted of the same offence committed in similar circumstances;
>
> (b) the sentence must be similar to the sentences imposed in the region on similar young persons found guilty of the same offence committed in similar circumstances;
>
> (c) the sentence must be proportionate to the seriousness of the offence and the degree of responsibility of the young person for that offence;

> (d) all available sanctions other than custody that are reasonable in the cir-
> cumstances should be considered for all young persons, with particular attention
> to the circumstances of aboriginal young persons; and
>
> (e) subject to paragraph (c), the sentence must
>
> > (i) be the least restrictive sentence that is capable of achieving the pur-
> > pose [of sentencing],
> >
> > (ii) be the one that is most likely to rehabilitate the young person and
> > reintegrate him or her into society, and
> >
> > (iii) promote a sense of responsibility in the young person, and an
> > acknowledgement of the harm done to victims and the community.

Clearly, the drafters of the YCJA have attempted to address the criticism levelled at sentencing practices under the YOA. Section 38(2)(b), for example, is an
attempt to diminish the variability in sentences for young persons who commit
similar offences (although this principle was weakened in the final draft by the
addition of "in the region"). As well, s. 38(2)(c) addresses the relatively lengthy
sentences that were being prescribed for certain offenders under the YOA. However, only time will tell to what degree these new sentencing principles will alter
established sentencing patterns for youth.

Sentencing will be covered in greater detail in chapter 11.

PART 5: CUSTODY AND SUPERVISION

Part 5 of the YCJA contains provisions dealing with the administration of custodial
sentences, including the appointment of youth workers, programs for reintegration of offenders into the community, the review of custodial sentences, and
facility choices and/or transfers (open or secure custody, youth or adult facility,
and so on). These issues are dealt with separately from the sentencing provisions
largely because post-sentencing decisions are often made not by the youth court
(although certain decisions do require court approval or involvement) but by
administrators in the youth custody system, who have considerable discretion with
regard to how a court-imposed sentence will be carried out.

PART 6: PUBLICATION, RECORDS, AND INFORMATION

Restrictions on the disclosure of youth records have existed since the *Juvenile
Delinquents Act*. This practice was intended to protect the privacy of youth in
conflict with the law. It was thought that minimizing stigmatization or "labelling"
would increase the likelihood of rehabilitating these youths. The YOA, as originally
enacted, continued this trend with provisions that narrowly restricted the publication of young offender records. One provision, for example, restricted the media
from publishing "any information serving to identify" any person under 18 years of
age involved in youth court proceedings. This included the accused, the victims, or
any witnesses. The provision was interpreted broadly to include not only names,
but also photographs for publication. Any individual who contravened this provision could face prosecution. However, such a ban excluded deceased youths and
youths who had been transferred to adult court under the YOA.

The limitations on the media to publish identifying information about young
offenders were constitutionally challenged in *Southam Inc. v. The Queen*.[1] The newspaper corporation argued that the provisions contravened freedom of the press.

The Ontario Court of Appeal, however, upheld the YOA provisions on the basis that the provisions did not completely ban publication. Information about young offender cases that did not identify the youths in the proceeding were permissible for publication. Furthermore, the objective of protecting vulnerable youths was recognized.

But the publication ban continued to attract criticism. The public believed that it had a right to such information for the purpose of protection. The media viewed the restrictive provisions as a restraint on freedom of the press. Also, mental health professionals and school officials felt that disclosure of youth records was vital for effective rehabilitation and reintegration into the community. As a result, several amendments were made during the tenure of the YOA, paving the way for the publication provisions in the YCJA.

Provisions permitting the publication of identifying information about young persons in the YCJA have become even more liberal. Section 110(1) of the YCJA establishes that "no person shall publish the name of a young person, or any other information related to a young person, if it would identify the young person as a young person dealt with under this Act." However, the publication ban is not absolute. Section 110(2) contains three major exceptions: (a) where a young person is subject to an adult sentence; (b) where a young person is subject to a youth sentence for a "presumptive offence" (see definition in s. 2—certain violent offences) or is designated a "**violent offender**"; and (c) where the publication of information is "made in the course of the administration of justice, if it is not the purpose of the publication to make the information known in the community." For example, the police may be required to publicize identifying information about a young person at large if it will aid them in their search and ultimate arrest of an alleged offender. In all three of these cases, the ban on publication does not apply.

The general ban on publication of identifying information also applies to victims and witnesses who are under 18 years of age and who are involved in youth court proceedings (s. 111(1)). Once the victim or witness turns 18 years of age, he or she is entitled to publish or "cause to be published" such information.

Sections 114 to 124 specify who may keep or have access to youth records. A youth justice court, a review board, or any other court may keep a record of any case that comes before it. A record of any alleged offence may be kept by any police force that participated in the investigation of a young person. These police records may also be kept by the Royal Canadian Mounted Police in a central repository for the purpose of keeping criminal history files. The government or any agency of the government may keep records for the purpose of investigating an alleged offence, for use in youth court proceedings, for determining sentencing and the appropriateness of extrajudicial measures, or as a result of administering extrajudicial measures. A person or organization that helps implement an extrajudicial measure may also keep a record.

Similar provisions apply to providing others access to records about young persons. Section 118(1) orders that no access should ever be given unless authorized under the YCJA. This does not apply, however, to youths subjected to adult sentencing. Section 119(1) provides an extensive list of individuals, agencies, and institutions that may have limited access to court and/or police records about young persons (for example, a person carrying out a criminal record check for government employment purposes).

violent offender
under the YCJA, a judicial designation—that is, a judge designates a person a violent offender, and the designation has various implications under the legislation

Section 119(2) provides limitations on the period available for the access to records that depend on the sentence imposed on the young person. If extrajudicial sanctions are imposed, access to records is terminated two years following the imposition of sanctions. If the young person is acquitted of the offence, the access ends two months after the expiry of the time to appeal passes. If an absolute discharge is ordered, the period ends one year after a finding of guilt. In the case of a conditional discharge, access to records will be denied as of three years following the verdict. When there is a finding of guilt for a summary conviction offence, the period lasts three years after the sentence has been completed. Finally, in the case of an indictable offence, an authorized individual may be provided with access to records up to five years following the completion of the sentence.

Even if the authorized period of access to records about young persons passes, the interest of justice may require some flexibility. Accordingly, s. 123(1) provides exceptional circumstances under which an individual may acquire access to a record following the time period. Furthermore, a young person to whom a record relates may have access to the record at any time.

There are also particular individuals and institutions who may receive information that is contained in a record. A police officer, for example, can disclose information that is contained within a record to any person if it is necessary in the course of an investigation (s. 125). As under the YOA, schools and other institutions and professionals working with young persons may obtain information about a record. Here, disclosure must be necessary to ensure compliance with probation or conditional sentencing, to ensure the safety of others, or to help rehabilitate the young person. However, if information is accessed for these purposes, the information must be kept separate from any records of the young person, no other person may be permitted to access it, and it must be destroyed once the purpose for which it was obtained has passed. Information cannot be disclosed after the time for access to records has passed.

Section 127(1) empowers the youth court to enable the provincial director, a peace officer, or the attorney general to disclose information about a youth record to anyone. The applicant must demonstrate to the court that the young person has caused serious personal injury and continues to pose a serious risk to others. The applicant must also prove that disclosure is necessary to avoid such risk. The youth court must give the young person, the parent of the young person, and the attorney general an opportunity to be heard before rendering its decision. An application for disclosure can be made in the absence of a young person if all reasonable efforts have been made to locate him or her.

PART 7: GENERAL PROVISIONS

This part deals with procedural issues such as the disqualification of judges after a change of plea, exclusion of certain individuals from the courtroom (including the young person himself or herself, under certain circumstances), and out-of-province transfers of jurisdiction. It creates an offence based on assisting escape from youth custody or for interfering with a youth's compliance with sentence conditions, and another based on non-compliance with the publication ban (s. 138).

Part 7 also establishes the general applicability of the *Criminal Code* to the youth criminal justice system, subject to certain exceptions[2] "with any modifications that the circumstances require" (ss. 140 to 142).

Sections 146 to 153 deal with evidence in the youth justice system and are covered in later chapters of this book.

Finally, s. 157 authorizes the attorney general of Canada or a minister designated by the lieutenant governor in council of a province to establish certain "community-based programs":

(a) programs that are an alternative to judicial proceedings, such as victim–offender reconciliation programs, mediation programs and restitution programs;

(b) programs that are an alternative to detention before sentencing, such as bail supervision programs; and

(c) programs that are an alternative to custody, such as intensive support and supervision programs, and programs to carry out attendance orders.

Chapter Summary

This chapter provided a broad and shallow overview of the *Youth Criminal Justice Act*. After introducing the guiding principles of the legislation expressed in s. 3, the various major parts of the Act were introduced, including extrajudicial measures, organization, judicial measures, sentencing, custody and supervision, publication of records, and general provisions. Within these broad categories, reference was made to some of the most important issues addressed by this legislation, such as age jurisdiction, parental involvement, right to counsel, and sentencing principles. By providing a "map" of the YCJA, this chapter laid a foundation upon which specific issues of interest to police will be more fully explored in later chapters.

KEY TERMS

preamble

statutory prioritization

reparation

liberal construction

extrajudicial measures

caution

sanction

disposition

violent offender

NOTES

1. *Southam Inc. v. The Queen* (1984), 48 OR (2d) 678; 42 CR (3d) 336 (CA).

2. Notably with respect to the system of caps on detention for mentally disordered persons: s. 141 of the YCJA.

EXERCISES AND REVIEW

Review Questions

1. What is the effective difference between the paragraphs in the preamble of the YCJA and the principles set out in the declaration of principle (s. 3)?

2. How are legislative "principles" applied by judges?

3. Are any other sets of "principles" created by the YCJA? Where do they appear and for what purpose?

4. How does the YCJA purport to achieve its objective of proportional accountability?

5. Which provision of the YCJA sets out the legislation's age jurisdiction?

6. Which section of the YCJA provides that youthful accuseds are entitled to be tried by a judge and jury for certain offences?

7. Why do certain "notice to parent" provisions of the YCJA also require notice to the parent of the youth's right to counsel?

8. Why does s. 35 of the YCJA provide for a judicial referral of a youth suspect/accused to a child welfare agency? How do you think this section will be used in practice?

9. Why does the legislation have separate parts for sentencing (part 4) and for custody and supervision (part 5)?

10. What is the rationale behind the ban on publication of the identity of youthful accused/offenders?

11. Why can an accused's record of sanctions under the extrajudicial measures section be disclosed to the victim of an offence (s. 12)?

12. What are the exceptions to the rule that bans publication of a youthful suspect's identity?

13. What does "publication" mean for the purpose of the publication ban sections? Does the YCJA prohibit speaking the suspect's name into a police vehicle radio?

Discussion Questions

Certain provisions of the YCJA are directed at youth who have been designated as "serious violent offenders."

1. How is a youth so designated?

2. Who makes the designation? On what basis?

3. Having regard to the definition of "serious violent offence" in s. 2, what sort of acts might you define as "serious violent offences"? Do other members of your discussion group agree with you?

CHAPTER 8

Police Procedures and the Youthful Suspect: Extrajudicial Measures, Charging, Arrest, and Interviewing

■ CHAPTER OBJECTIVES

After completing this chapter, you should be able to:

- List some strategic decisions that must be made by police personnel during first or early contacts with a youthful suspect.

- Explain what is meant by "extrajudicial measures" and list three types of such measures.

- Understand at what point in an investigation police personnel are required to comply with s. 146 of the *Youth Criminal Justice Act* (YCJA).

- Describe the points that must be included in a rights caution to a young offender.

- Explain police responsibilities with respect to notice to parents/access to parents upon the charging or arrest of a young offender.

- Describe the components of a young offender's right to counsel.

- Describe the features of a valid waiver of the right to silence/right to counsel by a young suspect.

- Define "spontaneous statement" for the purpose of the YCJA.

Introduction

The arrest, questioning, and detention of adolescents suspected of committing criminal offences in Canada is governed by three[1] major sources of legislation: the *Canadian Charter of Rights and Freedoms*, the *Criminal Code*, and the *Youth Criminal Justice Act*.

The Charter and the Code apply equally to both adults and young persons. The YCJA guarantees special rights and protections to young persons in addition to those applicable to adults. These additional rights are prescribed based on an understanding that adolescents are more vulnerable and generally less mature and sophisticated than adults, and are not as well informed about their procedural rights or about the justice system in general.

Besides these enhanced procedural rights, certain provisions of the YCJA are intended to promote parental involvement throughout the youth criminal justice process. This involvement is sought for several reasons. Parental involvement can be a means of providing youth with a measure of adult guidance, which can be helpful when it comes to securing (and paying for) legal representation, and can also be a much-needed source of emotional support at a difficult time. Parental involvement throughout the adolescent's prosecution can also be a way to provide for reintegration of the youth into the community after a sentence is complete. Needless to say, youthful offenders whose parents are unable or unwilling to support them during the investigation and prosecution of an offence can be at a significant disadvantage.

Before we examine in detail the specific provisions relating to the investigation and arrest of young people, it is appropriate to introduce the subject of initial police contact with youthful suspects, and the importance of decisions made in the course of these encounters.

Police and the Young Suspect: First Contacts

A SUSPECT'S AGE

Police personnel may become involved with young suspects in a number of different ways: a police officer may observe a crime in progress and may intervene, or may discover evidence of a crime when speaking with teens about another matter (after pulling over a car, for example). More frequently, however, police will be called to attend at the scene of an incident, whether by a victim, by parents, or by others such as school or store personnel.

Police officers must keep in mind that at the first stage of arrest, which can be a simple encounter on the street, they need to be aware of a young person's rights lest an unwitting Charter violation jeopardize a subsequent prosecution; any time an officer stops someone, it is considered a detention. Even routine traffic stops amount to a detention. If an officer needs to conduct a more thorough investigation (longer than 15 minutes), the officer can detain someone for up to 24 hours, but this time period can be stretched to 36 hours under reasonable circumstances, such as long weekends or the unavailability of a justice of the peace. A key difference between arresting young people and arresting adults is that police must advise the young person's parents of the circumstances. Even if an officer arrests a young person for one hour and releases him/her, the officer must contact the parents and tell them what happened. If police take custody of the child and bring him/her to a cell block or police station, they must contact the parents immediately to let them know their son or daughter is being detained. Once police decide there are grounds to lay an information, the next step is to make a decision regarding pre-trial detention.

In the course of an initial contact, police officers should have had sufficient training to be alert to the age of suspects and potential suspects. Because there are special rules governing the use of statements by a young person, police should always keep in mind the possibility that a suspect is within the age jurisdiction of the YCJA. Appearances can be deceptive; many teenagers take pains to look older than their years, so it is wise for officers to err on the side of caution and to assume that a young adult suspect (or witness) is 17 years of age or younger. The matter is easier if the suspect is known to the person who calls the police, but it always makes sense to make "how old are you?" and "may I see some ID?" two of the first questions asked of a suspect apparently under age 25.

Where officers mistake suspects for adults, or where youthful suspects misrepresent their age as 18 or older, the YCJA provides a curative provision:

> 146(8) A youth justice court judge may in any proceedings under this Act rule admissible any statement or waiver by a young person if, at the time of the making of the statement or waiver,
>
> (a) the young person held himself or herself to be eighteen years old or older;
>
> (b) the person to whom the statement or waiver was made conducted reasonable inquiries as to the age of the young person and had reasonable grounds for believing that the young person was eighteen years old or older; and
>
> (c) in all other circumstances the statement or waiver would otherwise be admissible.

But as noted in paragraph (b), in order for a statement to have a chance at admissibility, the questioning officer must have made reasonable inquiries. Where a young-looking suspect cannot or will not produce proof of age, his or her age may ultimately be proven in court by means of parental testimony; until that time, investigators should treat him or her as a person under age 18.

WITNESS OR SUSPECT?

Another early issue that investigating officers must consider is whether a young person being questioned about an incident is a witness, a victim, or a suspect (or any combination of these). In addition to the well-known Charter protections that are triggered by arrest, the evidence provisions of s. 146 of the YCJA (to be discussed more fully below) must be considered, and the relevant caution(s) must be administered, from the moment that investigators develop "reasonable grounds for believing that the young person has committed an offence," if the admissibility of a statement is to be preserved.

There is some limited case law that supports the position that, where a youth is just casually being questioned as a witness, victim, or "potential suspect," s. 146 does not apply.[2] Although these cases appear to give officers a little relief from the strictures of the legislation, questioning on this basis should proceed with extreme caution, especially where evidence is moving in the direction of reasonable grounds. Investigators should also be aware that if, in questioning a young "witness," that witness suddenly makes an incriminating statement, the statement is unlikely to be admissible under s. 146(3), which protects **spontaneous statements**. Statements made in response to police questions have been held by the courts not to qualify as spontaneous.[3]

TO ARREST OR NOT? DECISION TO ARREST

When dealing with an adult suspect, the decision whether to arrest generally turns on the nature of the offence. Indictable and hybrid offences are arrestable without a warrant; summary conviction offences are normally dealt with by service of an appearance notice.

When dealing with young suspects there are additional considerations. The detention of a young person in police custody triggers a range of police responsibilities, including the need to **caution**, the need for detention separate from adults (s. 30(3)), and the requirement of immediate efforts to contact the youth's parents (s. 26(1)). Because of the vulnerable nature of teenagers, there is a strong legislative bias against their pre-trial detention. However, police may have legitimate concerns about the safety of an unsupervised youth and may be motivated to detain him or her for safety reasons. When dealing with a teenager in trouble, the line between criminal justice and child protection can often be blurred. But it is important that officers be clear about their motivations, because the courts have no power to continue a detention based on child protection motives:

> 29(1) A youth justice court judge or a justice shall not detain a young person in custody prior to being sentenced as a substitute for appropriate child protection, mental health or other social measures.[4]

In circumstances where investigators are concerned for the safety of a young person but where arrest is not permitted by law or does not otherwise seem appropriate, police personnel may suggest that the young person accompany them on a consensual basis to a place of safety, either to the home of a parent or guardian, or to the police station to await the arrival of such a person. In a circumstance such as this, it is always a good idea to inform the young person that any statements he or she makes may be admissible in court.

Where the offence being investigated is of a less serious nature and there is no question of arrest, police still have some decisions to make. They can serve the suspect with a notice to appear in court if the suspect is found committing an offence, or serve the suspect with a criminal summons when they do not find the suspect committing the offence. A criminal summons is an order, sworn before a justice of the peace, commanding someone to appear in court. In both instances, police must advise the suspect of his or her right to counsel,[5] and the police must comply with the YCJA requirement to contact parents (s. 26(2)), but they must first consider the appropriateness of the resort to extrajudicial measures. This exercise of discretion will in some cases be very informal—the investigating officer may decide not to charge the youth at all, dismissing him or her with a simple verbal warning to stay out of trouble. This situation is comparable to circumstances in which an adult suspect is not charged on the basis of the officer's determination

spontaneous statement
a statement by a youth that is offered without being prompted by police questions or comments and before police have had a chance to advise the youth of his or her s. 146 rights

caution
in the arrest context, a formal warning, often in a rehearsed or set form, delivered to a person under arrest or being questioned, for the purpose of advising that person of his or her rights

that the evidence available does not support the necessary "reasonable grounds." However, as will be explained below, in the case of youth, there is explicit authority or discretion not to charge even if reasonable grounds do, in fact, exist. When an investigating officer has reasonable grounds that will support a charge, but is considering exercising his or her discretion to forgo resort to the judicial process, the case falls squarely into the realm of "extrajudicial measures."

EXTRAJUDICIAL MEASURES

While the resort to extrajudicial measures involves the exercise of significant discretion, the decision to *consider* such measures is *not* discretionary:

> 6(1) A police officer shall, before starting judicial proceedings or taking any other measures under this Act against a young person alleged to have committed an offence, consider whether it would be sufficient, having regard to the principles set out in section 4, to take no further action, warn the young person, administer a caution, if a program has been established under section 7, or, with the consent of the young person, refer the young person to a program or agency in the community that may assist the young person not to commit offences.

Although s. 6(2) provides that the failure of police to consider extrajudicial measures (sometimes known as "diversion") does not invalidate a subsequent charge, it is clear that the intent of the legislature is that resort to extrajudicial measures be automatically considered in *every* case. In fact, to comply with this provision, many police departments throughout the country have incorporated into their charge packages a section detailing why criminal charges were laid rather than resorting to extrajudicial measures.

In cases involving serious violence or aggravating factors such as hate motivations, diversion "considerations" may be perfunctory at best; but note that s. 6(1) creates no specific exception for crimes of violence. In some Canadian jurisdictions, police do, in fact, use extrajudicial measures to deal with mildly or moderately violent incidents, such as school yard fights. Other considerations that will influence an officer's decision to attempt extrajudicial measures include the suspect's age, demeanour, and record of prior offences. The experience of police personnel in dealing with young offenders makes many of them quite well placed to make a determination of whether "it would be sufficient ... to take no further action ... or to [resort to a caution and/or a referral]" (s. 6(1)). Less experienced officers will benefit from the advice of more senior colleagues in making their first such determinations.

Extrajudicial measures fall into three broad categories: warnings, cautions, and referrals. Section 9 provides that evidence that a youth was given a warning, caution, or referral is inadmissible to prove prior offending behaviour. It is interesting to note that there is no such restriction with regard to extrajudicial sanctions (subject, of course, to restrictions on access to records). Acceptance of responsibility by the young person for her or his behaviour is a precondition to an extrajudicial sanction, but not to a warning, caution, or referral.

While virtually all of the extrajudicial measures permitted under the YCJA were available to police under the YOA, such diversion was unfortunately underused. It surprises many people that Canada compares poorly to other countries throughout the world with regard to its diversion rates for young people. Under the YOA, Canada diverted about 23 percent of its prospective criminal charges involving young people in comparison with 53 percent in the United States, 57 percent in Great Britain, and 61 percent in New Zealand.

Sections 4 and 5 provide that there is a presumption that extrajudicial measures are adequate to hold young people accountable for non-violent offences if they have no prior convictions. Even with young people who have "priors," meaning prior criminal convictions, extrajudicial measures should still be used if such a measure would prove adequate to hold the young person accountable. In essence, the objectives of extrajudicial measures centre on the relationship between the young person and her or his community, her or his family, and the victim.

As mentioned, extrajudicial measures include all forms of police diversion, informal police warnings, formal police cautions, Crown counsel cautions, and police referral to community-based programs, such as attendance centres and other social service agencies. Sections 7 and 8 permit the establishment of formal police or Crown counsel caution programs, through an order of the lieutenant governor in council. In the province of Ontario, there have been no such formal programs created.

While s. 6(1) seems to suggest that the young person's consent is only required for the extrajudicial measure, in practice it makes good sense to obtain a youth's consent to have parents or others present at a caution meeting. Although the youth's acceptance of responsibility for the chargeable act is not an explicit precondition to the giving of a caution, s. 4, which sets out the principles of the extrajudicial measures program, states that encouraging such acceptance is an important objective of the program. Obviously, a youth's refusal to take responsibility for the alleged act will be an important consideration with respect to whether a caution is appropriate.

It is unclear why the drafters of the YCJA believed it necessary to give legislative effect to the process of delivering police cautions; it is hoped that ss. 6, 7, and 8 do not in any way serve to complicate a process that appears to already work well. In writing about police cautioning, Nicholas Bala notes:

> [B]ut this may be related to ... poor stats. ... Often it represents the most effective, most humane, and least expensive way of dealing with an adolescent who has made a mistake. The informal, immediate response of a police officer, especially one with sensitivity and experience in dealing with youths, can have as much or more impact in terms of deterrence and accountability than a much delayed, often perfunctory appearance in youth court.[6]

Referrals

Also mentioned in s. 6(1) is the option of "referring" a youth to a program or agency in the community. Sections 10, 18, and 157 are complementary to this provision in that they allow for provinces and the federal government to set up community-based programs designed to provide alternatives to the formal court process.

According to Bala, while such referrals were employed in other provinces under the YOA, they were rarely used in Ontario, owing to a concern that the "treatment" that might be prescribed might well prove, unfairly, to be more onerous than the sentence imposed by a youth court upon conviction.[7] However, since the coming into force of the YCJA, numerous agencies and initiatives in Ontario have been granted funding by the Ministry of Children and Youth Services to provide options for police and courts to refer and divert adolescents from the formal court system. These programs are quite diverse in their mandates and range from attendance centres to clinical supports and residential treatment options. Because these programs are community-based, the nature of the programs vary. Attendance centres are places where youths must go if so ordered. They are often similar to schools or community centres, where adolescents are offered rehabilitation and, especially, a place to stay out of trouble in the after-school and evening hours. Clinical supports offer treatment by professionals such as psychologists. Residential treatment options include group homes or foster care facilities with particular resources tailored to meet the needs of certain groups of youth at risk. Overall, many of these programs have experienced great success; however, some police officers report that many young people continue to fall through the cracks in the system because they don't keep their appointments or they end up on long waiting lists. Community-based alternative measures are discussed in more detail in chapter 12.

Sanctions

The more onerous type of extrajudicial measure (and the one most familiar to those who worked with s. 4—Alternative Measures—of the YOA) is the **extrajudicial sanction**, established by s. 10 of the YCJA. Sanctions are used with young people who cannot be "adequately" dealt with by warning, caution, or referral:

extrajudicial sanctions in the context of the YCJA, extrajudicial measures that go beyond cautions to impose compliance with a rehabilitative or community service program

10(1) An extrajudicial sanction may be used to deal with a young person alleged to have committed an offence only if the young person cannot be adequately dealt with by a warning, caution or referral mentioned in section 6, 7 or 8 because of the seriousness of the offence, the nature and number of previous offences committed by the young person or any other aggravating circumstances.

(2) An extrajudicial sanction may be used only if

(a) it is part of a program of sanctions that may be authorized by the Attorney General or authorized by a person, or a member of a class of persons, designated by the lieutenant governor in council of the province;

(b) the person who is considering whether to use the extrajudicial sanction is satisfied that it would be appropriate, having regard to the needs of the young person and the interests of society;

(c) the young person, having been informed of the extrajudicial sanction, fully and freely consents to be subject to it;

(d) the young person has, before consenting to be subject to the extrajudicial sanction, been advised of his or her right to be represented by counsel and been given a reasonable opportunity to consult with counsel;

(e) the young person accepts responsibility for the act or omission that forms the basis of the offence that he or she is alleged to have committed;

(f) there is, in the opinion of the Attorney General, sufficient evidence to proceed with the prosecution of the offence; and

(g) the prosecution of the offence is not in any way barred at law.

(3) An extrajudicial sanction may not be used in respect of a young person who

(a) denies participation or involvement in the commission of the offence; or

(b) expresses the wish to have the charge dealt with by a youth justice court.

The nature of "sanction" programs and the sanctions that they impose vary widely across the country. These programs are funded provincially and therefore are dependent on a provincial government's will and allocation of funding for their development. Examples of such programs include victim–offender reconciliation programs, community service programs, and aboriginal community councils. Youth who participate in these programs may be required to perform some sort of community or personal service, make apologies, or make reparations. Formal counselling or treatment is less common.

Sanctions can be used on either a pre- or a post-charge basis, and most provinces have a policy about this, as well as eligibility guidelines. In Ontario, a charge is generally laid first, and police personnel make recommendations to the Crown where they believe that extrajudicial measures may be appropriate (or the Crown may make this decision independently). The Crown then typically refers the youth to a program, and a meeting is called with the youth (and sometimes the parents, the victim, or others) to develop a proposal for the sanction. If the sanction is acceptable to the youth and is complied with, the charge is dropped. Youth may be deemed suitable for extrajudicial sanctions despite a record of previous police warnings, cautions, or referrals to community-based programs, previous extrajudicial sanctions, or findings of guilt.

Although youth and parents who go through the sanction process often report satisfaction, some critics warn that these programs are not necessarily in the best interests of youth because the programs are delivered in the absence of a finding of guilt, and may actually result in more onerous "penalties" than would be imposed by the court on a youth's conviction.

While the delivery of a caution does not have future implications for a youth (s. 9 provides it is not admissible in later proceedings), participation in a sanction program might: failure to complete the program can result in the laying of a charge, and evidence of any participation is admissible for certain purposes—for example, at the time of sentencing for a later offence. Records, pursuant to s. 123, relating to extrajudicial sanctions, are kept for two years from the date that the young person consents to become involved in the program.

As provided by s. 10(2)(c), a sanction can be prescribed only on a consent basis, and the youth must know the nature of the particular sanction proposed before consenting. The decision to attempt to deal with a youth by means of a sanction triggers the right to counsel (s. 10(2)(d)) and the requirement to give notice to a parent (s. 11).

Unlike the administration of a caution, under s. 10(2)(e), eligibility for the administration of a sanction is dependent on the youth's acknowledgment of "responsibility" for the relevant act or omission. It is this requirement that most strongly forms the basis for the requirement of the right to counsel, because while statements made to satisfy this requirement are not technically admissible in an eventual proceeding (s. 10(4)), the fact that a youth has participated in such a program obviously implies the receipt of such a statement.

Finally, especially in jurisdictions in which post-charge sanctions are used, police personnel must remember that the use of a sanction is not an appropriate alternative to charging where a case is weak or does not give rise to reasonable grounds. In those cases, as always, no charge can be laid and no extrajudicial measure ought to be taken. Also, in deciding about which course to take—whether to charge or to recommend extrajudicial measures—police must be vigilant not to allow a bias on the basis of race, sex, social class, or any other inappropriate ground to affect their exercise of discretion.

The victim, under s. 12, has the right to some information about the extrajudicial sanctions being contemplated, including the name of the youth, conditions of the agreement, and the consequences of non-compliance.

The Admissibility of Youth Statements

Once a decision to charge has been made, protecting the value of investigative evidence, and especially statements by the accused, becomes extremely important.

Confessions and other statements are probably the most important source of evidence in the trial of a youth. For better or for worse, youth tend to be intimidated by adult interviewers (especially police), and both youth witnesses and youth suspects are more likely than adults to make statements to police or to answer police questions. Commentators have noted that youth tend to perceive the justice system differently from the way adults do. Teenagers' understanding of guilt and innocence tends to be rudimentary, and they may believe that there is no hope for them (and no reason to exercise their rights, such as the right not to make a statement) if they are guilty in the factual—and not necessarily legal—sense of the word. Conversely, youths are more likely than adults to believe that there is something to be gained—leniency, for example—through cooperation and disclosure to a degree that is not necessarily consistent with their best interests.

The YCJA, to some extent, acknowledges these differences and attempts to compensate for them by means of strict statement rules and requirements with respect to informing youth of their right to counsel. These strict requirements pose a challenge for police, who sometimes feel that, as easy as it is to get a youth to speak, the system makes it nearly impossible to ensure the admissibility of a youth statement. The YCJA places the onus on the prosecution to prove that police personnel complied with the requirements. This must be proven beyond a reasonable doubt, making it very difficult for a statement to be admitted and requiring a very high standard of compliance on the part of police personnel. This is consistent with adult criminal law, where the onus is also on the prosecution to establish, beyond a reasonable doubt, the voluntariness and admissibility of any statement to be tendered.

Inadmissibility, of course, is the biggest threat to statement evidence. Most police personnel are very familiar with Charter restraints on the admissibility of evidence.

If a police officer violates an accused's rights (to be free from self-incrimination, or the right to counsel, for example) under the Charter, any evidence that is subsequently discovered as a result of the statement during the investigation can be ruled inadmissible in court. In making a determination of admissibility under the Charter, a judge considers whether "having regard to all the circumstances, the admission ... would bring the administration of justice into disrepute."[8] This involves an assessment of the seriousness of the infringement of rights as well as a consideration of whether the police officer was acting in "good faith." The essential elements of the law pertaining to Charter violations in the context of the discovery of evidence were recently confirmed by the Supreme Court of Canada in the case of *R v. Rodgers*.[9]

With adult statements, if a judge determines that the evidence would have been obtained even without the rights violation, it is more likely that it will be admissible. In the case of youth, however, s. 146 of the YCJA (the successor to s. 56 of the YOA) creates an *automatic* exclusion of evidence obtained after breach of the rules, without resort to a Charter analysis. Because of this, officers who are well schooled in compliance with the Charter and with other sources of rules with respect to the collection of evidence (such as the *Criminal Code* or the common law) may nevertheless lack the training to successfully interview young suspects. Case law has repeatedly illustrated that the courts will protect the rights of an accused young person and encourage police compliance with the law even if this means that youths who are "in fact guilty" are acquitted. These cases exemplify the principle that the rights of young persons in conflict with the law are more important than the guilt of any individual offender.

While s. 146 of the YCJA is quite similar to its predecessor, s. 56 of the YOA, it incorporates an important new exception to the system of strict compliance:

> 146(6) When there has been a technical irregularity in complying with paragraphs (2)(b) to (d) [the provisions that set out the statement-taking rules], the youth justice court may admit into evidence a statement referred to in subsection (2), if satisfied that the admission of the statement would not bring into disrepute the principle that young persons are entitled to enhanced procedural protection to ensure that they are treated fairly and their rights are protected.

The wording in s. 146(6) is opposite to the wording in s. 24(2) of the Charter, which would be at play in the adult criminal context. This section of the Charter requires that evidence be excluded if it is established that the administration of justice would be brought into disrepute. The wording in s. 146(6) seems to place the burden of proof on the Crown. However, s. 146(6) is clearly intended to ensure admissibility of some statements that would have been excluded under the YOA, thereby decreasing the protection accorded young persons making statements to persons in authority.

While s. 146(6) of the YCJA is thus intended to allow for the admissibility of statements that might have previously been excluded, the provision has been interpreted relatively narrowly so far. What constitutes a "technical irregularity" has been considered in several cases, and the meaning of the term is narrowly circumscribed in this case law. For example, in *R v. O.K.*,[10] the court did not admit a young person's statement because the failure on the part of the police to provide the accused an opportunity to speak with counsel was not a mere "technical irregularity." In this case, three young people and one adult were charged with orchestrating what is commonly called a "grow rip"—that is, a theft of marijuana from a grow operation. In the course of this theft, they were alleged to have assaulted the grower and caused him serious injuries. On arrest, the various accuseds made statements to police, certain of which were admissible and others of which were not. In particular, the court stressed the need for young persons to understand their rights "in a meaningful way" and the obligation of police to inform them of these rights "carefully."

Searches and Charter Rights at the Time of Arrest

The police can search any person who has been arrested in order to preserve evidence that might otherwise be lost and to ensure the officer's safety. To commence this search, the officer is not required to have a reason to believe that anything will be discovered. So long as the arrest was lawful, anything discovered in the search can generally be used as evidence against the individual in court. For summary conviction offences, unless the police officer observes a person committing the offence, he or she must obtain a warrant to arrest the person from a justice of the peace or issue a criminal summons.

The Charter protects the rights of individuals who have been detained or arrested:

  8. Everyone has the right to be secure against unreasonable search and seizure.
  9. Everyone has the right not to be arbitrarily detained or imprisoned.
  10. Everyone has the right on arrest or detention
     (a) to be informed promptly of the reasons therefor;
     (b) to retain and instruct counsel without delay and to be informed of that right; and
     (c) to have the validity of the detention determined ... and to be released if the detention is not lawful.

As in the case of adults, evidence uncovered during an unreasonable or unlawful search may be excluded in court after a Charter analysis.

The above Charter protections are in addition to the rights guaranteed by the YCJA. Pre-trial detention is covered in the next chapter. Because the provisions of the YCJA with respect to the right to information/counsel are at least equal to or more stringent than these Charter rights, s. 10 of the Charter will be discussed below in relation to the YCJA.

Questioning Upon and After Arrest

PRELIMINARY ISSUES

As noted earlier, before questioning a youth in connection with an incident, officers should be clear about whether the youth is a witness or a suspect. Under the YOA, police officers or other "persons in authority" were required to comply with s. 56(2), whether the statement was taken from a young person who was regarded as a suspect or merely a witness at the time the statement was taken. The YCJA, however, restricts the applicability of the section to arrest situations or "circumstances where the peace officer or other person has reasonable grounds for believing that the young person has committed an offence" (s. 146(2)). If a youth is caught in the commission of an offence, officers should be careful not to eliminate chances for a spontaneous statement by asking premature questions.

Investigators should also remember to make first or new inquiries about a suspect's age. This should be done not only to ensure that the YCJA is applied to a youth under 18, but also in case the youth, who is about to be interviewed, has turned 18 since the commission (or suspected commission) of the offence: although in the latter case, the offence would be triable in youth court, the special YCJA provisions with respect to statements do *not* apply to suspects who have turned 18.

But once the decision is made to arrest (and even before this point if a youth is detained for some reason without being arrested), reasonable grounds for a charge will be made out and the duty to follow the provisions of s. 146 of the YCJA will be triggered.

SECTION 146: TIMING OF CAUTIONS

Section 146 reads, in part, as follows:

146(1) Subject to this section, the law relating to the admissibility of statements made by persons accused of committing offences applies in respect of young persons.

(2) No oral or written statement made by a young person who is less than eighteen years old, to a peace officer or to any other person who is, in law, a person in authority, on the arrest or detention of the young person or in circumstances where the peace officer or other person has reasonable grounds for believing that the young person has committed an offence is admissible against the young person unless

(a) the statement was voluntary;

(b) the person to whom the statement was made has, before the statement was made, clearly explained to the young person, in language appropriate to his or her age and understanding, that

(i) the young person is under no obligation to make a statement,

(ii) any statement made by the young person may be used as evidence in proceedings against him or her,

(iii) the young person has the right to consult counsel and a parent or other person in accordance with paragraph (c), and

(iv) any statement made by the young person is required to be made in the presence of counsel and any other person consulted in accordance with paragraph (c), if any, unless the young person desires otherwise;

(c) the young person has, before the statement was made, been given a reasonable opportunity to consult

(i) with counsel, and

(ii) with a parent or, in the absence of a parent, an adult relative or, in the absence of a parent and an adult relative, any other appropriate adult chosen by the young person, as long as that person is not a co-accused, or under investigation, in respect of the same offence; and

(d) if the young person consults a person in accordance with paragraph (c), the young person has been given a reasonable opportunity to make the statement in the presence of that person.

(3) The requirements set out in paragraphs (2)(b) to (d) do not apply in respect of oral statements if they are made spontaneously by the young person to a peace officer or other person in authority before that person has had a reasonable opportunity to comply with those requirements.

(4) A young person may waive the rights under paragraph (2)(c) or (d) but any such waiver

(a) must be recorded on video tape or audio tape; or

(b) must be in writing and contain a statement signed by the young person that he or she has been informed of the right being waived.

(5) When a waiver of rights under paragraph (2)(c) or (d) is not made in accordance with subsection (4) owing to a technical irregularity, the youth justice court may determine that the waiver is valid if it is satisfied that the young person was informed of his or her rights, and voluntarily waived them.

(6) When there has been a technical irregularity in complying with paragraphs (2)(b) to (d), the youth justice court may admit into evidence a statement referred to in subsection (2), if satisfied that the admission of the statement would not bring into disrepute the principle that young persons are entitled to enhanced procedural protection to ensure that they are treated fairly and their rights are protected.

In practice, the triggering of s. 146 means that a caution must be delivered without delay.

Even if there is no time to give a youth a full caution (or in circumstances in which the attending officer is unsure about all of the caution requirements), a partial caution should be given. The youth then can and should be re-cautioned later, especially if there were doubts about the validity of the earlier caution; if there is a gap in time between delivery of the caution and questioning; and if there is a change in interviewer, a change in place of detention, a change in the starting of a videotape or audio recording, or any other significant change in circumstances. The youth should also be re-cautioned if he or she begins to talk about involvement in a separate offence.

WHO IS A PERSON IN AUTHORITY?

A "**person in authority**," for the purposes of s. 146(2), is any person that a reasonable young person might perceive as a potential agent of the criminal justice system. "Peace officer" is specifically included in the section and, therefore, the section applies to all police officers.

Whether individuals other than police officers can be persons in authority is a more complicated issue. While parents often have considerable influence over their children, the legislation makes it clear (s. 146(9)) that they are not ordinarily persons in authority for the purpose of s. 146, which means that theoretically (putting aside the issue of hearsay for a moment) a parent to whom a child has confessed will be able to testify about that confession and it is admissible. If a parent were called to testify against a child, the defence would almost certainly argue that the parent is or has become a person in authority. By the same token, where parents are co-opted by investigators, or where they take an active role in the interrogation of their children, the presumption in s. 146(9) (parents, if consulted, are deemed not to be a person in authority) would easily be overcome.

Youths, more so than adults, are often open with their friends and siblings about involvement in criminal activities. For example, in virtually all school shootings that took place in Canada and the United States in the past decade or so, including the infamous massacre at Columbine High School in Littleton, Colorado, the adolescent perpetrators of the crimes told friends, teachers, or family members about the impending events before they took place.[11] Peers are not persons in authority, and statements to friends have the potential to get youths into a lot of trouble, especially since youth witnesses are often as intimidated by police as are youth suspects, and may readily answer police questions.

person in authority
for the purpose of the YCJA, any person that a reasonable young person might perceive as a potential agent of the criminal justice system

While parents and peers are rarely persons in authority, teachers and school personnel are occasionally found to be. Where a teacher, for example, is enlisted by police personnel to assist directly in an investigation, or where the matter being investigated by a teacher is serious enough (involving drug dealing, for example, or a serious assault) that it will inevitably lead to criminal justice proceedings, the teacher (and the police) should be aware that school staff have in the past been deemed to be persons in authority.

In contrast, doctors and psychologists are not deemed to be persons in authority, even when they are treating or assessing a youth pursuant to a court order. The testimony of these professionals is generally admissible for a range of purposes that include sentencing and sentencing reviews. The fact that a youth's statements made to a doctor are not necessarily confidential is worrisome to some commentators who feel that the benefit of any help that these professionals may be able to offer a youth comes at too high a potential price with respect to self-incrimination.

VOLUNTARINESS

Section 146(2)(a) requires that, in order to be admissible, a statement by a youth must be voluntary. Although "voluntary" is a term that can be easily defined in ordinary usage, the legal concept of "voluntariness" is very complicated and has been built up over decades and by layers and layers of case law.

Voluntariness has always been at the heart of the admissibility issue, and in a way s. 146(2)(a) cannot be satisfied unless every other part of s. 146 is complied with.

Essentially, a youth's statement is voluntary if it is made (1) freely by a youth who (2) understands and has been made aware of his or her rights and (3) is competent, sane, and capable of understanding the consequences of making the statement; (4) in the absence of promise of favour; (5) in the absence of threat of (further) sanctions or other negative consequences; and (6) in an atmosphere free of oppression, intimidation, or other discomfort. And even then, many lawyers and judges argue that voluntariness is still a subjective matter of fact, and a statement can be involuntary despite the satisfaction of all of these conditions. A review of the case law behind this "definition" is well beyond the scope of this text; suffice it to say that voluntariness must be informed and uncoerced, and is even more controversial than usual in the youth context.

From a practical standpoint, however, doing one's best to ensure the voluntariness of a youth's statement requires sensitivity to the characteristics of teenagers and a good measure of common sense. Ideally, the interviewer should be specially trained in speaking with youth and should be non-intimidating. The youth should be thoroughly cautioned, any waiver should be properly recorded, and all other elements of s. 146 should be satisfied. The interview environment should be non-intimidating, and the youth should be as comfortable as possible[12]—not exhausted, not naked, not starving, not alone, not sick, and not in pain. And not afraid, although the reality is that most youths are afraid of the police.

The lengths to which it is necessary to go to protect the voluntariness of even a street-smart youth's statement are frustrating to police, and the temptation may exist to set up a situation in which it will be possible to "overhear" a cellblock confession to, for example, a peer. However, such tactics have led, in the past, to the exclusion of evidence.

RIGHT TO INFORMATION AND AN
AGE-APPROPRIATE EXPLANATION

Although not specifically mentioned in s. 146, a youth, like an adult, has the right upon his or her arrest to know the nature of the crime for which he or she is being charged. This right flows from s. 10(a) of the Charter. Some judges have even suggested that parents have a right to the same information in order to be able to consult effectively with their child at the police station.

A youth also has a right, under s. 146(2)(b), to considerable information with respect to his or her procedural rights. Section 146(2)(b) sets out the rights that determine much of the content of a youth caution. As discussed previously, s. 146(2)(b) provides a detailed listing of the requisite minimum contents of a caution.

According to s. 146(2), the officer must have explained to the young person his or her rights in "language appropriate to his or her age and understanding." This requires that the police officer assess the level of understanding of the young person before obtaining the statement, a requirement that is unique to the youth context and absent from the Charter rules or from the *Criminal Code*. In *R v. C.G.*,[13] the judge described some of the evidence required to establish a youth's "age and understanding":

> Under section 56(2) [of the YOA], persons in authority taking statements must learn something about the educational level of the child, the language and vocabulary skills of the child, his faculties of understanding, his emotional state at the time. These inquiries do not call for the intervention of [a] psychologist, or a telephone call to the school teacher, or even to a parent. But they do require enough conversation with the young person to permit the officer to determine how many phrases must be explained and to what extent he must use ordinary or street language or even slang to be sure the child understands what is being said.

An investigating officer must use greater diligence in dealing with young accused and accused who have no previous experience with the criminal justice system. Learning disabilities and behavioural problems will be evidence weighed by the court. The police officer, when testifying, must be prepared to comprehensively explain how he or she formed his or her opinion about the young person's level of understanding:

> He will have to be able to say how he formed that opinion. And he will have to satisfy the court that he then clearly explained the necessary rules and rights to the young person in language that was consciously chosen to be appropriate for the young person's age and understanding.[14]

Following these inquiries, the officer must state the young person's rights in language that corresponds to this level of understanding. In practice, it may be a good idea for the officer to ask the youth to repeat, or even to transcribe, in his or her own words, the rights conveyed to him or her.

In determining whether the officer's language was appropriate, the court will assess not whether the particular child actually understood the rights that were read to him or her, but rather whether the rights were explained in language appropriate to his or her understanding. The case law has demonstrated that a "high standard of performance" is expected of the investigating officer in this regard.[15]

RIGHT TO SILENCE

Although, in practice, adult arrestees are typically cautioned about the effect of making statements, Nicholas Bala reminds us that, although the Charter prescribes a right to freedom from self-incrimination, Canadian law with respect to adults does not actually recognize a right to be informed of "the right to remain silent."[16] Section 146(2)(b), however, effectively does guarantee that right to young people.

waiver
the verbal or written giving up or dispensing with the exercise of a legal right

While an adult may waive his or her right to silence verbally, or sometimes even by implication—that is, by simply answering police questions—a youth's **waiver** is a much more formal affair. As discussed, s. 146(4) requires that a waiver be recorded and that the young person make clear that he or she understands the rights waived.

Obviously, the requirements imposed by s. 146(4) place a substantial constraint on police questioning. For example, it would be almost impossible to obtain a valid waiver at a crime scene or in a police cruiser. So, statements made in these places would be automatically lost. Where a youth is eager to make a statement (for example, if the youth is spilling over with protestations of innocence but is, in fact, incriminating himself or herself), police personnel may find themselves in a mad rush to set up recording technology, or to find a waiver form and pen. The delay involved in making these preparations may well give the talkative youth enough time to reconsider his or her candour. But, as explained above, it is exactly this increased openness that makes youth more vulnerable, and s. 146(4) is designed to compensate for this added vulnerability.

In fact, even where police administer a carefully thought out "youth caution" and produce a waiver form in simple language, there is no guarantee that youth will actually understand their rights and the consequences of their statements. In a study by Ontario researchers Abramovitch, Higgins-Biss, and Biss,[17] (innocent) male and female students in grades 6, 8, 10, and 12 (that is, aged about 11 to 17 years) were asked to imagine that they had been arrested for shoplifting and were administered a police-sanctioned caution including portions designed for youth (the Peel Regional Police Standard Cautions and Warnings, 1998). The children were then given a typical youth waiver document in the form below (see the box below). They were then asked whether they would sign the waiver.

PEEL REGIONAL POLICE FORCE

Waiver:

I, _____ , understand I have the right to call a lawyer or[a] call my parents or some other relative or some other adult. I also understand I can have any of these persons present with me now if I wish.

I do not want to call anyone or have anyone here with me now.

Dated the _____ day of _____ 19_____ .

Signed _____

Witnessed _____

ᵃ Note that under the YOA, it was unclear whether there was a right to call a lawyer *and* a parent or adult, or a lawyer *or* a parent or adult.

Afterward, the students were questioned by the researchers about their understanding of the effect of the waiver. The study determined that, while a weak majority (61 percent) of the students understood the waiver form, *the LESS a student understood about the form, the MORE likely he or she was to sign it.* Furthermore, while a majority of students understood the basic meaning of the waiver, fewer than 50 percent understood that if they signed the waiver, police questioning would follow. Because this study was designed to minimize stress for the participants, Abramovitch, Higgins-Biss, and Biss suggest that, in real arrest conditions, the expected rate of understanding of the waiver can be expected to be even lower. A representative of the Ontario youth advocate agency Justice for Children and Youth noted that, in practice,

> [o]ften there are youth who sign the waivers and don't know why they are doing so or can't recall whether or not they have signed anything.[18]

While it would be completely unfair to hold police responsible for delivering a full legal and human rights education to a youthful suspect before attempting to investigate a crime, police should remember that their own understanding of legal rights, waivers, and the like is considerably more sophisticated than that of most offenders, let alone teenage ones. When this is taken into account, the strictures of s. 146 may seem a little less unreasonable.

RIGHT TO CONSULT WITH COUNSEL AND PARENTS

There is a significant difference between the wording of the consultation provisions of the YOA and the YCJA. Under the YOA, the young person, before making a statement, had the right "to consult with counsel or a parent." Under s. 146(2)(c) of the YCJA, the wording has been changed to "consult with counsel *and* a parent." It is now clear that a young person can elect to consult with both counsel and a parent rather than having to choose one or the other. The legislation further specifies that, if a parent is unavailable, the young person may consult with an adult relative. In the absence of an adult relative, the youth may consult with any other appropriate adult that is not a co-accused or under investigation for the same offence.

The right to counsel under s. 146(2)(c) includes the right to be informed of that right (s. 146(2)(b)(iii)). Full compliance with the protection of this right includes the provision of a phone and privacy to make the initial call(s), (ideally) the provision of a local list of criminal defence counsel, and information about the availability of legal aid and the relevant phone number.

As mentioned above, a young person may waive his or her right to consult with counsel and a parent under s. 146(4). However, the investigating officer must meet a high standard of evidence for the waiver to be legitimately obtained. The young person should fully understand the right he or she is waiving and the consequences of doing so. Furthermore, the police officer might even be required to advise the young person of the reasons why he or she may wish to consult with counsel and/or a parent and that consultation is in his or her best interest. The judge in *R v. M.A.M.*[19] explained the test of a valid waiver:

> There should be a genuine endeavour by the person in authority to describe the function of the lawyer and the benefits to the young person of having a lawyer, or parents or relatives or an adult friend present. That endeavour should be designed

to lead to an appreciation on the part of the young person of the consequences of the choices that he makes.

Again, the court will not look at whether the young person subjectively understood the rights that were waived and the consequences of waiving them, but rather at whether the requirements of s. 146—for example, the need to give an age-appropriate explanation—were followed to the letter. Often, police, overwhelmed by the requirements of s. 146, choose not to rely on a waiver. Instead, they encourage the youth to consult with a lawyer and a parent.

In addition to the right to counsel, a youth is entitled to consult a parent or, if a parent is not available, another adult relative or acquaintance. When a young person has been arrested and detained, the police are obligated to inform a parent as soon as reasonably possible. The young person's wish to have his or her parent contacted is irrelevant in this situation. Case law has established that if a youth whom the police want to question expresses a desire to see a parent, the police must permit a meeting as soon as a parent is available.[20] Even if a youth is arrested but not detained pending trial, the police officer or Crown prosecutor must notify the parent in writing of the date of the youth court hearing. However, if a child is arrested and immediately released, there is no present requirement to notify a parent.

Many parents who are contacted by police when their child has been arrested become concerned and rush to the police station where their child has been detained. The youth, who is in a holding cell, is often unaware that his or her parents are in the station and would like to just get on with the process without the bother of consulting with a parent. In some cases, the youth waives his or her right to consult a parent and the police question him or her about the events. In this situation, it is the duty of the police officer to inform the young person that his or her parent has arrived at the station and give them an opportunity to meet before questioning, even if the youth previously waived the right to consult. The youth may want to exercise the right to consult a parent if he or she knows that a parent is readily available.

Understandably, parents will be quite upset upon hearing that their child has been detained for allegedly committing an offence. If the police officer recognizes that the parent is very angry, it may be a good idea to ask the child if he or she would prefer to contact a lawyer or another adult.

Some well-meaning parents who are present during police questioning and do not know the particulars of the investigation against their child may be harmful to their child's case. Recognizing this, the law requires police officers to provide an opportunity for the parent and child to meet alone before questioning. Before this meeting, the police officer should fully inform the parent of the charges and the nature of the investigation in order to facilitate a meaningful consultation between the parent and child. Police officers should be cautious in their attempt to "team up" with the parent in an attempt to extract a confession from the child. Although parents are generally not considered "persons in authority" (and therefore not required to meet the preconditions before obtaining a statement from the accused), the court may rule inadmissible any evidence obtained by a parent who is seemingly part of the "investigation team." When a child is a ward, the child protection worker or foster parent is considered a parent for the purpose of the investigation. Thus, all the procedural requirements applicable to parents apply to child protection workers or foster parents when a child is a ward.

There are some consequences that follow the failure of a police officer to contact a parent or allow for consultation. If the police officer does not provide a parent with appropriate notice, the court proceedings may be adjourned until notice is given. If notice is highly impractical, the court may dispense with the notice requirements or direct the police officer to give notice to another person. Generally, the court proceedings are not invalidated by the police officer's failure to give notice. However, it is advisable for police officers who are investigating an accused young person to comply with the notice provisions to the extent that it is possible. Compliance would spare everyone unnecessary delays in the proceedings and would avoid the potential that the young person's right is breached, which may result in the inadmissibility of vital evidence. Again, judges would rather acquit a "guilty youth" than permit the infringement of an essential right.

SPONTANEOUS STATEMENTS

According to s. 146(3), if a statement by a young person to a police officer is made spontaneously, the procedural requirements do not apply and the statement will be admissible in court. A significant factor in determining whether a statement is made spontaneously is the timing of the statement in relation to the time of arrest. If the statement is made before arrest or detention—before the police officer had a "reasonable opportunity" to comply with the procedures—then it is more likely to be viewed as spontaneous and thus admissible in court. However, where reasonable grounds to arrest or charge have been established, a young person's statement responding to a police officer's question is not "spontaneous."[21]

Another factor with respect to spontaneity is whether the police officer prompted the statement. If a police officer asks a question, regardless of its innocence, and it elicits an incriminating response from the youth, the statement is not "spontaneous." The appropriate test, then, is whether the utterance is "blurted out" without the prompting of a police officer in circumstances in which there is no opportunity to follow the appropriate procedures.[22]

In any event, the case law demonstrates that the spontaneity of statements will be construed narrowly—that is, where there is any doubt, the issue will be decided in favour of the young person, and not the person seeking to admit the statement.

Chapter Summary

This chapter began with a review of the determinations an investigator must make in the course of a first encounter with a young suspect, including age and status as suspect or witness. This was followed by a review of decisions to be made: whether to warn and dismiss, whether to charge and/or arrest, and whether to refer a youth (or to recommend his or her referral) to an extrajudicial measures program. A discussion of extrajudicial measures and the preconditions for participation followed.

Discussion then focused on arrest and the requirement of compliance with s. 146, including: voluntariness, age-appropriate explanations, the right to counsel, the right to consult with parents, and the requirements for a valid waiver. Finally, the admissibility of spontaneous statements was reviewed.

KEY TERMS

spontaneous statement

caution

extrajudicial sanctions

person in authority

waiver

NOTES

1. There are also some limited powers of arrest/detention with respect to provincial offences; these are prescribed in Ontario by the *Provincial Offences Act*, discussed in chapter 5.

2. See, for example, *R v. W.(J.)* (1996), 30 OR (3d) 342 (CA).

3. Ibid.

4. This provision is balanced by the innovative s. 35, which provides:

    In addition to any order that it is authorized to make, a youth justice court may, at any stage of proceedings against a young person, refer the young person to a child welfare agency for assessment to determine whether the young person is in need of child welfare services.

5. According to s. 25(1) of the YCJA, the right to counsel arises very early, even while the decision to charge is being made:

    A young person has the right to retain and instruct counsel without delay, and to exercise that right personally, at any stage of proceedings against the young person and before and during any consideration of whether, instead of starting or continuing judicial proceedings against the young person under this Act, to use an extrajudicial sanction to deal with the young person.

6. N. Bala, *Young Offenders Law* (Concord, ON: Irwin Law, 1997), 152-53.

7. Ibid., at 161.

8. *Canadian Charter of Rights and Freedoms*, part I of the *Constitution Act, 1982*, RSC 1985, app. II, no. 44, s. 24(2).

9. *R v. Rogers*, [2006] 1 SCR 55.

10. *R v. O.K.*, [2004] BCJ no. 1458 (BCPC) (QL).

11. For discussion on this point, see K. Newman, *Rampage: The Social Roots of School Shootings* (New York: Perseus Books, 2004).

12. According to Justice Cory in *R v. J.(J.T.)*, [1990] 2 SCR 755, at 766, "Teenagers may be more susceptible to subtle threats arising from their surroundings and the presence of persons in authority."

13. *R v. C.G.* (1986), 16 WCB 323 (Ont. Prov. Ct.).

14. Ibid.

15. *R v. P.B.* (1984), 44 CR (3d) 24, at 27 (BCPC).

16. Bala, supra note 6, at 107.

17. R. Abramovitch, K. Higgins-Biss, and S. Biss, "Young Persons' Comprehension of Waivers in Criminal Proceedings" (July 1993), *Canadian Journal of Criminology* 309-22.

18. *Justice for Children and Youth* (1995), submission of the Canadian Foundation for Children, Youth and the Law on the importance of statement protections under the *Young Offenders Act*, s. 56.

19. *R v. M.A.M.* (1986), 32 CCC (3d) 566, at 573 (BCCA).

20. *R v. P.(S.)* (1991), 44 OAC 316, at 317.

21. Supra note 2, at 349.

22. J. Hanson, "Youth Confessions: Section 56 of the Young Offenders Act" (1987), vol. 6, no. 2 *Canadian Journal of Family Law* 199.

EXERCISES AND REVIEW
Review Questions

1. Why must an officer establish a suspect's age at the earliest opportunity?

2. How is a criminal proceeding commenced for a summary conviction offence? Must a youth's parents be notified?

3. If a youth is not necessarily in criminal trouble, but is in a risky situation, how (name legislation) might police deal with him or her?

4. Does receiving a s. 6 caution give a youth a criminal (youth court) record?

5. How many s. 6 cautions can a youth receive before police are forced to lay a charge?

6. If a youth confesses before police have a chance to advise her of her rights, will the statement be admissible in court?

7. Does the Charter apply to youths?

8. How soon after detaining a youth must the police contact a parent? What if a youth has no available parent?

9. How must police record a youth's waiver of the right to counsel?

10. What if, unbeknownst to police, the tape recorder jams while recording a waiver?

11. Must a detained youth choose between contacting a lawyer and contacting a parent?

12. Is a school principal a person in authority for the purpose of s. 146? Why or why not?

13. Why might a youth wish to consult counsel before participating in a (pre-charge) sanction program under the extrajudicial measures section?

Discussion Questions

1. Find out how extrajudicial measures are administered in your community. Are referrals typically made at the pre- or post-charge stage? What is a typical extrajudicial sanction in your community?

2. What kinds of physical detention or interrogation conditions might invalidate the voluntariness of a youth's statement?

3. Draft the wording of a sample youth caution (assume that you are dealing with a typical 17-year-old suspect).

4. Draft the wording of a sample youth caution for a crying, 12-year-old suspect who is in grade 5.

5. Should police be required to explain to an arrested youth why contacting a lawyer is in his or her best interests? Defend your answer.

CHAPTER 9

The Pre-Trial Period

■ CHAPTER OBJECTIVES

After completing this chapter, you should be able to:

■ List the grounds for pre-trial detention under the *Criminal Code*.

■ List the rules pertaining to pre-trial detention added to the *Criminal Code* regime by the *Youth Criminal Justice Act* (YCJA).

■ Describe the information collected by police that is relevant to the decision to detain an accused pending trial.

■ Describe the basic process of a show-cause hearing and the burden of proof borne by Crown counsel.

■ List three conditions that may be imposed on a youth who is released at the end of a show-cause hearing.

■ Explain the consequences of a youth's failure to comply with release conditions.

■ Explain the role of police with respect to schools upon the interim release of a suspected young offender.

■ Describe the YCJA rules with respect to place of pre-trial detention for youth.

■ Critically assess the extent to which the YCJA regime for pre-trial detention has been put into practice so far.

In the majority of cases, an initial contact between police personnel and a young suspect will end in the release of the youth, either after an informal warning or upon service (or promised service) of a document compelling the youth's appearance in court. In more serious cases, police will need to consider whether it is appropriate to detain the youth—either for questioning, or for longer—pending a decision on **judicial interim release**.

The *Youth Criminal Justice Act* (YCJA) is intended to reduce the system's reliance on the use of custody as a sanction and to reserve it for the most serious cases, both upon sentencing and at the pre-trial stage. The YCJA incorporates the holding preconditions expressed in the *Criminal Code* and, in addition, further limits the use of pre-trial custody by requiring the satisfaction of the conditions set out in its own s. 39(1).

judicial interim release
also know as "bail," the release of an accused from pre-trial custody, often on condition of compliance with court-imposed conditions

Guidelines for Pre-Trial Detention

The YCJA rules contained in s. 28 for pre-trial detention, **show-cause hearings**, and judicial interim release incorporate the adult system expressed in the *Criminal Code*:

> Except to the extent that they are inconsistent with or excluded by this Act, the provisions of Part XVI (compelling appearance of an accused and interim release) of the *Criminal Code* apply to the detention and release of young persons under this Act.

Sections 515(10) and 495(2) of the *Criminal Code* are significant in this regard.

One effect of this provision is to apply to youths the adult pre-trial detention provisions in s. 515 of the *Criminal Code*:

> 515(10) For the purposes of this section, the detention of an accused in custody is justified only on one or more of the following grounds:
>
> (a) where the detention is necessary to ensure his or her attendance in court in order to be dealt with according to law;
>
> (b) where the detention is necessary for the protection or safety of the public, including any victim of or witness to the offence, having regard to all the circumstances including any substantial likelihood that the accused will, if released from custody, commit a criminal offence or interfere with the administration of justice; and
>
> (c) on any other just cause being shown and, without limiting the generality of the foregoing, where the detention is necessary in order to maintain confidence in the administration of justice, having regard to all the circumstances, including the apparent strength of the prosecution's case, the gravity of the nature of the offence, the circumstances surrounding its commission and the potential for a lengthy term of imprisonment.

Section 495(2) of the Code is also significant to youth as well as to adults in that it allows for detention of accused persons in the public interest, to avoid repetition of the offence, to identify the accused, or if evidence demands it. Section 495(2) provides as follows:

> 495(2) A peace officer shall not arrest a person without warrant for
>
> (a) an indictable offence mentioned in section 553,
>
> (b) an offence for which the person may be prosecuted by indictment or for which he is punishable on summary conviction, or
>
> (c) an offence punishable on summary conviction,
>
> in any case where
>
> (d) he believes on reasonable grounds that the public interest, having regard to all the circumstances including the need to
>
> (i) establish the identity of the person,
>
> (ii) secure or preserve evidence of or relating to the offence, or
>
> (iii) prevent the continuation or repetition of the offence or the commission of another offence,
>
> may be satisfied without so arresting the person, and
>
> (e) he has no reasonable grounds to believe that, if he does not so arrest the person, the person will fail to attend court in order to be dealt with according to law.

However, police who are familiar with the application of s. 515(10) and s. 495(2) cannot safely stop there, because the YCJA (s. 29(2)) adds another level of complexity to the analysis:

29(2) In considering whether the detention of a young person is necessary for the protection of the safety of the public under paragraph 515(10)(b) ... of the *Criminal Code*, a youth justice court or a justice shall presume that detention is not necessary under that paragraph if the young person could not, on being found guilty, be committed to custody on the grounds set out in paragraphs 39(1)(a) to (c) (restrictions on committal to custody).

These "restrictions on committal to custody" read as follows:

39(1) A youth justice court shall not commit a young person to custody under section 42 (youth sentences) unless

(a) the young person has committed a violent offence;

(b) the young person has failed to comply with non-custodial sentences;

(c) the young person has committed an indictable offence for which an adult would be liable to imprisonment for a term of more than two years and has a history that indicates a pattern of findings of guilt under this Act or the *Young Offenders Act*, chapter Y-1 of the Revised Statutes of Canada, 1985.

Note that the fourth justification for custody created by s. 39(1)(d), which allows for custody orders based on "aggravating circumstances," does *not* justify detention at the pre-trial stage.

This *Criminal Code* and YCJA legislative weave may appear confusing at first glance, but the bottom line is simple: where young people are concerned, pre-trial detention is rarely appropriate in the absence of violence, breach of probation, the combination of a serious offence and a criminal record, or serious concerns about failure to appear that could not be remedied by resort to s. 31 (care of responsible person), which will be discussed below.

The anti-custody emphasis of the YCJA is in large part a response to concerns that arose over the rate of custodial dispositions under the YOA. In practice, a youth who is subject to pre-trial custody is more likely to receive a custodial sentence upon conviction. And even where pre-trial custody was given as a reason to limit post-conviction custody, there was some concern that police might use pre-trial custody as a means of ensuring that an offender received some punishment.[1]

Critics of the YOA also had concerns about the use of detention for unintended purposes, such as child welfare placements. In enacting the YCJA, the legislators paid particular attention to unwarranted detention. Specifically, they included s. 29(1) as a preventive measure:

29(1) A youth justice court judge or a justice shall not detain a young person in custody prior to being sentenced as a substitute for appropriate child protection, mental health or other social measures.

From a practical standpoint, factors that police personnel will take into account in deciding whether to hold a young person briefly, at the police station, may include

- the need to secure or preserve evidence, including the need to interview the young person;

- the need to confirm identity/residency/age or other relevant information; and

- an immediate risk to the young person's safety—most provincial child protection legislation requires that youth under age 16 be released into the care of a responsible adult.

These short-term police station detentions are governed by s. 30(7) of the YCJA.

Factors that may prompt police to hold a young person long enough to bring him or her for a show-cause hearing might include

- symptoms or behaviour that suggest a need to seek a court-ordered medical or psychological assessment under s. 34,

- the need to make arrangements for placement "into the care of a responsible person" under s. 31,

- an offence involving violence,

- a breach of probation or of conditional supervision,

- the commission of a serious offence (for which an adult might receive a sentence of two years or more) combined with a record of prior convictions,

- a serious offence combined with a history of failure to attend for trial, and

- an inability, after reasonable efforts, to establish residency—for example, in the case of homeless youth.

Notwithstanding the foregoing, the YCJA does not specifically allow police to temporarily detain street youth just because they have nowhere to go, unless there are reasonable and probable grounds to suspect the youth has committed an offence warranting detention. Some provinces have legislation that allows for the detention of vagrant youth, but not through criminalizing their homelessness. For example, in 1999 Alberta enacted the *Protection of Children Involved in Prostitution Act*, which permits police to pick up and detain children for 72 hours without charging them. Proponents of the legislation argue that such action allows the youngsters to escape from their pimps and enables them to receive medical, psychological, and addiction counselling, and special legal services. Critics of the legislation decry it as a further abuse of marginalized teenaged girls that will further alienate them from mainstream society.

PLACE OF PRE-TRIAL DETENTION

Once at least one of the above factors is found to be present, police may consider, instead of detention, the placement of the youth in "the care of a responsible adult" pending trial under s. 31. This measure is far less intrusive because the youth can remain within the community. Section 31 does not limit the definition of "responsible person" to the youth's parents. It simply stipulates that the person must be "willing and able to take care of and exercise control over the young person." Both the youth and the responsible person must consent in writing to the arrangement. At all times, the youth court judge has the discretion to remove the youth from the care of the responsible person and issue a warrant for his or her arrest. Section 33 permits an application to a youth court for early release from detention.

Crown brief
document or package prepared by the police for the benefit of Crown counsel, which sets out the evidence the Crown needs to discharge a burden of proof—for example, the proof required to detain a youth in custody

Once a decision has been made to detain a youth, police personnel will prepare a Crown package, which includes the **Crown brief**. This package will contain any police evidence that will be useful to the Crown in discharging the burden of proving, at a show-cause hearing, that continued detention is appropriate.

Certain provisions are in place to protect the young person who is detained pending trial. Section 30(3), for example, establishes that a young person must be held in custody in a separate facility from adults. This is qualified, however, where the young person poses a risk to himself or herself or others while in a youth facility. In addition, if there is no place of detention for young persons within a reasonable distance, the youth may be placed in an adult facility. Unlike the YOA, the YCJA further stipulates that if the young person is 20 years old or over, he or she will be placed in an adult detention facility (s. 30(5)).

Upon arrest, young suspects are transported initially to a place of open detention. Once in this centre, the young person is typically classified and assigned to open or closed detention by the provincial director or his or her agent(s).

The Show-Cause Hearing

Youths who are detained must be brought to youth justice court within 24 hours of their arrest for a judicial interim release or show-cause hearing as described in s. 515 of the *Criminal Code*. For practical purposes, because of long weekends and other factors (particularly in remote areas) if a youth is arrested late in the week, he or she may not appear before a judge until Monday morning. This is changing to some extent because of the relatively new practice of courts conducting show-cause hearings remotely, either by video conference or audio tape. At this hearing, the judge determines whether the youth should continue to be detained pending trial or be released back into his or her community until the trial date.

In most cases, the burden of proof is on the Crown prosecutor (armed with the Crown brief) to "show cause" why the accused should be detained pending trial. However, in certain circumstances, as set out in s. 515(6) of the *Criminal Code*, it will be up to counsel for the accused to show cause why the young person should be released. Examples of such "reverse onus" situations include where the young person is charged with failing to attend court, breach of undertaking or recognizance, murder, or perhaps, most commonly, in situations where the young person is under release for an indictable offence and is then charged with a new indictable offence. Although the prosecutor must meet a high standard of proof to get an order for detention, the rules of evidence are relaxed in a pre-trial detention hearing. This means that evidence that otherwise would not be admitted in a trial is admitted at a pre-trial detention hearing as long as it is "credible or trustworthy."[2] Therefore, traditional "hearsay" evidence is admissible, as long as the criteria of credibility and trustworthiness are met.

Also, if the court deems it necessary, it can order under s. 34, in the course of a show-cause hearing or at any other stage in the proceedings, that the young person be subject to a medical or psychological assessment. This order is made with the young person's consent unless certain statutory criteria are met. The report of this assessment can be admitted and considered for the purpose of making the detention or release decision.

Section 19 of the YCJA, which allows for "conferences," can also be engaged at the bail stage of the youth criminal justice process. A conference, broadly defined under the law, is a group of people convened or called together to give advice to, or assist, someone named as a decision maker under the YCJA. Conferences will be discussed in more detail in chapter 10. Conferences often prove invaluable at the bail-hearing stage, because the involved parties (defence counsel, Crown, judge, sometimes children's aid workers, and parents) can depart from their formal roles to work together in struggling to find an appropriate placement for an at-risk young person. Interested parties can thus strategize to implement measures that will prove effective in stabilizing the young person's behaviours and ensure that she or he will not reoffend while awaiting trial. Conferences held at the bail stage can be particularly valuable in facilitating the brainstorming of creative solutions for young people who are runaways who have experienced placement problems, or who are experiencing difficulties with following the orders of the court to the point where further charges are continually being laid against them (they are incurring breach charges).

If the youth is ordered to be detained and the trial date is not in the near future, provisions in the *Criminal Code* require periodic rehearing of the detention decision every 30 days for a summary conviction offence and every 90 days for a hybrid or indictable offence.

Either the Crown or the accused young person may appeal any bail decision before the Ontario Court of Justice. Such "bail review" applications occur in situations where either party is displeased with a decision to either release or detain a young person in custody.

Judicial Interim Release

A justice of the peace (or a judge) who decides to release a youthful accused has the discretion to impose conditions in an attempt to control the youth's behaviour while in the community. The nature of these conditions (a long, inexhaustive list) is described in s. 515(4) of the *Criminal Code*. Common examples of conditions include a requirement to report to a police officer, to remain in the jurisdiction, and to avoid people or places connected with the offence. In the case of youth, there is sometimes a condition that the youth attend school.

Once the youth has been released into the community, the police are responsible for ensuring that these conditions are complied with and for responding appropriately if they are breached. The police have the authority, under s. 524 of the *Criminal Code*, to arrest and return the young person to custody for breach of a condition undertaken.

When a young person is released with conditions, it may be important for the police to maintain contact with the young person's school. The police are entitled, under s. 125(6) of the YCJA, to share information with school officials about the involvement of a young person in the justice system if it is necessary to ensure compliance with bail conditions or to ensure the safety of other students or staff. Such information must be kept separate from other information about the student, and access to it is restricted to necessary staff. Any record of information about a student who has had involvement with the youth court system must be destroyed by school officials when it is no longer required.

When an offence under investigation appears to relate to a young person's school, it is desirable for a police officer to consult with school authorities before the show-cause hearing. This will allow a judge to use information to set appropriate conditions upon release. For example, if the accused is charged with assaulting another student, an appropriate condition might be an order transferring the youth to another school. When a judge orders a youth to attend school as a condition of release, the police should be in contact with school officials to make appropriate educational and safety plans and to ensure that compliance is monitored. As schools continue to establish programs to deal with aggression and bullying, the police are generally becoming involved in working more closely with teachers and schools. Many schools now have school resource officers, especially in larger centres such as Ottawa, Toronto, Calgary, and Vancouver. These officers are assigned to specific schools within their patrol area, and each school has the officer's pager number. In emergencies, the school still calls 911. These new police roles must, like all other police functions, be carried out with sensitivity and confidentiality.

Sometimes, to ensure the protection of the public, a judge recommends or orders that a young person seek psychiatric assistance as a term of their release. This can become problematic when resources are not available. Waiting times for psychiatric help can be long. However, where mental health and community measures are not available, the YCJA clearly prohibits pre-trial detention as a substitute for child welfare, mental health, or other social measures. Where such measures are appropriate, police should contact the appropriate provincial ministries or community service providers, such as the Children's Aid Society.

Pre-Trial Detention in Practice Under the YCJA

In cases decided under the YCJA, judges have made it clear that the presumption against detention in s. 29(2) of the Act is a very significant departure from the previous legislation. It is expected that many young persons who would have been held pending trial under the YOA will be released under the new legislation. However, most of the case law has centred around the question of what constitutes a "violent" offence for the purposes of the provision, and, in that case law, "violence" has often been defined expansively to include, for example, arson and dangerous driving.[3] While courts in some jurisdictions have defined "violence" in a more limited way for the purposes of the provision,[4] this expansive approach seems to imply a desire on the part of the courts to detain more youths than the framers of the YCJA may have intended.

Statistically speaking, the impact of the YCJA on the treatment of adolescents in the pre-trial period is not altogether clear. As of 2005, statistical data kept by the Department of Justice do not clearly indicate whether detention of youth by police has decreased or increased as a result of the coming into force of the YCJA. To the contrary, evidence indicates no significant change in police detention of young persons charged with indictable offences or in the types of release used by police.[5] Similarly, courts do not appear to be changing their treatment of youths at bail hearings in a manner that is statistically significant. The number of admissions of youths to pre-trial detention (detained by police pending bail hearings) did decrease under the YCJA, but the proportion of youths detained after bail hearings did not change significantly. By 2005, the number of youths detained for committing minor offences or administration of justice offences, such as a breach of probation, had not changed significantly from the rates shown under the YOA.[6]

While statistical data about pre-trial detention under the YCJA do not provide a particularly clear picture of the impact of the new legislation, anecdotal evidence indicates that pre-trial detention is now at least perceived to be used in fewer cases. Police and Crown prosecutors have expressed frustration with the fact that the YCJA provisions relating to bail and young persons make it exceptionally difficult for authorities to successfully detain a young person in custody, even after a protracted show-cause hearing. Because of the combined effect of ss. 29 and 39(1) on detention under s. 515(10) of the *Criminal Code* on the second ground (for public protection or safety), the Crown relies more and more on the first ground (to ensure attendance at court) and the third ground (for "any other just cause") in seeking a detention order. Under these grounds, no youth can be detained before trial unless there is evidence of a real risk that the accused young person will fail to attend court as and when required, or that the public will be outraged by her or his release into the community given the serious nature of the charges. Prosecutors are concerned that the community is not being adequately protected while accused youths await trial in cases of serious violence, particularly where the accused young person has no significant prior record.

So far, the important players seem to be resisting the YCJA drafters' intention to substantially reduce reliance on pre-trial detention: the courts seem to be accepting a broader definition of "violent" under s. 29(2) than the YCJA drafters intended; police and the Crown express frustration with the stricter detention requirements; and there is no statistical evidence that shows fewer young people are being held before trial. As time progresses, clearer data will emerge and we will begin to determine whether the intention as expressed in the Act is being carried out.

Chapter Summary

In this chapter, we introduced the legal framework for the decision to detain or to release a suspected young offender before trial. The *Criminal Code* grounds for pre-trial detention were reviewed, in addition to the YCJA philosophy with respect to youth detention. We then discussed the inappropriateness of detention for social services purposes.

After covering the police decision-making process, we went on to outline the basic procedure in a show-cause hearing. Release with conditions, enforcement of conditions, and the police role in this process were discussed. The chapter ended with a discussion of the YCJA's focus on reducing reliance on pre-trial detention.

KEY TERMS

judicial interim release

show-cause hearing

Crown brief

NOTES

1. This concern appears to be refuted by research such as that reported in chapter 3, which showed that police tend to favour a restrained use of custodial dispositions.

2. *Criminal Code*, RSC 1985, c. C-46, s. 518(1)(e).

3. See, respectively, *R v. C.D.*, [2003] AJ no. 179 (CA) (QL) and *R v. C.D.K.*, [2004] AJ no. 237 (CA) (QL).

4. See, for example, *R v. J.J.C.*, [2003] PEIJ no. 99 (CA) (QL).

5. Department of Justice Canada, "Youth Criminal Justice Act, 2005 Annual Statement," online at http://justicecanada.ca/en/ps/yj/ycja/statement.

6. Ibid.

EXERCISES AND REVIEW

Review Questions

1. Section 515(10)(b) of the *Criminal Code* contemplates pre-trial detention for the "protection of the public." Does this ground include protection of the public from anticipated property crimes, or just crimes of violence?

2. If you were a police officer and had just arrested a youth who is suspected of committing a minor disturbance but who appears to be suffering from a serious schizophrenic episode, what would you do with respect to pre-trial detention? To which provisions/legislation would you turn for guidance on this issue?

3. If you were a member of a small police force in a remote area, what practical challenges might you face with respect to the requirement to hold a young offender separate from adults? How might you attempt to overcome those challenges?

4. What considerations might motivate a police officer to release a youth into the "care of a responsible person" under s. 31 of the YCJA instead of placing the youth in formal detention?

5. Is a history of cautions and/or sanctions under the extrajudicial sanctions part of the YCJA admissible at a show-cause hearing?

6. If you were an inner-city police officer accustomed to dealing with homeless "street youth," what particular pre-trial detention issues might you encounter?

Discussion Questions

1. The YCJA incorporates, in ss. 29 and 35, a new "refer-don't-detain" system for dealing with youths who do not meet the criteria for pre-trial detention but who could benefit from social services assistance. What concerns do you think prompted the introduction of these provisions? Do you think the new protocol raises any concerns of its own? What are the economic implications?

2. This chapter briefly discussed some ways in which police who deal with young offenders might find themselves involved with the school system. Can you think of some positive and some negative implications of increased police involvement in the school system?

CHAPTER 10

The Trial of a Young Accused

■ CHAPTER OBJECTIVES

After completing this chapter, you should be able to:

- Describe the jurisdiction of the youth justice court.

- Explain the youthful accused's right to counsel.

- List three *Youth Criminal Justice Act* (YCJA) provisions designed to support a youth's right to counsel.

- Describe YCJA procedures for accepting a youth's guilty plea.

- Explain what is meant by a "preliminary motion."

- Explain the procedure under which youthful convicts can receive adult sentences.

Jurisdiction of the Youth Court

Section 13 of the *Youth Criminal Justice Act* (YCJA) provides for the establishment, in each province of Canada, of **youth justice courts**. These courts deal with all matters in which a young person is charged under the *Criminal Code* or with another federal offence. A youth justice court can be either a separately constituted court reserved only for the purpose of hearing youth cases, or an existing court "designated" as a youth justice court. For example, according to s. 13(3):

> 13(3) When a young person elects or is deemed to have elected to be tried by a court composed of a judge and jury, the superior court of criminal jurisdiction in the province in which the election is made or deemed to have been made is deemed to be a youth justice court for the purpose of the proceeding, and the superior court judge is deemed to be a youth justice court judge.

"Young person" for the purpose of youth court **jurisdiction** is defined in s. 2:

> "young person" means a person who is or, in the absence of evidence to the contrary, appears to be twelve years old or older, but less than eighteen years old and, if the context requires, includes any person who is charged under this Act with

youth justice court
either a court specifically constituted for the purpose of hearing youth trials, or an existing adult court designated (temporarily or permanently) for that purpose

jurisdiction
the scope of authority of a court; jurisdiction can be based on a defined territory (Ontario court), a defined age range (youth court), a defined class of offences (small claims court), a defined area of law (family court), and so on.

having committed an offence while he or she was a young person or who is found guilty of an offence under this Act.

As a result, where there is no evidence to the contrary, a person who looks to be between the ages of 12 and 17 will be deemed to be a young person, and any person who is alleged to have committed an offence while under the age of 18 is under the jurisdiction of the youth justice court even if he or she is 18 or over at the time of trial. Finally, where there is conflicting evidence about the age of the young person at the time the offence was alleged to be committed, or where the offence took place over a period of time that included the young person's 18th birthday, the youth justice court has jurisdiction (s. 16).

No Transfer to Adult Court

Under the YOA, youth who were over a certain age and who were charged with certain serious offences could be "transferred" to adult court for the hearing of their trial and then subjected, if convicted in adult court, to an adult sentence. This transfer procedure was controversial, and is discussed in chapter 11. Pre-trial transfer of adolescents to adult court generated a line of case law with respect to various issues, such as whether there was a duty, upon arrest, to advise a youth about his or her potential for transfer.

The YCJA has abolished this transfer procedure. Now, instead of "transferring" an eligible youth to adult court where a stiffer sentence is available, a youth justice court judge can, in certain circumstances, impose an "adult sentence" in youth justice court without losing jurisdiction over the matter. This new procedure is an attempt on the part of the framers of the new Act to reduce considerable delay and administrative complication while providing sentencing flexibility and eliminating legal issues related to the decision to transfer.

The topic of sentencing, including the imposition of adult sentences in youth court, is discussed further in chapter 11.

The Youthful Accused's Right to Counsel

Under the welfare-oriented *Juvenile Delinquents Act* (JDA), the participation of lawyers in youth justice cases was strongly discouraged. While the legislation fell short of actually prohibiting the presence of lawyers in juvenile courts, there was no mention of legal representation in the JDA because the court process called for "informality." Lawyers were often viewed as roadblocks to the joint intentions of parents, judges, and prosecutors who were seen as working together to seek to advance the "best interests" of the child. Initially, even the majority of youth court judges lacked any legal training. Increasingly, from the mid-1960s through the 1970s, judges in the youth court system were legally trained and legal representation became more popular. There was, and today remains, some sentiment, however, that legal representation was and is not appropriate in the majority of cases coming before the juvenile court.

The introduction of a due process model of youth justice under the YOA introduced a right to counsel as one of the most fundamental rights accorded to youth. Section 56 of the YOA required that a police officer who wanted to question a young suspect first inform the suspect of his or her right to counsel. A youth could waive his or her right to counsel, but such a waiver will be accepted by the court only with strong evidence supporting the youth's full understanding of the waiver of this right. When the youth waived his or her right to counsel, a signed or video-taped waiver was required. Even if a police officer did not want to question the youth, there was an independent obligation (both under the YOA and the Charter) to inform the youth of his or her right to contact a lawyer.

Section 11(3) of the YOA required judges to inform the youth of his or her right to obtain counsel. If the youth wished to exercise this right, the judge was required to allow for a reasonable amount of time to obtain counsel. If a youth was financially unable to obtain counsel, s. 11(4)(b) of the YOA required the judge to refer the accused to a legal aid program. Furthermore, if no legal aid program was willing to provide services to the youth because he or she did not meet their financial criteria, s. 11(4)(b) further stipulated that the judge "shall … direct that the young person be represented by counsel." This meant that the government was burdened with the youth's legal fees.

Provincial governments became increasingly concerned with the financial burden of legal services for young people in conflict with the law. Some provinces, most notably Alberta, forced youths and their parents to repay the legal costs incurred by the government. There was growing resentment of the absolute right to counsel accorded to youths that was not available to adults in the ordinary criminal justice system.

The drafters of the YCJA felt that this right is so important in the youth court process that s. 25(4) of the YCJA is identically worded to s. 11(3) of the YOA. This reflects a widespread sentiment that, independently, young people lack an adequate understanding of the justice system and they are vulnerable to abuse throughout the process. In enacting s. 25(10), the YCJA does, however, recognize the provinces' concerns about legal costs:

> 25(10) Nothing in this Act prevents the lieutenant governor in council of a province … from establishing a program to authorize the recovery of the costs of a young person's counsel from the young person or the parents of the young person …

This provision was enacted as a result of increasing pressure from the provincial governments and their attempts to create provincial legislation to validate the recovery of legal costs from youths and their parents. Another YCJA innovation is s. 25(11), which provides an exception to a youth's absolute right to counsel. If the accused, who was under the age of 18 at the time of the offence, is 20 or over at the time of his or her first appearance before a youth justice court, the special notice provisions dealing with the right to counsel do not apply.

Law enforcement personnel should note that there is also a requirement, under s. 25(9), that notice of the right to counsel be included in many documents issued to youth, including appearance notices, summonses, and warrants.

Lawyers taking on the task of representing youths charged under the YCJA have a sensitive, as well as an important, role to play. The lawyer must always strive to represent the views and preferences of the adolescent, and not what the lawyer's vision of what is the best interests of the client. Further, it is important to remember that the adolescent is the client, even if it is the parents who are paying the lawyer's bill. Thus, it is from the adolescent whom the lawyer takes instructions.

The adolescent client enjoys the same rights as an adult client would in his or her relationship with the lawyer. Significant among these rights is the client's entitlement to confidentiality. The lawyer is not permitted to reveal to the adolescent's parents confidential information. Where the wishes and interests of the parents and the adolescent conflict, the lawyer is often in a difficult position.

Despite a strongly worded protection of the youthful accuseds' right to counsel, there is no requirement that a young person be represented by a lawyer. Under the YOA, most youths came to their first court appearance without a lawyer and the passage of the YCJA has not changed this. A large proportion of youthful accused continue to be represented only by their parents or **duty counsel** throughout the proceedings in relation to charges against them. While many may still believe that lawyers stand in the way of dealing with adolescents in a manner that serves their best interests, it is important to keep in mind that lawyers are "officers of the court" as well as representatives of their clients. Lawyers often assist in explaining proceedings to adolescents and can hasten the processing of cases by acting for their clients in resolution meetings and other negotiations held with the Crown. Others would therefore argue that the presence of lawyers in the youth justice court is a benefit to the administration of justice and should be assured by more comprehensive and accessible legal aid plans across the country.

duty counsel
lawyer, either the employee of a court or working under contract for a court, who provides on-the-spot, no-charge (although there may be an eventual charge) advice to unrepresented accused

Youth Justice Committees and Conferences

The YCJA provides in s. 18 that each province may establish one or more "youth justice committees" that are made up of "citizens" who support various aspects of the youth justice system by

- giving advice on the choice of extrajudicial measures,
- "supporting" victims and facilitating victim–offender reconciliation,
- arranging for community support services and mentoring relationships for the young offender,
- coordinating the interaction of child protection agencies and the youth criminal justice system,
- monitoring government compliance with the YCJA and advising government about improvements, and
- planning public education campaigns about the youth criminal justice system.

Because the responsibility for the establishment and administration of provincial youth justice committees lies with the provinces, the availability of these committees is quite varied across Canada, and the activities that they undertake also varies provincially.

Youth justice committees are also authorized to "act as a conference" for the purpose of s. 19, which provides in part:

19(1) A youth justice court judge, the provincial director, a police officer, a justice of the peace, a prosecutor or a youth worker may convene or cause to be convened a conference for the purpose of making a decision required to be made under this Act.

(2) The mandate of a conference may be, among other things, to give advice on appropriate extrajudicial measures, conditions for judicial interim release, sentences, including the review of sentences, and reintegration plans.

A conference may be called by a youth justice court judge, the provincial director (a representative of the Probation Services department), a police officer, a justice of the peace, a prosecutor, or a youth worker (another name for a youth probation officer). Advice may be sought on appropriate extradjudicial measures, bail conditions, sentences, review of sentences, and reintegration.

There are different types of conferences that may be convened. One type is a case planning conference. This type of conference brings together a team of professionals to discuss programs and services that may be available for the young person within his or her community. The conferences can take place at any stage in the YCJA process. However, an officer cannot compel a young person to participate in a program involuntarily unless this is done after a charge has been laid. A second type of conference is a restorative justice conference. The purpose of this conference is to hold the young person accountable for his or her actions and to help promote reparation for the harm done to the victim and to the community. This latter type of conference exemplifies the principles of the YCJA and promotes the objectives of sentencing too. Restorative justice is discussed in more detail in Chapter 12. Restorative justice conferences take place pre-charge and post-charge, and provincial funders allocate monies to them under the heading of extrajudicial measures/sanctions.

The mandated conferencing provisions allow for a creative, innovative, community-based approach to the problem of youth crime. The effectiveness of this concept lies in the development of links between the young person, the justice system, and community agencies and counselling services. Thus, through conferencing, a truly multidisciplinary approach to youth crime is achieved. The use of conferencing varies widely throughout the country. Some jurisdictions, including large centres, have yet to call a single conference, while others are holding conferences on a daily basis. Preliminary studies suggest that conferences are an effective way of striking at the causal factors underpinning youth crime, thus promoting and assuring public safety.

Diversion to Extrajudicial Measures and Sanctions

While the YCJA affords youth charged with criminal offences more due process protections than were conferred by either of its predecessor statutes, it is not the intention of the drafters of the Act that more youth should be dealt with formally. Quite the contrary, as is discussed in detail in chapter 12, one key goal of the YCJA is to divert youth who commit minor offences from the formal justice system by means of either extrajudicial measures or extrajudicial sanctions. Recall that extrajudicial measures are an alternative available to police instead of laying a charge and that extrajudicial sanctions are an alternative available to the Crown after a charge has been laid.

Generally speaking, the purposes of extrajudicial measures and sanctions are to logically link consequences to a crime while providing a creative, cost-effective means of dealing with minor youthful offending that addresses the needs not just of the offender but also of the victim, families, and communities. For example, if the charge was one of shoplifting, the sanction imposed might involve participation in an educational anti-shoplifting program, an apology to the store from which the item was stolen, and the writing of an essay explaining the costs of shoplifting. A charge of simple assault might involve participation in an anger management program, in the hope that the offender will come to terms with the impact of his or her behaviour and learn how to better manage his or her behaviour.

Pleas in Youth Justice Court

Where a youthful accused pleads not guilty to a charge, a trial will be held. Where the accused pleads guilty, and the court is satisfied that the facts (as read in by the prosecutor) support the charge, the accused will be convicted. However, if a youth pleads guilty and the court is *not* satisfied that the facts support the charge, according to s. 36(2) of the YCJA, a trial will proceed anyway. This "second guessing" of a youth's guilty plea is intended as a special protection, and is carried over from the historical *parens patriae* philosophy of the youth court, which has roots that are almost a century old.

As is required for adults, justices presiding in youth criminal justice court are required to conduct a "plea inquiry" before entertaining a plea of guilty. This requires that the court make inquiries of the young person to ensure that his or her plea is voluntary, and that he or she understands that he or she is admitting the essential elements of the offence and that the court is not bound by any plea agreement that may have been negotiated between the defence counsel and prosecutor (*Criminal Code*, s. 606(1)).

Preliminary Motions

motions and applications
mini-hearings, separate from the main trial, to resolve preliminary, usually procedural, issues

Preliminary **motions and applications** involve issues raised by the defence or the Crown before the commencement of the trial. These motions often involve procedural matters and, occasionally, Charter applications. Some of the most common preliminary motions include change of venue, joinder/separation of counts or accused, and disclosure orders. While preliminary motions are quite common in adult proceedings, they are less common in youth criminal justice proceedings. Reasons for this difference may include more frequent representation by legal aid and duty counsel in the youth justice system, limited knowledge of the legislation on the part of lawyers, and the misconception that the youth justice court imposes minimal penalties and, therefore, preliminary motions are unnecessary. Inadequate legal representation is a cause for concern, in light of the increased vulnerability of these clients. While youth may be intimidated by lawyers and may have more difficulty giving specific instructions with respect to their wishes, lawyers working in the youth justice system have a duty to serve their young clients well, and should provide increased assistance to young people when it comes to identifying their wishes and best interests.

Youth Court Trial Process

A major structural difference between the YOA and the YCJA with respect to the court system is the availability of trial by jury. Youth charged with indictable offences, where the penalty on conviction is five years or more in total custody and supervision time, can now elect to be tried by jury in the youth criminal justice court. Essentially, this applies to offences for which the youth can receive an adult sentence and the offences of first- or second-degree murder, even if a youth sentence would be ultimately imposed. To understand the difference between jury trials and trials by judge alone, it is also important to understand the difference between a summary conviction offence and an indictable offence under the *Criminal Code.*

When an adult is charged with the commission of a crime, he or she is accused of either a summary conviction offence or, in the minority of cases, an indictable offence. Some offences, called "hybrid" under the Code, can be dealt with either summarily or by indictment at the discretion of the Crown. Note that for arrest purposes, police treat all hybrid offences as indictable. A summary conviction offence is simply a less serious offence, and the court procedure is less formal. In this way, the court system can run more efficiently by reserving its resources for more serious cases. Specifically, all summary conviction offences are heard before a judge alone with no option of a jury.

In contrast, indictable offences, such as murder, are far more serious. Because there is substantially more at stake for the defendant and for the state, the trial process is more comprehensive with extensive preliminary inquiries and many witnesses. The trial of an indictable offence may be heard before a judge and a jury.

Under the YOA, all offences (whether summary conviction or indictable under the *Criminal Code*) were originally treated as summary conviction and proceeded as such. This meant that, for all charges, young persons did not have the right to a trial by jury. The rationale was that court proceedings were an intrusion into the child's life and should, therefore, be resolved quickly. This was thought to be an advantage to the child in terms of his or her reintegration into society.

In *R v. L.(R.),*[1] the denial of the right to a jury trial was constitutionally challenged by an accused. The Ontario Court of Appeal, however, upheld the provisions challenged. The judge stated that sentencing under the YOA is much less severe compared with sentencing under the adult system and that the rationale behind the YOA warrants this differential treatment.

In 1995, however, the YOA was amended to raise the maximum custodial sentence for murder from 5 years less a day to 10 years. As a result, youths charged with murder were allowed to elect whether they wished to be tried by a judge alone or by a judge and jury. This was necessary to comply with s. 11(f) of the Charter, which guarantees a person facing a maximum possible sentence of five years or longer the right to "the benefit of trial by jury."

In contrast, under the YCJA, there is no provision stating that all offences are to be treated as summary conviction offences. It is presumed that the same provisions dealing with summary conviction and indictable offences under the *Criminal Code* apply to offences under the YCJA. This means that, for indictable offences, youths in conflict with the law are, like adults, entitled to a trial by jury. For summary conviction offences, the youth is tried by a judge only and does not have the right to a trial by jury. Because the YCJA does not make all youth criminal justice proceedings summary conviction, it is argued that a higher degree of due process protection is now accorded to accused youth than was the case under the YOA.

Appeals

As with any criminal proceeding, decisions made in the youth justice court are subject to appeal. Any decision by a trial court that has criminal consequences can be appealed to a higher court. In the YCJA, section 37 outlines the appeal provisions. This section sets out the routes of appeal. It also states that decisions made under the review of sentence provisions—ss. 94 to 96—cannot be appealed. Youth courts in the province of Ontario are generally constituted at the Ontario Court of Justice level, and, therefore, the first level of appeal is to the Superior Court of Justice and from there to the Ontario Court of Appeal. Section 37(10) allows the appeal of a finding of guilt to the Supreme Court of Canada, but only with leave to appeal from that court. This requirement for leave to appeal means that the Supreme Court will look at the matter in brief and make a determination whether the case merits an appeal before it decides to hear the matter in full. This leave process is not required in some limited situations that give rise to an appeal "as of right," where the Supreme Court is obliged to hear the appeal without pre-screening cases the court believes are unworthy of its time.

Chapter Summary

This chapter introduced the offence jurisdiction and age jurisdiction of youth justice courts and noted that youth courts are now authorized to order adult sentences in certain cases. Post-charge diversion was reviewed, and youth justice committees and conferences introduced. The right to counsel provisions under s. 25 were reviewed and were compared with those in the YOA. Finally, pre-trial motions, the youth court trial process, and appeals were discussed.

KEY TERMS

youth justice court

jurisdiction

duty counsel

motions and applications

NOTES

1. *R v. L.(R.)* (1986), 52 CR (3d) 209 (Ont. CA).

EXERCISES AND REVIEW
Review Questions

1. Is a youthful accused entitled to a trial by jury? Under what circumstances?

2. In which court will a youth trial by jury be held?

3. Can a youth bring an application under the Charter?

4. Can a youth be made to stand trial even after pleading guilty? Why or why not?

5. What is a s. 19 conference? Under what circumstances might a police officer convene such a conference?

6. Under the YCJA, can a youth be "tried and convicted as an adult"?

7. What is the legal authority for requiring youths or their parents to repay the costs of duty counsel?

Discussion Questions

1. Imagine you are a 40-year-old male criminal defence lawyer hired by (or by the parents of) a 13-year-old girl charged with first-time arson. How might you treat this client differently from an adult repeat offender? How would you get representation instructions from her?

2. Can a youth be made to stand trial after partial completion or non-completion of an extrajudicial sanction (which requires an acknowledgment of responsibility for the act forming the basis of the charge)? Why or why not? How is a youth's right to be free from self-incrimination protected in this situation?

CHAPTER 11

Sentencing

■ CHAPTER OBJECTIVES

After completing this chapter, you should be able to:

- Locate and describe the legislative principles that guide sentencing under the *Youth Criminal Justice Act* (YCJA).

- Explain what element of the legislation gives rise to an anti-custody presumption, and locate provisions designed to support that presumption.

- List the types of sentences that can be imposed under the YCJA.

- Assess the degree to which the courts' sentencing practices for youths since the passage of the YCJA are consistent with the objectives and principles of the legislation.

- Identify particular offences that attract special sentencing under the YCJA.

- Identify situations in which a youth might be sentenced as an adult under the YCJA.

- Explain what is meant by conditional supervision.

- Describe the schedule and process by which non-custodial sentences are reviewed.

- Explain how and by whom the decision about the appropriate level of custody for a convicted youth is made.

Introduction

Sentencing is a central and crucial component of our youth justice legislation. The sentencing, custody, and supervision provisions that make up parts 4 and 5 of the *Youth Criminal Justice Act* (YCJA) are complex and unique, and they form nearly 50 percent of the total content of the legislation. The issue of how best to punish and/or rehabilitate young offenders has been, and continues to be, extremely contro- versial. Despite ongoing discussion and an abundance of writing about how to best sentence youths, writers and critics disagree dramatically about how youths should best be sanctioned after a finding of guilt. Not only is current research about the effectiveness of various sentences seriously inadequate, but there is also a signifi- cant political component to the debate about appropriate sentences. The YCJA's sentencing provisions are an attempt both to deal fairly with youth who offend and to provide accountability to the general public.

The sentencing provisions of the YCJA were created in response to public demands to reform the *Young Offenders Act* (YOA), which was perceived by many to be too lenient, despite evidence to the contrary. This concern is discussed in more detail below as well as in chapter 1. The architects of our justice system have long understood that not only must justice be done, it must be *seen to be done*—meaning that the public always demands some evidence of accountability that offenders are being punished, or at least that they are being "taken out of commission."

Public and media cries for "harsher" sentences under the YOA were almost invariably justified by the reasoning that offenders and other youths need to be specifically and generally deterred, or discouraged, from criminal behaviour. A corollary to the principle of visible justice is the principle of deterrence: most people believe that the threat of sanction will deter others from committing crimes, and without evidence that offenders are being punished—and reasonably harshly—there is no credible threat of sanction and, arguably, no deterrence.

Unfortunately, research has shown that the sentences that seem to most readily satisfy the need for public accountability—typically custody—are not necessarily the same ones most likely to actually accomplish the goal of rehabilitation and protection of society. Despite the fact that the effectiveness of the "short-sharp-shock" approach to custody—short terms of imprisonment, readily handed out—has been widely discredited by experts as a rehabilitative technique, and despite the fact that under the YOA, the per capita rate of youth imprisonment in Canada exceeded the US rate and was one of the highest in developed countries around the world, segments of the Canadian public continue to call for "tougher sentences for youth." While this call is probably based on significant misperceptions of what actually goes on in the youth justice system, it persists, and most politicians accept that it would be arrogant to ignore its proponents. As a result, the YCJA's sentencing philosophy requires an almost acrobatic balance of a presumption against custodial sentences and a commitment to impose meaningful sentences and to make offending youth truly accountable to their victims and to society for the harm they have done.

Not only the drafters of the YCJA, but also the justice system actors, such as judges, Crown prosecutors, and police, who are charged with the task of putting the legislation into effect, are faced with the acrobatic task of balancing the goals of the YCJA with the needs and circumstances of particular offenders and the demands of victims and families. Remember too that, while a new youth justice law has been passed, mostly the same people are enforcing and applying it as did so under the YOA. The extent to which philosophical shifts in the approach to youth justice crafted by the drafters of the YCJA are actually reflected in the treatment of individual youths depends on the actions of judges, lawyers, and police in each individual case.

Purpose and Principles of Sentencing

According to s. 38(1), the purpose of sentencing—the objectives it is intended to achieve—is:

> 38(1) ... to hold a young person accountable for an offence through the imposition of just sanctions that have meaningful consequences for the young person

and that promote his or her rehabilitation and reintegration into society, thereby contributing to the long-term protection of the public.

This "purpose" is relatively simply stated; but by other words, the YCJA suggests that the route to achieving the public-centred goal of protection—the bottom-line goal of most modern justice systems—must pass by several offender-centred signposts: accountability, meaningful consequences, rehabilitation, and supported reintegration.

In order to assist judges in following the prescribed route to public protection, the legislation provides "principles" in s. 38(2). These are complicated and warrant reference to the legislation itself, but in summary,

- a youth sentence cannot be greater than the adult sentence for the same offence committed in similar circumstances;

- the sentence must be similar to others handed out to other youth in the same region[1] for similar offences (that is, sentences are to be consistent);

- the sentence must be proportionate to the seriousness of the crime and the youth's degree of responsibility; and

- the sentence must, subject to the proportionality issue, be the least restrictive one capable of satisfying the s. 38(1) purpose, be the most rehabilitative/ reintegrative choice, and promote a sense of responsibility and acknowledgment of harm in the young person.

Besides these principles, s. 38(3) outlines **mitigating** and **aggravating factors** that the judge should consider in determining the appropriate sentence. These factors include the young person's degree of participation in committing the crime, the harm done to the victim, anything the young person has done to repair the harm done to the victim and community, the time already spent in detention, prior criminal history, and any other relevant circumstances related to the purpose and principles of sentencing.

mitigating factor
a circumstance or action during or after the commission of an offence that supports a lighter sentence—for example, sincere and expressed remorse for harm done

aggravating factor
a circumstance or action during or after the commission of an offence that supports a more onerous sentence—for example, "gay bashing" (a hate-motivated crime)

COMMON-LAW SENTENCING PRINCIPLES

Besides the purpose and principles set out in s. 38, youth sentencing is to be informed by the general Statement of Principle for the Act set out in s. 3 and to be guided by common-law principles—that is, principles that have developed through case decisions, either independently or through the interpretation of statutory provisions. However, in doing so, judges cannot apply any principle that is in conflict with the provisions of the YCJA itself. And, in practice, most common-law principles of sentencing (such as denunciation, deterrence, and parity) have already been codified in the provisions of the YCJA.

THE ROLE OF DETERRENCE IN YOUTH CRIMINAL JUSTICE SENTENCING

Across the country, there is significant diversity of opinion with respect to the value of deterrence in sentencing young people. In some respects, there has been a "showdown" occurring in courts across our nation, all of which are struggling with this issue.

Courts in different provinces have dealt with the relevance of deterrence under the YCJA in divergent ways. The British Columbia Court of Appeal held that general deterrence remains a factor under the YCJA, albeit one of diminished importance.[2] In contrast, the Manitoba Court of Appeal held that although the judicial process may have a deterrent effect on the young person and others, neither general nor specific deterrence is a relevant YCJA sentencing principle.[3]

In *T.M.*, one of the first decisions under the YCJA dealing with this issue, the Ontario Court of Appeal held that general deterrence has less importance but has not been entirely diminished.[4] The court went on to ask "What do accountability, meaningful consequences, and long-term protection of the public go to if not to specific deterrence?"

In 2005, the Supreme Court of Canada resolved much of the controversy pertaining to the role of deterrence under the YCJA when it heard appeals of *B.V.N.* and *B.W.P.* together.[5] A majority of the Supreme Court held that the YCJA introduced a new sentencing regime, and its wording can only support the conclusion that Parliament deliberately excluded general deterrence as a factor of youth sentencing. The court admonished lower level decision makers to focus on the young person before the court. As a result, general deterrence is no longer to be considered when an adolescent is sentenced in Canada.

However, despite this ruling of the Supreme Court, the role of deterrence in the sentencing of young persons will likely continue to be one of the most controversial issues in years to come, given the public and police outcry for tougher sentencing, and the very real issues of youth violence, youth gangs, and the proliferation of firearms on the streets of our country.

Limits on Custodial Sentences

To reach the goal of limiting custodial sentences, s. 39(1) of the YCJA limits the use of custody to circumstances that meet the following criteria:

- where a youth has committed a violent offence;[6]

- where a youth has failed to comply with previous non-custodial sentences;

- where a youth who has a criminal history commits an indictable offence for which an adult could be sentenced for more than two years; and

- where, according to the evidence and the discretion of the sentencing judge, a non-custodial sentence is inconsistent with the stated purposes and principles of sentencing under s. 38 of the YCJA.

Even where these criteria are met, a youth court judge must always consider the use of alternative sentencing measures and the likely effectiveness of this in the particular case before the imposition of a custodial sentence (ss. 39(2) and (3)). As at the pre-trial level, the court cannot commit a youth to custody for child protection, mental health, or social welfare purposes (s. 39(5)).

Before sentencing, the judge should "consider a pre-sentence report and any sentencing proposal made by the young person or his or her counsel" (s. 39(6)) unless the use of a report is waived by the young person and/or his or her counsel and the court is satisfied that a report is not necessary. (Pre-sentence reports and the rules relating to them are explained in s. 40, discussed below.) Finally, if after all of this analysis the judge still believes that custody is necessary, s. 39(9) provides that he or she must give written reasons for the decision to impose a custodial sentence.

THE STRUGGLE TO DEFINE WHAT CONSTITUTES A "VIOLENT OFFENCE"

As we have learned in this chapter, given the restrictions on the use of custody contained in s. 39(1), a youth justice court is not to commit a young person to custody unless the young person has committed a violent offence. What constitutes a violent offence has been one of the most hotly contested issues in youth criminal justice. Similar to the issue of the significance of deterrence in youth sentencing, there has been disagreement among courts across the country on this issue that has been only very recently resolved by the Supreme Court of Canada.

Clearly, where someone causes or attempts to cause serious bodily harm to another in the commission of an offence, this is a violent offence. For example, the Nova Scotia Court of Appeal ruled that a "serious violent offence" is an offence in the commission of which a young person causes or attempts to cause serious bodily harm.[7] The court held that a "violent offence," accordingly, is an offence in the commission of which the young person causes or attempts to cause bodily harm. The court also found that an offence is not "violent" simply because of the section of the *Criminal Code* that defines it.

However, some courts have extended the definition of violent offence to include situations where no serious bodily harm is suffered, but the victim suffered some harm as a result of the accused's actions. For example, the Prince Edward Island Court of Appeal held that a "violent offence" means an offence in which bodily harm (but not necessarily "serious bodily harm") has been caused to the victim.[8]

The Supreme Court of Canada, in 2005, made it clear that the harm must be serious bodily harm and not merely psychological.[9] The court held that the definition of "violent" under the YCJA should be interpreted narrowly, in order to give effect to the framers' intention of reducing Canada's over-reliance on custodial sentences for young persons convicted of criminal offences. To avoid locking up large numbers of youth, fewer offences should be considered a "violent offence" for the purpose of this provision.

Pre-Sentence Reports

Section 40 provides for the preparation (by the **provincial director**) and admissibility of a "pre-sentence report": a (usually) written summary of information relevant to the sentencing decision. This report can contain, among other things, information from interviews with the offender, the victim, and other interested parties; general information about the offender's background, character, living situation, and commitment to treatment and rehabilitation; school information; information about available rehabilitative/community programs; and a restricted summary of the accused's criminal history (see s. 40(2)(d)(iii)).

A pre-sentence report *must* be admitted if the youth wants it to be and custody is being considered. If a non-custodial sentence is being considered, the court *may* order one to be prepared for consideration.

provincial director
for the purpose of the YCJA, a person or "a group or class of persons"—that is, certain members of the provincial corrections administration—designated by a provincial government to perform a wide range of functions under the legislation (for example, assigning the level of custody placements and ensuring that pre-sentence reports are completed)

Victim Impact Statements

The court can also consider a report from the prosecution side in the form of a **victim impact statement**. These are provided for by s. 722 of the *Criminal Code* and have been made a part of the youth justice court process by s. 50 of the YCJA. Victim impact statements represent a new (and sometimes controversial) focus on the victim that has recently been evident in the court system in general.

In some jurisdictions, police are instrumental in the preparation of such statements, because they will generally be the primary contact with victims. In other areas, the statements may be prepared by victim–offender reconciliation agencies, or by the Victim Witness Assistance Program. Where victim impact statements are prepared by police, they must form part of the disclosure given to the accused by the Crown. However, where they are prepared by third party agencies, they need not be given to the accused before trial. Obtaining a useful victim impact statement requires sensitivity, a commitment to accuracy, and good interviewing skills.

In most cases, these statements will be filed with the court, but occasionally a victim may wish to read the statement aloud in court.

Sentences in Youth Justice Court

The youth justice court judge has a very wide range of sentencing options from which to choose. He or she must keep in mind the YCJA purpose and principles of sentencing and consider the pre-sentence report, victim impact statements, recommendations from counsel on both sides, and representations by parents. The options are described in s. 42(2) and include:

- reprimand—s. 42(2)(a)
- absolute discharge—s. 42(2)(b)
- conditional discharge—s. 42(2)(c)
- fine not exceeding $1,000—s. 42(2)(d)
- special (not general) damages—s. 42(2)(e)
- restitution of stolen property—s. 42(2)(f)
- restitution to an innocent purchaser of stolen goods—s. 42(2)(g)
- compensation through personal service—s. 42(2)(h)
- community service, for up to 240 hours/within 12 months—s. 42(2)(i) and s. 54
- prohibition/seizure/forfeiture order—s. 42(2)(j) and s. 51
- probation for up to 2 years—s. 42(2)(k) and ss. 55 and 56
- intensive support and supervision—s. 42(2)(l)
- non-residential program, for up to 240 hours/6 months—s. 42(2)(m)
- custody and supervision, for up to 2 years total, or up to 3 years for *Criminal Code* "life" offences—s. 42(2)(n)

- custody and supervision, for up to 3 years total for certain "presumptive" offences (YCJA s. 2, "presumptive offence," subs. (a)(ii)-(iv)—s. 42(2)(o))

- deferred custody and supervision not exceeding 6 months—s. 42(2)(p)

- for first-degree murder, up to 10 years total custody and supervision (maximum 6 years custody and 4 years supervision)—s. 42(2)(q)(i)

- for second-degree murder, up to 7 years total custody and supervision (maximum 4 years custody and 3 years supervision)—s. 42(2)(q)(ii)

- intensive rehabilitative custody and supervision not to exceed 2 years, or 3 years for a *Criminal Code* "life" offence—s. 42(2)(r)(i)

- intensive rehabilitative custody and supervision not to exceed 10 years for first-degree murder (maximum 6 years custody and 4 years supervision)—s. 42(2)(r)(ii)

- intensive rehabilitative custody and supervision not to exceed 7 years for second-degree murder (maximum 4 years custody and 3 years supervision)—s. 42(2)(r)(iii)

- conditions—s. 42(2)(s)

Clearly, there is no shortage of options for a youth court judge, but it is important to remember that any sentence imposed must be consistent with the principles of consistency and proportionality expressed in s. 38; therefore, once a regional precedent is taken into account, the range of available sentences will be limited by the type of offence committed and the circumstances.

In appropriate cases, typically involving young persons with no prior criminal history who have committed minor offences, the judge can order an absolute discharge. This means the youth will be set free without a traditional "criminal record." However, a finding of guilt will be recorded and can be used for certain limited purposes within the criminal justice system.

The judge may also order a conditional discharge. Here, the youth will be free of a criminal record following compliance with any conditions that are imposed by the court. The conditions available to a judge to impose on a young person are outlined in s. 55 of the YCJA.

The youth court also has jurisdiction to impose a maximum fine of $1,000 on a young person. There are rules relating to the imposition of fines, and judges must not impose a fine where the youth has no realistic ability to pay it without hardship. The same goes for orders of damages or restitution. If the young person is in possession of any person's property as a result of the offence, the judge can order him or her to return or replace the stolen goods.

The young person may even be ordered to perform a personal service to a victim in lieu of monetary compensation, but such orders will depend on the consent of the victim, and in these cases, police may be relied upon to assist in the victim–offender relationship. The judge may also order up to 240 hours of community service as a form of compensation to the community.

In more serious cases, the judge can impose a probation order on a young person. Such an order must be for a specified period and cannot exceed 2 years. A youth may also be faced with a disposition requiring him or her to attend a specified non-residential program for support and supervision. These programs, which include attendance centres, are highly innovative and are proven to assist with the reduction of recidivism risk.

Section 42(2)(n) provides for a combined custody and supervision order. It specifies that, following custody, a young person is subject to supervision in the community with conditions for a period that is half the length of time of custody. The combined period cannot exceed 2 years for most offences. For offences that, under the Code, could lead to imprisonment for life, a 3-year maximum custody and supervision order can be made. If the young person fails to comply with any conditions while under supervision, he or she may be ordered to serve the remainder of the sentence in custody.

In *B.W.P.*,[10] the Manitoba Court of Appeal held that the court has complete discretion to determine the ratio of custody and supervision. In that case, the court found that the trial judge did not err in sentencing a young person to one day in custody and the remainder of 15 months conditional supervision for manslaughter. In that case, the youth charged was aboriginal and had, after killing another youth in a fight, plead guilty to manslaughter. The case was appealed to the Supreme Court of Canada, and the court upheld the lower court's decision to vary the proportion of time spent in a custodial setting under a custody and supervision sentence. The court made it clear that the trier of fact is entitled to impose a lesser amount of time in custody if he or she sees fit to do so.

Section 42(2)(q) provides for the maximum sentences that can be imposed on young persons for committing murder. In the case of first-degree murder, a young person can be sentenced up to 10 years. The 10-year sentence is composed of 6 years in custody and 4 years of **conditional supervision** served in the community. In the case of second-degree murder, the judge can order a maximum sentence of 7 years in a combination of 4 years in custody and 3 years of conditional supervision.

In keeping with the rehabilitation principle of the YCJA, a youth court judge may order that a young person be placed in custody for "intensive rehabilitation" followed by conditional supervision. This order can be made only where (1) the young person has committed a presumptive offence (first- or second-degree murder, attempted murder, manslaughter, aggravated sexual assault, or an offence deemed seriously violent); (2) he or she is suffering from a mental illness; (3) an effective treatment and supervision plan has been developed; and (4) consent has been obtained from the provincial director.

An **intensive rehabilitation and supervision sentence** ordinarily cannot exceed 2 years. However, if the offence under the Code would lead to life imprisonment, a 3-year rehabilitative custody order may be made. If the young person has been found guilty of first-degree murder, he or she may be subject to custody for intensive rehabilitation for 6 years and conditional supervision in the community for 4 years. In the case of second-degree murder, the young person may face a maximum of 4 years of intensive rehabilitation in custody and 3 years of conditional supervision in the community. This section is an attempt to ensure that where a mentally ill youth (who may not be ill enough to be committed under the mental disorder provisions of the *Criminal Code*) has committed a serious crime attracting custody, he or she can be required to participate in appropriate rehabilitation or treatment.

If a young person is convicted of a criminal offence, his or her record does not simply disappear. Youth records are expunged after three to five years, depending

conditional supervision
a portion of a custodial sentence that is served outside custody and during which a youth is subject to strict conditions of behaviour

intensive rehabilitation and supervision sentence
custody and/or supervision that involves participation in treatment or rehabilitation programs designed to treat the causes of offending in mentally ill youth

upon the seriousness of the offence, but if a further offence is committed by someone with such a record before the time has passed, the record can be kept open beyond the three to five year period. Further, if a person over 18 years of age commits an offence while his or her youth record is still open, the youth record becomes part of his or her adult record.

REVIEW OF A NON-CUSTODIAL SENTENCE

Section 59 of the YCJA provides that with the exception of custodial sentences, youth sentences are subject to review at the request of the youth, the youth's parent, the attorney general, or the provincial director, six months following their imposition. With leave of the court, this review can come earlier than the six-month date. There are several grounds on which a youth sentence may be reviewed: the circumstances that led to the sentence have changed materially, the youth is unable to perform or is having great difficulty performing the conditions, the conditions are inhibiting positive opportunities available to the young person, and any other relevant factor at the discretion of the youth court. Following a sentence review, the youth court judge may order that the sentence continue unchanged, terminate the youth sentence, or vary the sentence (but the court may not make the sentence more onerous than the original sentence).

The Imposition of Adult Sentences

All justice systems of the western world deal with adolescents differently than adults in general, but also allow for the prospect of treating the few youths who commit particularly heinous or shocking crimes as adults.[11] Some countries go to the extreme of imposing capital punishment on adolescents. For example, the death penalty was available for adolescents in 20 American states until March 2005 when, in the case of *Roper v. Simmons*,[12] the Supreme Court of the United States struck down the death penalty as an inappropriate sanction for "juveniles."[13] This decision commuted the death sentences of 72 juvenile offenders on death row in American prisons. While Canada does not allow capital punishment for adolescent or adult offenders, we do allow for certain youth to be treated as seriously as they could be if they were adult offenders. Our justice system allows, under the YCJA, for the sentencing of certain youthful offenders as adults. The YCJA makes such treatment likely in a wider range of cases than did the YOA. So far, this aspect of the YCJA has proven to be very controversial.

When a young person commits a violent offence, there is widespread public support for the notion that he or she should be subject to a more punitive sentence than any youth sentence available under the YCJA, under which the maximum penalty is 10 years in custody. Section 42(9) of the YCJA permits the attorney general to designate a youth's offence as a "serious violent offence" and "endorse the information accordingly." Such an endorsement will, obviously, have an effect on sentencing and will carry some significance in terms of future use of the youth justice court record.

Even then, some heinous crimes require a more substantial societal reaction. In these few cases, youth sentences cannot satisfy the principle of "proportionate accountability." Under the YOA, the justice system had the power to transfer certain youths accused of serious crimes to adult court for trial and sentencing. Under the YCJA, youths can be subject to adult sentences after a trial in youth court.

Under the YOA, a transfer hearing was held to determine whether it would be appropriate to transfer the youth to adult court. If the youth was transferred, he or she was within the jurisdiction of the adult system, subject to adult sentencing. Much criticism centred on the inefficiency of transfer hearings to determine whether a youth should be tried in youth court or adult court. The notion that the court would make a determination about what sort of treatment was warranted by the facts and circumstances of the case, combined with the attributes of the youth charged, *before* trial was particularly disturbing to some commentators as an affront to the constitutional presumption of innocence.[14]

Under the YOA, transfer of youth under 16 but over 14 years of age could take place at the initiative of the prosecution only in the case of murder, manslaughter, attempted murder, or aggravated sexual assault. However, a young person who was 16 or 17 years of age and who was charged with one of these offences was presumptively transferred to adult court. The reverse onus created by this presumption made it necessary for the 16- or 17-year-old to apply to have his or her case remain within the youth court jurisdiction. For other offences, the young person normally remained within the jurisdiction of the youth court.

The adult sentencing provisions[15] of the YCJA differ from the YOA with respect to age jurisdiction. In what was a very controversial change made by the new legislation, the scope of what constituted a "presumptive offence" was expanded by the drafters of the YJCA. The age for adult sentencing for a youth who commits a "presumptive offence" (defined in s. 2) was lowered by the new Act. Under s. 61, a youth who is found guilty of such an offence at 14 years of age can be presumptively subjected to an adult sentence, at provincial discretion. The youth bears a reverse onus when applying to be subject to youth sentencing instead (s. 63). For other offences, the attorney general can apply under s. 64 to have an adult sentence imposed on a young person who has attained the age of 14 years and whose offence has been designated a "serious violent offence" under s. 42(9).

It is not just commentators but also the courts who have taken issue with this expanded reverse onus. Shortly after the YCJA came into effect, Quebec courts made it clear that presumptive adult sentencing was not acceptable in that province. More recently, the Ontario Court of Appeal, in the decision *R v. B.D.*,[16] struck down the reverse onus provisions regarding presumptive adult sentencing in the YCJA as unconstitutionally violating the young person's rights.[17] Consequently, in Canada's largest province, adult sentences are not presumptively available for adolescents who offend, although they may be available if the Crown is able to prove them necessary. At the time of writing, this decision has yet to be considered by the Supreme Court of Canada, so the status of presumptive adult sentencing in the rest of Canada is unclear, though Ontario's decision is certain to be influential.

Under the YOA, transfer hearings took place before the actual trial. A hearing was held to determine whether the youth should be transferred to adult court. The focus was not on the guilt or innocence of the youth, but rather on the appropriateness of adult court compared with youth court, and on the best interests of the young person and the public. Evidence that would ordinarily be inadmissible at trial was permitted at this stage. Hearsay evidence and opinions about the youth, for example, could be used in the prosecutor's argument. Any such evidence could not later be used, regardless of the determined jurisdiction. Although the onus of proof rested with the prosecutor (or the applicant for transfer), the burden was relatively easy to meet.

In contrast, an advantage of adult sentencing under the YCJA is that there is no need for a separate hearing to determine the appropriate jurisdiction. If the young person is over 14 years of age and is found guilty of a presumptive offence, the YCJA provides that he or she is automatically eligible to be sentenced as an adult if the attorney general applies. Proponents of this approach argue that it allows for predictability and impartiality. Whether or not presumptive offences are retained, efficiency is a general advantage because a separate "mini-trial" is no longer necessary. However, such efficiency coupled with a lower minimum age for adult sentencing will likely mean an increase in adult sentencing for young persons.

Under the YCJA, if the young person or the attorney general wishes to challenge the choice of sentencing, a pre-sentencing hearing is to be held. The YCJA provides a relatively structured test to determine whether a youth, following an application, should be subject to a youth or adult sentence. Section 72 prescribes that a youth court judge, in making his or her decision, should consider:

> 72(1) … the seriousness and circumstances of the offence, and the age, maturity, character, background and previous record of the young person and any other factors that the court considers relevant, and
>
>> (a) if it is of the opinion that a youth sentence imposed in accordance with the purpose and principles set out in subparagraph 3(1)(b)(ii) and section 38 would have sufficient length to hold the young person accountable for his or her offending behaviour, it shall order that the young person is not liable to an adult sentence and that a youth sentence must be imposed; and
>
>> (b) if it is of the opinion that a youth sentence imposed in accordance with the purpose and principles set out in subparagraph 3(1)(b)(ii) and section 38 would not have sufficient length to hold the young person accountable for his or her offending behaviour, it shall order that an adult sentence be imposed.

Another controversial issue surrounding adult sentencing is the placement of young persons in adult facilities. According to s. 76, the youth court has the discretion to either (1) place the youth in a youth custody facility separate from adults; (2) place the youth in an adult correctional facility; or (3) if the sentence is more than 2 years, place the youth in a penitentiary. Generally, young persons who are under 18 years of age at the time of sentencing should be placed in a youth custody facility. However, young persons who are over 18 at the time of sentencing are normally placed in an adult correctional facility.

After the youth has begun serving his or her sentence, s. 76(6) allows for an application to be made to place the youth in another facility. Generally, a young person who has attained the age of 20 should not remain in a youth facility unless it "would be in the best interests of the young person and would not jeopardize the safety of others" (s. 76(9)).

CUSTODY

Custodial dispositions and conditional supervision are, arguably, the most intrusive aspects of the youth criminal justice system. Many experts believe that custodial placements are in the best interests of young people only in certain narrow circumstances, and those who have studied youth criminal behaviour typically believe that "to not only effectively understand but to treat anti-social youth it is necessary to maintain them in their natural ecology."[18]

As mentioned earlier, the YCJA, in both the preamble and in s. 39, expresses a central goal of reducing the number and proportion of custodial sentences dealt to youth. The legislation also contains many provisions dealing with young persons' rights and responsibilities while serving a sentence. Section 83 sets out the purpose and principles of the youth custody and supervision system:

> 83(1) The purpose of the youth custody and supervision system is to contribute to the protection of society by
> > (a) carrying out sentences imposed by courts through the safe, fair and humane custody and supervision of young persons; and
> > (b) assisting young persons to be rehabilitated and reintegrated into the community as law-abiding citizens, by providing effective programs to young persons in custody and while under supervision in the community.

Section 83(2) provides that, in addition to the general YCJA legislative principles set out in s. 3, several custody principles are to be followed, and lists first the "least restrictive measures" that provide appropriate protection for the public. Young persons in custody maintain the same rights as other young persons except those that are necessary for serving the sentence. Involvement of family and other members of the young person's community is to be encouraged. Ongoing decisions relating to custody and supervision and sentencing review should be fair. Finally, when a youth is placed in an adult facility, he or she should not be disadvantaged when it comes to eligibility for and conditions of release.

Each province is required, under s. 85, to establish at least two levels of youth facilities. These levels, usually described as "open" and "secure" custody, are differentiated by the degree of restraint on the young person. When a young person has been sentenced to serve time in custody, the provincial director has the authority to determine the level at which the young person will be admitted. He or she also has the authority to transfer the young person to a different level of custody if it would be in the interest of society and the young person.

Section 85(5) establishes the factors that the provincial director must consider in determining the level of custody or the appropriateness of a transfer. Placement should be the least restrictive to the young person having regard to the prescribed factors. These factors include the seriousness of the offence and the circumstances surrounding it, the needs and circumstances of the youth, the safety of other young persons in custody, and societal interests. The level of custody decision must also take into account the appropriateness of programs available to the young person while in a particular facility or level of facility. The likelihood of escape is a relevant factor as well.

Consistent with the due process theme of the YCJA, several provisions protect the rights of a young person while he or she is serving a custodial sentence. Under s. 86, young persons shall be provided with information throughout the process and shall be given an opportunity to be heard. The young person also has the right to a review of decisions with regard to initial placement or transfer under s. 87. Reviews are conducted by an independent review board.

REVIEW OF CUSTODIAL SENTENCE

Section 94(1) provides that a review of a custodial sentence must take place before the youth court at least annually for the duration of the sentence. In addition, s. 94(3) enables the young person or his or her parent to request a review at any time on the grounds outlined as follows in s. 94(6):

> 94(6) … (a) on the ground that the young person has made sufficient progress to justify a change in the youth sentence;
> (b) on the ground that the circumstances that led to the youth sentence have changed materially;
> (c) on the ground that new services or programs are available that were not available at the time of the youth sentence;
> (d) on the ground that the opportunities for rehabilitation are now greater in the community; or
> (e) on any other ground that the youth justice court considers appropriate.

After giving the young person, his or her parents, the attorney general, and the provincial director an opportunity to be heard at a custody review, the youth court judge renders a decision. The judge may order no changes or may release the young person from custody and place him or her under conditional supervision for a period not exceeding the remainder of the sentence.

Over-Age Transfer

Under s. 89 of the YCJA, when a young person attains 20 years of age at the time of sentencing or while in custody, he or she is automatically ordered to serve the duration of the sentence in a provincial correctional facility for adults. (Adults sentenced after they turn 18 for crimes committed as youth are tried as young people but serve their sentences in adult facilities.) Section 89(2) enables the provincial director to apply to the youth justice court to transfer over-age young persons to a penitentiary for the remainder of their sentence if it would be in the young person's or society's "best interests" and if there are at least 2 years left on the sentence.

Young persons who began their custodial sentence under 20 years of age may also be transferred to an adult facility. Section 92(1) enables a provincial director, upon application to the youth court, to transfer a young person who has attained the age of 18 to an adult correctional facility for the remainder of his or her sentence. Furthermore, a young person may be transferred from an adult correctional facility to a penitentiary in some circumstances.

Reintegration into the Community

The principles of rehabilitation and reintegration are central to a custodial disposition under the YCJA. Section 90(1) orders the provincial director to designate a youth worker to a young person in custody "without delay." A young person who is serving a sentence in the community is also assigned a youth worker for support, supervision, and encouragement while completing the imposed conditions. Furthermore, s. 91 authorizes the provincial director to implement a **reintegration leave**,

reintegration leave
a period spent out of custody, with leave of the provincial director, for making arrangements or participating in activities that will facilitate the youth's reintegration into the community

releasing the young person from custody for periods of time for the purposes of, among other things, attending school, obtaining employment, and attending community programs.

Several provisions apply to young persons who are under conditional supervision following their custodial sentence. Section 105(2) lists the standard conditions imposed on all young persons under conditional supervision. Section 105(3) enumerates additional conditions that may be imposed at the order of the youth court. This list is extremely broad and includes school attendance, obtaining employment, residing with a parent, and remaining within a specified territory. Paragraph (g) authorizes judicial discretion to impose "any other conditions" deemed appropriate.

If it is suspected that a young person is about to breach or has breached a condition, the provincial director is empowered under s. 106 to suspend the conditional supervision and place the young person in custody pending judicial review. When the suspension of conditional supervision is ordered, the youth may, if necessary, be apprehended by police pursuant to a warrant issued under s. 107. The youth court judge then has the option of either cancelling suspension of the conditional supervision, varying the existing conditions or creating new ones, or ordering the young person to remain in custody for a period not exceeding his or her original sentence.

Termination of a Youth Sentence

Under s. 82(1), with certain exceptions, a youth's criminal record need not be disclosed for most purposes when he or she has been discharged absolutely or has completed serving the sentence. The record *can* be used within the youth criminal justice system—for example, for the purpose of determining sentences and whether to sentence as a youth or as an adult, to decide whether a subsequent offence is a presumptive offence, or to decide whether pre-trial custody is appropriate.

The limitations on the public use of a young person's criminal record are intended to protect the youth and allow for easier reintegration into the community. Section 82(3), for example, specifically deals with public employment applications. It prohibits questions that relate to disclosure of a prior record.

YCJA Sentencing Principles as Applied So Far: A Critical Assessment

Clearly, as is discussed above, the sentencing provisions of the YCJA are at the crucial core of its content. As is the case in general with all of the Act's provisions, given the short time period during which it has been in force, it is difficult to assess how effectively its sentencing provisions are being implemented. It is also difficult to determine to what extent changes to the diversion provisions relating to extrajudicial measures and sanctions (to be discussed in chapter 12) rather than reliance on the sentencing principles, is behind changes to numbers of youth sent to custody. However, early data indicate that the sentencing principles are being put into practice and that there is, in fact, a reduction in the number of custodial sentences.

Information gathered by the Department of Justice Canada indicates that, in the very first year of the YCJA's operation (2003–2004), there was a drop in the rate of youths sent to custody. In 2002–2003, the rate of sentencing youths to custody was 5.64, whereas in 2003–2004, the rate decreased to 3.78 per 100,000. This translates into a drop of 33 percent in custody use.[19] This drop is characterized by the department as "dramatic." This information is general and does not indicate the extent to which regional variation in sentencing practices is continuing, but the trend is encouraging.

Even before this research was released, like a canary in a mineshaft, vacant beds and closures of youth custodial facilities across Canada were a signal that courts were in fact starting to give effect to the intentions of the drafters of the YCJA by reducing custody levels.[20]

While rates of custody use can be fairly easily tracked, it is more difficult to determine whether the broader goals set out in the YCJA's sentencing principles are being met. It is, for example, not easy to assess whether the public is being better protected or whether the underlying causes of youth crime are being addressed. However, the decrease in the rate of youth crime discussed in chapters 1 and 13 is encouraging.

Chapter Summary

This chapter introduced the purpose and principles of sentencing as expressed in s. 38 of the YCJA. The legislation's restrictions on the use of custodial sentences followed, and the very wide range of sentencing options available under the legislation were examined. The optional review of non-custodial sentences was considered, as was the compulsory review of custodial ones.

A comparison followed of the YCJA regime of adult sentencing in youth justice court with the YOA system of transfers to adult court. The administration of custodial sentences was then discussed, as was the effect of termination of a youth sentence.

The chapter closes with a discussion of available data indicating that the sentencing principles set out in the YCJA are being put into practice by the courts, as evidenced by the reduction in the number and proportion of custodial sentences being used.

KEY TERMS

mitigating factor

aggravating factor

provincial director

victim impact statement

conditional supervision

intensive rehabilitation and supervision sentence

reintegration leave

NOTES

1. An earlier draft of the legislation referred to "Canada" instead of the "same region." This principle was therefore weakened during legislative debate.

2. *B.V.N.*, [2004] BCJ no. 974 (CA) (QL).

3. *B.W.P.*, [2004] MJ no. 267 (CA) (QL).

4. *T.M.*, [2003] OJ no. 4120 (CA) (QL).

5. *B.V.N.*, *B.W.P.*, 2006 SCC 27.

6. A violent offence is one against the person, not purely against property—for example, robbery and assault.

7. *T.M.D.*, [2003] NSJ no. 488 (CA) (QL).

8. *J.J.C.*, [2003] PEIJ no. 99 (CA) (QL).

9. *C.D.; C.D.K.*, [2005] 3 SCR 668; 2005 SCC 78.

10. *B.W.P.*, [2004] MJ no. 267 (CA) (QL).

11. For an international comparison, see, for example, N. Bala and R. Jaremko, "Youth Justice—Historical and International Perspectives," in N. Bala, J. Hornick, and H. Snyder, eds., *Approaches to Youth Justice International Comparisons* (Toronto: Thompson Educational Publishing, 2002), chapter 1.

12. *Roper v. Simmons*, 543 US 551 (2005).

13. See, for example, "U.S. Supreme Court Declares Juvenile Death Penalty Unconstitutional," *PBS News* (March 3, 2005), online at http://www.pbs.org/newshour/extra/features/jan-june05/death_3-02.html.

14. For a discussion of this criticism as well as an examination in more detail of adult sentencing in general, see R. Bromwich, "Compassion, Human Rights and Adult Sentencing under the Y.C.J.A." (2002), 14 *Windsor Review of Legal and Social Issues* 71.

15. Sections 62, 63, 64(1) and (5), 70, 72(1) and (2), and 73(1).

16. *R v. B.D.*, March 24, 2006, docket nos. C42719 and C42923 (Ont. CA).

17. Section 7 of the *Canadian Charter of Rights and Freedoms*, part I of the *Constitution Act, 1982*, RSC 1985, app. II, no. 44.

18. A.W. Leschied, "Implementing Alternatives to Custody in Addressing Youth Crime: Applications of the Multisystemic Therapy Approach in Canada," article for a presentation made at *Beyond Prisons*, an international symposium hosted by Corrections Canada, CIDA, and Queen's University in Kingston, Ontario, March 1998, at 4.

19. Department of Justice Canada, "The Use of Custody Under the Youth Criminal Justice Act" (November 2005), online at http://justice.gc.ca/en/ps/yj/research/doob-sprott/section1.html.

20. See, for example, "McGuinty Government Slashes Youth Custody Beds," *OPSEU News Release* (May 2, 2005), online at http://www.opseu.org/news/Press2005/may22005.htm.

EXERCISES AND REVIEW

Review Questions

1. Where in the YCJA are the purpose and principles of sentencing expressed? Where else in the legislation is sentencing mentioned?

2. When (if ever) must a non-custodial sentence be reviewed? What about a custodial sentence?

3. Name four situations in which a youth might be sentenced to custody.

   a.

   b.

c.

d.

4. List two mitigating factors that a judge might consider (under s. 38(3)) in deciding to impose a lighter youth sentence.

   a.

   b.

5. List two aggravating factors that a judge might consider (under s. 38(3)) in deciding to impose a harsher youth sentence.

   a.

   b.

6. How long can a youth, sentenced as a youth, be committed to custody for first-degree murder?

7. How long can a youth, sentenced as an adult, be placed in custody for a conviction for first-degree murder?

8. What is the maximum fine a youth can be ordered to pay?

9. Must a youth participate in rehabilitative treatment while in custody? In what circumstances?

Discussion Questions

1. Under the YCJA, a court can sentence a youth convicted of a serious crime to "intensive rehabilitative custody." A youth who meets the criteria for such sentencing need not consent to this kind of sentence. Do you think forced participation in treatment or rehabilitation programs is a good idea? List some advantages and disadvantages.

2. The YCJA allows for the use of victim impact statements in youth justice court. This change from the previous regime has been somewhat controversial. Do you know the reasons for the controversy? If not, identify some possible advantages and disadvantages of increased victim participation in the sentencing process.

3. Some experts believe that probation is actually the most effective sentence when it comes to reducing youth recidivism. The research about probation is partly credited with providing an impetus to support other justice system initiatives such as conditional supervision and reintegration leave. Why might probation or other forms of supervision work particularly well for youths?

PART IV

Emerging Trends in the Youth Criminal Justice System

CHAPTER 12

Restorative Justice and the Young Offender

■ CHAPTER OBJECTIVES

After completing this chapter, you should be able to:

- Describe the history of diversion in the young offender criminal justice system.

- Describe the fundamental principles of alternative dispute resolution (ADR), restorative justice, and mediation.

- Describe the principles of diversion and restorative justice set out in the *Youth Criminal Justice Act.*

- Explain the difference between extrajudicial measures and extrajudicial sanctions.

- Describe the key principles of interest-based mediation, sentencing circles, and family group conferencing.

- List some primary criticisms made of alternative dispute resolution (ADR)–based programs.

- Critically assess current outcomes of restorative justice practices under the YCJA.

Introduction

In its decision in *Gladue v. The Queen*,[1] the Supreme Court of Canada endorsed the concept of **restorative justice** and the use of community-based alternatives to imprisonment. The court was asked to consider the meaning of s. 718.2(e) of the *Criminal Code*, which states that judges are to consider all reasonable alternatives to incarceration for all offenders, but "with particular attention to the circumstances of aboriginal offenders." The court ruled that this passage imposes a duty upon judges to recognize factors that affect offenders, particularly aboriginal people, such as poverty, substance abuse, and lack of education or employment opportunities, and to consider the role these factors may play in bringing the offender before the courts. In determining a sentence, judges must consider the types of sanctions that might be appropriate for an offender given his or her heritage.

restorative justice
an approach to justice that focuses on repairing the harm caused by crime; the intention is to hold the offender responsible for his or her actions by providing an opportunity for the parties directly affected by the crime (i.e., victim(s), offender, and community) to seek a resolution that affords healing and reparation

Any sentencing decision should take into account whether there is community support for the offender and community programs that provide alternatives to incarceration. The court recognized that restorative justice approaches may differ from one community to another, but that they tend to be community-based.

Although the *Gladue* case specifically dealt with aboriginal offenders, the court clearly indicated that the aims of restorative justice should apply to all offenders. The court also rejected the view that a restorative approach is a more lenient approach to crime, or that a sentence focusing on restorative justice is necessarily a lighter sentence. Restoring harmony involves determining sentences that respond to the needs of the victim, the community, and the offender.

Clearly, it is in the best interests of society to support offenders in turning away from crime and in learning to behave in socially acceptable ways when they return to the community. Groups concerned with the rehabilitation of offenders have tended to promote restorative justice approaches, arguing that they encourage offenders to feel and express remorse, to recognize the harm they have done to their victims, and to accept responsibility for their actions. Moreover, restorative processes can provide an opportunity to address underlying causes, although this can occur only if the community has programs to address issues such as alcohol and substance abuse, anger management, and mental illness.

alternative dispute resolution (ADR)
a range of processes for dispute resolution that are truly alternative to the existing judicial system, as well as processes that modify or improve upon practices and procedures currently in use within the existing court system (i.e., mediation)

Restorative justice by its nature is a form of **alternative dispute resolution (ADR)**. The most reported forms of restorative justice come from the aboriginal or First Nations cultures and can best be described as "healing circles." Another form is found in the Victim Offender Reconciliation Programs (VORP). While the techniques used in each form may differ, the ultimate goal remains the same: repairing and restoring severed relationships and enabling healing. Restorative justice programs recognize that there is a relational rift that occurs when a wrong is committed. This rift occurs between the offender and his or her victim, the victim's family, the broader community, and lastly the offender and his or her family. Reconciliation or the healing of these relationships is vital for the rehabilitation of all affected parties.

The forms of truth and justice sought in restorative justice processes are quite different from what is handed out in a traditional court of justice. The adversarial system's focus is on the determination of factual truth. The judge achieves this by considering the presented evidence and ensuring trial fairness. A restorative justice process is not only interested in factual truth, but also in assisting in the healing of the relationships that were effected by the offender's actions.

It is this focus on healing that made restorative justice particularly attractive to the drafters of the YCJA. The YCJA recognizes the social and psychological benefits of reconciling young offenders to the individuals—whether victims, family members, community members, or others—and groups that are affected by their criminal behaviour.

Restorative Justice and the Young Offender

Since Canadian youth criminal law was first conceived in the early 1900s, federal legislators have promoted the use of strategies for dealing with adolescent offenders outside of the formal justice system (known broadly as "alternative measures") as an appropriate means to address youth crime.

The *Juvenile Delinquents Act* (JDA), with its strong patriarchal approach, promoted "training and support" as the way to reduce youth criminality. As a result, early diversion programs focused on discipline and modelling normative behaviour. In 1984, the *Young Offenders Act* (YOA) emphasized the protection of offenders' rights by employment of criminal procedures and due process. The YOA emphasized the importance of using alternative measures and the least intrusive interventions when dealing with youth crime. In the Alternative Measures Program under the YOA, the Crown attorney decided which offenders would be referred to the program, based upon the offender's history and the type of charge laid by police. If the offender was successful, then the charge would be "stayed" by the Crown.

If we were to place the JDA and YOA on a continuum with the far left emphasizing a child-welfare-based law with minimal rights protection and the far right of the continuum categorized as a criminalized process with an emphasis on offender rights and due process, the JDA would be at the far left of the continuum and the YOA at the right. The *Youth Criminal Justice Act* (YCJA) would be just right of centre because it represents an attempt to balance offender rights and due process, with an emphasis on finding the least intrusive intervention appropriate to an offender's needs.

However, it is also important to note that most, if not all, of the alternative measures available under the YCJA were also allowed under the YOA; at least arguably, all of Canada's youth justice statutes have attempted similarly to divert adolescents from the criminal process, despite differences in the way they have been applied. Despite their differences, all three acts emphasize the importance of using alternative, non-judicial methods to try and reduce youth crime. The question that researchers now ask is not whether non-judicial interventions reduce recidivism in young offenders, but which program designs are the most effective.

Restorative Justice and the YCJA

The YCJA allows for essentially two forms of alternative dispute resolution: pre-charge (**extrajudicial measures** [EJM]) and post-charge (**extrajudicial sanctions** [EJS]). The YCJA sets out program design criteria that stress both "restorative justice" and "interest-based alternative dispute resolution" principles.

Section 5 of the YCJA sets out the objectives for EJM and EJS programs. These objectives are to

(a) provide an effective and timely response to offending behaviour outside the bounds of judicial measures,

(b) encourage young persons to acknowledge and repair the harm caused to the victim and the community,

(c) encourage families of young persons—including extended families where appropriate—and the community to become involved in the design and implementation of those measures,

(d) provide an opportunity for victims to participate in decisions related to the measures selected and to receive reparation, and

(e) respect the rights and freedoms of young persons and be proportionate to the seriousness of the offence.

These objectives are consistent with the federal Department of Justice's definition of restorative justice, which includes the following goals:

extrajudicial measures ways used by police to divert young people who are (pre-charged) suspected of committing a crime from the criminal justice system

extrajudicial sanctions post-charge programs designed for young people, when there is sufficient evidence for prosecution, that address a young person's criminal activities without resort to traditional sentences

1. repairing harm caused by the crime,

2. collaboration and inclusion (for example, victims, family, police, judges, probation), and

3. healing/forgiveness.

While the YCJA confirms the validity of ADR and restorative justice principles, there remains very few of these programs in existence. In fact, of the programs that do exist, the majority pre-date the YCJA. These programs are completely voluntary and generally are the result of a post-charge referral. At present, Ontario has only pilot EJS programs running in a few of the major urban centres. There are no provincially funded EJM programs in Ontario at the time of writing.

Restorative Justice: A Form of ADR

"Alternative dispute resolution" is a broad term used to describe any method that employs a non-adversarial approach to resolve disputes. The adversarial system relies upon a neutral "trier of fact" (judge) to determine either guilt or innocence of an accused in criminal proceedings or liability of a defendant in civil proceedings. These determinations are based on evidence and findings of fact. As a result, this system is very formal and procedural in nature. ADR systems tend to be less formal and not as backward-looking as the adversarial system. ADR methods are more process oriented. They often make use of a neutral third party who assists the disputants in resolving their conflict.

An ADR program can involve the use of several different methods, including negotiation, facilitation, mediation, and arbitration. Negotiation is the process whereby interested parties resolve disputes, agree upon courses of action, bargain for individual or collective advantage, and/or attempt to craft outcomes that serve their mutual interests. Facilitation involves the design and overseeing of a process that assists parties in achieving their interests. In arbitration, a neutral third party is empowered by the parties to decide the outcome of a dispute. The decision of the arbitrator can be in the form of a final order (binding arbitration) or be a suggested resolution (non-binding arbitration). Mediation is a dispute resolution process that assists parties in finding their own way to resolve conflicts.

Some ADR programs can be highly informal and disputant-centred (facilitation), while others are highly structured (arbitration). Mediation falls somewhere in the middle.

Interest-Based Mediation

**interest-based
mediation**
a type of mediation
based on a third-party
neutral assisting the
parties to understand
the needs and desires
of each other in order to
resolve a dispute

As discussed above, mediation is a dispute resolution process that assists affected parties in finding their own way to resolve conflicts. Unlike the adversarial system, where a neutral third party (the judge) imposes a ruling, mediation allows the parties to determine and impose their own solution. In **interest-based mediation**, the primary focus of the mediator is not to judge each side's position but to assist each party in grasping the other's interests (needs and desires) and then assist the parties in tailoring a solution that meets these interests.

Aspects of interest-based mediation make it a viable restorative justice/ADR process that can be applied in young offender cases. This is particularly true for situations where there is a clear victim. Property offences (for example, vandalism, theft, and mischief) and minor assaults are situations that can be dealt with through this form of ADR. An example where this has successfully worked is in the Victim Offender Reconciliation Program. The program was introduced in Kitchener, Ontario in 1974 by Mark Jantzi and the Mennonite Central Committee (MCC) and has been adopted by different agencies across Canada. The program is offered on a voluntary basis to both adults and young persons and can be used at both the pre-charge and post-charge stage.

Sentencing Circles

While the majority of cases where **sentencing circles** have been used involved aboriginal offenders and victims,[2] there has been increasing evidence that this model can and should be available to all offenders. Sentencing circles are part of the court process and, as the name implies, occur after a finding of guilt.

Sentencing circles generally operate in the following manner. After a finding or admission of guilt, the court invites interested members of the community to join the judge, prosecutor, defence counsel, police, social service providers, and community elders, along with the offender, the victim, and their families and supporters, to meet in a circle to discuss the offence, the factors that may have contributed to it, sentencing options, and ways of reintegrating the offender into the community. Everyone is given the chance to speak. Often the circle will suggest a restorative community sentence involving some form of restitution to the victim, community service, and/or treatment or counselling. Sometimes members of the circle will offer to help ensure that the offender lives up to the obligations of the community sentence, while others may offer to provide support to the victim.

The circle process can be a valuable means of getting input and advice from the community to help the judge set an appropriate and effective sentence. It is important to note, though, that while sentencing circles can make recommendations, including a period of custody, the judge is not bound to accept the circle's recommendations.

sentencing circle
a group of people, including the accused, the victim, families, justice system players, and members of the community who make recommendations to the court regarding appropriate sentencing

Family Group Conferencing

Family group conferencing (FGC) was originally developed as part of the criminal justice system in the Australasian countries.[3] This ADR process focuses on joint decision making by bringing together the victim, the offender, and their families to address the harm caused by the criminal behaviour. The purpose of the conference is to provide an opportunity for healing and to promote the development of a plan to avoid reoffending. Similar to mediation-based programs, family group conferencing suggests that the offender needs to realize the impact that his or her behaviour has had on the victim and participate in finding a solution to restore the damage. Family group conferencing acknowledges the need for the offender to go through this process with adequate support from his or her family.

family group conferencing
an ADR process with Australian origins that brings together the offender, the victim, and their families to promote healing and to develop a plan to prevent reoffending

Proponents of FGC suggest the following reasons why it may be a more valid process than the criminal justice system for certain crimes:

- It gives families the opportunity to participate in the decision making and care of their children.

- It offers a collaborative, strengths-based, and culturally sensitive approach in helping families.

- Neutral facilitation is provided by community service agencies.

- It creates plans that are realistic, achievable, and long lasting.

- It enables youth to strengthen relationships and vital attachments with family, community, and culture.

- It restores balance and harmony for families and promotes understanding.

Criticisms of Restorative Justice/ADR

The restorative justice/ADR process is not without its critics, especially in the context of criminal proceedings. Criminal matters involve disputes with the courts focusing on issues of guilt, punishment, and justice. The state in the criminal context is charged with ensuring that justice is served and that the overall safety of citizens is preserved. Conversely, civil disputes are seen as private in nature—between individual parties—and deal with such issues as negligence and compensation. ADR, and in particular mediation, has been successfully employed in civil matters; the main reason is that both processes seek the same outcome, which is settlement. Settlement is not the primary goal of criminal law and the criminal justice system. This system is required to take into account the public's interests, safety, and justice.

The use of restorative justice/ADR may resolve matters between the offender and victim but fail in addressing broader public interests. Similarly, ADR processes such as mediation and sentencing circles are seen as private processes, and therefore admissions and settlements are often sealed or subject to binding "gag" orders that limit the public admission of wrongdoing, further eroding the public perception that a just outcome was achieved.

Even with these criticisms, mediation-based programs, sentencing circles, and family group conferencing have important roles to play in the rehabilitation of young offenders. These programs have had success in meeting the needs of offenders and victims while imposing conditions that are meaningful to the offender and the broader community.

Restorative Justice Under the YCJA: A Critical Assessment

There are several reasons it is difficult to accurately assess the effectiveness of the operation of restorative justice measures under the YCJA. First, the statute is still quite new. At the time of writing, the YCJA has been in force for only about three years. As a result, information about the effectiveness of the law is still emerging. Second, the informal nature of restorative justice measures means that accurate data about the extent to which they are used are not always kept. For example, police may not keep or publish statistical data about how many warnings, cautions, or referrals officers make under the YCJA. Furthermore, the outcomes of informal interventions, such as extrajudicial measures, are hard to track. It is difficult to say with certainty whether adolescents given such sanctions are less likely to reoffend, especially because recidivism by a person originally dealt with informally may be recorded as a first offence.

Despite these difficulties with data collection, it does seem that we can say with some certainty that, overall, police and Crown prosecutors are using the alternative measures available to them under the YCJA more frequently than they made use of parallel provisions under the YOA. It is evident from available information that a large number of adolescents are being dealt with informally under the YCJA. Statistics Canada reports indicate that, in 2004, more than 101,000 youths were "cleared by other means" rather than being charged, compared with the 78,000 youths who received criminal charges.[4] There remains, however, inconsistency in the use of the extrajudicial provisions of the YCJA across the country. Different provinces have very different rates of recorded youth crime and of adolescents charged.[5] Research by the Department of Justice Canada into annual rates and proportions of young persons charged showed large reductions in charge rates. In 2002 and 2003, in Manitoba, Ontario, New Brunswick, Alberta, Nova Scotia, and British Columbia, police and Crown prosecutors appeared to be making good use of the YCJA's alternative measures provisions. However, the same study showed that Saskatchewan and the Northwest Territories showed no evidence of a change in approach by officials as a result of the passage of the new Act. The evidence from Quebec, Prince Edward Island, and Newfoundland and Labrador showed little reduction, but, especially in the case of Quebec, this may be due to a predisposition on the part of justice system officials in those provinces to deal with youth informally under the YOA.[6]

Still more difficult to assess than the level of use of ADR processes under the YCJA is the effectiveness of these measures. However, the information that is available does imply that use of these measures meets the principled objectives of the legislation, particularly in addressing underlying causes of youth crime, while reducing recidivism rates in a cost-effective manner. Comprehensive information about the effectiveness of such programs is simply not available. However, individual agencies and jurisdictions are endeavouring to provide data in this regard. St. Leonard's Society of London, Ontario is one agency that provides pre-charge extrajudicial measures and post-charge extrajudicial sanctions programs to youth who commit offences. Services provided by the agency include sentencing circles, administration of family group conferences, and supervision of community service hours. A study conducted to evaluate the effectiveness of these programs showed that, through them, a "significant number of youth were being diverted from the youth criminal justice system" and thereafter not continuing through the courts. The study also showed a close match between the stated objectives of diversion in the legislation and the program's elements.[7]

Chapter Summary

This chapter outlined the history and general principles behind restorative justice and ADR in the context of youth criminal justice. A key purpose of the YCJA is to increase the use of ADR-based approaches to deal with more adolescents outside the formal court system. While different jurisdictions within Canada have put these approaches into effect to varying degrees, it appears that, overall, many adolescents are being dealt with informally as a result. Available evidence indicates that these approaches are having the intended effect of reducing youth recidivism and incarceration rates. As youth courts adapt to the custody-limiting provisions of the YCJA, it must turn to appropriate alternatives to incarceration. As a result, more ADR-based programs are being developed by community agencies and other service providers.

KEY TERMS

restorative justice

alternative dispute resolution (ADR)

extrajudicial measures

extrajudicial sanctions

interest-based meditation

sentencing circle

family group conferencing

NOTES

1. *Gladue v. The Queen*, [1999] 1 SCR 688.

2. See Department of Justice Canada, "Rethinking Access to Criminal Justice in Canada: A Critical Review of Needs, Responses and Restorative Justice Initiatives," online at http://justice.gc.ca/en/ps/rs/rep/2003/rr03-2.pdf.

3. C. Adler and J. Wundersitz, eds., *Family Group Conferencing and Juvenile Justice: The Way Forward or Misplaced Optimism?* (Canberra, Australia: Australian Institute of Criminology, 1994).

4. Statistics Canada, *The Daily*, July 21, 2005, data available on CANSIM tables 252-0013 and 252-0014; see also (2004), vol. 25, no. 5 *Juristat: Crime Statistics in Canada.*

5. See Department of Justice Canada, "The Impact of the Youth Criminal Justice Act on Police Charging Practices," online at http://www.canadajustice.ca/en/ps/yj/research/pcarrington-jschulenberg/section3a.html#r32.

6. Ibid.

7. P. Radley, *St. Leonard's Society of London Evaluation of Extrajudicial Measures Program: Final Report* (London, ON: Public Partner Inc., 2006).

EXERCISES AND REVIEW

True or False Questions

_____ 1. The use of restorative justice in young offender matters only began with the introduction of the YOA.

_____ 2. The notion of the use of restorative justice in criminal proceedings is set out in the *Criminal Code*.

_____ 3. EJM and EJS are programs set out in the YOA.

_____ 4. Reparation of harm and healing is the primary goal of restorative justice.

_____ 5. EJM and EJS are not voluntary programs.

_____ 6. Family group conferencing is a different name for a sentencing circle.

_____ 7. The main criticism of ADR is that it costs too much.

_____ 8. The YCJA emphasizes the use of the justice system more than the YOA did.

_____ 9. There were no diversion programs under the JDA.

_____ 10. There is still debate regarding whether restorative justice works.

Review Questions

1. Explain the significance of *Gladue v. The Queen* and the impact it has had on criminal proceedings.

2. Describe what is meant by the abbreviation ADR.

3. Explain the fundamental purpose(s) of restorative justice.

4. Describe the difference between extrajudicial measures and extrajudicial sanctions.

5. Discuss the philosophical differences between interest-based mediation and the criminal justice system.

6. What is the main criticism of ADR being used in a court proceeding?

Discussion Questions

1. You have been hired by a local community organization to assist in the development of a new extrajudicial measures program. Based on the principles of the YCJA, develop the key guiding principles for the new program.

2. You are the community representative on a provincial government committee charged with creating government-funded extrajudicial sanctions. As a member of the committee, your first task is to present to the other members a description of the various types of programs that are available.

3. Some observers have argued that the YCJA, in trying to balance the diversion philosophies of the JDA and the YOA, has led to an unresponsive and less effective Act. Consider the philosophies of each Act and discuss whether you agree or disagree with this statement.

4. Do you think the use of ADR is appropriate when addressing young offenders? List some advantages and disadvantages.

CHAPTER 13

Emerging Issues and Youth Crime: Changing Social Realities and Public Perceptions

▇ CHAPTER OBJECTIVES

After completing this chapter, you should be able to:

- Identify emerging public perceptions and new realities relating to youth crime, particularly with respect to gangs and guns, globalization, technological changes, shifting immigration patterns, changing gender roles, and international tensions.

- Understand problems relating to the difference between public perceptions and realities indicated by available evidence.

- Describe potential ways to address the social factors that contribute to violent youth crime.

Introduction

As discussed briefly in chapter 1, youth crime and its public perception are issues with both ongoing and emerging dimensions. Certain aspects of adolescence as a developmental stage have not changed, and likely will not change, over time. Adolescents have always had certain attributes, such as their physical and psychological immaturity and lack of experience, that lead them to take more risks than adults and to push social boundaries. Adolescents are also vulnerable in ways that adults are less so, and as a result suffer victimization by crime disproportionately.

However, while adolescence as a phase of human development, and certain general patterns of adolescent offending, do not appear to have changed nearly as much as the media would lead us to believe, our social understanding of adolescence does change, as does our society. As a result, certain aspects of adolescence and youth crime do show historical changes. Also, several changes in particular to our society have led to changes in both the public's perception of youth crime and the reality of that crime. Changes in the real nature of youth crime do not always correspond to how the public *thinks* it is changing. Gangs and guns, globalization, technological changes, shifting immigration patterns, changing gender roles, and tensions in international politics are emerging factors contributing to anti-youth sentiment on the part of the Canada public. However, the perception that youth crime is a growing problem is not borne out by statistics.

Gangs and Guns

In recent years, certain high-profile cases of gun violence have given rise to a great deal of public concern about increases in the use of guns and the proliferation of youth gangs in Canada. Much of this concern was led by media reports about Toronto, Canada's largest city. Toronto's rate of gun-related homicides increased rapidly in the early years of the 21st century,[1] reaching a record year in 2005. The shooting death of a 15-year-old girl, Jane Creba, and injuries suffered by six other bystanders who were struck by stray bullets in a gang shooting while shopping on Yonge Street on Boxing Day 2005,[2] gave rise to a media and political outcry. The shootings were associated with gang activity by young males, and young black men in particular; of the eight people charged in connection with Creba's death, three were dealt with under the *Youth Criminal Justice Act* (YCJA) because they were adolescents. This outcry resulted in gun control becoming a major issue in the debates leading up to Canada's January 23, 2006 federal election. Toronto's mayor led the call for the banning of handguns.[3]

It is not only the availability of guns that has been blamed by commentators for Toronto's surge in gun violence. Many see at the root of the problems a celebration of guns and violence in our culture. Music, particularly some varieties of the rap and heavy metal genres, entertainment, video games, and war toys have been blamed for gun violence and gang activity. Anecdotally, police report incidents involving teens using toy or imitation guns during criminal activity, such as "armed robbery." Several Greater Toronto Area (GTA) mayors are considering banning toy guns; Scugog Township, located north of Oshawa, became the first Ontario municipality to ban minors from playing with toy guns in public places.[4] Other commentators focus on economic disadvantage and social marginalization suffered by minority youth, and particularly black youth, as a key cause of gang activity.[5]

It is difficult to say with certainty what social, cultural, or other factors cause increases in gang activity and gun violence like that being experienced in Toronto. However, where empirical data are available, they do not support the proposition that gun violence and gang activity are dramatically on the rise in Canada. As discussed elsewhere in this chapter and in chapter 1, far from showing such an increase, data from 2005 show that Canada's rates of violent crime and youth crime have fallen. It is possible that fears by youth of retaliation by gang members have prevented the reporting of significant amounts of gang activity. Available, reliable information about youth gangs in Canada is relatively scarce. Police and the general public anecdotally share perceptions that youth gang activity and gun violence are on the increase. However, empirical data do not yet support this belief. It is clear that there are pockets of gun violence of great concern in Toronto. However, it is not evident from available data that violent crime, gun violence, or gang activity are dramatically on the rise overall in Canada. Media reports about gun violence and gang activity are uneven; where the victims are middle class and white, the stories receive more coverage, giving rise to potentially misguided understandings about the extent of these problems.[6] Comprehensive data on youth gang activity have not been compiled for very long. The 2002 Canadian Police Survey on Youth Gangs was the first survey of its kind conducted on a national scale. The existence of 434 youth gangs was reported, with a membership of 7,071 adolescents, comprising only 0.24 percent of the youth population.[7] Nonetheless, a troubling aspect of Canada's youth gang membership is the disproportionately high representation of visible minority youth—particularly African Canadian—and aboriginal youth in the gangs. Also troubling is the wide range of gang activity reported, from assault to drug trafficking to burglary. Nonetheless, the survey's findings indicated more concern about possible future problems with gangs and guns in Canada than it did about the current situation.

A large part of Canada's perceived and real problem with gangs and guns seems to be American in origin. According to the investigative findings of Toronto police, many, if not most, of the handguns used in Toronto's gun homicides are being smuggled in from the United States.[8] Just as the guns are imported from our southern neighbour, so too is our impression that gun use and gang activity are on the rise. While only a fractional percentage of Canadian youth reportedly participate in youth gangs, a far larger proportion of American youth are involved in such activity.[9] Because we are saturated with American media reports, it is easy for Canadians to mistakenly perceive gang violence to be a more immediate and local concern than it actually is.

Changing Gender Roles

It is a common perception of the Canadian public that adolescent girls have become more criminally active generally, and more prone to violent behaviour specifically, than girls in generations past. Police report that more girls are becoming involved in youth gangs across our country.[10] Anecdotally, police officers report girls taking on a more active role in gangs rather than being the classic "moll," or gangsta's girlfriend. Public concern about female aggression and violence has rarely been higher. Some of the recent concern about gang activity has been about the involvement of young women in gangs. Newspapers and TV newscasts regularly report stories about young girls involved in violence and, most recently, gang activity. For example, the 2003 murder by two adolescent girls of their mother in her bathtub, which led to their convictions for first-degree murder and receipt of ten-year jail sentences in June 2006, received nationwide media coverage.[11]

Available statistics, as discussed in chapters 1 and 2, do not generally support the perception that there has been a dramatic increase in youth crime by females. Despite subjective reports by officers that girls are committing a greater number of violent crimes, police figures estimate that young females comprise only 6 percent of gang membership throughout Canada. None of Canada's known gangs are composed exclusively of girls. Where females are gang members, they are not likely to occupy leadership positions in the criminal organization, however formally or informally it is structured. Young women are less likely to "graduate" from offending behaviour to adult criminality. There appears to be little evidence to support the belief that there are gangs of young women acting as conspicuously violent or as aggressive as their male counterparts. Even where females do commit violent crimes, the violence is generally less serious than that perpetrated by their male counterparts. An analysis of the type of violent offending by young female offenders reveals that two-thirds of female youths charged with a violent crime in 1999 were charged with common assault, compared with just under half (46 percent) of male youth.

It is not easy to determine how the current rate of crime by adolescent females compares with that of the past. Historically, females have always been largely absent from crime statistics and from studies of offending behaviour. It has often been assumed that young females do not engage in offences, but, as noted above with respect to the violent crime rate, this is not the case. Young women, like men, also commit minor property offences, such as shoplifting, with greater frequency than the uniform crime report data indicate, and with greater frequency than their male counterparts. This is also the case with prostitution. Females were more often charged as "runaways" under the *Juvenile Delinquents Act*, reflecting a greater familial protectiveness, or perhaps a more proprietary attitude toward young women.

Since girls still make up such a small minority of youth charged with offences, and particularly violent offences, the perception by police and the public that girls are "out of control" is not easily explained. However, certain other social factors, such as changes in gender roles, may shed light on why so many people share this misconception.

What our society expects of, and accepts from, women and girls in terms of their behaviour has changed markedly over the past 30 years or so. The overwhelming majority of females two generations ago were not educated to the same extent as males and were expected to have roles primarily in the home. As a result of cultural changes and feminist activism, women now enter the paid labour force in ever-increasing numbers, even taking on combat roles in the Canadian military. Females in Canada are entitled to equal treatment in education and under the law, and no longer expect to be treated as inferior to males. So, too, have the expectations of behaviour of adolescent girls changed. Girls are no longer expected to conduct themselves with timidity or subservience. This change in female roles and behaviour stands in contrast not only to Canada's past, but also to the expectations many new Canadians bring from their cultures of origin. Thus, the behaviour of young women can be surprising to adult members of our communities. It is likely, at least in part, as a result of these factors that the public increasingly perceives female youth to be unmanageable.

At least publicly and politically, most Canadians generally view women's advances toward equality in a positive light. Status of Women Canada, a federal government agency devoted to promoting gender equality and the full participation of women in the life of the country,[12] receives a good deal of public funding directed toward their goal, as do many similarly focused women's groups. Canada sees itself as an international leader in advancing women's equality. However, many people share varying levels of discomfort with the new roles taken on by women in our society. Their unease with this social change can underlie expressed sentiments that teenage girls are "out of control." Especially because women were historically primarily responsible for rearing children at home and have now moved on to broader roles in the public sphere, some people blame changing gender roles not only for a perceived increase in offending by girls, but also for an alleged increase in youth crime in general. Some writers expressly blame changing gender roles for perceived increases in adolescent offending, as well as a variety of other social ills. Stroud, for example, in *Contempt of Court* blames "feminists" and "deluded academic twits" for youth crime and for inadequacies he finds in laws designed to respond to it. He writes that the *Young Offenders Act* (YOA) is a "pure feminist dialectic" and "the product of a female fascist mindset."[13]

Even though crime by girls still constitutes a small proportion of overall offending by youth, it is significant and bears close consideration. Female youth crime poses unique problems for the Canadian justice and corrections systems, which are tailored primarily to male offenders. Rehabilitation programs, for example, are generally designed based on research about what treatments are most effective in controlling *male* violence. Custody facilities are generally not set up for handling inmates of both sexes. When female adolescents do offend, we are obligated to meet their **gender-specific** rehabilitative needs.

gender-specific
associated with persons of one gender to the exclusion of the other

Furthermore, although statistics do not currently support perceptions that girls are becoming increasingly involved in criminal activity as well as becoming more violent, there may indeed be such an increase on the horizon. Shifting gender roles might in fact be leading to an ultimate levelling of behaviour patterns between young males and females. It is possible that statistics are simply lagging behind in reflecting this new reality. Police anecdotally report that some of the change to girls' offending behaviour may be of a qualitative nature that may not be reflected in official statistics. Officers note that female offenders used to be "around the crime" instead of the ones actually committing the crimes. For example, they would wait outside while their boyfriends broke into a house. Now they are reportedly often the central players. It may also be that girls are more often dealt with informally, through extrajudicial measures or sanctions, than are boys, which may undermine the accuracy of available statistics. Close watch over the next few years of statistics, anecdotal reports, and other information sources respecting female offending behaviour is warranted in order for our justice system to deal appropriately with changes to female adolescents' behaviour—if such changes do take place.

However, on the basis of evidence now available, it appears that the relationship of real concern between young women and violence is not the perpetration of violent acts by girls but their victimization by violent males. It is particularly troubling that the public perceives young women to be increasingly perpetrators of violent behaviour when rates of victimization of teenage girls are considered. Young women are more likely to experience victimization by violence than any other category of person. While they are far less likely to commit crime than males, female youth are far more likely to be victimized by crime than male youth. In addition, female youth are more likely to be the victims of violence than male youth. It is hypothesized that the higher rates of victimization for female youth are attributable to their greater risk of sexual assault. Female young people aged 12 through 17 years were the primary victims in family assaults, including sexual assault and physical assault. These statistics speak to the continuing vulnerability of teenage females in the face of the growing social power of women in general; despite the gains attained by Canadian women in the last half-century, violence against women remains a serious social problem undermining women's equality that needs to be addressed.

Economic Globalization

globalization
the increasing economic interdependence of countries worldwide through a growing quantity and variety of cross-border transactions in goods and services, free international capital flows, and rapid, widespread distribution of technology

Economic **globalization** is increasing public perceptions of youth criminality and propensity for violence in important ways. With the increasing social and economic interaction and interdependence between people, organizations, and companies in disparate locations, globalization leads people to perceive themselves not just as members of a family, cultural group, or state but, increasingly, as citizens of a wider world. The saturation of television with several global news media networks has led to a greatly increased level of news reporting of violent crime, especially youth crime. We are now much more aware of incidents of violent crime by youth than we used to be. These reports give a sense of immediacy to such crimes, fostering in the public a sense that we have been victimized, or at least know someone who has been the victim of such crimes, when really the incidents have often taken place far away and affected no one to whom we are personally connected. This is most clearly the case regarding "school shootings," such as those at Columbine High in Littleton, Colorado and in Taber, Alberta in 1999 and, more recently, those in Montreal and Pennsylvania in 2006.[14]

In addition to the globalization of news media, we have advertising campaigns orchestrated by multinational companies that specifically target youth. As a result of these campaigns and global telecommunications via the Internet and other means, as described by Naomi Klein in *No Logo*,[15] youth subcultures in first world nations have global dimensions, identifying with and appearing more "like" each other than their forebears in any locality. Examples include "Goths," "punks," "skaters," and many more self-identified groups. These commodified subcultures contribute to perceptions on the part of the adult public that today's youth are alien to their elders, undesirable, and fundamentally unlike the youth of the past.

Technological Changes

"Thank God for high tech."

—Norman Olson, Commander of the Michigan Militia Corps,
an extreme right-wing group using the Internet[16]

Related to the globalization of youth culture are technological changes that play a significant new role in altering the nature of youth crime. In 2002, there were over two million Internet hosts and 840 million users around the world.[17] The importance of the Internet and other global telecommunications technology in changing Western society cannot be overestimated. The consequences of such changes are not all socially beneficial; new technologies have also made new kinds of crime possible and offered new ways for people to commit existing crimes worldwide. Law enforcement officials refer to these new types of criminal behaviour as **cybercrime**. Special units have been set up in police forces worldwide, including those in Canada, to deal with this cybercrime.

cybercrime
criminal activity committed on computers over the Internet

In chatrooms, on Internet "blog" sites, and by email people communicate with each other instantaneously around the globe. Although originally developed by the American military, the Internet has become a democratic information source and communications system. While this democratization of instantaneous communication is exciting and positive, it has also allowed for the international organization of criminal activity on a large scale. In 2004 alone, the FBI estimated cybercrime cost the United States about $400 billion. Unfortunately, the FBI also reported the same year that only about 5 percent of cybercriminals had been caught or convicted.[18]

As a result of the rapid development of new communications technologies, there is a large technological "generation gap." Youth, having grown up with these new technologies, tend to be far more computer literate than their parents. By virtue of their high level of computer literacy, adolescents have become involved in new varieties of criminal activity with surprising sophistication and dramatic consequences. **Hackers**—individuals who write malicious code to "break in" to and damage others' computers—have, in several high-profile cases, turned out to be adolescents.[19] For example, German youth Sven Juergens caused worldwide havoc with his "Sasser" worm virus, bringing banks, airlines, military bases, hospitals, and government buildings to a halt in 2004.[20] Juergens was relatively lucky in receiving only jail time for his crime; in 1997, two young Chinese hackers were sentenced to death.[21] High-speed **piracy**, involving the theft of downloaded entertainment materials such as music and movies, as well as the theft of software, especially by young people, also abounds.

Police officers also report the Internet has made it easy for alienated young people to connect with other disenfranchised youth and track down potentially harmful information. Anecdotally, police describe situations in which teens have created suicide pacts over the Internet, and report that, in extreme cases, teenagers have brought bombs to school after learning online how to build them. In addition, when online conversations between alienated young people focus on violent fantasies, the participants can get the impression that these acts are acceptable or justifiable because so many people seem to be agreeing. Also, when young people commit crimes of extreme violence, they often leave behind an electronic paper trail. For example, after 25-year-old Kimveer Gill embarked on a shooting spree at Dawson College in Montreal in 2006, killing one teenager and wounding 19 other people, his online diary, published on a "Goth" website, was widely publicized by the media. Gill posted photographs of himself pointing guns at the camera and wrote that he wanted to die in a hail of gunfire.

The Internet has also become a tool used by adolescents in simpler, more old-fashioned varieties of youth crime. Websites and email have been used by youth to bully, harass, and stalk other youth.

Despite public perception that adolescents are behind most cybercrime, evidence indicates it is actually adults who are responsible for much, if not the vast majority, of its more damaging varieties. While teenage hackers have committed high-profile mischief using malicious code, this often has had playful dimensions and was not generally intended to harm. For example, the Sasser worm, according to its inventor, was not intended to actually hurt anyone but rather to counter existing viruses. However, many adult career criminal entrepreneurs use the Internet for illicit purposes. Credit card fraud is one example of sophisticated crime facilitated by Internet use. Other examples of cybercrime committed by adults include hacking,

hackers
individuals who, by means of programming skills, gain illegal access to computer files or networks

piracy
unauthorized use or reproduction of copyrighted or patented software or other creative materials

the development of computer viruses, identity theft, and child pornography. In all of these sorts of cybercrime, adult career criminals engage in lucrative black market entrepeneurship electronically, gaining access to victims with whom they would not otherwise have contact.

In reality, a more compelling concern than that of adolescents using the Internet to commit crimes is that adolescents, by virtue of their high degree of computer literacy and frequent Internet use, are more likely than adults to fall victim to cybercrime. For example, adult sexual predators can gain access to young victims through Internet chatrooms. Another concern is that the Internet has provided a new venue for **hate crime**. The Internet has brought hate speech and hate literature to an audience who would not otherwise be exposed to it. Alienated adolescents who surf the Web will almost invariably come across hate sites. These adolescents are especially vulnerable to the messages in hate speech; their lack of life experience makes them less critical of what they read than adults. The influence of Internet hate speech on adolescents has even been linked to school shootings: Columbine students Dylan Klebold's and Eric Harris's killing spree was linked to their Internet use, particularly their interest in Neo-Nazi hate websites.[22] It therefore may be more appropriate to focus on ways of protecting adolescents from cybercrime rather than cracking down on their electronic offending.

hate crime
illegal activity motivated by prejudice against an identifiable group

Demographic Patterns

Patterns of immigration and birth rates have, in the past 30 or so years, dramatically affected the demographic makeup of North American nations and particularly the face of Canadian society. Young people make up a substantial proportion of Canada's population. In 2000, some 26 percent of Canada's population was composed of young people.[23] These young people, as a group, are visibly and culturally different from Canadian youth of past generations. Visible minority populations and populations of aboriginal people are increasing markedly relative to those of white Europeans. At the same time, Canada's white European population, and particularly the "baby boom" generation, is aging. Generally, non-aboriginal people whose families have been in Canada for more than one generation, and people of European descent in particular, tend to have lower birth rates.[24] As a consequence, we now have a large population of young people who are visibly culturally and racially different from the dominant mainstream of adults in Canadian society. Just as some 19th-century members of the Canadian public worried that orphans and non-British immigrants were of lesser "stock," many writers believe these differences contribute to racism and xenophobia—a fear of strangers or the unknown—lurking beneath today's public perceptions that we are facing a crisis of ever-increasing youth crime.

International Tensions

Perhaps the most troubling difference between contemporary perceptions of adolescent offending and those of the past relates to changes in international politics. While the late 20th century saw the emergence of global tourism on an unprecedented scale, with international borders decreasing in significance and relaxed international travel, our confidence in our safety at home and abroad has now been seriously undermined. The **al-Qaida** terrorist attacks of the early 21st century, most significantly those on September 11, 2001 in New York City, but also those that followed in London, England and Madrid, Spain, led to America's "war on terror" and tremendous public xenophobia about potential "terrorists," particularly those perceived to be Islamic. Although no al-Qaida attacks have taken place in Canada at the time of writing, in June 2006 mass arrests were made of 17 individuals who, as a "home-grown al-Qaida cell," were allegedly planning a series of major terrorist assaults on targets in southern Ontario. Five of the 17 people charged were youths at the time of their arrest. The Toronto-area arrests were preceded by 18 related arrests in the United States, Britain, Bosnia, Denmark, Sweden, and Bangladesh.[25] Those arrested in Canada self-identified with al-Qaida members abroad, had communicated via the Internet, and even ordered explosives online. This case is a significant example of technological changes and international politics as emerging factors that are changing the nature of contemporary youth crime and public perception of that crime.

It is likely that the June 2006 terrorism arrests will serve only to exacerbate public fears about alien, hostile youth living among us, and thereby increase public perception that youth violence in Canada is on the rise.

As is the case with other youth crime discussed in this chapter, adolescents are more likely to be victimized by people's fear of terrorism than they are to perpetrate it. Hate crime directed against youth perceived to be Islamic has increased since September 11, 2001, with young people at greater risk of victimization, such as assaults and bullying, than older adults.[26] Immediately following the 2006 arrests discussed above, a Toronto-area mosque was vandalized[27] in an act characterized by many as a response to the arrests. Furthermore, in all of the reported cases of planned al-Qaida terrorist attacks in New York, London, and most recently in Canada, the planning process involved one or more adults influencing impressionable adolescents and exploiting them to commit the crimes.[28] Thus, it may be more appropriate to focus on preventing such exploitation of adolescent alienation by adults than to concentrate on harsh consequences for adolescents who do offend.

> **al-Qaida**
> international terrorist network that has claimed responsibility for several attacks on western cities; "al-Qaida" means "the base"

Chapter Summary

Despite the media attention focused on youth crime, young people are not more likely to commit crimes than are adults, and youth crime and youth violence are not on the rise in Canada. However, adolescents are especially vulnerable and are more likely to be victimized by criminal offending than are adults. Available evidence indicates that this difference between public perceptions of adolescent offending and the reality of youth crime is as much of a problem for emerging issues relating to youth crime as it is for the more "old-fashioned" varieties. With respect to all of the emerging factors relating to youth crime discussed in this chapter—gangs and guns, globalization, shifting immigration patterns, tensions in international politics, changing gender roles, and technological changes—victimization and exploitation of youth by adult criminals appears to be a matter of greater concern than adolescent offending.

Of course, adolescent offending must also be addressed. However, it is evident that youth offending reflects a wide range of social problems, and should be approached within that broader context. Lawyers, judges, courts, community groups, social advocates, and politicians should seek to implement programs and initiatives that focus more on addressing these underlying social causes of youth crime than on forcefully "solving" the problem with the "long arm of the law."

KEY TERMS

gender-specific

globalization

cybercrime

hackers

piracy

hate crime

al-Qaida

NOTES

1. See, for example, R. Lamberti, "Gun Violence Is Way Up in Toronto This Year," *Toronto Sun*, December 31, 2003; "Three More Victims Die in Toronto Gun Violence," CTV.ca, September 18, 2005, online at http://www.ctv.ca.

2. See "8 Arrested in Jane Creba Shooting Death," CBC News, June 13, 2006, online at http://www.cbc.ca/toronto/story/to-creba20060613.html.

3. See "Support Ban on Handguns, Toronto's Mayor Urges," CBC News, December 31, 2005, online at http://www.cbc.ca/story/canada/national/2005/12/30/mayor_shootings051230.html.

4. See T. Woodcock, "Toy Gun Ban Goes Too Far," *Toronto Sun*, February 20, 2006.

5. See, for example, B. Powell, "After Jane, a Rallying Cry," *Toronto Star*, June 18, 2006, online at http://www.thestar.com.

6. Ibid.

7. Astwood Strategy Corporation, *2002 Canadian Police Survey on Youth Gangs*, Solicitor General Canada, catalogue no. PS4-4/2002.

8. See "Mayor Speaks Out Against Toronto Gun Violence," CTV.ca, August 8, 2005, online at http://www.ctv.ca.

9. Astwood Strategy Corporation, supra note 7.

10. "Number of Female Gang Members on the Rise: Police," CTV.ca, May 17, 2006, online at http://www.ctv.ca.

11. See "2 Sisters Get Maximum Penalty in Mother's Drowning," CBC News, June 20, 2006, online at http://www.cbc.ca/news/story/2006/06/30/bathtub-sisters.html.

12.   http://www.swc-cfc.gc.ca/index_e.html.

13.   C. Stroud, *Contempt of Court* (Toronto: Macmillan of Canada, 1992).

14.   For a thorough general discussion of school shootings, see, for example, K.S. Newman, *Rampage: The Social Roots of School Shootings* (New York: Perseus Books, 2004).

15.   N. Klein, *No Logo* (New York: HarperCollins, 2000).

16.   J. Sandberg, "Net Results: Some Nasty Creatures in Cyberspace," *The Globe and Mail*, December 13, 1994, reprinted from *The Wall Street Journal*.

17.   "Birth of the Internet," CBC News, March 7, 2006, online at http://www.cbc.ca/ news/background/internet.

18.   See "Lucrative Internet Crimes Difficult to Curb: Report," CBC News, July 5, 2005, online at http://www.cbc.ca/story/science/national/2005/07/05/ internet-crime050705.html.

19.   For example, the 2003 arrest by the RCMP of a 16-year-old Mississauga youth in connection with the Randex computer worm illustrates the ability of Canadian youth to commit criminal mischief by use of "malicious code." For discussion of this virus, see online at http://www.sophos.com/pressoffice/news/articles/2004/ 05/va_randexarrest.html.

20.   See Dalton and Hall, "Teenage Hacker Faces Jail for Global Net Virus," *The Scotsman*, May 10, 2004, online at http://news.scotsman.com/ topics.cfm?tid=45&id=531332004.

21.   Ibid.

22.   For discussion of Internet use by adolescent offenders, see D. Verton, *The Hacker Diaries: Confessions of Teenage Hackers* (New York: McGraw-Hill, 2002).

23.   Statistics Canada, "Children and Youth in Canada," Canadian Centre for Justice Statistics Profile Series, June 2001.

24.   For discussion of Canada's changing population demographics, see Statistics Canada, "Census of Population: Immigration, Birthplace and Birthplace of Parents, Citizenship, Ethnic Origin, Visible Minorities, and Aboriginal Peoples," *The Daily*, January 21, 2003, online at http://www.statcan.ca/Daily/English/ 030121/d030121a.htm.

25.   See, for example, Bell and Patrick, "Alleged Canadian Terror Plot Has Worldwide Links," *National Post*, June 4, 2006.

26.   See Statistics Canada, "Hate Crime in Canada: An Overview of Issues and Data Sources," Canadian Centre for Justice Statistics, 2001, catalogue no. 85-551-XIE.

27.   "Mosque Vandalized After Bomb Plot Sweep," CBC News, June 4, 2006, online at http://www.cbc.ca/story/canada/national/2006/06/04/mosque-vandalized.html.

28.   "Indepth: Toronto Bomb Plot Profiles of the Suspects," CBC News, June 12, 2006, online at http://www.cbc.ca/news/background/toronto-bomb-plot/suspects.html.

EXERCISES AND REVIEW
Review Questions

1. Describe what aspects of the nature of adolescence have not changed, and probably will not change, over time.

2. Discuss effective ways to reduce youth recidivism.

3. Describe some effects of economic globalization on the public's perceptions of, and realities in relation to, adolescent offending.

4. What sorts of social change are contributing to public and police perceptions that offending by adolescent females is on the rise?

5. Describe the different varieties of cybercrime and discuss ways in which adolescents are involved in, or affected by, each.

6. How are international tensions affecting public perceptions and realities about youth crime?

Discussion Questions

1. Using an Internet search engine, look up the terms "youth," "crime," and "violence" in combination. Conduct a review of the first 10 Web postings retrieved. Analyze the articles in terms of whether the article is concerned with, alludes to, mentions, or cites the following:

   a. gang activity

   b. race or ethnicity

   c. gender

   d. poverty

   e. social values

   f. adequacy of the law

   g. terrorism

   h. violence

   i. positive or negative views about youth

2. Discuss the implications to adolescents of the comment made by an extreme right-wing activist: "Thank God for high tech."

Youth Criminal Justice Act

An Act in respect of criminal justice for young persons and to amend and repeal other Acts

2002, c. 1

[Assented to February 19, 2002]

TABLE OF PROVISIONS

Preamble

SHORT TITLE

1. Short title

INTERPRETATION

2. Definitions

DECLARATION OF PRINCIPLE

3. Policy for Canada with respect to young persons

PART 1
EXTRAJUDICIAL MEASURES

Principles and Objectives

4. Declaration of principles
5. Objectives

Warnings, Cautions and Referrals

6. Warnings, cautions and referrals
7. Police cautions
8. Crown cautions
9. Evidence of measures is inadmissible

Extrajudicial Sanctions

10. Extrajudicial sanctions
11. Notice to parent
12. Victim's right to information

PART 2
ORGANIZATION OF YOUTH CRIMINAL JUSTICE SYSTEM

Youth Justice Court

13. Designation of youth justice court
14. Exclusive jurisdiction of youth justice court

15. Contempt against youth justice court
16. Status of offender uncertain
17. Youth justice court may make rules

Youth Justice Committees

18. Youth justice committees

Conferences

19. Conferences may be convened

Justices of the Peace

20. Certain proceedings may be taken before justices

Clerks of the Court

21. Powers of clerks

Provincial Directors

22. Powers, duties and functions of provincial directors

PART 3
JUDICIAL MEASURES

Consent to Prosecute

23. Pre-charge screening
24. Private prosecutions

Right to Counsel

25. Right to counsel

Notices to Parents

26. Notice in case of arrest or detention
27. Order requiring attendance of parent

Detention before Sentencing

28. Application of Part XVI of Criminal Code
29. Detention as social measure prohibited
30. Designated place of temporary detention

31. Placement of young person in care of responsible person

Appearance

32. Appearance before judge or justice

Release from or Detention in Custody

33. Application for release from or detention in custody

Medical and Psychological Reports

34. Medical or psychological assessment

Referral to Child Welfare Agency

35. Referral to child welfare agency

Adjudication

36. When young person pleads guilty

Appeals

37. Appeals

PART 4
SENTENCING

Purpose and Principles

38. Purpose
39. Committal to custody

Pre-sentence Report

40. Pre-sentence report

Youth Sentences

41. Recommendation of conference
42. Considerations as to youth sentence
43. Additional youth sentences
44. Custodial portion if additional youth sentence
45. Supervision when additional youth sentence extends the period in custody
46. Exception when youth sentence in respect of earlier offence
47. Committal to custody deemed continuous
48. Reasons for the sentence
49. Warrant of committal
50. Application of Part XXIII of *Criminal Code*
51. Mandatory prohibition order
52. Review of order made under section 51
53. Funding for victims
54. Where a fine or other payment is ordered
55. Conditions that must appear in orders
56. Communication of order
57. Transfer of youth sentence
58. Interprovincial arrangements
59. Review of youth sentences not involving custody
60. Provisions applicable to youth sentences on review

Adult Sentence and Election

61. Age for purpose of presumptive offences
62. Imposition of adult sentence

63. Application by young person
64. Application by Attorney General
65. Presumption does not apply
66. No election if youth sentence
67. Election—adult sentence
68. Proof of notice under subsection 64(4)
69. Paragraph (a) "presumptive offence"—included offences
70. Inquiry by court to young person
71. Hearing—adult sentences
72. Test—adult sentences
73. Court must impose adult sentence
74. Application of Parts XXIII and XXIV of *Criminal Code*
75. Inquiry by the court to the young person
76. Placement when subject to adult sentence
77. Obligation to inform—parole
78. Release entitlement
79. If person convicted under another Act
80. If person who is serving a sentence under another Act is sentenced to an adult sentence
81. Procedure for application or notice

Effect of Termination of Youth Sentence

82. Effect of absolute discharge or termination of youth sentence

PART 5
CUSTODY AND SUPERVISION

83. Purpose
84. Young person to be held apart from adults
85. Levels of custody
86. Procedural safeguards
87. Review
88. Functions to be exercised by youth justice court
89. Exception if young person is twenty years old or older
90. Youth worker
91. Reintegration leave
92. Transfer to adult facility
93. When young person reaches twenty years of age
94. Annual review
95. Orders are youth sentences
96. Recommendation of provincial director for conditional supervision of young person
97. Conditions to be included in custody and supervision order
98. Application for continuation of custody
99. Report
100. Reasons
101. Review of youth justice court decision
102. Breach of conditions
103. Review by youth justice court
104. Continuation of custody

105. Conditional supervision
106. Suspension of conditional supervision
107. Apprehension
108. Review by provincial director
109. Review by youth justice court

PART 6
PUBLICATION, RECORDS AND INFORMATION

Protection of Privacy of Young Persons
110. Identity of offender not to be published
111. Identity of victim or witness not to be published
112. Non-application

Fingerprints and Photographs
113. *Identification of Criminals Act* applies

Records That May Be Kept
114. Youth justice court, review board and other courts
115. Police records
116. Government records

Access to Records
117. Exception—adult sentence
118. No access unless authorized
119. Persons having access to records
120. Access to R.C.M.P. records
121. Deemed election
122. Disclosure of information and copies of record
123. Where records may be made available
124. Access to record by young person

Disclosure of Information in a Record
125. Disclosure by peace officer during investigation
126. Records in the custody, etc., of archivists
127. Disclosure with court order

Disposition or Destruction of Records and Prohibition on Use and Disclosure
128. Effect of end of access periods
129. No subsequent disclosure

PART 7
GENERAL PROVISIONS

Disqualification of Judge
130. Disqualification of judge

Substitution of Judge
131. Powers of substitute youth justice court judge

Exclusion from Hearing
132. Exclusion from hearing

Transfer of Charges
133. Transfer of charges

Forfeiture of Recognizances
134. Applications for forfeiture of recognizances
135. Proceedings in case of default

Offences and Punishment
136. Inducing a young person, etc.
137. Failure to comply with sentence or disposition
138. Offences
139. Offence and punishment

Application of Criminal Code
140. Application of *Criminal Code*
141. Sections of *Criminal Code* applicable
142. Part XXVII and summary conviction trial provisions of *Criminal Code* to apply

Procedure
143. Counts charged in information
144. Issue of subpoena
145. Warrant

Evidence
146. General law on admissibility of statements to apply
147. Statements not admissible against young person
148. Testimony of a parent
149. Admissions
150. Material evidence
151. Evidence of a child or young person
152. Proof of service
153. Seal not required

Forms, Regulations and Rules of Court
154. Forms
155. Regulations

Agreements with Provinces
156. Agreements with provinces

Programs
157. Community-based programs

PART 8
TRANSITIONAL PROVISIONS
158. Prohibition on proceedings
159. Proceedings commenced under *Young Offenders Act*
160. Offences committed before this section in force
161. Applicable sentence
162. Proceedings commence with information
163. Application to delinquency and other offending behaviour
164. Agreements continue in force
165. Designation of youth justice court

PART 9

CONSEQUENTIAL AMENDMENTS, REPEAL AND COMING INTO FORCE

Consequential Amendments

166. *Canada Evidence Act*

167-170. *Contraventions Act*

171-174. *Corrections and Conditional Release Act*

175-186. *Criminal Code*

187-189. *DNA Identification Act*

190-194. *Extradition Act*

195. *Mutual Legal Assistance in Criminal Matters Act*

196-197. *Prisons and Reformatories Act*

198. *Transfer of Offenders Act*

Repeal

199. Repeal of R.S., c. Y-1

Coming into Force

200. Coming into force

2002, c. 1

[Assented to February 19, 2002]

PREAMBLE

WHEREAS members of society share a responsibility to address the developmental challenges and the needs of young persons and to guide them into adulthood;

WHEREAS communities, families, parents and others concerned with the development of young persons should, through multi-disciplinary approaches, take reasonable steps to prevent youth crime by addressing its underlying causes, to respond to the needs of young persons, and to provide guidance and support to those at risk of committing crimes;

WHEREAS information about youth justice, youth crime and the effectiveness of measures taken to address youth crime should be publicly available;

WHEREAS Canada is a party to the United Nations Convention on the Rights of the Child and recognizes that young persons have rights and freedoms, including those stated in the *Canadian Charter of Rights and Freedoms* and the *Canadian Bill of Rights*, and have special guarantees of their rights and freedoms;

AND WHEREAS Canadian society should have a youth criminal justice system that commands respect, takes into account the interests of victims, fosters responsibility and ensures accountability through meaningful consequences and effective rehabilitation and reintegration, and that reserves its most serious intervention for the most serious crimes and reduces the over-reliance on incarceration for non-violent young persons;

NOW, THEREFORE, Her Majesty, by and with the advice and consent of the Senate and House of Commons of Canada, enacts as follows:

SHORT TITLE

1. This Act may be cited as the *Youth Criminal Justice Act.*

INTERPRETATION

2. (1) The definitions in this subsection apply in this Act.

"adult" means a person who is neither a young person nor a child.

"adult sentence," in the case of a young person who is found guilty of an offence, means any sentence that could be imposed on an adult who has been convicted of the same offence.

"Attorney General" means the Attorney General as defined in section 2 of the *Criminal Code*, read as if the reference in that definition to "proceedings" were a reference to "proceedings or extrajudicial measures," and includes an agent or delegate of the Attorney General.

"child" means a person who is or, in the absence of evidence to the contrary, appears to be less than twelve years old.

"conference" means a group of persons who are convened to give advice in accordance with section 19.

"confirmed delivery service" means certified or registered mail or any other method of service that provides proof of delivery.

"custodial portion," with respect to a youth sentence imposed on a young person under paragraph 42(2)(n), (o), (q) or (r), means the period of time, or the portion of the young person's youth sentence, that must be served in custody before he or she begins to serve the remainder under supervision in the community subject to conditions under paragraph 42(2)(n) or under conditional supervision under paragraph 42(2)(o), (q) or (r).

"disclosure" means the communication of information other than by way of publication.

"extrajudicial measures" means measures other than judicial proceedings under this Act used to deal with a young person alleged to have committed an offence and includes extrajudicial sanctions.

"extrajudicial sanction" means a sanction that is part of a program referred to in section 10.

"offence" means an offence created by an Act of Parliament or by any regulation, rule, order, by-law or ordinance made under an Act of Parliament other than an ordinance of the Yukon Territory or the Northwest Territories or a law of the Legislature for Nunavut.

"parent" includes, in respect of a young person, any person who is under a legal duty to provide for the young person or any person who has, in law or in fact, the custody or control of the young person, but does not include a person who has the custody or control of the young person by reason only of proceedings under this Act.

"pre-sentence report" means a report on the personal and family history and present environment of a young person made in accordance with section 40.

"presumptive offence" means

(a) an offence committed, or alleged to have been committed, by a young person who has attained the age of fourteen years, or, in a province where the lieutenant governor in council has fixed an age greater than fourteen years under section 61, the age so fixed, under one of the following provisions of the *Criminal Code*:

(i) section 231 or 235 (first degree murder or second degree murder within the meaning of section 231),

(ii) section 239 (attempt to commit murder),

(iii) section 232, 234 or 236 (manslaughter), or

(iv) section 273 (aggravated sexual assault); or

(b) a serious violent offence for which an adult is liable to imprisonment for a term of more than two years committed, or alleged to have been committed, by a young person after the coming into force of section 62 (adult sentence) and after the young person has attained the age of fourteen years, or, in a province where the lieutenant governor in council has fixed an age greater than fourteen years under section 61, the age so fixed, if at the time of the commission or alleged commission of the offence at least two judicial determinations have been made under subsection 42(9), at different proceedings, that the young person has committed a serious violent offence.

"provincial director" means a person, a group or class of persons or a body appointed or designated by or under an Act of the legislature of a province or by the lieutenant governor in council of a province or his or her delegate to perform in that province, either generally or in a specific case, any of the duties or functions of a provincial director under this Act.

"publication" means the communication of information by making it known or accessible to the general public through any means, including print, radio or television broadcast, telecommunication or electronic means.

"record" includes any thing containing information, regardless of its physical form or characteristics, including microform, sound recording, videotape, machine-readable record, and any copy of any of those things, that is created or kept for the purposes of this Act or for the investigation of an offence that is or could be prosecuted under this Act.

"review board" means a review board referred to in subsection 87(2).

"serious violent offence" means an offence in the commission of which a young person causes or attempts to cause serious bodily harm.

"young person" means a person who is or, in the absence of evidence to the contrary, appears to be twelve years old or older, but less than eighteen years old and, if the context requires, includes any person who is charged under this Act with having committed an offence while he or she was a young person or who is found guilty of an offence under this Act.

"youth custody facility" means a facility designated under subsection 85(2) for the placement of young persons and, if so designated, includes a facility for the secure restraint of young persons, a community residential centre, a group home, a child care institution and a forest or wilderness camp.

"youth justice court" means a youth justice court referred to in section 13.

"youth justice court judge" means a youth justice court judge referred to in section 13.

"youth sentence" means a sentence imposed under section 42, 51 or 59 or any of sections 94 to 96 and includes a confirmation or a variation of that sentence.

"youth worker" means any person appointed or designated, whether by title of youth worker or probation officer or by any other title, by or under an Act of the legislature of a province or by the lieutenant governor in council of a province or his or her delegate to perform in that province, either generally or in a specific case, any of the duties or functions of a youth worker under this Act.

WORDS AND EXPRESSIONS

(2) Unless otherwise provided, words and expressions used in this Act have the same meaning as in the *Criminal Code*.

DESCRIPTIVE CROSS-REFERENCES

(3) If, in any provision of this Act, a reference to another provision of this Act or a provision of any other Act is followed by words in parentheses that are or purport to be descriptive of the subject-matter of the provision referred to, those words form no part of the provision in which they occur but are inserted for convenience of reference only.

DECLARATION OF PRINCIPLE

POLICY FOR CANADA WITH RESPECT TO YOUNG PERSONS

3. (1) The following principles apply in this Act:

(a) the youth criminal justice system is intended to

(i) prevent crime by addressing the circumstances underlying a young person's offending behaviour,

(ii) rehabilitate young persons who commit offences and reintegrate them into society, and

(iii) ensure that a young person is subject to meaningful consequences for his or her offence

in order to promote the long-term protection of the public;

(b) the criminal justice system for young persons must be separate from that of adults and emphasize the following:

(i) rehabilitation and reintegration,

(ii) fair and proportionate accountability that is consistent with the greater dependency of young persons and their reduced level of maturity,

(iii) enhanced procedural protection to ensure that young persons are treated fairly and that their rights, including their right to privacy, are protected,

(iv) timely intervention that reinforces the link between the offending behaviour and its consequences, and

(v) the promptness and speed with which persons responsible for enforcing this Act must act, given young persons' perception of time;

(c) within the limits of fair and proportionate accountability, the measures taken against young persons who commit offences should

(i) reinforce respect for societal values,

(ii) encourage the repair of harm done to victims and the community,

(iii) be meaningful for the individual young person given his or her needs and level of development and, where appropriate, involve the parents, the extended family, the community and social or other agencies in the young person's rehabilitation and reintegration, and

(iv) respect gender, ethnic, cultural and linguistic differences and respond to the needs of aboriginal young persons and of young persons with special requirements; and

(d) special considerations apply in respect of proceedings against young persons and, in particular,

(i) young persons have rights and freedoms in their own right, such as a right to be heard in the course of and to participate in the processes, other than the decision to prosecute, that lead to decisions that affect them, and young persons have special guarantees of their rights and freedoms,

(ii) victims should be treated with courtesy, compassion and respect for their dignity and privacy and should suffer the minimum degree of inconvenience as a result of their involvement with the youth criminal justice system,

(iii) victims should be provided with information about the proceedings and given an opportunity to participate and be heard, and

(iv) parents should be informed of measures or proceedings involving their children and encouraged to support them in addressing their offending behaviour.

ACT TO BE LIBERALLY CONSTRUED

(2) This Act shall be liberally construed so as to ensure that young persons are dealt with in accordance with the principles set out in subsection (1).

PART 1
EXTRAJUDICIAL MEASURES

Principles and Objectives

DECLARATION OF PRINCIPLES

4. The following principles apply in this Part in addition to the principles set out in section 3:

(a) extrajudicial measures are often the most appropriate and effective way to address youth crime;

(b) extrajudicial measures allow for effective and timely interventions focused on correcting offending behaviour;

(c) extrajudicial measures are presumed to be adequate to hold a young person accountable for his or her offending behaviour if the young person has committed a non-violent offence and has not previously been found guilty of an offence; and

(d) extrajudicial measures should be used if they are adequate to hold a young person accountable for his or her offending behaviour and, if the use of extrajudicial measures is consistent with the principles set out in this section, nothing in this Act precludes their use in respect of a young person who

(i) has previously been dealt with by the use of extrajudicial measures, or

(ii) has previously been found guilty of an offence.

OBJECTIVES

5. Extrajudicial measures should be designed to

(a) provide an effective and timely response to offending behaviour outside the bounds of judicial measures;

(b) encourage young persons to acknowledge and repair the harm caused to the victim and the community;

(c) encourage families of young persons—including extended families where appropriate—and the community to become involved in the design and implementation of those measures;

(d) provide an opportunity for victims to participate in decisions related to the measures selected and to receive reparation; and

(e) respect the rights and freedoms of young persons and be proportionate to the seriousness of the offence.

Warnings, Cautions and Referrals

WARNINGS, CAUTIONS AND REFERRALS

6. (1) A police officer shall, before starting judicial proceedings or taking any other measures under this Act against a young person alleged to have committed an offence, consider whether it would be sufficient, having regard to the principles set out in section 4, to take no further action, warn the young person, administer a caution, if a program has been established under section 7, or, with the consent of the young person, refer the young person to a program or agency in the community that may assist the young person not to commit offences.

SAVING

(2) The failure of a police officer to consider the options set out in subsection (1) does not invalidate any subsequent charges against the young person for the offence.

POLICE CAUTIONS

7. The Attorney General, or any other minister designated by the lieutenant governor of a province, may establish a program authorizing the police to administer cautions to young persons instead of starting judicial proceedings under this Act.

CROWN CAUTIONS

8. The Attorney General may establish a program authorizing prosecutors to administer cautions to young persons instead of starting or continuing judicial proceedings under this Act.

EVIDENCE OF MEASURES IS INADMISSIBLE

9. Evidence that a young person has received a warning, caution or referral mentioned in section 6, 7 or 8 or that a police officer has taken no further action in respect of an offence, and evidence of the offence, is inadmissible for the purpose of proving prior offending behaviour in any proceedings before a youth justice court in respect of the young person.

Extrajudicial Sanctions

EXTRAJUDICIAL SANCTIONS

10. (1) An extrajudicial sanction may be used to deal with a young person alleged to have committed an offence only if the young person cannot be adequately dealt with by a warning, caution or referral mentioned in section 6, 7 or 8 because of the seriousness of the offence, the nature and number of previous offences committed by the young person or any other aggravating circumstances.

CONDITIONS

(2) An extrajudicial sanction may be used only if

(a) it is part of a program of sanctions that may be authorized by the Attorney General or authorized by a person, or a member of a class of persons, designated by the lieutenant governor in council of the province;

(b) the person who is considering whether to use the extrajudicial sanction is satisfied that it would be appropriate, having regard to the needs of the young person and the interests of society;

(c) the young person, having been informed of the extrajudicial sanction, fully and freely consents to be subject to it;

(d) the young person has, before consenting to be subject to the extrajudicial sanction, been advised of his or her right to be represented by counsel and been given a reasonable opportunity to consult with counsel;

(e) the young person accepts responsibility for the act or omission that forms the basis of the offence that he or she is alleged to have committed;

(f) there is, in the opinion of the Attorney General, sufficient evidence to proceed with the prosecution of the offence; and

(g) the prosecution of the offence is not in any way barred at law.

RESTRICTION ON USE

(3) An extrajudicial sanction may not be used in respect of a young person who

(a) denies participation or involvement in the commission of the offence; or

(b) expresses the wish to have the charge dealt with by a youth justice court.

ADMISSIONS NOT ADMISSIBLE IN EVIDENCE

(4) Any admission, confession or statement accepting responsibility for a given act or omission that is made by a young person as a condition of being dealt with by extrajudicial measures is inadmissible in evidence against any young person in civil or criminal proceedings.

NO BAR TO JUDICIAL PROCEEDINGS

(5) The use of an extrajudicial sanction in respect of a young person alleged to have committed an offence is not a bar to judicial proceedings under this Act, but if a charge is laid against the young person in respect of the offence,

(a) the youth justice court shall dismiss the charge if it is satisfied on a balance of probabilities that the young person has totally complied with the terms and conditions of the extrajudicial sanction; and

(b) the youth justice court may dismiss the charge if it is satisfied on a balance of probabilities that the young person has partially complied with the terms and conditions of the extrajudicial sanction and if, in the opinion of the court, prosecution of the charge would be unfair having regard to the circumstances and the young person's performance with respect to the extrajudicial sanction.

LAYING OF INFORMATION, ETC.

(6) Subject to subsection (5) and section 24 (private prosecutions only with consent of Attorney General), nothing in this section shall be construed as preventing any person from laying an information or indictment, obtaining the issue or confirmation of any process or proceeding with the prosecution of any offence in accordance with law.

NOTICE TO PARENT

11. If a young person is dealt with by an extrajudicial sanction, the person who administers the program under which the sanction is used shall inform a parent of the young person of the sanction.

VICTIM'S RIGHT TO INFORMATION

12. If a young person is dealt with by an extrajudicial sanction, a police officer, the Attorney General, the provincial director or any organization established by a province to provide assistance to victims shall, on request, inform the victim of the identity of the young person and how the offence has been dealt with.

PART 2
ORGANIZATION OF YOUTH CRIMINAL JUSTICE SYSTEM

Youth Justice Court

DESIGNATION OF YOUTH JUSTICE COURT

13. (1) A youth justice court is any court that may be established or designated by or under an Act of the legislature of a province, or designated by the Governor in Council or the lieutenant governor in council of a province, as a youth justice court for the purposes of this Act, and a youth justice court judge is a person who may be appointed or designated as a judge of the youth justice court or a judge sitting in a court established or designated as a youth justice court.

DEEMED YOUTH JUSTICE COURT

(2) When a young person elects to be tried by a judge without a jury, the judge shall be a judge as defined in section 552 of the *Criminal Code*, or if it is an offence set out in section 469 of that Act, the judge shall be a judge of the superior court of criminal jurisdiction in the province in which the election is made. In either case, the judge is deemed to be a youth justice court judge and the court is deemed to be a youth justice court for the purpose of the proceeding.

DEEMED YOUTH JUSTICE COURT

(3) When a young person elects or is deemed to have elected to be tried by a court composed of a judge and jury, the superior court of criminal jurisdiction in the province in which the election is made or deemed to have been made is deemed to be a youth justice court for the purpose of the proceeding, and the superior court judge is deemed to be a youth justice court judge.

COURT OF RECORD

(4) A youth justice court is a court of record.

EXCLUSIVE JURISDICTION OF YOUTH JUSTICE COURT

14. (1) Despite any other Act of Parliament but subject to the *Contraventions Act* and the *National Defence Act*, a youth justice court has exclusive jurisdiction in respect of any offence alleged to have been committed by a person while he or she was a young person, and that person shall be dealt with as provided in this Act.

ORDERS

(2) A youth justice court has jurisdiction to make orders against a young person under sections 810 (recognizance—fear of injury or damage), 810.01 (recognizance—fear of criminal organization offence) and 810.2 (recognizance—fear of serious personal injury offence) of the *Criminal Code*. If the young person fails or refuses to enter into a recognizance referred to in any of those sections, the court may impose any one of the sanctions set out in subsection 42(2) (youth sentences) except that, in the case of an order under paragraph 42(2)(n) (custody and supervision order), it shall not exceed thirty days.

PROSECUTION PROHIBITED

(3) Unless the Attorney General and the young person agree, no extrajudicial measures shall be taken or judicial proceedings commenced under this Act in respect of an offence after the end of the time limit set out in any other Act of Parliament or any regulation made under it for the institution of proceedings in respect of that offence.

CONTINUATION OF PROCEEDINGS

(4) Extrajudicial measures taken or judicial proceedings commenced under this Act against a young person may be continued under this Act after the person attains the age of eighteen years.

YOUNG PERSONS OVER THE AGE OF EIGHTEEN YEARS

(5) This Act applies to persons eighteen years old or older who are alleged to have committed an offence while a young person.

POWERS OF YOUTH JUSTICE COURT JUDGE

(6) For the purpose of carrying out the provisions of this Act, a youth justice court judge is a justice and a provincial court judge and has the jurisdiction and powers of a summary conviction court under the *Criminal Code*.

POWERS OF A JUDGE OF A SUPERIOR COURT

(7) A judge of a superior court of criminal jurisdiction, when deemed to be a youth justice court judge for the purpose of a proceeding, retains the jurisdiction and powers of a superior court of criminal jurisdiction.

CONTEMPT AGAINST YOUTH JUSTICE COURT

15. (1) Every youth justice court has the same power, jurisdiction and authority to deal with and impose punishment for contempt against the court as may be exercised by the superior court of criminal jurisdiction of the province in which the court is situated.

JURISDICTION OF YOUTH JUSTICE COURT

(2) A youth justice court has jurisdiction in respect of every contempt of court committed by a young person against the youth justice court whether or not committed in the face of the court, and every contempt of court committed by a young person against any other court otherwise than in the face of that court.

CONCURRENT JURISDICTION OF YOUTH JUSTICE COURT

(3) A youth justice court has jurisdiction in respect of every contempt of court committed by a young person against any other court in the face of that court and every contempt of court committed by an adult against the youth justice court in the face of the youth justice court, but nothing in this subsection affects the power, jurisdiction or authority of any other court to deal with or impose punishment for contempt of court.

YOUTH SENTENCE—CONTEMPT

(4) When a youth justice court or any other court finds a young person guilty of contempt of court, it may impose as a youth sentence any one of the sanctions set out in subsection 42(2) (youth sentences), or any number of them that are not inconsistent with each other, but no other sentence.

SECTION 708 OF *CRIMINAL CODE* APPLIES IN RESPECT OF ADULTS

(5) Section 708 (contempt) of the *Criminal Code* applies in respect of proceedings under this section in youth justice court against adults, with any modifications that the circumstances require.

STATUS OF OFFENDER UNCERTAIN

16. When a person is alleged to have committed an offence during a period that includes the date on which the person attains the age of eighteen years, the youth justice court has jurisdiction in respect of the offence and shall, after putting the person to their election under section 67 (adult sentence) if applicable, and on finding the person guilty of the offence,

(a) if it has been proven that the offence was committed before the person attained the age of eighteen years, impose a sentence under this Act;

(b) if it has been proven that the offence was committed after the person attained the age of eighteen years, impose any sentence that could be imposed under the *Criminal Code* or any other Act of Parliament on an adult who has been convicted of the same offence; and

(c) if it has not been proven that the offence was committed after the person attained the age of eighteen years, impose a sentence under this Act.

YOUTH JUSTICE COURT MAY MAKE RULES

17. (1) The youth justice court for a province may, subject to the approval of the lieutenant governor in council of the province, establish rules of court not inconsistent with this Act or any other Act of Parliament or with any regulations made under section 155 regulating proceedings within the jurisdiction of the youth justice court.

RULES OF COURT

(2) Rules under subsection (1) may be made

(a) generally to regulate the duties of the officers of the youth justice court and any other matter considered expedient to attain the ends of justice and carry into effect the provisions of this Act;

(b) subject to any regulations made under paragraph 155(b), to regulate the practice and procedure in the youth justice court; and

(c) to prescribe forms to be used in the youth justice court if they are not otherwise provided for by or under this Act.

PUBLICATION OF RULES

(3) Rules of court that are made under the authority of this section shall be published in the appropriate provincial gazette.

Youth Justice Committees

YOUTH JUSTICE COMMITTEES

18. (1) The Attorney General of Canada or a province or any other minister that the lieutenant governor in council of the province may designate may establish one or more committees of citizens, to be known as youth justice committees, to assist in any aspect of the administration of this Act or in any programs or services for young persons.

ROLE OF COMMITTEE

(2) The functions of a youth justice committee may include the following:

(a) in the case of a young person alleged to have committed an offence,

(i) giving advice on the appropriate extrajudicial measure to be used in respect of the young person,

(ii) supporting any victim of the alleged offence by soliciting his or her concerns and facilitating the reconciliation of the victim and the young person,

(iii) ensuring that community support is available to the young person by arranging for the use of services from within the community, and enlisting members of the community to provide short-term mentoring and supervision, and

(iv) when the young person is also being dealt with by a child protection agency or a community group, helping to coordinate the interaction of the agency or group with the youth criminal justice system;

(b) advising the federal and provincial governments on whether the provisions of this Act that grant rights to young persons, or provide for the protection of young persons, are being complied with;

(c) advising the federal and provincial governments on policies and procedures related to the youth criminal justice system;

(d) providing information to the public in respect of this Act and the youth criminal justice system;

(e) acting as a conference; and

(f) any other functions assigned by the person who establishes the committee.

Conferences

CONFERENCES MAY BE CONVENED

19. (1) A youth justice court judge, the provincial director, a police officer, a justice of the peace, a prosecutor or a youth worker may convene or cause to be convened a conference for the purpose of making a decision required to be made under this Act.

MANDATE OF A CONFERENCE

(2) The mandate of a conference may be, among other things, to give advice on appropriate extrajudicial measures, conditions for judicial interim release, sentences, including the review of sentences, and reintegration plans.

RULES FOR CONFERENCES

(3) The Attorney General or any other minister designated by the lieutenant governor in council of a province may establish rules for the convening and conducting of conferences other than conferences convened or caused to be convened by a youth justice court judge or a justice of the peace.

RULES TO APPLY

(4) In provinces where rules are established under subsection (3), the conferences to which those rules apply must be convened and conducted in accordance with those rules.

Justices of the Peace

CERTAIN PROCEEDINGS MAY BE TAKEN BEFORE JUSTICES

20. (1) Any proceeding that may be carried out before a justice under the *Criminal Code*, other than a plea, a trial or an adjudication, may be carried out before a justice in respect of an offence alleged to have been committed by a young person, and any process that may be issued by a justice under the *Criminal Code* may be issued by a justice in respect of an offence alleged to have been committed by a young person.

ORDERS UNDER SECTION 810 OF *CRIMINAL CODE*

(2) A justice has jurisdiction to make an order under section 810 (recognizance—fear of injury or damage) of the *Criminal Code* in respect of a young person. If the young person fails or refuses to enter into a recognizance referred to in that section, the justice shall refer the matter to a youth justice court.

Clerks of the Court

POWERS OF CLERKS

21. In addition to any powers conferred on a clerk of a court by the *Criminal Code*, a clerk of the youth justice court may exercise the powers ordinarily exercised by a clerk of a court, and, in particular, may

(a) administer oaths or solemn affirmations in all matters relating to the business of the youth justice court; and

(b) in the absence of a youth justice court judge, exercise all the powers of a youth justice court judge relating to adjournment.

Provincial Directors

POWERS, DUTIES AND FUNCTIONS OF PROVINCIAL DIRECTORS

22. The provincial director may authorize any person to exercise the powers or perform the duties or functions of the provincial director under this Act, in which case the powers, duties or functions are deemed to have been exercised or performed by the provincial director.

PART 3
JUDICIAL MEASURES

Consent to Prosecute

PRE-CHARGE SCREENING

23. (1) The Attorney General may establish a program of pre-charge screening that sets out the circumstances in which the consent of the Attorney General must be obtained before a young person is charged with an offence.

PRE-CHARGE SCREENING PROGRAM

(2) Any program of pre-charge screening of young persons that is established under an Act of the legislature of a province or by a directive of a provincial government, and that is in place before the coming into force of this section, is deemed to be a program of pre-charge screening for the purposes of subsection (1).

PRIVATE PROSECUTIONS

24. No prosecutions may be conducted by a prosecutor other than the Attorney General without the consent of the Attorney General.

Right to Counsel

RIGHT TO COUNSEL

25. (1) A young person has the right to retain and instruct counsel without delay, and to exercise that right personally, at any stage of proceedings against the young person and before and during any consideration of whether, instead of starting or continuing judicial proceedings against the young person under this Act, to use an extrajudicial sanction to deal with the young person.

ARRESTING OFFICER TO ADVISE YOUNG PERSON OF RIGHT TO COUNSEL

(2) Every young person who is arrested or detained shall, on being arrested or detained, be advised without delay by the arresting officer or the officer in charge, as the case may be, of the right to retain and instruct counsel, and be given an opportunity to obtain counsel.

JUSTICE, YOUTH JUSTICE COURT OR REVIEW BOARD TO ADVISE YOUNG PERSON OF RIGHT TO COUNSEL

(3) When a young person is not represented by counsel

(a) at a hearing at which it will be determined whether to release the young person or detain the young person in custody prior to sentencing,

(b) at a hearing held under section 71 (hearing—adult sentences),

(c) at trial,

(d) at any proceedings held under subsection 98(3) (continuation of custody), 103(1) (review by youth justice court), 104(1) (continuation of custody), 105(1) (conditional supervision) or 109(1) (review of decision),

(e) at a review of a youth sentence held before a youth justice court under this Act, or

(f) at a review of the level of custody under section 87,

the justice or youth justice court before which the hearing, trial or review is held, or the review board before which the review is held, shall advise the young person of the right to retain and instruct counsel and shall give the young person a reasonable opportunity to obtain counsel.

TRIAL, HEARING OR REVIEW BEFORE YOUTH JUSTICE COURT OR REVIEW BOARD

(4) When a young person at trial or at a hearing or review referred to in subsection (3) wishes to obtain counsel but is unable to

do so, the youth justice court before which the hearing, trial or review is held or the review board before which the review is held

(a) shall, if there is a legal aid program or an assistance program available in the province where the hearing, trial or review is held, refer the young person to that program for the appointment of counsel; or

(b) if no legal aid program or assistance program is available or the young person is unable to obtain counsel through the program, may, and on the request of the young person shall, direct that the young person be represented by counsel.

APPOINTMENT OF COUNSEL

(5) When a direction is made under paragraph (4)(b) in respect of a young person, the Attorney General shall appoint counsel, or cause counsel to be appointed, to represent the young person.

RELEASE HEARING BEFORE JUSTICE

(6) When a young person, at a hearing referred to in paragraph (3)(a) that is held before a justice who is not a youth justice court judge, wishes to obtain counsel but is unable to do so, the justice shall

(a) if there is a legal aid program or an assistance program available in the province where the hearing is held,

(i) refer the young person to that program for the appointment of counsel, or

(ii) refer the matter to a youth justice court to be dealt with in accordance with paragraph (4)(a) or (b); or

(b) if no legal aid program or assistance program is available or the young person is unable to obtain counsel through the program, refer the matter without delay to a youth justice court to be dealt with in accordance with paragraph (4)(b).

YOUNG PERSON MAY BE ASSISTED BY ADULT

(7) When a young person is not represented by counsel at trial or at a hearing or review referred to in subsection (3), the justice before whom or the youth justice court or review board before which the proceedings are held may, on the request of the young person, allow the young person to be assisted by an adult whom the justice, court or review board considers to be suitable.

COUNSEL INDEPENDENT OF PARENTS

(8) If it appears to a youth justice court judge or a justice that the interests of a young person and the interests of a parent are in conflict or that it would be in the best interests of the young person to be represented by his or her own counsel, the judge or justice shall ensure that the young person is represented by counsel independent of the parent.

STATEMENT OF RIGHT TO COUNSEL

(9) A statement that a young person has the right to be represented by counsel shall be included in

(a) any appearance notice or summons issued to the young person;

(b) any warrant to arrest the young person;

(c) any promise to appear given by the young person;

(d) any undertaking or recognizance entered into before an officer in charge by the young person;

(e) any notice given to the young person in relation to any proceedings held under subsection 98(3) (continuation of custody), 103(1) (review by youth justice court), 104(1) (continuation of custody), 105(1) (conditional supervision) or 109(1) (review of decision); or

(f) any notice of a review of a youth sentence given to the young person.

RECOVERY OF COSTS OF COUNSEL

(10) Nothing in this Act prevents the lieutenant governor in council of a province or his or her delegate from establishing a program to authorize the recovery of the costs of a young person's counsel from the young person or the parents of the young person. The costs may be recovered only after the proceedings are completed and the time allowed for the taking of an appeal has expired or, if an appeal is taken, all proceedings in respect of the appeal have been completed.

EXCEPTION FOR PERSONS OVER THE AGE OF TWENTY

(11) Subsections (4) to (9) do not apply to a person who is alleged to have committed an offence while a young person, if the person has attained the age of twenty years at the time of his or her first appearance before a youth justice court in respect of the offence; however, this does not restrict any rights that a person has under the law applicable to adults.

Notices to Parents

NOTICE IN CASE OF ARREST OR DETENTION

26. (1) Subject to subsection (4), if a young person is arrested and detained in custody pending his or her appearance in court, the officer in charge at the time the young person is detained shall, as soon as possible, give or cause to be given to a parent of the young person, orally or in writing, notice of the arrest stating the place of detention and the reason for the arrest.

NOTICE IN OTHER CASES

(2) Subject to subsection (4), if a summons or an appearance notice is issued in respect of a young person, the person who issued the summons or appearance notice, or, if a young person is released on giving a promise to appear or entering into an undertaking or recognizance, the officer in charge, shall, as soon as possible, give or cause to be given to a parent of the young person notice in writing of the summons, appearance notice, promise to appear, undertaking or recognizance.

NOTICE TO PARENT IN CASE OF TICKET

(3) Subject to subsection (4), a person who serves a ticket under the *Contraventions Act* on a young person, other than a ticket served for a contravention relating to parking a vehicle, shall, as soon as possible, give or cause to be given notice in writing of the ticket to a parent of the young person.

NOTICE TO RELATIVE OR OTHER ADULT

(4) If the whereabouts of the parents of a young person are not known or it appears that no parent is available, a notice under this section may be given to an adult relative of the young person who is known to the young person and is likely to assist the young person or, if no such adult relative is available, to any other adult who is known to the young person and is likely to assist the young person and who the person giving the notice considers appropriate.

NOTICE ON DIRECTION OF YOUTH JUSTICE COURT JUDGE OR JUSTICE

(5) If doubt exists as to the person to whom a notice under this section should be given, a youth justice court judge or, if a youth justice court judge is, having regard to the circumstances, not reasonably available, a justice may give directions as to the person to whom the notice should be given, and a notice given in accordance with those directions is sufficient notice for the purposes of this section.

CONTENTS OF NOTICE

(6) Any notice under this section shall, in addition to any other requirements under this section, include

(a) the name of the young person in respect of whom it is given;

(b) the charge against the young person and, except in the case of a notice of a ticket served under the *Contraventions Act*, the time and place of appearance; and

(c) a statement that the young person has the right to be represented by counsel.

NOTICE OF TICKET UNDER *CONTRAVENTIONS ACT*

(7) A notice under subsection (3) shall include a copy of the ticket.

SERVICE OF NOTICE

(8) Subject to subsections (10) and (11), a notice under this section that is given in writing may be served personally or be sent by confirmed delivery service.

PROCEEDINGS NOT INVALID

(9) Subject to subsections (10) and (11), failure to give a notice in accordance with this section does not affect the validity of proceedings under this Act.

EXCEPTION

(10) Failure to give a notice under subsection (2) in accordance with this section in any case renders invalid any subsequent proceedings under this Act relating to the case unless

(a) a parent of the young person attends court with the young person; or

(b) a youth justice court judge or a justice before whom proceedings are held against the young person

(i) adjourns the proceedings and orders that the notice be given in the manner and to the persons that the judge or justice directs, or

(ii) dispenses with the notice if the judge or justice is of the opinion that, having regard to the circumstances, the notice may be dispensed with.

WHERE NOTICE IS NOT SERVED

(11) Where there has been a failure to give a notice under subsection (1) or (3) in accordance with this section and none of the persons to whom the notice may be given attends court with the young person, a youth justice court judge or a justice before whom proceedings are held against the young person may

(a) adjourn the proceedings and order that the notice be given in the manner and to the persons that the judge or justice directs; or

(b) dispense with the notice if the judge or justice is of the opinion that, having regard to the circumstances, the notice may be dispensed with.

EXCEPTION FOR PERSONS OVER THE AGE OF TWENTY

(12) This section does not apply to a person who is alleged to have committed an offence while a young person, if the person has attained the age of twenty years at the time of his or her first appearance before a youth justice court in respect of the offence.

ORDER REQUIRING ATTENDANCE OF PARENT

27. (1) If a parent does not attend proceedings held before a youth justice court in respect of a young person, the court may, if in its opinion the presence of the parent is necessary or in the best interests of the young person, by order in writing require the parent to attend at any stage of the proceedings.

NO ORDER IN TICKET PROCEEDINGS

(2) Subsection (1) does not apply in proceedings commenced by filing a ticket under the *Contraventions Act*.

SERVICE OF ORDER

(3) A copy of the order shall be served by a peace officer or by a person designated by a youth justice court by delivering it personally to the parent to whom it is directed, unless the youth justice court authorizes service by confirmed delivery service.

FAILURE TO ATTEND

(4) A parent who is ordered to attend a youth justice court under subsection (1) and who fails without reasonable excuse, the proof of which lies on the parent, to comply with the order

(a) is guilty of contempt of court;

(b) may be dealt with summarily by the court; and

(c) is liable to the punishment provided for in the *Criminal Code* for a summary conviction offence.

WARRANT TO ARREST PARENT

(5) If a parent who is ordered to attend a youth justice court under subsection (1) does not attend when required by the order or fails to remain in attendance as required and it is proved that a copy of the order was served on the parent, a youth justice court may issue a warrant to compel the attendance of the parent.

Detention before Sentencing

APPLICATION OF PART XVI OF *CRIMINAL CODE*

28. Except to the extent that they are inconsistent with or excluded by this Act, the provisions of Part XVI (compelling appearance of an accused and interim release) of the *Criminal Code* apply to the detention and release of young persons under this Act.

DETENTION AS SOCIAL MEASURE PROHIBITED

29. (1) A youth justice court judge or a justice shall not detain a young person in custody prior to being sentenced as a substitute for appropriate child protection, mental health or other social measures.

DETENTION PRESUMED UNNECESSARY

(2) In considering whether the detention of a young person is necessary for the protection or safety of the public under paragraph 515(10)(b) (substantial likelihood—commit an offence or interfere with the administration of justice) of the *Criminal Code*, a youth justice court or a justice shall presume that detention is not necessary under that paragraph if the young person could not, on being found guilty, be committed to custody on the grounds set out in paragraphs 39(1)(a) to (c) (restrictions on committal to custody).

DESIGNATED PLACE OF TEMPORARY DETENTION

30. (1) Subject to subsection (7), a young person who is arrested and detained prior to being sentenced, or who is detained in accordance with a warrant issued under subsection 59(6) (compelling appearance for review of sentence), shall be detained in any place of temporary detention that may be designated by the lieutenant governor in council of the province or his or her delegate or in a place within a class of places so designated.

EXCEPTION

(2) A young person who is detained in a place of temporary detention under subsection (1) may, in the course of being transferred from that place to the court or from the court to that place, be held under the supervision and control of a peace officer.

DETENTION SEPARATE FROM ADULTS

(3) A young person referred to in subsection (1) shall be held separate and apart from any adult who is detained or held in custody unless a youth justice court judge or a justice is satisfied that, having regard to the best interests of the young person,

(a) the young person cannot, having regard to his or her own safety or the safety of others, be detained in a place of detention for young persons; or

(b) no place of detention for young persons is available within a reasonable distance.

TRANSFER TO ADULT FACILITY

(4) When a young person is detained under subsection (1), the youth justice court may, on application of the provincial director made at any time after the young person attains the age of eighteen years, after giving the young person an opportunity to be heard, authorize the provincial director to direct, despite subsection (3), that the young person be temporarily detained in a provincial correctional facility for adults, if the court considers it to be in the best interests of the young person or in the public interest.

WHEN YOUNG PERSON IS TWENTY YEARS OLD OR OLDER

(5) When a young person is twenty years old or older at the time his or her temporary detention under subsection (1) begins, the young person shall, despite subsection (3), be temporarily detained in a provincial correctional facility for adults.

TRANSFER BY PROVINCIAL DIRECTOR

(6) A young person who is detained in custody under subsection (1) may, during the period of detention, be transferred by the provincial director from one place of temporary detention to another.

EXCEPTION RELATING TO TEMPORARY DETENTION

(7) Subsections (1) and (3) do not apply in respect of any temporary restraint of a young person under the supervision and control of a peace officer after arrest, but a young person who is so restrained shall be transferred to a place of temporary detention referred to in subsection (1) as soon as is practicable, and in no case later than the first reasonable opportunity after the appearance of the young person before a youth justice court judge or a justice under section 503 of the *Criminal Code*.

AUTHORIZATION OF PROVINCIAL AUTHORITY FOR DETENTION

(8) In any province for which the lieutenant governor in council has designated a person or a group of persons whose authorization is required, either in all circumstances or in circumstances specified by the lieutenant governor in council, before a young person who has been arrested may be detained in accordance with this section, no young person shall be so detained unless the authorization is obtained.

DETERMINATION BY PROVINCIAL AUTHORITY OF PLACE OF DETENTION

(9) In any province for which the lieutenant governor in council has designated a person or a group of persons who may determine the place where a young person who has been arrested may be detained in accordance with this section, no young person may be so detained in a place other than the one so determined.

PLACEMENT OF YOUNG PERSON IN CARE OF RESPONSIBLE PERSON

31. (1) A young person who has been arrested may be placed in the care of a responsible person instead of being detained in custody if a youth justice court or a justice is satisfied that

(a) the young person would, but for this subsection, be detained in custody under section 515 (judicial interim release) of the *Criminal Code*;

(b) the person is willing and able to take care of and exercise control over the young person; and

(c) the young person is willing to be placed in the care of that person.

INQUIRY AS TO AVAILABILITY OF A RESPONSIBLE PERSON

(2) If a young person would, in the absence of a responsible person, be detained in custody, the youth justice court or the justice shall inquire as to the availability of a responsible person and whether the young person is willing to be placed in that person's care.

CONDITION OF PLACEMENT

(3) A young person shall not be placed in the care of a person under subsection (1) unless

(a) that person undertakes in writing to take care of and to be responsible for the attendance of the young person in court when required and to comply with any other conditions that the youth justice court judge or the justice may specify; and

(b) the young person undertakes in writing to comply with the arrangement and to comply with any other conditions that the youth justice court judge or the justice may specify.

REMOVING YOUNG PERSON FROM CARE

(4) A young person, a person in whose care a young person has been placed or any other person may, by application in writing to a youth justice court judge or a justice, apply for an order under subsection (5) if

(a) the person in whose care the young person has been placed is no longer willing or able to take care of or exercise control over the young person; or

(b) it is, for any other reason, no longer appropriate that the young person remain in the care of the person with whom he or she has been placed.

ORDER

(5) When a youth justice court judge or a justice is satisfied that a young person should not remain in the custody of the person in whose care he or she was placed under subsection (1), the judge or justice shall

(a) make an order relieving the person and the young person of the obligations undertaken under subsection (3); and

(b) issue a warrant for the arrest of the young person.

EFFECT OF ARREST

(6) If a young person is arrested in accordance with a warrant issued under paragraph (5)(b), the young person shall be taken before a youth justice court judge or a justice without delay and dealt with under this section and sections 28 to 30.

Appearance

APPEARANCE BEFORE JUDGE OR JUSTICE

32. (1) A young person against whom an information or indictment is laid must first appear before a youth justice court judge or a justice, and the judge or justice shall

(a) cause the information or indictment to be read to the young person;

(b) if the young person is not represented by counsel, inform the young person of the right to retain and instruct counsel;

(c) if notified under subsection 64(2) (intention to seek adult sentence) or if section 16 (status of accused uncertain) applies, inform the young person that the youth justice court might, if the young person is found guilty, order that an adult sentence be imposed; and

(d) if the young person is charged with having committed an offence set out in paragraph (a) of the definition "presumptive offence" in subsection 2(1), inform the young person in the following words of the consequences of being charged with such an offence:

An adult sentence will be imposed if you are found guilty unless the court orders that you are not liable to an adult sentence and that a youth sentence must be imposed.

WAIVER

(2) A young person may waive the requirements of subsection (1) if the young person is represented by counsel and counsel advises the court that the young person has been informed of that provision.

YOUNG PERSON NOT REPRESENTED BY COUNSEL

(3) When a young person is not represented by counsel, the youth justice court, before accepting a plea, shall

(a) satisfy itself that the young person understands the charge;

(b) if the young person is liable to an adult sentence, explain to the young person the consequences of being liable to an adult sentence and the procedure by which the young person may apply for an order that a youth sentence be imposed; and

(c) explain that the young person may plead guilty or not guilty to the charge or, if subsection 67(1) (election of court for trial—adult sentence) or (3) (election of court for trial in Nunavut—adult sentence) applies, explain that the young person may elect to be tried by a youth justice court judge without a jury and without having a preliminary inquiry, or to have a preliminary inquiry and be tried by a judge without a jury, or to have a preliminary inquiry and be tried by a court composed of a judge and jury.

IF YOUTH JUSTICE COURT NOT SATISFIED

(4) If the youth justice court is not satisfied that a young person understands the charge, the court shall, unless the young person must be put to his or her election under subsection 67(1) (election of court for trial—adult sentence) or, with respect to Nunavut, subsection 67(3) (election of court for trial in Nunavut—adult sentence), enter a plea of not guilty on behalf of the young person and proceed with the trial in accordance with subsection 36(2) (young person pleads not guilty).

IF YOUTH JUSTICE COURT NOT SATISFIED

(5) If the youth justice court is not satisfied that a young person understands the matters set out in subsection (3), the court shall direct that the young person be represented by counsel.

Release from or Detention in Custody

APPLICATION FOR RELEASE FROM OR DETENTION IN CUSTODY

33. (1) If an order is made under section 515 (judicial interim release) of the *Criminal Code* in respect of a young person by a justice who is not a youth justice court judge, an application may, at any time after the order is made, be made to a youth justice court for the release from or detention in custody of the young person, as the case may be, and the youth justice court shall hear the matter as an original application.

NOTICE TO PROSECUTOR

(2) An application under subsection (1) for release from custody shall not be heard unless the young person has given the prosecutor at least two clear days notice in writing of the application.

NOTICE TO YOUNG PERSON

(3) An application under subsection (1) for detention in custody shall not be heard unless the prosecutor has given the young person at least two clear days notice in writing of the application.

WAIVER OF NOTICE

(4) The requirement for notice under subsection (2) or (3) may be waived by the prosecutor or by the young person or his or her counsel, as the case may be.

APPLICATION FOR REVIEW UNDER SECTION 520 OR 521 OF *CRIMINAL CODE*

(5) An application under section 520 or 521 of the *Criminal Code* for a review of an order made in respect of a young person by a youth justice court judge who is a judge of a superior court shall be made to a judge of the court of appeal.

NUNAVUT

(6) Despite subsection (5), an application under section 520 or 521 of the *Criminal Code* for a review of an order made in respect of

a young person by a youth justice court judge who is a judge of the Nunavut Court of Justice shall be made to a judge of that court.

NO REVIEW

(7) No application may be made under section 520 or 521 of the *Criminal Code* for a review of an order made in respect of a young person by a justice who is not a youth justice court judge.

INTERIM RELEASE BY YOUTH JUSTICE COURT JUDGE ONLY

(8) If a young person against whom proceedings have been taken under this Act is charged with an offence referred to in section 522 of the *Criminal Code*, a youth justice court judge, but no other court, judge or justice, may release the young person from custody under that section.

REVIEW BY COURT OF APPEAL

(9) A decision made by a youth justice court judge under subsection (8) may be reviewed in accordance with section 680 of the *Criminal Code* and that section applies, with any modifications that the circumstances require, to any decision so made.

Medical and Psychological Reports

MEDICAL OR PSYCHOLOGICAL ASSESSMENT

34. (1) A youth justice court may, at any stage of proceedings against a young person, by order require that the young person be assessed by a qualified person who is required to report the results in writing to the court,

(a) with the consent of the young person and the prosecutor; or

(b) on its own motion or on application of the young person or the prosecutor, if the court believes a medical, psychological or psychiatric report in respect of the young person is necessary for a purpose mentioned in paragraphs (2)(a) to (g) and

(i) the court has reasonable grounds to believe that the young person may be suffering from a physical or mental illness or disorder, a psychological disorder, an emotional disturbance, a learning disability or a mental disability,

(ii) the young person's history indicates a pattern of repeated findings of guilt under this Act or the *Young Offenders Act*, chapter Y-1 of the Revised Statutes of Canada, 1985, or

(iii) the young person is alleged to have committed a serious violent offence.

PURPOSE OF ASSESSMENT

(2) A youth justice court may make an order under subsection (1) in respect of a young person for the purpose of

(a) considering an application under section 33 (release from or detention in custody);

(b) making its decision on an application heard under section 71 (hearing—adult sentences);

(c) making or reviewing a youth sentence;

(d) considering an application under subsection 104(1) (continuation of custody);

(e) setting conditions under subsection 105(1) (conditional supervision);

(f) making an order under subsection 109(2) (conditional supervision); or

(g) authorizing disclosure under subsection 127(1) (information about a young person).

CUSTODY FOR ASSESSMENT

(3) Subject to subsections (4) and (6), for the purpose of an assessment under this section, a youth justice court may remand a young person to any custody that it directs for a period not exceeding thirty days.

PRESUMPTION AGAINST CUSTODIAL REMAND

(4) A young person shall not be remanded in custody in accordance with an order made under subsection (1) unless

(a) the youth justice court is satisfied that

(i) on the evidence custody is necessary to conduct an assessment of the young person, or

(ii) on the evidence of a qualified person detention of the young person in custody is desirable to conduct the assessment of the young person, and the young person consents to custody; or

(b) the young person is required to be detained in custody in respect of any other matter or by virtue of any provision of the *Criminal Code*.

REPORT OF QUALIFIED PERSON IN WRITING

(5) For the purposes of paragraph (4)(a), if the prosecutor and the young person agree, evidence of a qualified person may be received in the form of a report in writing.

APPLICATION TO VARY ASSESSMENT ORDER IF CIRCUMSTANCES CHANGE

(6) A youth justice court may, at any time while an order made under subsection (1) is in force, on cause being shown, vary the terms and conditions specified in the order in any manner that the court considers appropriate in the circumstances.

DISCLOSURE OF REPORT

(7) When a youth justice court receives a report made in respect of a young person under subsection (1),

(a) the court shall, subject to subsection (9), cause a copy of the report to be given to

(i) the young person,

(ii) any parent of the young person who is in attendance at the proceedings against the young person,

(iii) any counsel representing the young person, and

(iv) the prosecutor; and

(b) the court may cause a copy of the report to be given to

(i) a parent of the young person who is not in attendance at the proceedings if the parent is, in the opinion of the court, taking an active interest in the proceedings, or

(ii) despite subsection 119(6) (restrictions respecting access to certain records), the provincial director, or the director of the provincial correctional facility for adults or the penitentiary at which the young person is serving a youth sentence, if, in the opinion of the court, withholding the report would jeopardize the safety of any person.

CROSS-EXAMINATION

(8) When a report is made in respect of a young person under subsection (1), the young person, his or her counsel or the adult assisting the young person under subsection 25(7) and the prosecutor shall, subject to subsection (9), on application to the youth justice court, be given an opportunity to cross-examine the person who made the report.

NON-DISCLOSURE IN CERTAIN CASES

(9) A youth justice court shall withhold all or part of a report made in respect of a young person under subsection (1) from a private prosecutor, if disclosure of the report or part, in the opinion of the court, is not necessary for the prosecution of the case and might be prejudicial to the young person.

NON-DISCLOSURE IN CERTAIN CASES

(10) A youth justice court shall withhold all or part of a report made in respect of a young person under subsection (1) from the

young person, the young person's parents or a private prosecutor if the court is satisfied, on the basis of the report or evidence given in the absence of the young person, parents or private prosecutor by the person who made the report, that disclosure of the report or part would seriously impair the treatment or recovery of the young person, or would be likely to endanger the life or safety of, or result in serious psychological harm to, another person.

EXCEPTION—INTERESTS OF JUSTICE

(11) Despite subsection (10), the youth justice court may release all or part of the report to the young person, the young person's parents or the private prosecutor if the court is of the opinion that the interests of justice make disclosure essential.

REPORT TO BE PART OF RECORD

(12) A report made under subsection (1) forms part of the record of the case in respect of which it was requested.

DISCLOSURE BY QUALIFIED PERSON

(13) Despite any other provision of this Act, a qualified person who is of the opinion that a young person held in detention or committed to custody is likely to endanger his or her own life or safety or to endanger the life of, or cause bodily harm to, another person may immediately so advise any person who has the care and custody of the young person whether or not the same information is contained in a report made under subsection (1).

DEFINITION OF "QUALIFIED PERSON"

(14) In this section, "qualified person" means a person duly qualified by provincial law to practice medicine or psychiatry or to carry out psychological examinations or assessments, as the circumstances require, or, if no such law exists, a person who is, in the opinion of the youth justice court, so qualified, and includes a person or a member of a class of persons designated by the lieutenant governor in council of a province or his or her delegate.

Referral to Child Welfare Agency

REFERRAL TO CHILD WELFARE AGENCY

35. In addition to any order that it is authorized to make, a youth justice court may, at any stage of proceedings against a young person, refer the young person to a child welfare agency for assessment to determine whether the young person is in need of child welfare services.

Adjudication

WHEN YOUNG PERSON PLEADS GUILTY

36. (1) If a young person pleads guilty to an offence charged against the young person and the youth justice court is satisfied that the facts support the charge, the court shall find the young person guilty of the offence.

WHEN YOUNG PERSON PLEADS NOT GUILTY

(2) If a young person charged with an offence pleads not guilty to the offence or pleads guilty but the youth justice court is not satisfied that the facts support the charge, the court shall proceed with the trial and shall, after considering the matter, find the young person guilty or not guilty or make an order dismissing the charge, as the case may be.

Appeals

APPEALS

37. (1) An appeal in respect of an indictable offence or an offence that the Attorney General elects to proceed with as an indictable offence lies under this Act in accordance with Part XXI (appeals—indictable offences) of the *Criminal Code*, which Part applies with any modifications that the circumstances require.

APPEALS FOR CONTEMPT OF COURT

(2) A finding of guilt under section 15 for contempt of court or a sentence imposed in respect of the finding may be appealed as if the finding were a conviction or the sentence were a sentence in a prosecution by indictment.

APPEAL

(3) Section 10 of the *Criminal Code* applies if a person is convicted of contempt of court under subsection 27(4) (failure of parent to attend court).

APPEALS TO BE HEARD TOGETHER

(4) A judicial determination under subsection 42(9) (judicial determination of serious violent offence), or an order under subsection 72(1) (court order—adult or youth sentence), 75(3) (ban on publication) or 76(1) (placement when subject to adult sentence), may be appealed as part of the sentence and, unless the court to which the appeal is taken otherwise orders, if more than one of these is appealed they must be part of the same appeal proceeding.

APPEALS FOR SUMMARY CONVICTION OFFENCES

(5) An appeal in respect of an offence punishable on summary conviction or an offence that the Attorney General elects to proceed with as an offence punishable on summary conviction lies under this Act in accordance with Part XXVII (summary conviction offences) of the *Criminal Code*, which Part applies with any modifications that the circumstances require.

APPEALS WHERE OFFENCES ARE TRIED JOINTLY

(6) An appeal in respect of one or more indictable offences and one or more summary conviction offences that are tried jointly or in respect of which youth sentences are jointly imposed lies under this Act in accordance with Part XXI (appeals—indictable offences) of the *Criminal Code*, which Part applies with any modifications that the circumstances require.

DEEMED ELECTION

(7) For the purpose of appeals under this Act, if no election is made in respect of an offence that may be prosecuted by indictment or proceeded with by way of summary conviction, the Attorney General is deemed to have elected to proceed with the offence as an offence punishable on summary conviction.

IF THE YOUTH JUSTICE COURT IS A SUPERIOR COURT

(8) In any province where the youth justice court is a superior court, an appeal under subsection (5) shall be made to the court of appeal of the province.

NUNAVUT

(9) Despite subsection (8), if the Nunavut Court of Justice is acting as a youth justice court, an appeal under subsection (5) shall be made to a judge of the Nunavut Court of Appeal, and an appeal of that judge's decision shall be made to the Nunavut Court of Appeal in accordance with section 839 of the *Criminal Code*.

APPEAL TO THE SUPREME COURT OF CANADA

(10) No appeal lies under subsection (1) from a judgment of the court of appeal in respect of a finding of guilt or an order dismissing an information or indictment to the Supreme Court of Canada unless leave to appeal is granted by the Supreme Court of Canada.

NO APPEAL FROM YOUTH SENTENCE ON REVIEW

(11) No appeal lies from a youth sentence under section 59 or any of sections 94 to 96.

PART 4
SENTENCING

Purpose and Principles

PURPOSE

38. (1) The purpose of sentencing under section 42 (youth sentences) is to hold a young person accountable for an offence through the imposition of just sanctions that have meaningful consequences for the young person and that promote his or her rehabilitation and reintegration into society, thereby contributing to the long-term protection of the public.

SENTENCING PRINCIPLES

(2) A youth justice court that imposes a youth sentence on a young person shall determine the sentence in accordance with the principles set out in section 3 and the following principles:

(a) the sentence must not result in a punishment that is greater than the punishment that would be appropriate for an adult who has been convicted of the same offence committed in similar circumstances;

(b) the sentence must be similar to the sentences imposed in the region on similar young persons found guilty of the same offence committed in similar circumstances;

(c) the sentence must be proportionate to the seriousness of the offence and the degree of responsibility of the young person for that offence; and

(d) subject to paragraph (c), the sentence must

(i) be the least restrictive sentence that is capable of achieving the purpose set out in subsection (1),

(ii) be the one that is most likely to rehabilitate the young person and reintegrate him or her into society, and

(iii) promote a sense of responsibility in the young person, and an acknowledgement of the harm done to victims and the community.

FACTORS TO BE CONSIDERED

(3) In determining a youth sentence, the youth justice court shall take into account

(a) the degree of participation by the young person in the commission of the offence;

(b) the harm done to victims and whether it was intentional or reasonably foreseeable;

(c) any reparation made by the young person to the victim or the community;

(d) the time spent in detention by the young person as a result of the offence;

(e) the previous findings of guilt of the young person; and

(f) any other aggravating and mitigating circumstances related to the young person or the offence that are relevant to the purpose and principles set out in this section.

COMMITTAL TO CUSTODY

39. (1) A youth justice court shall not commit a young person to custody under section 42 (youth sentences) unless

(a) the young person has committed a violent offence;

(b) the young person has failed to comply with non-custodial sentences;

(c) the young person has committed an indictable offence for which an adult would be liable to imprisonment for a term of more than two years and has a history that indicates a pattern of findings of guilt under this Act or the *Young Offenders Act*, chapter Y-1 of the Revised Statutes of Canada, 1985; or

(d) in exceptional cases where the young person has committed an indictable offence, the aggravating circumstances of the offence are such that the imposition of a non-custodial sentence would be inconsistent with the purpose and principles set out in section 38.

ALTERNATIVES TO CUSTODY

(2) If any of paragraphs (1)(a) to (c) apply, a youth justice court shall not impose a custodial sentence under section 42 (youth sentences) unless the court has considered all alternatives to custody raised at the sentencing hearing that are reasonable in the circumstances, and determined that there is not a reasonable alternative, or combination of alternatives, that is in accordance with the purpose and principles set out in section 38.

FACTORS TO BE CONSIDERED

(3) In determining whether there is a reasonable alternative to custody, a youth justice court shall consider submissions relating to

(a) the alternatives to custody that are available;

(b) the likelihood that the young person will comply with a non-custodial sentence, taking into account his or her compliance with previous non-custodial sentences; and

(c) the alternatives to custody that have been used in respect of young persons for similar offences committed in similar circumstances.

IMPOSITION OF SAME SENTENCE

(4) The previous imposition of a particular non-custodial sentence on a young person does not preclude a youth justice court from imposing the same or any other non-custodial sentence for another offence.

CUSTODY AS SOCIAL MEASURE PROHIBITED

(5) A youth justice court shall not use custody as a substitute for appropriate child protection, mental health or other social measures.

PRE-SENTENCE REPORT

(6) Before imposing a custodial sentence under section 42 (youth sentences), a youth justice court shall consider a pre-sentence report and any sentencing proposal made by the young person or his or her counsel.

REPORT DISPENSED WITH

(7) A youth justice court may, with the consent of the prosecutor and the young person or his or her counsel, dispense with a pre-sentence report if the court is satisfied that the report is not necessary.

LENGTH OF CUSTODY

(8) In determining the length of a youth sentence that includes a custodial portion, a youth justice court shall be guided by the purpose and principles set out in section 38, and shall not take into consideration the fact that the supervision portion of the sentence may not be served in custody and that the sentence may be reviewed by the court under section 94.

REASONS

(9) If a youth justice court imposes a youth sentence that includes a custodial portion, the court shall state the reasons why it has determined that a non-custodial sentence is not adequate to achieve the purpose set out in subsection 38(1), including, if applicable, the reasons why the case is an exceptional case under paragraph (1)(d).

Pre-sentence Report

PRE-SENTENCE REPORT

40. (1) Before imposing sentence on a young person found guilty of an offence, a youth justice court

(a) shall, if it is required under this Act to consider a pre-sentence report before making an order or a sentence in respect of a young person, and

(b) may, if it considers it advisable,

require the provincial director to cause to be prepared a pre-sentence report in respect of the young person and to submit the report to the court.

CONTENTS OF REPORT

(2) A pre-sentence report made in respect of a young person shall, subject to subsection (3), be in writing and shall include the following, to the extent that it is relevant to the purpose and principles of sentencing set out in section 38 and to the restrictions on custody set out in section 39:

(a) the results of an interview with the young person and, if reasonably possible, the parents of the young person and, if appropriate and reasonably possible, members of the young person's extended family;

(b) the results of an interview with the victim in the case, if applicable and reasonably possible;

(c) the recommendations resulting from any conference referred to in section 41;

(d) any information that is applicable to the case, including

(i) the age, maturity, character, behaviour and attitude of the young person and his or her willingness to make amends,

(ii) any plans put forward by the young person to change his or her conduct or to participate in activities or undertake measures to improve himself or herself,

(iii) subject to subsection 119(2) (period of access to records), the history of previous findings of delinquency under the *Juvenile Delinquents Act*, chapter J-3 of the Revised Statutes of Canada, 1970, or previous findings of guilt for offences under the *Young Offenders Act*, chapter Y-1 of the Revised Statutes of Canada, 1985, or under this or any other Act of Parliament or any regulation made under it, the history of community or other services rendered to the young person with respect to those findings and the response of the young person to previous sentences or dispositions and to services rendered to him or her,

(iv) subject to subsection 119(2) (period of access to records), the history of alternative measures under the *Young Offenders Act*, chapter Y-1 of the Revised Statutes of Canada, 1985, or extrajudicial sanctions used to deal with the young person and the response of the young person to those measures or sanctions,

(v) the availability and appropriateness of community services and facilities for young persons and the willingness of the young person to avail himself or herself of those services or facilities,

(vi) the relationship between the young person and the young person's parents and the degree of control and influence of the parents over the young person and, if appropriate and reasonably possible, the relationship between the young person and the young person's extended family and the degree of control and influence of the young person's extended family over the young person, and

(vii) the school attendance and performance record and the employment record of the young person;

(e) any information that may assist the court in determining under subsection 39(2) whether there is an alternative to custody; and

(f) any information that the provincial director considers relevant, including any recommendation that the provincial director considers appropriate.

ORAL REPORT WITH LEAVE

(3) If a pre-sentence report cannot reasonably be committed to writing, it may, with leave of the youth justice court, be submitted orally in court.

REPORT FORMS PART OF RECORD

(4) A pre-sentence report shall form part of the record of the case in respect of which it was requested.

COPIES OF PRE-SENTENCE REPORT

(5) If a pre-sentence report made in respect of a young person is submitted to a youth justice court in writing, the court

(a) shall, subject to subsection (7), cause a copy of the report to be given to

(i) the young person,

(ii) any parent of the young person who is in attendance at the proceedings against the young person,

(iii) any counsel representing the young person, and

(iv) the prosecutor; and

(b) may cause a copy of the report to be given to a parent of the young person who is not in attendance at the proceedings if the parent is, in the opinion of the court, taking an active interest in the proceedings.

CROSS-EXAMINATION

(6) If a pre-sentence report made in respect of a young person is submitted to a youth justice court, the young person, his or her counsel or the adult assisting the young person under subsection 25(7) and the prosecutor shall, subject to subsection (7), on application to the court, be given the opportunity to cross-examine the person who made the report.

REPORT MAY BE WITHHELD FROM PRIVATE PROSECUTOR

(7) If a pre-sentence report made in respect of a young person is submitted to a youth justice court, the court may, when the prosecutor is a private prosecutor and disclosure of all or part of the report to the prosecutor might, in the opinion of the court, be prejudicial to the young person and is not, in the opinion of the court, necessary for the prosecution of the case against the young person,

(a) withhold the report or part from the prosecutor, if the report is submitted in writing; or

(b) exclude the prosecutor from the court during the submission of the report or part, if the report is submitted orally in court.

REPORT DISCLOSED TO OTHER PERSONS

(8) If a pre-sentence report made in respect of a young person is submitted to a youth justice court, the court

(a) shall, on request, cause a copy or a transcript of the report to be supplied to

(i) any court that is dealing with matters relating to the young person, and

(ii) any youth worker to whom the young person's case has been assigned; and

(b) may, on request, cause a copy or a transcript of all or part of the report to be supplied to any person not otherwise authorized under this section to receive a copy or a transcript of the report if, in the opinion of the court, the person has a valid interest in the proceedings.

DISCLOSURE BY THE PROVINCIAL DIRECTOR

(9) A provincial director who submits a pre-sentence report made in respect of a young person to a youth justice court may make all or part of the report available to any person in whose custody or under whose supervision the young person is placed or to any other person who is directly assisting in the care or treatment of the young person.

INADMISSIBILITY OF STATEMENTS

(10) No statement made by a young person in the course of the preparation of a pre-sentence report in respect of the young person is admissible in evidence against any young person in civil or criminal proceedings except those under section 42 (youth sentences), 59 (review of non-custodial sentence) or 71 (hearing—adult sentences) or any of sections 94 to 96 (reviews and other proceedings related to custodial sentences).

Youth Sentences

RECOMMENDATION OF CONFERENCE

41. When a youth justice court finds a young person guilty of an offence, the court may convene or cause to be convened a conference under section 19 for recommendations to the court on an appropriate youth sentence.

CONSIDERATIONS AS TO YOUTH SENTENCE

42. (1) A youth justice court shall, before imposing a youth sentence, consider any recommendations submitted under section 41, any pre-sentence report, any representations made by the parties to the proceedings or their counsel or agents and by the parents of the young person, and any other relevant information before the court.

YOUTH SENTENCE

(2) When a youth justice court finds a young person guilty of an offence and is imposing a youth sentence, the court shall, subject to this section, impose any one of the following sanctions or any number of them that are not inconsistent with each other and, if the offence is first degree murder or second degree murder within the meaning of section 231 of the *Criminal Code*, the court shall impose a sanction set out in paragraph (q) or subparagraph (r)(ii) or (iii) and may impose any other of the sanctions set out in this subsection that the court considers appropriate:

(a) reprimand the young person;

(b) by order direct that the young person be discharged absolutely, if the court considers it to be in the best interests of the young person and not contrary to the public interest;

(c) by order direct that the young person be discharged on any conditions that the court considers appropriate and may require the young person to report to and be supervised by the provincial director;

(d) impose on the young person a fine not exceeding $1,000 to be paid at the time and on the terms that the court may fix;

(e) order the young person to pay to any other person at the times and on the terms that the court may fix an amount by way of compensation for loss of or damage to property or for loss of income or support, or an amount for, in the Province of Quebec, pre-trial pecuniary loss or, in any other province, special damages, for personal injury arising from the commission of the offence if the value is readily ascertainable, but no order shall be made for other damages in the Province of Quebec or for general damages in any other province;

(f) order the young person to make restitution to any other person of any property obtained by the young person as a result of the commission of the offence within the time that the court may fix, if the property is owned by the other person or was, at the time of the offence, in his or her lawful possession;

(g) if property obtained as a result of the commission of the offence has been sold to an innocent purchaser, where restitution of the property to its owner or any other person has been made or ordered, order the young person to pay the purchaser, at the time and on the terms that the court may fix, an amount not exceeding the amount paid by the purchaser for the property;

(h) subject to section 54, order the young person to compensate any person in kind or by way of personal services at the time and on the terms that the court may fix for any loss, damage or injury suffered by that person in respect of which an order may be made under paragraph (e) or (g);

(i) subject to section 54, order the young person to perform a community service at the time and on the terms that the court may fix, and to report to and be supervised by the provincial director or a person designated by the youth justice court;

(j) subject to section 51 (mandatory prohibition order), make any order of prohibition, seizure or forfeiture that may be imposed under any Act of Parliament or any regulation made under it if an accused is found guilty or convicted of that offence, other than an order under section 161 of the *Criminal Code*;

(k) place the young person on probation in accordance with sections 55 and 56 (conditions and other matters related to probation orders) for a specified period not exceeding two years;

(l) subject to subsection (3) (agreement of provincial director), order the young person into an intensive support and supervision program approved by the provincial director;

(m) subject to subsection (3) (agreement of provincial director) and section 54, order the young person to attend a non-residential program approved by the provincial director, at the times and on the terms that the court may fix, for a maximum of two hundred and forty hours, over a period not exceeding six months;

(n) make a custody and supervision order with respect to the young person, ordering that a period be served in custody and that a second period—which is one half as long as the first—be served, subject to sections 97 (conditions to be included) and 98 (continuation of custody), under supervision in the community subject to conditions, the total of the periods not to exceed two years from the date of the coming into force of the order or, if the young person is found guilty of an offence for which the punishment provided by the *Criminal Code* or any other Act of Parliament is imprisonment for life, three years from the date of coming into force of the order;

(o) in the case of an offence set out in subparagraph (a)(ii), (iii) or (iv) of the definition "presumptive offence" in subsection 2(1), make a custody and supervision order in respect of the young person for a specified period not exceeding three years from the date of committal that orders the young person to be committed into a continuous period of custody for the first portion of the sentence and, subject to subsection 104(1) (continuation of custody), to serve the remainder of the sentence under conditional supervision in the community in accordance with section 105;

(p) subject to subsection (5), make a deferred custody and supervision order that is for a specified period not exceeding six months, subject to the conditions set out in subsection 105(2), and to any conditions set out in subsection 105(3) that the court considers appropriate;

(q) order the young person to serve a sentence not to exceed

(i) in the case of first degree murder, ten years comprised of

(A) a committal to custody, to be served continuously, for a period that must not, subject to subsection 104(1) (continuation of custody), exceed six years from the date of committal, and

(B) a placement under conditional supervision to be served in the community in accordance with section 105, and

(ii) in the case of second degree murder, seven years comprised of

(A) a committal to custody, to be served continuously, for a period that must not, subject to subsection 104(1) (continuation of custody), exceed four years from the date of committal, and

(B) a placement under conditional supervision to be served in the community in accordance with section 105;

(r) subject to subsection (7), make an intensive rehabilitative custody and supervision order in respect of the young person

(i) that is for a specified period that must not exceed

(A) two years from the date of committal, or

(B) if the young person is found guilty of an offence for which the punishment provided by the *Criminal Code* or any other Act of Parliament is imprisonment for life, three years from the date of committal,

and that orders the young person to be committed into a continuous period of intensive rehabilitative custody for the first portion of the sentence and, subject to subsection 104(1) (continuation of custody), to serve the remainder under conditional supervision in the community in accordance with section 105,

(ii) that is for a specified period that must not exceed, in the case of first degree murder, ten years from the date of committal, comprising

(A) a committal to intensive rehabilitative custody, to be served continuously, for a period that must not exceed six years from the date of committal, and

(B) subject to subsection 104(1) (continuation of custody), a placement under conditional supervision to be served in the community in accordance with section 105, and

(iii) that is for a specified period that must not exceed, in the case of second degree murder, seven years from the date of committal, comprising

(A) a committal to intensive rehabilitative custody, to be served continuously, for a period that must not exceed four years from the date of committal, and

(B) subject to subsection 104(1) (continuation of custody), a placement under conditional supervision to be served in the community in accordance with section 105; and

(s) impose on the young person any other reasonable and ancillary conditions that the court considers advisable and in the best interests of the young person and the public.

AGREEMENT OF PROVINCIAL DIRECTOR

(3) A youth justice court may make an order under paragraph (2)(l) or (m) only if the provincial director has determined that a program to enforce the order is available.

YOUTH JUSTICE COURT STATEMENT

(4) When the youth justice court makes a custody and supervision order with respect to a young person under paragraph (2)(n), the court shall state the following with respect to that order:

You are ordered to serve (state the number of days or months to be served) in custody, to be followed by (state one-half of the number of days or months stated above) to be served under supervision in the community subject to conditions.

If you breach any of the conditions while you are under supervision in the community, you may be brought back into custody and required to serve the rest of the second period in custody as well.

You should also be aware that, under other provisions of the *Youth Criminal Justice Act*, a court could require you to serve the second period in custody as well.

The periods in custody and under supervision in the community may be changed if you are or become subject to another sentence.

DEFERRED CUSTODY AND SUPERVISION ORDER

(5) The court may make a deferred custody and supervision order under paragraph (2)(p) if

(a) the young person is found guilty of an offence that is not a serious violent offence; and

(b) it is consistent with the purpose and principles set out in section 38 and the restrictions on custody set out in section 39.

APPLICATION OF SECTIONS 106 TO 109

(6) Sections 106 to 109 (suspension of conditional supervision) apply to a breach of a deferred custody and supervision order made under paragraph (2)(p) as if the breach were a breach of an order for conditional supervision made under subsection 105(1) and, for the purposes of sections 106 to 109, supervision under a deferred custody and supervision order is deemed to be conditional supervision.

INTENSIVE REHABILITATIVE CUSTODY AND SUPERVISION ORDER

(7) A youth justice court may make an intensive rehabilitative custody and supervision order under paragraph (2)(r) in respect of a young person only if

(a) either

(i) the young person has been found guilty of an offence under one of the following provisions of the *Criminal Code*, namely, section 231 or 235 (first degree murder or second degree murder within the meaning of section 231), section 239 (attempt to commit murder), section 232, 234 or 236 (manslaughter) or section 273 (aggravated sexual assault), or

(ii) the young person has been found guilty of a serious violent offence for which an adult is liable to imprisonment for a term of more than two years, and the young person had previously been found guilty at least twice of a serious violent offence;

(b) the young person is suffering from a mental illness or disorder, a psychological disorder or an emotional disturbance;

(c) a plan of treatment and intensive supervision has been developed for the young person, and there are reasonable grounds to believe that the plan might reduce the risk of the young person repeating the offence or committing a serious violent offence; and

(d) the provincial director has determined that an intensive rehabilitative custody and supervision program is available and that the young person's participation in the program is appropriate.

SAFEGUARD OF RIGHTS

(8) Nothing in this section abrogates or derogates from the rights of a young person regarding consent to physical or mental health treatment or care.

DETERMINATION BY COURT

(9) On application of the Attorney General after a young person is found guilty of an offence, and after giving both parties an opportunity to be heard, the youth justice court may make a judicial determination that the offence is a serious violent offence and endorse the information or indictment accordingly.

APPEALS

(10) For the purposes of an appeal in accordance with section 37, a determination under subsection (9) is part of the sentence.

INCONSISTENCY

(11) An order may not be made under paragraphs (2)(k) to (m) in respect of an offence for which a conditional discharge has been granted under paragraph (2)(c).

COMING INTO FORCE OF YOUTH SENTENCE

(12) A youth sentence or any part of it comes into force on the date on which it is imposed or on any later date that the youth justice court specifies.

CONSECUTIVE YOUTH SENTENCES

(13) Subject to subsections (15) and (16), a youth justice court that sentences a young person may direct that a sentence imposed on the young person under paragraph (2)(n), (o), (q) or (r) be served consecutively if the young person

(a) is sentenced while under sentence for an offence under any of those paragraphs; or

(b) is found guilty of more than one offence under any of those paragraphs.

DURATION OF YOUTH SENTENCE FOR A SINGLE OFFENCE

(14) No youth sentence, other than an order made under paragraph (2)(j), (n), (o), (q) or (r), shall continue in force for more than two years. If the youth sentence comprises more than one sanction imposed at the same time in respect of the same offence, the combined duration of the sanctions shall not exceed two years, unless the sentence includes a sanction under paragraph (2)(j), (n), (o), (q) or (r) that exceeds two years.

DURATION OF YOUTH SENTENCE FOR DIFFERENT OFFENCES

(15) Subject to subsection (16), if more than one youth sentence is imposed under this section in respect of a young person with respect to different offences, the continuous combined duration of those youth sentences shall not exceed three years, except if one of the offences is first degree murder or second degree murder within the meaning of section 231 of the *Criminal Code*, in which case the continuous combined duration of those youth sentences shall not exceed ten years in the case of first degree murder, or seven years in the case of second degree murder.

DURATION OF YOUTH SENTENCES MADE AT DIFFERENT TIMES

(16) If a youth sentence is imposed in respect of an offence committed by a young person after the commencement of, but before the completion of, any youth sentences imposed on the young person,

(a) the duration of the sentence imposed in respect of the subsequent offence shall be determined in accordance with subsections (14) and (15);

(b) the sentence may be served consecutively to the sentences imposed in respect of the previous offences; and

(c) the combined duration of all the sentences may exceed three years and, if the offence is, or one of the previous offences was,

(i) first degree murder within the meaning of section 231 of the *Criminal Code*, the continuous combined duration of the youth sentences may exceed ten years, or

(ii) second degree murder within the meaning of section 231 of the *Criminal Code*, the continuous combined duration of the youth sentences may exceed seven years.

SENTENCE CONTINUES WHEN ADULT

(17) Subject to sections 89, 92 and 93 (provisions related to placement in adult facilities) of this Act and section 743.5 (transfer of jurisdiction) of the *Criminal Code*, a youth sentence imposed on a young person continues in effect in accordance with its terms after the young person becomes an adult.

ADDITIONAL YOUTH SENTENCES

43. Subject to subsection 42(15) (duration of youth sentences), if a young person who is subject to a custodial sentence imposed under paragraph 42(2)(n), (o), (q) or (r) that has not expired receives an additional youth sentence under one of those paragraphs, the young person is, for the purposes of the *Corrections and Conditional Release Act*, the *Criminal Code*, the *Prisons and Reformatories Act* and this Act, deemed to have been sentenced to one youth sentence commencing at the beginning of the first of those youth sentences to be served and ending on the expiry of the last of them to be served.

CUSTODIAL PORTION IF ADDITIONAL YOUTH SENTENCE

44. Subject to subsection 42(15) (duration of youth sentences) and section 46 (exception when youth sentence in respect of earlier offence), if an additional youth sentence under paragraph 42(2)(n), (o), (q) or (r) is imposed on a young person on whom a youth sentence had already been imposed under one of those paragraphs that has not expired and the expiry date of the youth sentence that includes the additional youth sentence, as determined in accordance with section 43, is later than the expiry date of the youth sentence that the young person was serving before the additional youth sentence was imposed, the custodial portion of the young person's youth sentence is, from the date the additional sentence is imposed, the total of

(a) the unexpired portion of the custodial portion of the youth sentence before the additional youth sentence was imposed, and

(b) the relevant period set out in subparagraph (i), (ii) or (iii):

(i) if the additional youth sentence is imposed under paragraph 42(2)(n), the period that is two thirds of the period that constitutes the difference between the expiry of the youth sentence as determined in accordance with section 43 and the expiry of the youth sentence that the young person was serving before the additional youth sentence was imposed,

(ii) if the additional youth sentence is a concurrent youth sentence imposed under paragraph 42(2)(o), (q) or (r), the custodial portion of the youth sentence imposed under that paragraph that extends beyond the expiry date of the custodial portion of the sentence being served before the imposition of the additional sentence, or

(iii) if the additional youth sentence is a consecutive youth sentence imposed under paragraph 42(2)(o), (q) or (r), the custodial portion of the additional youth sentence imposed under that paragraph.

SUPERVISION WHEN ADDITIONAL YOUTH SENTENCE EXTENDS THE PERIOD IN CUSTODY

45. (1) If a young person has begun to serve a portion of a youth sentence in the community subject to conditions under paragraph 42(2)(n) or under conditional supervision under paragraph 42(2)(o), (q) or (r) at the time an additional youth sentence is imposed under one of those paragraphs, and, as a result of the application of section 44, the custodial portion of the young person's youth sentence ends on a day that is later than the day on which the young person received the additional youth sentence, the serving of a portion of the youth sentence under supervision in the community subject to conditions or under conditional supervision shall become inoperative and the young person shall be committed to custody under paragraph 102(1)(b) or 106(b) until the end of the extended portion of the youth sentence to be served in custody.

SUPERVISION WHEN ADDITIONAL YOUTH SENTENCE DOES NOT EXTEND THE PERIOD IN CUSTODY

(2) If a youth sentence has been imposed under paragraph 42(2)(n), (o), (q) or (r) on a young person who is under supervision in the community subject to conditions under paragraph 42(2)(n) or under conditional supervision under paragraph 42(2)(o), (q) or (r), and the additional youth sentence would not modify the expiry date of the youth sentence that the young person was serving at the time the additional youth sentence was imposed, the young person may be remanded to the youth custody facility that the provincial director considers appropriate. The provincial director shall review the case and,

no later than forty-eight hours after the remand of the young person, shall either refer the case to the youth justice court for a review under section 103 or 109 or release the young person to continue the supervision in the community or the conditional supervision.

SUPERVISION WHEN YOUTH SENTENCE ADDITIONAL TO SUPERVISION

(3) If a youth sentence has been imposed under paragraph 42(2)(n), (o), (q) or (r) on a young person who is under conditional supervision under paragraph 94(19)(b) or subsection 96(5), the young person shall be remanded to the youth custody facility that the provincial director considers appropriate. The provincial director shall review the case and, no later than forty-eight hours after the remand of the young person, shall either refer the case to the youth justice court for a review under section 103 or 109 or release the young person to continue the conditional supervision.

EXCEPTION WHEN YOUTH SENTENCE IN RESPECT OF EARLIER OFFENCE

46. The total of the custodial portions of a young person's youth sentences shall not exceed six years calculated from the beginning of the youth sentence that is determined in accordance with section 43 if

(a) a youth sentence is imposed under paragraph 42(2)(n), (o), (q) or (r) on the young person already serving a youth sentence under one of those paragraphs; and

(b) the later youth sentence imposed is in respect of an offence committed before the commencement of the earlier youth sentence.

COMMITTAL TO CUSTODY DEEMED CONTINUOUS

47. (1) Subject to subsections (2) and (3), a young person who is sentenced under paragraph 42(2)(n) is deemed to be committed to continuous custody for the custodial portion of the sentence.

INTERMITTENT CUSTODY

(2) If the sentence does not exceed ninety days, the youth justice court may order that the custodial portion of the sentence be served intermittently if it is consistent with the purpose and principles set out in section 38.

AVAILABILITY OF PLACE OF INTERMITTENT CUSTODY

(3) Before making an order of committal to intermittent custody, the youth justice court shall require the prosecutor to make available to the court for its consideration a report of the provincial director as to the availability of a youth custody facility in which an order of intermittent custody can be enforced and, if the report discloses that no such youth custody facility is available, the court shall not make the order.

REASONS FOR THE SENTENCE

48. When a youth justice court imposes a youth sentence, it shall state its reasons for the sentence in the record of the case and shall, on request, give or cause to be given a copy of the sentence and the reasons for the sentence to

(a) the young person, the young person's counsel, a parent of the young person, the provincial director and the prosecutor; and

(b) in the case of a committal to custody under paragraph 42(2)(n), (o), (q) or (r), the review board.

WARRANT OF COMMITTAL

49. (1) When a young person is committed to custody, the youth justice court shall issue or cause to be issued a warrant of committal.

CUSTODY DURING TRANSFER

(2) A young person who is committed to custody may, in the course of being transferred from custody to the court or from the court to custody, be held under the supervision and control of a peace officer or in any place of temporary detention referred to in subsection 30(1) that the provincial director may specify.

SUBSECTION 30(3) APPLIES

(3) Subsection 30(3) (detention separate from adults) applies, with any modifications that the circumstances require, in respect of a person held in a place of temporary detention under subsection (2).

APPLICATION OF PART XXIII OF *CRIMINAL CODE*

50. (1) Subject to section 74 (application of *Criminal Code* to adult sentences), Part XXIII (sentencing) of the *Criminal Code* does not apply in respect of proceedings under this Act except for sections 722 (victim impact statements), 722.1 (copy of statement) and 722.2 (inquiry by court), subsection 730(2) (court process continues in force) and sections 748 (pardons and remissions), 748.1 (remission by the Governor in Council) and 749 (royal prerogative) of that Act, which provisions apply with any modifications that the circumstances require.

SECTION 787 OF *CRIMINAL CODE* DOES NOT APPLY

(2) Section 787 (general penalty) of the *Criminal Code* does not apply in respect of proceedings under this Act.

MANDATORY PROHIBITION ORDER

51. (1) Despite section 42 (youth sentences), when a young person is found guilty of an offence referred to in any of paragraphs 109(1)(a) to (d) of the *Criminal Code*, the youth justice court shall, in addition to imposing a sentence under section 42 (youth sentences), make an order prohibiting the young person from possessing any firearm, cross-bow, prohibited weapon, restricted weapon, prohibited device, ammunition, prohibited ammunition or explosive substance during the period specified in the order as determined in accordance with subsection (2).

DURATION OF PROHIBITION ORDER

(2) An order made under subsection (1) begins on the day on which the order is made and ends not earlier than two years after the young person has completed the custodial portion of the sentence or, if the young person is not subject to custody, after the time the young person is found guilty of the offence.

DISCRETIONARY PROHIBITION ORDER

(3) Despite section 42 (youth sentences), where a young person is found guilty of an offence referred to in paragraph 110(1)(a) or (b) of the *Criminal Code*, the youth justice court shall, in addition to imposing a sentence under section 42 (youth sentences), consider whether it is desirable, in the interests of the safety of the young person or of any other person, to make an order prohibiting the young person from possessing any firearm, cross-bow, prohibited weapon, restricted weapon, prohibited device, ammunition, prohibited ammunition or explosive substance, or all such things, and where the court decides that it is so desirable, the court shall so order.

DURATION OF PROHIBITION ORDER

(4) An order made under subsection (3) against a young person begins on the day on which the order is made and ends not later than two years after the young person has completed the custodial portion of the sentence or, if the young person is not subject to custody, after the time the young person is found guilty of the offence.

REASONS FOR THE PROHIBITION ORDER

(5) When a youth justice court makes an order under this section, it shall state its reasons for making the order in the record of the case and shall give or cause to be given a copy of the order and, on request, a transcript or copy of the reasons to the young person against whom the order was made, the counsel and a parent of the young person and the provincial director.

REASONS

(6) When the youth justice court does not make an order under subsection (3), or when the youth justice court does make such an order but does not prohibit the possession of everything referred to in that subsection, the youth justice court shall include in the record a statement of the youth justice court's reasons.

APPLICATION OF *CRIMINAL CODE*

(7) Sections 113 to 117 (firearm prohibition orders) of the *Criminal Code* apply in respect of any order made under this section.

REPORT

(8) Before making an order referred to in section 113 (lifting firearms order) of the *Criminal Code* in respect of a young person, the youth justice court may require the provincial director to cause to be prepared, and to submit to the youth justice court, a report on the young person.

REVIEW OF ORDER MADE UNDER SECTION 51

52. (1) A youth justice court may, on application, review an order made under section 51 at any time after the end of the period set out in subsection 119(2) (period of access to records) that applies to the record of the offence that resulted in the order being made.

GROUNDS

(2) In conducting a review under this section, the youth justice court shall take into account

(a) the nature and circumstances of the offence in respect of which the order was made; and

(b) the safety of the young person and of other persons.

DECISION OF REVIEW

(3) When a youth justice court conducts a review under this section, it may, after giving the young person, a parent of the young person, the Attorney General and the provincial director an opportunity to be heard,

(a) confirm the order;

(b) revoke the order; or

(c) vary the order as it considers appropriate in the circumstances of the case.

NEW ORDER NOT TO BE MORE ONEROUS

(4) No variation of an order made under paragraph (3)(c) may be more onerous than the order being reviewed.

APPLICATION OF PROVISIONS

(5) Subsections 59(3) to (5) apply, with any modifications that the circumstances require, in respect of a review under this section.

FUNDING FOR VICTIMS

53. (1) The lieutenant governor in council of a province may order that, in respect of any fine imposed in the province under paragraph 42(2)(d), a percentage of the fine as fixed by the lieutenant governor in council be used to provide such assistance to victims of offences as the lieutenant governor in council may direct from time to time.

VICTIM FINE SURCHARGE

(2) If the lieutenant governor in council of a province has not made an order under subsection (1), a youth justice court that imposes a fine on a young person under paragraph 42(2)(d) may, in addition to any other punishment imposed on the young person, order the young person to pay a victim fine surcharge in an amount not exceeding fifteen per cent of the fine. The surcharge shall be used to provide such assistance to victims of offences as the lieutenant governor in council of the province in which the surcharge is imposed may direct from time to time.

WHERE A FINE OR OTHER PAYMENT IS ORDERED

54. (1) The youth justice court shall, in imposing a fine under paragraph 42(2)(d) or in making an order under paragraph 42(2)(e) or (g), have regard to the present and future means of the young person to pay.

DISCHARGE OF FINE OR SURCHARGE

(2) A young person on whom a fine is imposed under paragraph 42(2)(d), including any percentage of a fine imposed under subsection 53(1), or on whom a victim fine surcharge is imposed under subsection 53(2), may discharge the fine or surcharge in whole or in part by earning credits for work performed in a program established for that purpose

(a) by the lieutenant governor in council of the province in which the fine or surcharge was imposed; or

(b) by the lieutenant governor in council of the province in which the young person resides, if an appropriate agreement is in effect between the government of that province and the government of the province in which the fine or surcharge was imposed.

RATES, CREDITING AND OTHER MATTERS

(3) A program referred to in subsection (2) shall determine the rate at which credits are earned and may provide for the manner of crediting any amounts earned against the fine or surcharge and any other matters necessary for or incidental to carrying out the program.

REPRESENTATIONS RESPECTING ORDERS UNDER PARAGRAPHS 42(2)(E) TO (H)

(4) In considering whether to make an order under any of paragraphs 42(2)(e) to (h), the youth justice court may consider any representations made by the person who would be compensated or to whom restitution or payment would be made.

NOTICE OF ORDERS UNDER PARAGRAPHS 42(2)(E) TO (H)

(5) If the youth justice court makes an order under any of paragraphs 42(2)(e) to (h), it shall cause notice of the terms of the order to be given to the person who is to be compensated or to whom restitution or payment is to be made.

CONSENT OF PERSON TO BE COMPENSATED

(6) No order may be made under paragraph 42(2)(h) unless the youth justice court has secured the consent of the person to be compensated.

ORDERS UNDER PARAGRAPH 42(2)(H), (I) OR (M)

(7) No order may be made under paragraph 42(2)(h), (i) or (m) unless the youth justice court is satisfied that

(a) the young person against whom the order is made is a suitable candidate for such an order; and

(b) the order does not interfere with the normal hours of work or education of the young person.

DURATION OF ORDER FOR SERVICE

(8) No order may be made under paragraph 42(2)(h) or (i) to perform personal or community services unless those services can be completed in two hundred and forty hours or less and within twelve months after the date of the order.

COMMUNITY SERVICE ORDER

(9) No order may be made under paragraph 42(2)(i) unless

(a) the community service to be performed is part of a program that is approved by the provincial director; or

(b) the youth justice court is satisfied that the person or organization for whom the community service is to be performed has agreed to its performance.

APPLICATION FOR FURTHER TIME TO COMPLETE YOUTH SENTENCE

(10) A youth justice court may, on application by or on behalf of the young person in respect of whom a youth sentence has been imposed under any of paragraphs 42(2)(d) to (i), allow further time for the completion of the sentence subject to any regulations made under paragraph 155(b) and to any rules made by the youth justice court under subsection 17(1).

CONDITIONS THAT MUST APPEAR IN ORDERS

55. (1) The youth justice court shall prescribe, as conditions of an order made under paragraph 42(2)(k) or (l), that the young person

(a) keep the peace and be of good behaviour; and

(b) appear before the youth justice court when required by the court to do so.

CONDITIONS THAT MAY APPEAR IN ORDERS

(2) A youth justice court may prescribe, as conditions of an order made under paragraph 42(2)(k) or (l), that a young person do one or more of the following that the youth justice court considers appropriate in the circumstances:

(a) report to and be supervised by the provincial director or a person designated by the youth justice court;

(b) notify the clerk of the youth justice court, the provincial director or the youth worker assigned to the case of any change of address or any change in the young person's place of employment, education or training;

(c) remain within the territorial jurisdiction of one or more courts named in the order;

(d) make reasonable efforts to obtain and maintain suitable employment;

(e) attend school or any other place of learning, training or recreation that is appropriate, if the youth justice court is satisfied that a suitable program for the young person is available there;

(f) reside with a parent, or any other adult that the youth justice court considers appropriate, who is willing to provide for the care and maintenance of the young person;

(g) reside at a place that the provincial director may specify;

(h) comply with any other conditions set out in the order that the youth justice court considers appropriate, including conditions for securing the young person's good conduct and for preventing the young person from repeating the offence or committing other offences; and

(i) not own, possess or have the control of any weapon, ammunition, prohibited ammunition, prohibited device or explosive substance, except as authorized by the order.

COMMUNICATION OF ORDER

56. (1) A youth justice court that makes an order under paragraph 42(2)(k) or (l) shall

(a) cause the order to be read by or to the young person bound by it;

(b) explain or cause to be explained to the young person the purpose and effect of the order, and confirm that the young person understands it; and

(c) cause a copy of the order to be given to the young person, and to any parent of the young person who is in attendance at the sentencing hearing.

COPY OF ORDER TO PARENT

(2) A youth justice court that makes an order under paragraph 42(2)(k) or (l) may cause a copy to be given to a parent of the young person who is not in attendance at the proceedings if the parent is, in the opinion of the court, taking an active interest in the proceedings.

ENDORSEMENT OF ORDER BY YOUNG PERSON

(3) After the order has been read and explained under subsection (1), the young person shall endorse on the order an acknowledgement that the young person has received a copy of the order and had its purpose and effect explained.

VALIDITY OF ORDER

(4) The failure of a young person to endorse the order or of a parent to receive a copy of the order does not affect the validity of the order.

COMMENCEMENT OF ORDER

(5) An order made under paragraph 42(2)(k) or (l) comes into force

(a) on the date on which it is made; or

(b) if a young person receives a sentence that includes a period of continuous custody and supervision, at the end of the period of supervision.

EFFECT OF ORDER IN CASE OF CUSTODY

(6) If a young person is subject to a sentence that includes both a period of continuous custody and supervision and an order made under paragraph 42(2)(k) or (l), and the court orders under subsection 42(12) a delay in the start of the period of custody, the court may divide the period that the order made under paragraph 42(2)(k) or (l) is in effect, with the first portion to have effect from the date on which it is made until the start of the period of custody, and the remainder to take effect at the end of the period of supervision.

NOTICE TO APPEAR

(7) A young person may be given notice either orally or in writing to appear before the youth justice court under paragraph 55(1)(b).

WARRANT IN DEFAULT OF APPEARANCE

(8) If service of a notice in writing is proved and the young person fails to attend court in accordance with the notice, a youth justice court may issue a warrant to compel the appearance of the young person.

TRANSFER OF YOUTH SENTENCE

57. (1) When a youth sentence has been imposed under any of paragraphs 42(2)(d) to (i), (k), (l) or (s) in respect of a young person and the young person or a parent with whom the young person resides is or becomes a resident of a territorial division outside the jurisdiction of the youth justice court that imposed the youth sentence, whether in the same or in another province, a youth justice court judge in the territorial division in which the youth sentence was imposed may, on the application of the Attorney General or on the application of the young person or the young person's parent, with the consent of the Attorney General, transfer to a youth justice court in another territorial division the youth sentence and any portion of the record of the case that is appropriate. All subsequent proceedings relating to the case shall then be carried out and enforced by that court.

NO TRANSFER OUTSIDE PROVINCE BEFORE APPEAL COMPLETED

(2) No youth sentence may be transferred from one province to another under this section until the time for an appeal against the youth sentence or the finding on which the youth sentence was based has expired or until all proceedings in respect of any such appeal have been completed.

TRANSFER TO A PROVINCE WHEN PERSON IS ADULT

(3) When an application is made under subsection (1) to transfer the youth sentence of a young person to a province in which the young person is an adult, a youth justice court judge may, with the

consent of the Attorney General, transfer the youth sentence and the record of the case to the youth justice court in the province to which the transfer is sought, and the youth justice court to which the case is transferred shall have full jurisdiction in respect of the youth sentence as if that court had imposed the youth sentence. The person shall be further dealt with in accordance with this Act.

INTERPROVINCIAL ARRANGEMENTS

58. (1) When a youth sentence has been imposed under any of paragraphs 42(2)(k) to (r) in respect of a young person, the youth sentence in one province may be dealt with in any other province in accordance with any agreement that may have been made between those provinces.

YOUTH JUSTICE COURT RETAINS JURISDICTION

(2) Subject to subsection (3), when a youth sentence imposed in respect of a young person is dealt with under this section in a province other than that in which the youth sentence was imposed, the youth justice court of the province in which the youth sentence was imposed retains, for all purposes of this Act, exclusive jurisdiction over the young person as if the youth sentence were dealt with within that province, and any warrant or process issued in respect of the young person may be executed or served in any place in Canada outside the province where the youth sentence was imposed as if it were executed or served in that province.

WAIVER OF JURISDICTION

(3) When a youth sentence imposed in respect of a young person is dealt with under this section in a province other than the one in which the youth sentence was imposed, the youth justice court of the province in which the youth sentence was imposed may, with the consent in writing of the Attorney General of that province and the young person, waive its jurisdiction, for the purpose of any proceeding under this Act, to the youth justice court of the province in which the youth sentence is dealt with, in which case the youth justice court in the province in which the youth sentence is dealt with shall have full jurisdiction in respect of the youth sentence as if that court had imposed the youth sentence.

REVIEW OF YOUTH SENTENCES NOT INVOLVING CUSTODY

59. (1) When a youth justice court has imposed a youth sentence in respect of a young person, other than a youth sentence under paragraph 42(2)(n), (o), (q) or (r), the youth justice court shall, on the application of the young person, the young person's parent, the Attorney General or the provincial director, made at any time after six months after the date of the youth sentence or, with leave of a youth justice court judge, at any earlier time, review the youth sentence if the court is satisfied that there are grounds for a review under subsection (2).

GROUNDS FOR REVIEW

(2) A review of a youth sentence may be made under this section

(a) on the ground that the circumstances that led to the youth sentence have changed materially;

(b) on the ground that the young person in respect of whom the review is to be made is unable to comply with or is experiencing serious difficulty in complying with the terms of the youth sentence;

(c) on the ground that the young person in respect of whom the review is to be made has contravened a condition of an order made under paragraph 42(2)(k) or (l) without reasonable excuse;

(d) on the ground that the terms of the youth sentence are adversely affecting the opportunities available to the young person to obtain services, education or employment; or

(e) on any other ground that the youth justice court considers appropriate.

PROGRESS REPORT

(3) The youth justice court may, before reviewing under this section a youth sentence imposed in respect of a young person, require the provincial director to cause to be prepared, and to submit to the youth justice court, a progress report on the performance of the young person since the youth sentence took effect.

SUBSECTIONS 94(10) TO (12) APPLY

(4) Subsections 94(10) to (12) apply, with any modifications that the circumstances require, in respect of any progress report required under subsection (3).

SUBSECTIONS 94(7) AND (14) TO (18) APPLY

(5) Subsections 94(7) and (14) to (18) apply, with any modifications that the circumstances require, in respect of reviews made under this section and any notice required under subsection 94(14) shall also be given to the provincial director.

COMPELLING APPEARANCE OF YOUNG PERSON

(6) The youth justice court may, by summons or warrant, compel a young person in respect of whom a review is to be made under this section to appear before the youth justice court for the purposes of the review.

DECISION OF THE YOUTH JUSTICE COURT AFTER REVIEW

(7) When a youth justice court reviews under this section a youth sentence imposed in respect of a young person, it may, after giving the young person, a parent of the young person, the Attorney General and the provincial director an opportunity to be heard,

(a) confirm the youth sentence;

(b) terminate the youth sentence and discharge the young person from any further obligation of the youth sentence; or

(c) vary the youth sentence or impose any new youth sentence under section 42, other than a committal to custody, for any period of time, not exceeding the remainder of the period of the earlier youth sentence, that the court considers appropriate in the circumstances of the case.

NEW YOUTH SENTENCE NOT TO BE MORE ONEROUS

(8) Subject to subsection (9), when a youth sentence imposed in respect of a young person is reviewed under this section, no youth sentence imposed under subsection (7) shall, without the consent of the young person, be more onerous than the remainder of the youth sentence reviewed.

EXCEPTION

(9) A youth justice court may under this section extend the time within which a youth sentence imposed under paragraphs 42(2)(d) to (i) is to be complied with by a young person if the court is satisfied that the young person requires more time to comply with the youth sentence, but in no case shall the extension be for a period of time that expires more than twelve months after the date the youth sentence would otherwise have expired.

PROVISIONS APPLICABLE TO YOUTH SENTENCES ON REVIEW

60. This Part and Part 5 (custody and supervision) apply with any modifications that the circumstances require to orders made in respect of reviews of youth sentences under sections 59 and 94 to 96.

Adult Sentence and Election

AGE FOR PURPOSE OF PRESUMPTIVE OFFENCES

61. The lieutenant governor in council of a province may by order fix an age greater than fourteen years but not more than sixteen years for the purpose of the application of the provisions of this Act relating to presumptive offences.

IMPOSITION OF ADULT SENTENCE

62. An adult sentence shall be imposed on a young person who is found guilty of an indictable offence for which an adult is liable to imprisonment for a term of more than two years in the following cases:

(a) in the case of a presumptive offence, if the youth justice court makes an order under subsection 70(2) or paragraph 72(1)(b); or

(b) in any other case, if the youth justice court makes an order under subsection 64(5) or paragraph 72(1)(b) in relation to an offence committed after the young person attained the age of fourteen years.

APPLICATION BY YOUNG PERSON

63. (1) A young person who is charged with, or found guilty of, a presumptive offence may, at any time before evidence is called as to sentence or, where no evidence is called, before submissions are made as to sentence, make an application for an order that he or she is not liable to an adult sentence and that a youth sentence must be imposed.

APPLICATION UNOPPOSED

(2) If the Attorney General gives notice to the youth justice court that the Attorney General does not oppose the application, the youth justice court shall, without a hearing, order that the young person, if found guilty, is not liable to an adult sentence and that a youth sentence must be imposed.

APPLICATION BY ATTORNEY GENERAL

64. (1) The Attorney General may, following an application under subsection 42(9) (judicial determination of serious violent offence), if any is made, and before evidence is called as to sentence or, where no evidence is called, before submissions are made as to sentence, make an application for an order that a young person is liable to an adult sentence if the young person is or has been found guilty of an offence, other than a presumptive offence, for which an adult is liable to imprisonment for a term of more than two years, that was committed after the young person attained the age of fourteen years.

NOTICE OF INTENTION TO SEEK ADULT SENTENCE

(2) If the Attorney General intends to seek an adult sentence for an offence by making an application under subsection (1), or by establishing that the offence is a presumptive offence within the meaning of paragraph (b) of the definition "presumptive offence" in subsection 2(1), the Attorney General shall, before the young person enters a plea or with leave of the youth justice court before the commencement of the trial, give notice to the young person and the youth justice court of the intention to seek an adult sentence.

INCLUDED OFFENCES

(3) A notice of intention to seek an adult sentence given in respect of an offence is notice in respect of any included offence of which the young person is found guilty for which an adult is liable to imprisonment for a term of more than two years.

NOTICE TO YOUNG PERSON

(4) If a young person is charged with an offence, other than an offence set out in paragraph (a) of the definition "presumptive offence" in subsection 2(1), and the Attorney General intends to establish, after a finding of guilt, that the offence is a serious violent offence and a presumptive offence within the meaning of paragraph (b) of the definition "presumptive offence" in subsection 2(1) for which the young person is liable to an adult sentence, the Attorney General shall, before the young person enters a plea or, with leave of the youth justice court under subsection (2), before the commencement of the trial, give notice of that intention to the young person.

APPLICATION UNOPPOSED

(5) If the young person gives notice to the youth justice court that the young person does not oppose the application for an adult sentence, the youth justice court shall, without a hearing, order that if the young person is found guilty of an offence for which an adult is liable to imprisonment for a term of more than two years, an adult sentence must be imposed.

PRESUMPTION DOES NOT APPLY

65. If the Attorney General at any stage of proceedings gives notice to the youth justice court that an adult sentence will not be sought in respect of a young person who is alleged to have committed an offence set out in paragraph (a) of the definition "presumptive offence" in subsection 2(1), the court shall order that the young person is not liable to an adult sentence, and the court shall order a ban on publication of information that would identify the young person as having been dealt with under this Act.

NO ELECTION IF YOUTH SENTENCE

66. If the youth justice court has made an order under subsection 63(2) or section 65 before a young person is required to be put to an election under section 67, the young person shall not be put to an election unless the young person is alleged to have committed first degree murder or second degree murder within the meaning of section 231 of the *Criminal Code*.

ELECTION—ADULT SENTENCE

67. (1) Subject to section 66, the youth justice court shall, before a young person enters a plea, put the young person to his or her election in the words set out in subsection (2) if

(a) the young person is charged with having committed an offence set out in paragraph (a) of the definition "presumptive offence" in subsection 2(1);

(b) the Attorney General has given notice under subsection 64(2) of the intention to seek an adult sentence for an offence committed after the young person has attained the age of fourteen years;

(c) the young person is charged with having committed first or second degree murder within the meaning of section 231 of the *Criminal Code* before the young person has attained the age of fourteen years; or

(d) the person to whom section 16 (status of accused uncertain) applies is charged with having, after attaining the age of fourteen years, committed an offence for which an adult would be entitled to an election under section 536 of the *Criminal Code*, or over which a superior court of criminal jurisdiction would have exclusive jurisdiction under section 469 of that Act.

WORDING OF ELECTION

(2) The youth justice court shall put the young person to his or her election in the following words:

You have the option to elect to be tried by a youth justice court judge without a jury and without having had a preliminary inquiry; or you may elect to have a preliminary inquiry and to be tried by a judge without a jury; or you may elect to have a preliminary inquiry and to be tried by a court composed of a judge and jury. If you do not elect now, you shall be deemed to have elected to have a preliminary inquiry and to be tried by a court composed of a judge and jury. How do you elect to be tried?

ELECTION—NUNAVUT

(3) Subject to section 66, in respect of proceedings in Nunavut, the youth justice court shall, before a young person enters a plea, put the young person to his or her election in the words set out in subsection (4) if

(a) the young person is charged with having committed an offence set out in paragraph (a) of the definition "presumptive offence" in subsection 2(1);

(b) the Attorney General has given notice under subsection 64(2) of the intention to seek an adult sentence for an offence committed after the young person has attained the age of fourteen years;

(c) the young person is charged with having committed first or second degree murder within the meaning of section 231 of the *Criminal Code* before the young person has attained the age of fourteen years; or

(d) the person to whom section 16 (status of accused uncertain) applies is charged with having, after attaining the age of fourteen years, committed an offence for which an adult would be entitled to an election under section 536.1 of the *Criminal Code*.

WORDING OF ELECTION

(4) The youth justice court shall put the young person to his or her election in the following words:

You have the option to elect to be tried by a judge of the Nunavut Court of Justice alone, acting as a youth justice court without a jury and without a preliminary inquiry; or you may elect to have a preliminary inquiry and to be tried by a judge of the Nunavut Court of Justice, acting as a youth justice court without a jury; or you may elect to have a preliminary inquiry and to be tried by a judge of the Nunavut Court of Justice, acting as a youth justice court with a jury. If you do not elect now, you shall be deemed to have elected to have a preliminary inquiry and to be tried by a court composed of a judge and jury. How do you elect to be tried?

MODE OF TRIAL WHERE CO-ACCUSED ARE YOUNG PERSONS

(5) When two or more young persons who are charged with the same offence, who are jointly charged in the same information or indictment or in respect of whom the Attorney General seeks joinder of counts that are set out in separate informations or indictments are put to their election, then, unless all of them elect or re-elect or are deemed to have elected, as the case may be, the same mode of trial, the youth justice court judge

(a) may decline to record any election, re-election or deemed election for trial by a youth justice court judge without a jury, a judge without a jury or, in Nunavut, a judge of the Nunavut Court Justice without a jury; and

(b) if the judge declines to do so, shall hold a preliminary inquiry unless a preliminary inquiry has been held prior to the election, re-election or deemed election.

ATTORNEY GENERAL MAY REQUIRE TRIAL BY JURY

(6) The Attorney General may, even if a young person elects under subsection (1) or (3) to be tried by a youth justice court judge without a jury or a judge without a jury, require the young person to be tried by a court composed of a judge and jury.

PRELIMINARY INQUIRY

(7) When a young person elects to be tried by a judge without a jury, or elects or is deemed to have elected to be tried by a court composed of a judge and jury, the youth justice court referred to in subsection 13(1) shall conduct a preliminary inquiry and if, on its conclusion, the young person is ordered to stand trial, the proceedings shall be conducted

(a) before a judge without a jury or a court composed of a judge and jury, as the case may be; or

(b) in Nunavut, before a judge of the Nunavut Court of Justice acting as a youth justice court, with or without a jury, as the case may be.

PRELIMINARY INQUIRY PROVISIONS OF *CRIMINAL CODE*

(8) The preliminary inquiry shall be conducted in accordance with the provisions of Part XVIII (procedure on preliminary inquiry) of the *Criminal Code*, except to the extent that they are inconsistent with this Act.

PARTS XIX AND XX OF *CRIMINAL CODE*

(9) Proceedings under this Act before a judge without a jury or a court composed of a judge and jury or, in Nunavut, a judge of the Nunavut Court of Justice acting as a youth justice court, with or without a jury, as the case may be, shall be conducted in accordance with the provisions of Parts XIX (indictable offences—trial without jury) and XX (procedure in jury trials and general provisions) of the *Criminal Code*, with any modifications that the circumstances require, except that

(a) the provisions of this Act respecting the protection of privacy of young persons prevail over the provisions of the *Criminal Code*; and

(b) the young person is entitled to be represented in court by counsel if the young person is removed from court in accordance with subsection 650(2) of the *Criminal Code*.

PROOF OF NOTICE UNDER SUBSECTION 64(4)

68. (1) When a young person is found guilty of an offence, other than an offence set out in paragraph (a) of the definition "presumptive offence" in subsection 2(1), committed after he or she attained the age of fourteen years, and the Attorney General seeks to establish that the offence is a serious violent offence and a presumptive offence within the meaning of paragraph (b) of the definition "presumptive offence" in subsection 2(1), the Attorney General must satisfy the youth justice court that the young person, before entering a plea, was given notice under subsection 64(4) (intention to prove prior serious violent offences).

DETERMINATION OF SERIOUS VIOLENT OFFENCE

(2) If the youth justice court is satisfied that the young person was given notice under subsection 64(4) (intention to prove prior serious violent offences), the Attorney General may make an application in accordance with subsection 42(9) (judicial determination of serious violent offence).

INQUIRY BY COURT AND PROOF

(3) If the youth justice court determines that the offence is a serious violent offence, it shall ask whether the young person admits to the previous judicial determinations of serious violent offences made at different proceedings. If the young person does not admit to any of it, the Attorney General may adduce evidence as proof of the previous judicial determinations in accordance with section 667 of the *Criminal Code*, with any modifications that the circumstances require. For the purposes of that section, a certified copy of the information or indictment endorsed in accordance with subsection 42(9) (judicial determination of serious violent offence) or a certified copy of a court decision is deemed to be a certificate.

DETERMINATION BY COURT

(4) If the youth justice court, after making its inquiry under subsection (3), is satisfied that the offence is a presumptive offence within the meaning of paragraph (b) of the definition "presumptive offence" in subsection 2(1), the youth justice court shall endorse the information or indictment accordingly.

DETERMINATION BY COURT

(5) If the youth justice court, after making its inquiry under subsection (3), is not satisfied that the offence is a presumptive offence within the meaning of paragraph (b) of the definition "presumptive offence" in subsection 2(1), the Attorney General may make an application under subsection 64(1) (application for adult sentence).

PARAGRAPH (A) "PRESUMPTIVE OFFENCE"—INCLUDED OFFENCES

69. (1) If a young person who is charged with an offence set out in paragraph (a) of the definition "presumptive offence" in subsection 2(1) is found guilty of committing an included offence for which an adult is liable to imprisonment for a term of more than two years, other than another presumptive offence set out in that paragraph,

(a) the Attorney General may make an application under subsection 64(1) (application for adult sentence) without the necessity of giving notice under subsection 64(2), if the finding of guilt is for an offence that is not a presumptive offence; or

(b) subsections 68(2) to (5) apply without the necessity of the Attorney General giving notice under subsection 64(2) (intention to seek adult sentence) or (4) (intention to prove prior serious violent offences), if the finding of guilt is for an offence that would be a presumptive offence within the meaning of paragraph (b) of the definition "presumptive offence" in subsection 2(1) if a judicial determination is made that the offence is a serious violent offence and on proof of previous judicial determinations of a serious violent offence.

OTHER SERIOUS OFFENCES—INCLUDED OFFENCES

(2) If the Attorney General has given notice under subsection 64(2) of the intention to seek an adult sentence and the young person, after he or she has attained the age of fourteen years, is found guilty of committing an included offence for which an adult is liable to imprisonment for a term of more than two years, the Attorney General may make an application under subsection 64(1) (application for adult sentence) or seek to apply the provisions of section 68.

INQUIRY BY COURT TO YOUNG PERSON

70. (1) The youth justice court, after hearing an application under subsection 42(9) (judicial determination of serious violent offence), if any is made, and before evidence is called or, where no evidence is called, before submissions are made as to sentence, shall inquire whether a young person wishes to make an application under subsection 63(1) (application for youth sentence) and if so, whether the Attorney General would oppose it, if

(a) the young person has been found guilty of a presumptive offence;

(b) the young person has not already made an application under subsection 63(1); and

(c) no order has been made under section 65 (young person not liable to adult sentence).

NO APPLICATION BY YOUNG PERSON

(2) If the young person indicates that he or she does not wish to make an application under subsection 63(1) (application for youth sentence) or fails to give an indication, the court shall order that an adult sentence be imposed.

HEARING—ADULT SENTENCES

71. The youth justice court shall, at the commencement of the sentencing hearing, hold a hearing in respect of an application under subsection 63(1) (application for youth sentence) or 64(1) (application for adult sentence), unless the court has received notice that the application is not opposed. Both parties and the parents of the young person shall be given an opportunity to be heard at the hearing.

TEST—ADULT SENTENCES

72. (1) In making its decision on an application heard in accordance with section 71, the youth justice court shall consider the seriousness and circumstances of the offence, and the age, maturity, character, background and previous record of the young person and any other factors that the court considers relevant, and

(a) if it is of the opinion that a youth sentence imposed in accordance with the purpose and principles set out in subparagraph 3(1)(b)(ii) and section 38 would have sufficient length to hold the young person accountable for his or her offending behaviour, it shall order that the young person is not liable to an adult sentence and that a youth sentence must be imposed; and

(b) if it is of the opinion that a youth sentence imposed in accordance with the purpose and principles set out in subparagraph 3(1)(b)(ii) and section 38 would not have sufficient length to hold the young person accountable for his or her offending behaviour, it shall order that an adult sentence be imposed.

ONUS

(2) The onus of satisfying the youth justice court as to the matters referred to in subsection (1) is with the applicant.

PRE-SENTENCE REPORTS

(3) In making its decision, the youth justice court shall consider a pre-sentence report.

COURT TO STATE REASONS

(4) When the youth justice court makes an order under this section, it shall state the reasons for its decision.

APPEALS

(5) For the purposes of an appeal in accordance with section 37, an order under subsection (1) is part of the sentence.

COURT MUST IMPOSE ADULT SENTENCE

73. (1) When the youth justice court makes an order under subsection 64(5) or 70(2) or paragraph 72(1)(b) in respect of a young person, the court shall, on a finding of guilt, impose an adult sentence on the young person.

COURT MUST IMPOSE YOUTH SENTENCE

(2) When the youth justice court makes an order under subsection 63(2), section 65 or paragraph 72(1)(a) in respect of a young person, the court shall, on a finding of guilt, impose a youth sentence on the young person.

APPLICATION OF PARTS XXIII AND XXIV OF *CRIMINAL CODE*

74. (1) Parts XXIII (sentencing) and XXIV (dangerous and long-term offenders) of the *Criminal Code* apply to a young person in respect of whom the youth justice court has ordered that an adult sentence be imposed.

FINDING OF GUILT BECOMES A CONVICTION

(2) A finding of guilt for an offence in respect of which an adult sentence is imposed becomes a conviction once the time allowed for the taking of an appeal has expired or, if an appeal is taken, all proceedings in respect of the appeal have been completed and the appeal court has upheld an adult sentence.

INTERPRETATION

(3) This section does not affect the time of commencement of an adult sentence under subsection 719(1) of the *Criminal Code.*

INQUIRY BY THE COURT TO THE YOUNG PERSON

75. (1) If the youth justice court imposes a youth sentence in respect of a young person who has been found guilty of having committed a presumptive offence set out in paragraph (a) of the definition "presumptive offence" in subsection 2(1), or an offence under paragraph (b) of that definition for which the Attorney General has given notice under subsection 64(2) (intention to seek adult sentence), the court shall at the sentencing hearing inquire whether the young person or the Attorney General wishes to make an application under subsection (3) for a ban on publication.

NO APPLICATION FOR A BAN

(2) If the young person and the Attorney General both indicate that they do not wish to make an application under subsection (3), the court shall endorse the information or indictment accordingly.

ORDER FOR A BAN

(3) On application of the young person or the Attorney General, a youth justice court may order a ban on publication of information that would identify the young person as having been dealt with under this Act if the court considers it appropriate in the circumstances, taking into account the importance of rehabilitating the young person and the public interest.

APPEALS

(4) For the purposes of an appeal in accordance with section 37, an order under subsection (3) is part of the sentence.

PLACEMENT WHEN SUBJECT TO ADULT SENTENCE

76. (1) Subject to subsections (2) and (9) and sections 79 and 80 and despite anything else in this Act or any other Act of Parliament, when a young person who is subject to an adult sentence in respect of an offence is sentenced to a term of imprisonment for the offence, the youth justice court shall order that the young person serve any portion of the imprisonment in

(a) a youth custody facility separate and apart from any adult who is detained or held in custody;

(b) a provincial correctional facility for adults; or

(c) if the sentence is for two years or more, a penitentiary.

WHEN YOUNG PERSON SUBJECT TO ADULT PENALTIES

(2) The youth justice court that sentences a young person under subsection (1) shall, unless it is satisfied that to do so would not be in the best interests of the young person or would jeopardize the safety of others,

(a) if the young person is under the age of eighteen years at the time that he or she is sentenced, order that he or she be placed in a youth custody facility; and

(b) if the young person is eighteen years old or older at the time that he or she is sentenced, order that he or she not be placed in a youth custody facility and order that any portion of the sentence be served in a provincial correctional facility for adults or, if the sentence is two years or more, in a penitentiary.

OPPORTUNITY TO BE HEARD

(3) Before making an order under subsection (1), the youth justice court shall give the young person, a parent of the young person, the Attorney General, the provincial director and representatives of the provincial and federal correctional systems an opportunity to be heard.

REPORT NECESSARY

(4) Before making an order under subsection (1), the youth justice court shall require that a report be prepared for the purpose of assisting the court.

APPEALS

(5) For the purposes of an appeal in accordance with section 37, an order under subsection (1) is part of the sentence.

REVIEW

(6) On application, the youth justice court shall review the placement of a young person under this section and, if satisfied that the circumstances that resulted in the initial order have changed materially, and after having given the young person, a parent of the young person, the Attorney General, the provincial director and the representatives of the provincial and federal correctional systems an

opportunity to be heard, the court may order that the young person be placed in

(a) a youth custody facility separate and apart from any adult who is detained or held in custody;

(b) a provincial correctional facility for adults; or

(c) if the sentence is for two years or more, a penitentiary.

WHO MAY MAKE APPLICATION

(7) An application referred to in this section may be made by the young person, one of the young person's parents, the provincial director, representatives of the provincial and federal correctional systems and the Attorney General, after the time for all appeals has expired.

NOTICE

(8) When an application referred to in this section is made, the applicant shall cause a notice of the application to be given to the other persons referred to in subsection (7).

LIMIT—AGE TWENTY

(9) No young person shall remain in a youth custody facility under this section after the young person attains the age of twenty years, unless the youth justice court that makes the order under subsection (1) or reviews the placement under subsection (6) is satisfied that remaining in the youth custody facility would be in the best interests of the young person and would not jeopardize the safety of others.

OBLIGATION TO INFORM—PAROLE

77. (1) When a young person is ordered to serve a portion of a sentence in a youth custody facility under paragraph 76(1)(a) (placement when subject to adult sentence), the provincial director shall inform the appropriate parole board.

APPLICABILITY OF *CORRECTIONS AND CONDITIONAL RELEASE ACT*

(2) For greater certainty, Part II of the *Corrections and Conditional Release Act* applies, subject to section 78, with respect to a young person who is the subject of an order under subsection 76(1) (placement when subject to adult sentence).

APPROPRIATE PAROLE BOARD

(3) The appropriate parole board for the purposes of this section is

(a) if subsection 112(1) of the *Corrections and Conditional Release Act* would apply with respect to the young person but for the fact that the young person was ordered into a youth custody facility, the parole board mentioned in that subsection; and

(b) in any other case, the National Parole Board.

RELEASE ENTITLEMENT

78. (1) For greater certainty, section 6 of the *Prisons and Reformatories Act* applies to a young person who is ordered to serve a portion of a sentence in a youth custody facility under paragraph 76(1)(a) (placement when subject to adult sentence) only if section 743.1 (rules respecting sentences of two or more years) of the *Criminal Code* would direct that the young person serve the sentence in a prison.

RELEASE ENTITLEMENT

(2) For greater certainty, section 127 of the *Corrections and Conditional Release Act* applies to a young person who is ordered to serve a portion of a sentence in a youth custody facility under paragraph 76(1)(a) (placement when subject to adult sentence) only if section 743.1 (rules respecting sentences of two or more years) of the *Criminal Code* would direct that the young person serve the sentence in a penitentiary.

IF PERSON CONVICTED UNDER ANOTHER ACT

79. If a person who is serving all or a portion of a sentence in a youth custody facility under paragraph 76(1)(a) (placement when

subject to adult sentence) is sentenced to a term of imprisonment under an Act of Parliament other than this Act, the remainder of the portion of the sentence being served in the youth custody facility shall be served in a provincial correctional facility for adults or a penitentiary, in accordance with section 743.1 (rules respecting sentences of two or more years) of the *Criminal Code.*

IF PERSON WHO IS SERVING A SENTENCE UNDER ANOTHER ACT IS SENTENCED TO AN ADULT SENTENCE

80. If a person who has been serving a sentence of imprisonment under an Act of Parliament other than this Act is sentenced to an adult sentence of imprisonment under this Act, the sentences shall be served in a provincial correctional facility for adults or a penitentiary, in accordance with section 743.1 (rules respecting sentences of two or more years) of the *Criminal Code.*

PROCEDURE FOR APPLICATION OR NOTICE

81. An application or a notice to the court under section 63, 64, 65 or 76 must be made or given orally, in the presence of the other party, or in writing with a copy served personally on the other party.

Effect of Termination of Youth Sentence

EFFECT OF ABSOLUTE DISCHARGE OR TERMINATION OF YOUTH SENTENCE

82. (1) Subject to section 12 (examination as to previous convictions) of the *Canada Evidence Act*, if a young person is found guilty of an offence, and a youth justice court directs under paragraph 42(2)(b) that the young person be discharged absolutely, or the youth sentence, or any disposition made under the *Young Offenders Act*, chapter Y-1 of the Revised Statutes of Canada, 1985, has ceased to have effect, other than an order under section 51 (mandatory prohibition order) of this Act or section 20.1 (mandatory prohibition order) of the *Young Offenders Act*, the young person is deemed not to have been found guilty or convicted of the offence except that

(a) the young person may plead autrefois convict in respect of any subsequent charge relating to the offence;

(b) a youth justice court may consider the finding of guilt in considering an application under subsection 63(1) (application for youth sentence) or 64(1) (application for adult sentence);

(c) any court or justice may consider the finding of guilt in considering an application for judicial interim release or in considering what sentence to impose for any offence; and

(d) the National Parole Board or any provincial parole board may consider the finding of guilt in considering an application for conditional release or pardon.

DISQUALIFICATIONS REMOVED

(2) For greater certainty and without restricting the generality of subsection (1), an absolute discharge under paragraph 42(2)(b) or the termination of the youth sentence or disposition in respect of an offence for which a young person is found guilty removes any disqualification in respect of the offence to which the young person is subject under any Act of Parliament by reason of a finding of guilt.

APPLICATIONS FOR EMPLOYMENT

(3) No application form for or relating to the following shall contain any question that by its terms requires the applicant to disclose that he or she has been charged with or found guilty of an offence in respect of which he or she has, under this Act or the *Young Offenders Act*, chapter Y-1 of the Revised Statutes of Canada, 1985, been discharged absolutely, or has completed the youth sentence under this Act or the disposition under the *Young Offenders Act*:

(a) employment in any department, as defined in section 2 of the *Financial Administration Act*;

(b) employment by any Crown corporation, as defined in section 83 of the *Financial Administration Act*;

(c) enrolment in the Canadian Forces; or

employment on or in connection with the operation of any work, undertaking or business that is within the legislative authority of Parliament.

FINDING OF GUILT NOT A PREVIOUS CONVICTION

(4) A finding of guilt under this Act is not a previous conviction for the purposes of any offence under any Act of Parliament for which a greater punishment is prescribed by reason of previous convictions, except for

(a) the purpose of establishing that an offence is a presumptive offence within the meaning of paragraph (b) of the definition "presumptive offence" in subsection 2(1); or

(b) the purpose of determining the adult sentence to be imposed.

PART 5
CUSTODY AND SUPERVISION

PURPOSE

83. (1) The purpose of the youth custody and supervision system is to contribute to the protection of society by

(a) carrying out sentences imposed by courts through the safe, fair and humane custody and supervision of young persons; and

(b) assisting young persons to be rehabilitated and reintegrated into the community as law-abiding citizens, by providing effective programs to young persons in custody and while under supervision in the community.

PRINCIPLES TO BE USED

(2) In addition to the principles set out in section 3, the following principles are to be used in achieving that purpose:

(a) that the least restrictive measures consistent with the protection of the public, of personnel working with young persons and of young persons be used;

(b) that young persons sentenced to custody retain the rights of other young persons, except the rights that are necessarily removed or restricted as a consequence of a sentence under this Act or another Act of Parliament;

(c) that the youth custody and supervision system facilitate the involvement of the families of young persons and members of the public;

(d) that custody and supervision decisions be made in a forthright, fair and timely manner, and that young persons have access to an effective review procedure; and

(e) that placements of young persons where they are treated as adults not disadvantage them with respect to their eligibility for and conditions of release.

YOUNG PERSON TO BE HELD APART FROM ADULTS

84. Subject to subsection 30(3) (pre-trial detention), paragraphs 76(1)(b) and (c) (placement in adult facilities with adult sentence) and sections 89 to 93 (placement in adult facilities with youth sentence), a young person who is committed to custody shall be held separate and apart from any adult who is detained or held in custody.

LEVELS OF CUSTODY

85. (1) In the youth custody and supervision system in each province there must be at least two levels of custody for young persons distinguished by the degree of restraint of the young persons in them.

DESIGNATION OF YOUTH CUSTODY FACILITIES

(2) Every youth custody facility in a province that contains one or more levels of custody shall be designated by

(a) in the case of a youth custody facility with only one level of custody, being the level of custody with the least degree of restraint of the young persons in it, the lieutenant governor in council or his or her delegate; and

(b) in any other case, the lieutenant governor in council.

PROVINCIAL DIRECTOR TO SPECIFY CUSTODY LEVEL— COMMITTAL TO CUSTODY

(3) The provincial director shall, when a young person is committed to custody under paragraph 42(2)(n), (o), (q) or (r) or an order is made under subsection 98(3), paragraph 103(2)(b), subsection 104(1) or paragraph 109(2)(b), determine the level of custody appropriate for the young person, after having taken into account the factors set out in subsection (5).

PROVINCIAL DIRECTOR TO SPECIFY CUSTODY LEVEL—TRANSFER

(4) The provincial director may determine a different level of custody for the young person when the provincial director is satisfied that the needs of the young person and the interests of society would be better served by doing so, after having taken into account the factors set out in subsection (5).

FACTORS

(5) The factors referred to in subsections (3) and (4) are

(a) that the appropriate level of custody for the young person is the one that is the least restrictive to the young person, having regard to

(i) the seriousness of the offence in respect of which the young person was committed to custody and the circumstances in which that offence was committed,

(ii) the needs and circumstances of the young person, including proximity to family, school, employment and support services,

(iii) the safety of other young persons in custody, and

(iv) the interests of society;

(b) that the level of custody should allow for the best possible match of programs to the young person's needs and behaviour, having regard to the findings of any assessment in respect of the young person; and

(c) the likelihood of escape.

PLACEMENT AND TRANSFER AT APPROPRIATE LEVEL

(6) After the provincial director has determined the appropriate level of custody for the young person under subsection (3) or (4), the young person shall be placed in the youth custody facility that contains that level of custody specified by the provincial director.

NOTICE

(7) The provincial director shall cause a notice in writing of a determination under subsection (3) or (4) to be given to the young person and a parent of the young person and set out in that notice the reasons for it.

PROCEDURAL SAFEGUARDS

86. (1) The lieutenant governor in council of a province shall ensure that procedures are in place to ensure that the due process rights of the young person are protected with respect to a determination made under subsection 85(3) or (4), including that the young person be

(a) provided with any relevant information to which the provincial director has access in making the determination, subject to subsection (2);

(b) given the opportunity to be heard; and

(c) informed of any right to a review under section 87.

WITHHOLDING OF INFORMATION

(2) Where the provincial director has reasonable grounds to believe that providing the information referred to in paragraph (1)(a) would jeopardize the safety of any person or the security of a facility, he or she may authorize the withholding from the young person of as much information as is strictly necessary in order to protect such safety or security.

REVIEW

87. (1) A young person may apply for a review under this section of a determination

(a) under subsection 85(3) that would place the young person in a facility at a level of custody that has more than a minimal degree of restraint; or

(b) under subsection 85(4) that would transfer a young person to a facility at a level of custody with a higher degree of restraint or increase the degree of restraint of the young person in the facility.

PROCEDURAL SAFEGUARDS

(2) The lieutenant governor in council of a province shall ensure that procedures are in place for the review under subsection (1), including that

(a) the review board that conducts the review be independent;

(b) the young person be provided with any relevant information to which the review board has access, subject to subsection (3); and

(c) the young person be given the opportunity to be heard.

WITHHOLDING OF INFORMATION

(3) Where the review board has reasonable grounds to believe that providing the information referred to in paragraph (2)(b) would jeopardize the safety of any person or the security of a facility, it may authorize the withholding from the young person of as much information as is strictly necessary in order to protect such safety or security.

FACTORS

(4) The review board shall take into account the factors referred to in subsection 85(5) in reviewing a determination.

DECISION IS FINAL

(5) A decision of the review board under this section in respect of a particular determination is final.

FUNCTIONS TO BE EXERCISED BY YOUTH JUSTICE COURT

88. The lieutenant governor in council of a province may order that the power to make determinations of the level of custody for young persons and to review those determinations be exercised in accordance with the *Young Offenders Act*, chapter Y-1 of the Revised Statutes of Canada, 1985. The following provisions of that Act apply, with any modifications that the circumstances require, to the exercise of those powers:

(a) the definitions "review board" and "progress report" in subsection 2(1);

(b) section 11;

(c) sections 24.1 to 24.3; and

(d) sections 28 to 31.

EXCEPTION IF YOUNG PERSON IS TWENTY YEARS OLD OR OLDER

89. (1) When a young person is twenty years old or older at the time the youth sentence is imposed on him or her under paragraph 42(2)(n), (o), (q) or (r), the young person shall, despite section 85, be committed to a provincial correctional facility for adults to serve the youth sentence.

IF SERVING YOUTH SENTENCE IN A PROVINCIAL CORRECTIONAL FACILITY

(2) If a young person is serving a youth sentence in a provincial correctional facility for adults pursuant to subsection (1), the youth justice court may, on application of the provincial director at any time after the young person begins to serve a portion of the youth sentence in a provincial correctional facility for adults, after giving the young person, the provincial director and representatives of the provincial and federal correctional systems an opportunity to be heard, authorize the provincial director to direct that the young person serve the remainder of the youth sentence in a penitentiary if the court considers it to be in the best interests of the young person or in the public interest and if, at the time of the application, that remainder is two years or more.

PROVISIONS TO APPLY

(3) If a young person is serving a youth sentence in a provincial correctional facility for adults or a penitentiary under subsection (1) or (2), the *Prisons and Reformatories Act* and the *Corrections and Conditional Release Act*, and any other statute, regulation or rule applicable in respect of prisoners or offenders within the meaning of those Acts, statutes, regulations and rules, apply in respect of the young person except to the extent that they conflict with Part 6 (publication, records and information) of this Act, which Part continues to apply to the young person.

YOUTH WORKER

90. (1) When a youth sentence is imposed committing a young person to custody, the provincial director of the province in which the young person received the youth sentence and was placed in custody shall, without delay, designate a youth worker to work with the young person to plan for his or her reintegration into the community, including the preparation and implementation of a reintegration plan that sets out the most effective programs for the young person in order to maximize his or her chances for reintegration into the community.

ROLE OF YOUTH WORKER WHEN YOUNG PERSON IN THE COMMUNITY

(2) When a portion of a young person's youth sentence is served in the community in accordance with section 97 or 105, the youth worker shall supervise the young person, continue to provide support to the young person and assist the young person to respect the conditions to which he or she is subject, and help the young person in the implementation of the reintegration plan.

REINTEGRATION LEAVE

91. (1) The provincial director of a province may, subject to any terms or conditions that he or she considers desirable, authorize, for a young person committed to a youth custody facility in the province further to an order under paragraph 76(1)(a) (placement when subject to adult sentence) or a youth sentence imposed under paragraph 42(2)(n), (o), (q) or (r),

(a) a reintegration leave from the youth custody facility for a period not exceeding thirty days if, in the opinion of the provincial director, it is necessary or desirable that the young person be absent, with or without escort, for medical, compassionate or humanitarian reasons or for the purpose of rehabilitating the young person or reintegrating the young person into the community; or

(b) that the young person be released from the youth custody facility on the days and during the hours that the provincial director specifies in order that the young person may

(i) attend school or any other educational or training institution,

(ii) obtain or continue employment or perform domestic or other duties required by the young person's family,

(iii) participate in a program specified by the provincial director that, in the provincial director's opinion, will enable the young person to better carry out employment or improve his or her education or training, or

(iv) attend an out-patient treatment program or other program that provides services that are suitable to addressing the young person's needs.

RENEWAL OF REINTEGRATION LEAVE

(2) A reintegration leave authorized under paragraph (1)(a) may be renewed by the provincial director for one or more thirty-day periods on reassessment of the case.

REVOCATION OF AUTHORIZATION

(3) The provincial director of a province may, at any time, revoke an authorization made under subsection (1).

ARREST AND RETURN TO CUSTODY

(4) If the provincial director revokes an authorization under subsection (3) or if a young person fails to comply with any term or condition of a reintegration leave or a release from custody under this section, the young person may be arrested without warrant and returned to custody.

TRANSFER TO ADULT FACILITY

92. (1) When a young person is committed to custody under paragraph 42(2)(n), (o), (q) or (r), the youth justice court may, on application of the provincial director made at any time after the young person attains the age of eighteen years, after giving the young person, the provincial director and representatives of the provincial correctional system an opportunity to be heard, authorize the provincial director to direct that the young person, subject to subsection (3), serve the remainder of the youth sentence in a provincial correctional facility for adults, if the court considers it to be in the best interests of the young person or in the public interest.

IF SERVING YOUTH SENTENCE IN A PROVINCIAL CORRECTIONAL FACILITY

(2) The youth justice court may authorize the provincial director to direct that a young person, subject to subsection (3), serve the remainder of a youth sentence in a penitentiary

(a) if the youth justice court considers it to be in the best interests of the young person or in the public interest;

(b) if the provincial director applies for the authorization at any time after the young person begins to serve a portion of a youth sentence in a provincial correctional facility for adults further to a direction made under subsection (1);

(c) if, at the time of the application, that remainder is two years or more; and

(d) so long as the youth justice court gives the young person, the provincial director and representatives of the provincial and federal correctional systems an opportunity to be heard.

PROVISIONS TO APPLY

(3) If the provincial director makes a direction under subsection (1) or (2), the *Prisons and Reformatories Act* and the *Corrections and Conditional Release Act*, and any other statute, regulation or rule applicable in respect of prisoners and offenders within the meaning of those Acts, statutes, regulations and rules, apply in respect of the young person except to the extent that they conflict with Part 6 (publication, records and information) of this Act, which Part continues to apply to the young person.

PLACEMENT WHEN ADULT AND YOUTH SENTENCES

(4) If a person is subject to more than one sentence, at least one of which is a youth sentence imposed under paragraph 42(2)(n), (o), (q) or (r) and at least one of which is a sentence referred to in either paragraph (b) or (c), he or she shall serve, in a provincial correctional

facility for adults or a penitentiary in accordance with section 743.1 (rules respecting sentences of two or more years) of the *Criminal Code*, the following:

(a) the remainder of any youth sentence imposed under paragraph 42(2)(n), (o), (q) or (r);

(b) an adult sentence to which an order under paragraph 76(1)(b) or (c) (placement in adult facility) applies; and

(c) any sentence of imprisonment imposed otherwise than under this Act.

YOUTH SENTENCE AND ADULT SENTENCE

(5) If a young person is committed to custody under a youth sentence under paragraph 42(2)(n), (o), (q) or (r) and is also already subject to an adult sentence to which an order under paragraph 76(1)(a) (placement when subject to adult sentence) applies, the young person may, in the discretion of the provincial director, serve the sentences, or any portion of the sentences, in a youth custody facility, in a provincial correctional facility for adults or, if the unexpired portion of the sentence is two years or more, in a penitentiary.

WHEN YOUNG PERSON REACHES TWENTY YEARS OF AGE

93. (1) When a young person who is committed to custody under paragraph 42(2)(n), (o), (q) or (r) is in a youth custody facility when the young person attains the age of twenty years, the young person shall be transferred to a provincial correctional facility for adults to serve the remainder of the youth sentence, unless the provincial director orders that the young person continue to serve the youth sentence in a youth custody facility.

IF SERVING YOUTH SENTENCE IN A PROVINCIAL CORRECTIONAL FACILITY

(2) If a young person is serving a portion of a youth sentence in a provincial correctional facility for adults pursuant to a transfer under subsection (1), the youth justice court may, on application of the provincial director after the transfer, after giving the young person, the provincial director and representatives of the provincial and federal correctional systems an opportunity to be heard, authorize the provincial director to direct that the young person serve the remainder of the youth sentence in a penitentiary if the court considers it to be in the best interests of the young person or in the public interest and if, at the time of the application, that remainder is two years or more.

PROVISIONS TO APPLY

(3) If the provincial director makes the direction, the *Prisons and Reformatories Act* and the *Corrections and Conditional Release Act*, and any other statute, regulation or rule applicable in respect of prisoners and offenders within the meaning of those Acts, statutes, regulations and rules, apply in respect of the young person except to the extent that they conflict with Part 6 (publication, records and information) of this Act, which Part continues to apply to the young person.

ANNUAL REVIEW

94. (1) When a young person is committed to custody pursuant to a youth sentence under paragraph 42(2)(n), (o), (q) or (r) for a period exceeding one year, the provincial director of the province in which the young person is held in custody shall cause the young person to be brought before the youth justice court without delay at the end of one year from the date of the most recent youth sentence imposed in respect of the offence—and at the end of every subsequent year from that date—and the youth justice court shall review the youth sentence.

ANNUAL REVIEW

(2) When a young person is committed to custody pursuant to youth sentences imposed under paragraph 42(2)(n), (o), (q) or (r) in respect of more than one offence for a total period exceeding one year, the provincial director of the province in which the young person is held in custody shall cause the young person to be brought before the youth justice court without delay at the end of one year from the date of the earliest youth sentence imposed—and at the end of every subsequent year from that date—and the youth justice court shall review the youth sentences.

OPTIONAL REVIEW

(3) When a young person is committed to custody pursuant to a youth sentence imposed under paragraph 42(2)(n), (o), (q) or (r) in respect of an offence, the provincial director may, on the provincial director's own initiative, and shall, on the request of the young person, the young person's parent or the Attorney General, on any of the grounds set out in subsection (6), cause the young person to be brought before a youth justice court to review the youth sentence,

(a) when the youth sentence is for a period not exceeding one year, once at any time after the expiry of the greater of

(i) thirty days after the date of the youth sentence imposed under subsection 42(2) in respect of the offence, and

(ii) one third of the period of the youth sentence imposed under subsection 42(2) in respect of the offence; and

(b) when the youth sentence is for a period exceeding one year, at any time after six months after the date of the most recent youth sentence imposed in respect of the offence.

TIME FOR OPTIONAL REVIEW

(4) The young person may be brought before the youth justice court at any other time, with leave of the youth justice court judge.

REVIEW

(5) If a youth justice court is satisfied that there are grounds for review under subsection (6), the court shall review the youth sentence.

GROUNDS FOR REVIEW

(6) A youth sentence imposed in respect of a young person may be reviewed under subsection (5)

(a) on the ground that the young person has made sufficient progress to justify a change in the youth sentence;

(b) on the ground that the circumstances that led to the youth sentence have changed materially;

(c) on the ground that new services or programs are available that were not available at the time of the youth sentence;

(d) on the ground that the opportunities for rehabilitation are now greater in the community; or

(e) on any other ground that the youth justice court considers appropriate.

NO REVIEW IF APPEAL PENDING

(7) Despite any other provision of this section, no review of a youth sentence in respect of which an appeal has been taken shall be made under this section until all proceedings in respect of any such appeal have been completed.

YOUTH JUSTICE COURT MAY ORDER APPEARANCE OF YOUNG PERSON FOR REVIEW

(8) When a provincial director is required under subsections (1) to (3) to cause a young person to be brought before the youth justice court and fails to do so, the youth justice court may, on application made by the young person, his or her parent or the Attorney General, or on its own motion, order the provincial director to cause the young person to be brought before the youth justice court.

PROGRESS REPORT

(9) The youth justice court shall, before reviewing under this section a youth sentence imposed in respect of a young person, require the provincial director to cause to be prepared, and to submit

to the youth justice court, a progress report on the performance of the young person since the youth sentence took effect.

ADDITIONAL INFORMATION IN PROGRESS REPORT

(10) A person preparing a progress report in respect of a young person may include in the report any information relating to the personal and family history and present environment of the young person that he or she considers advisable.

WRITTEN OR ORAL REPORT

(11) A progress report shall be in writing unless it cannot reasonably be committed to writing, in which case it may, with leave of the youth justice court, be submitted orally in court.

SUBSECTIONS 40(4) TO (10) TO APPLY

(12) Subsections 40(4) to (10) (procedures respecting pre-sentence reports) apply, with any modifications that the circumstances require, in respect of progress reports.

NOTICE OF REVIEW FROM PROVINCIAL DIRECTOR

(13) When a youth sentence imposed in respect of a young person is to be reviewed under subsection (1) or (2), the provincial director shall cause any notice that may be directed by rules of court applicable to the youth justice court or, in the absence of such a direction, at least five clear days notice of the review to be given in writing to the young person, a parent of the young person and the Attorney General.

NOTICE OF REVIEW FROM PERSON REQUESTING IT

(14) When a review of a youth sentence imposed in respect of a young person is requested under subsection (3), the person requesting the review shall cause any notice that may be directed by rules of court applicable to the youth justice court or, in the absence of such a direction, at least five clear days notice of the review to be given in writing to the young person, a parent of the young person and the Attorney General.

STATEMENT OF RIGHT TO COUNSEL

(15) A notice given to a parent under subsection (13) or (14) shall include a statement that the young person whose youth sentence is to be reviewed has the right to be represented by counsel.

SERVICE OF NOTICE

(16) A notice under subsection (13) or (14) may be served personally or may be sent by confirmed delivery service.

NOTICE MAY BE WAIVED

(17) Any of the persons entitled to notice under subsection (13) or (14) may waive the right to that notice.

IF NOTICE NOT GIVEN

(18) If notice under subsection (13) or (14) is not given in accordance with this section, the youth justice court may

(a) adjourn the proceedings and order that the notice be given in the manner and to the persons that it directs; or

(b) dispense with the notice if, in the opinion of the court, having regard to the circumstances, notice may be dispensed with.

DECISION OF THE YOUTH JUSTICE COURT AFTER REVIEW

(19) When a youth justice court reviews under this section a youth sentence imposed in respect of a young person, it may, after giving the young person, a parent of the young person, the Attorney General and the provincial director an opportunity to be heard, having regard to the needs of the young person and the interests of society,

(a) confirm the youth sentence;

(b) release the young person from custody and place the young person under conditional supervision in accordance with

the procedure set out in section 105, with any modifications that the circumstances require, for a period not exceeding the remainder of the youth sentence that the young person is then serving; or

(c) if the provincial director so recommends, convert a youth sentence under paragraph 42(2)(r) to a youth sentence under paragraph 42(2)(q) if the offence was murder or to a youth sentence under paragraph 42(2)(n) or (o), as the case may be, if the offence was an offence other than murder.

ORDERS ARE YOUTH SENTENCES

95. Orders under subsections 97(2) (conditions) and 98(3) (continuation of custody), paragraph 103(2)(b) (continuation of custody), subsections 104(1) (continuation of custody) and 105(1) (conditional supervision) and paragraph 109(2)(b) (continuation of suspension of conditional supervision) are deemed to be youth sentences for the purposes of section 94 (reviews).

RECOMMENDATION OF PROVINCIAL DIRECTOR FOR CONDITIONAL SUPERVISION OF YOUNG PERSON

96. (1) When a young person is held in custody pursuant to a youth sentence under paragraph 42(2)(n), (o), (q) or (r), the provincial director may, if satisfied that the needs of the young person and the interests of society would be better served by doing so, make a recommendation to the youth justice court that the young person be released from custody and placed under conditional supervision.

NOTICE

(2) If the provincial director makes a recommendation, the provincial director shall cause a notice to be given in writing that includes the reasons for the recommendation and the conditions that the provincial director would recommend be set under section 105 to the young person, a parent of the young person and the Attorney General and give a copy of the notice to the youth justice court.

APPLICATION TO COURT FOR REVIEW OF RECOMMENDATION

(3) If notice of a recommendation is made under subsection (2) with respect to a youth sentence imposed on a young person, the youth justice court shall, if an application for review is made by the young person, the young person's parent or the Attorney General within ten days after service of the notice, review the youth sentence without delay.

SUBSECTIONS 94(7), (9) TO (12) AND (14) TO (19) APPLY

(4) Subject to subsection (5), subsections 94(7) (no review of appeal pending), (9) to (12) (progress reports) and (14) to (19) (provisions respecting notice and decision of the youth justice court) apply, with any modifications that the circumstances require, in respect of reviews made under this section and any notice required under subsection 94(14) shall also be given to the provincial director.

IF NO APPLICATION FOR REVIEW MADE UNDER SUBSECTION (3)

(5) A youth justice court that receives a notice under subsection (2) shall, if no application for a review is made under subsection (3),

(a) order the release of the young person and place the young person under conditional supervision in accordance with section 105, having regard to the recommendations of the provincial director; or

(b) if the court considers it advisable, order that the young person not be released.

For greater certainty, an order under this subsection may be made without a hearing.

NOTICE WHEN NO RELEASE ORDERED

(6) When a youth justice court orders that the young person not be released under paragraph (5)(b), it shall cause a notice of its order to be given to the provincial director without delay.

PROVINCIAL DIRECTOR MAY REQUEST REVIEW

(7) When the provincial director is given a notice under subsection (6), he or she may request a review under this section.

WHEN PROVINCIAL DIRECTOR REQUESTS A REVIEW

(8) When the provincial director requests a review under subsection (7),

(a) the provincial director shall cause any notice that may be directed by rules of court applicable to the youth justice court or, in the absence of such a direction, at least five clear days notice of the review to be given in writing to the young person, a parent of the young person and the Attorney General; and

(b) the youth justice court shall review the youth sentence without delay after the notice required under paragraph (a) is given.

CONDITIONS TO BE INCLUDED IN CUSTODY AND SUPERVISION ORDER

97. (1) Every youth sentence imposed under paragraph 42(2)(n) shall contain the following conditions, namely, that the young person, while serving the portion of the youth sentence under supervision in the community,

(a) keep the peace and be of good behaviour;

(b) report to the provincial director and then be under the supervision of the provincial director;

(c) inform the provincial director immediately on being arrested or questioned by the police;

(d) report to the police, or any named individual, as instructed by the provincial director;

(e) advise the provincial director of the young person's address of residence and report immediately to the provincial director any change

(i) in that address,

(ii) in the young person's normal occupation, including employment, vocational or educational training and volunteer work,

(iii) in the young person's family or financial situation, and

(iv) that may reasonably be expected to affect the young person's ability to comply with the conditions of the sentence; and

(f) not own, possess or have the control of any weapon, ammunition, prohibited ammunition, prohibited device or explosive substance, except as authorized in writing by the provincial director for the purposes of the young person participating in a program specified in the authorization.

OTHER CONDITIONS

(2) The provincial director may set additional conditions that support and address the needs of the young person, promote the reintegration of the young person into the community and offer adequate protection to the public from the risk that the young person might otherwise present. The provincial director shall, in setting the conditions, take into account the needs of the young person, the most effective programs for the young person in order to maximize his or her chances for reintegration into the community, the nature of the offence and the ability of the young person to comply with the conditions.

COMMUNICATION OF CONDITIONS

(3) The provincial director shall

(a) cause the conditions to be read by or to the young person bound by them;

(b) explain or cause to be explained to the young person the purpose and effect of the conditions, and confirm that the young person understands them; and

(c) cause a copy of the conditions to be given to the young person, and to a parent of the young person.

PROVISIONS TO APPLY

(4) Subsections 56(3) (endorsement of order by young person) and (4) (validity of order) apply, with any modifications that the circumstances require, in respect of conditions under this section.

APPLICATION FOR CONTINUATION OF CUSTODY

98. (1) Within a reasonable time before the expiry of the custodial portion of a young person's youth sentence, the Attorney General or the provincial director may apply to the youth justice court for an order that the young person remain in custody for a period not exceeding the remainder of the youth sentence.

CONTINUATION OF CUSTODY

(2) If the hearing for an application under subsection (1) cannot be completed before the expiry of the custodial portion of the youth sentence, the court may order that the young person remain in custody pending the determination of the application if the court is satisfied that the application was made in a reasonable time, having regard to all the circumstances, and that there are compelling reasons for keeping the young person in custody.

DECISION

(3) The youth justice court may, after giving both parties and a parent of the young person an opportunity to be heard, order that a young person remain in custody for a period not exceeding the remainder of the youth sentence, if it is satisfied that there are reasonable grounds to believe that

(a) the young person is likely to commit a serious violent offence before the expiry of the youth sentence he or she is then serving; and

(b) the conditions that would be imposed on the young person if he or she were to serve a portion of the youth sentence in the community would not be adequate to prevent the commission of the offence.

FACTORS

(4) For the purpose of determining an application under subsection (1), the youth justice court shall take into consideration any factor that is relevant to the case of the young person, including

(a) evidence of a pattern of persistent violent behaviour and, in particular,

(i) the number of offences committed by the young person that caused physical or psychological harm to any other person,

(ii) the young person's difficulties in controlling violent impulses to the point of endangering the safety of any other person,

(iii) the use of weapons in the commission of any offence,

(iv) explicit threats of violence,

(v) behaviour of a brutal nature associated with the commission of any offence, and

(vi) a substantial degree of indifference on the part of the young person as to the reasonably foreseeable consequences, to other persons, of the young person's behaviour;

(b) psychiatric or psychological evidence that a physical or mental illness or disorder of the young person is of such a nature that the young person is likely to commit, before the expiry of the youth sentence the young person is then serving, a serious violent offence;

(c) reliable information that satisfies the youth justice court that the young person is planning to commit, before the expiry of the youth sentence the young person is then serving, a serious violent offence;

(d) the availability of supervision programs in the community that would offer adequate protection to the public from the risk that the young person might otherwise present until the expiry of the youth sentence the young person is then serving;

(e) whether the young person is more likely to reoffend if he or she serves his or her youth sentence entirely in custody without the benefits of serving a portion of the youth sentence in the community under supervision; and

(f) evidence of a pattern of committing violent offences while he or she was serving a portion of a youth sentence in the community under supervision.

REPORT

99. (1) For the purpose of determining an application under section 98 (application for continuation of custody), the youth justice court shall require the provincial director to cause to be prepared, and to submit to the youth justice court, a report setting out any information of which the provincial director is aware with respect to the factors set out in subsection 98(4) that may be of assistance to the court.

WRITTEN OR ORAL REPORT

(2) A report referred to in subsection (1) shall be in writing unless it cannot reasonably be committed to writing, in which case it may, with leave of the youth justice court, be submitted orally in court.

PROVISIONS APPLY

(3) Subsections 40(4) to (10) (procedures respecting presentence reports) apply, with any modifications that the circumstances require, in respect of a report referred to in subsection (1).

NOTICE OF HEARING

(4) When an application is made under section 98 (application for continuation of custody) in respect of a young person, the provincial director shall cause to be given, to the young person and to a parent of the young person, at least five clear days notice of the hearing in writing.

STATEMENT OF RIGHT TO COUNSEL

(5) Any notice given to a parent under subsection (4) shall include a statement that the young person has the right to be represented by counsel.

SERVICE OF NOTICE

(6) A notice under subsection (4) may be served personally or may be sent by confirmed delivery service.

WHEN NOTICE NOT GIVEN

(7) When notice under subsection (4) is not given in accordance with this section, the youth justice court may

(a) adjourn the hearing and order that the notice be given in any manner and to any person that it directs; or

(b) dispense with the giving of the notice if, in the opinion of the youth justice court, having regard to the circumstances, the giving of the notice may be dispensed with.

REASONS

100. When a youth justice court makes an order under subsection 98(3) (decision for continued custody), it shall state its reasons for the order in the record of the case and shall provide, or cause to be provided, to the young person in respect of whom the order was made, the counsel and a parent of the young person, the Attorney General and the provincial director

(a) a copy of the order; and

(b) on request, a transcript or copy of the reasons for the order.

REVIEW OF YOUTH JUSTICE COURT DECISION

101. (1) An order made under subsection 98(3) (decision for continued custody) in respect of a young person, or the refusal to make such an order, shall, on application of the young person, the young person's counsel, the Attorney General or the provincial director made within thirty days after the decision of the youth justice court, be reviewed by the court of appeal, and that court may, in its discretion, confirm or reverse the decision of the youth justice court.

EXTENSION OF TIME TO MAKE APPLICATION

(2) The court of appeal may, at any time, extend the time within which an application under subsection (1) may be made.

NOTICE OF APPLICATION

(3) A person who proposes to apply for a review under subsection (1) shall give notice of the application in the manner and within the period of time that may be directed by rules of court.

BREACH OF CONDITIONS

102. (1) If the provincial director has reasonable grounds to believe that a young person has breached or is about to breach a condition to which he or she is subject under section 97 (conditions to be included in custody and supervision orders), the provincial director may, in writing,

(a) permit the young person to continue to serve a portion of his or her youth sentence in the community, on the same or different conditions; or

(b) if satisfied that the breach is a serious one that increases the risk to public safety, order that the young person be remanded to any youth custody facility that the provincial director considers appropriate until a review is conducted.

PROVISIONS APPLY

(2) Sections 107 (apprehension) and 108 (review by provincial director) apply, with any modifications that the circumstances require, to an order under paragraph (1)(b).

REVIEW BY YOUTH JUSTICE COURT

103. (1) When the case of a young person is referred to the youth justice court under section 108 (review by provincial director), the provincial director shall, without delay, cause the young person to be brought before the youth justice court, and the youth justice court shall, after giving the young person an opportunity to be heard,

(a) if the court is not satisfied on reasonable grounds that the young person has breached or was about to breach one of the conditions under which he or she was being supervised in the community, order that the young person continue to serve a portion of his or her youth sentence in the community, on the same or different conditions; or

(b) if the court is satisfied on reasonable grounds that the young person has breached or was about to breach one of the conditions under which he or she was being supervised in the community, make an order under subsection (2).

ORDER

(2) On completion of a review under subsection (1), the youth justice court

(a) shall order that the young person continue to serve the remainder of the youth sentence the young person is then serving in the community, and when the court does so, the court may vary the existing conditions or impose new conditions; or

(b) shall, despite paragraph 42(2)(n) (custody and supervision order), order that the young person remain in custody for a period that does not exceed the remainder of the youth sentence the young person is then serving, if the youth justice court is satisfied that the breach of the conditions was serious.

PROVISIONS APPLY

(3) Subsections 109(4) to (8) apply, with any modifications that the circumstances require, in respect of a review under this section.

CONTINUATION OF CUSTODY

104. (1) When a young person on whom a youth sentence under paragraph 42(2)(o), (q) or (r) has been imposed is held in custody and an application is made to the youth justice court by the Attorney General, within a reasonable time before the expiry of the custodial portion of the youth sentence, the provincial director of the province in which the young person is held in custody shall cause the young person to be brought before the youth justice court and the youth justice court may, after giving both parties and a parent of the young person an opportunity to be heard and if it is satisfied that there are reasonable grounds to believe that the young person is likely to commit an offence causing the death of or serious harm to another person before the expiry of the youth sentence the young person is then serving, order that the young person remain in custody for a period not exceeding the remainder of the youth sentence.

CONTINUATION OF CUSTODY

(2) If the hearing of an application under subsection (1) cannot be completed before the expiry of the custodial portion of the youth sentence, the court may order that the young person remain in custody until the determination of the application if the court is satisfied that the application was made in a reasonable time, having regard to all the circumstances, and that there are compelling reasons for keeping the young person in custody.

FACTORS

(3) For the purpose of determining an application under subsection (1), the youth justice court shall take into consideration any factor that is relevant to the case of the young person, including

(a) evidence of a pattern of persistent violent behaviour and, in particular,

(i) the number of offences committed by the young person that caused physical or psychological harm to any other person,

(ii) the young person's difficulties in controlling violent impulses to the point of endangering the safety of any other person,

(iii) the use of weapons in the commission of any offence,

(iv) explicit threats of violence,

(v) behaviour of a brutal nature associated with the commission of any offence, and

(vi) a substantial degree of indifference on the part of the young person as to the reasonably foreseeable consequences, to other persons, of the young person's behaviour;

(b) psychiatric or psychological evidence that a physical or mental illness or disorder of the young person is of such a nature that the young person is likely to commit, before the expiry of the youth sentence the young person is then serving, an offence causing the death of or serious harm to another person;

(c) reliable information that satisfies the youth justice court that the young person is planning to commit, before the expiry of the youth sentence the young person is then serving, an offence causing the death of or serious harm to another person; and

(d) the availability of supervision programs in the community that would offer adequate protection to the public from the risk that the young person might otherwise present until the expiry of the youth sentence the young person is then serving.

YOUTH JUSTICE COURT TO ORDER APPEARANCE OF YOUNG PERSON

(4) If a provincial director fails to cause a young person to be brought before the youth justice court under subsection (1), the youth justice court shall order the provincial director to cause the young person to be brought before the youth justice court without delay.

PROVISIONS TO APPLY

(5) Sections 99 to 101 apply, with any modifications that the circumstances require, in respect of an order made, or the refusal to make an order, under this section.

IF APPLICATION DENIED

(6) If an application under this section is denied, the court may, with the consent of the young person, the Attorney General and the provincial director, proceed as though the young person had been brought before the court as required under subsection 105(1).

CONDITIONAL SUPERVISION

105. (1) The provincial director of the province in which a young person on whom a youth sentence under paragraph 42(2)(o), (q) or (r) has been imposed is held in custody or, if applicable, with respect to whom an order has been made under subsection 104(1) (continuation of custody), shall cause the young person to be brought before the youth justice court at least one month before the expiry of the custodial portion of the youth sentence. The court shall, after giving the young person an opportunity to be heard, by order, set the conditions of the young person's conditional supervision.

CONDITIONS TO BE INCLUDED IN ORDER

(2) The youth justice court shall include in the order under subsection (1) the following conditions, namely, that the young person

(a) keep the peace and be of good behaviour;

(b) appear before the youth justice court when required by the court to do so;

(c) report to the provincial director immediately on release, and then be under the supervision of the provincial director or a person designated by the youth justice court;

(d) inform the provincial director immediately on being arrested or questioned by the police;

(e) report to the police, or any named individual, as instructed by the provincial director;

(f) advise the provincial director of the young person's address of residence on release and after release report immediately to the clerk of the youth justice court or the provincial director any change

(i) in that address,

(ii) in the young person's normal occupation, including employment, vocational or educational training and volunteer work,

(iii) in the young person's family or financial situation, and

(iv) that may reasonably be expected to affect the young person's ability to comply with the conditions of the order;

(g) not own, possess or have the control of any weapon, ammunition, prohibited ammunition, prohibited device or explosive substance, except as authorized by the order; and

(h) comply with any reasonable instructions that the provincial director considers necessary in respect of any condition of the conditional supervision in order to prevent a breach of that condition or to protect society.

OTHER CONDITIONS

(3) In setting conditions for the purposes of subsection (1), the youth justice court may include in the order the following conditions, namely, that the young person

(a) on release, travel directly to the young person's place of residence, or to any other place that is noted in the order;

(b) make reasonable efforts to obtain and maintain suitable employment;

(c) attend school or any other place of learning, training or recreation that is appropriate, if the court is satisfied that a suitable program is available for the young person at such a place;

(d) reside with a parent, or any other adult that the court considers appropriate, who is willing to provide for the care and maintenance of the young person;

(e) reside in any place that the provincial director may specify;

(f) remain within the territorial jurisdiction of one or more courts named in the order;

(g) comply with conditions set out in the order that support and address the needs of the young person and promote the reintegration of the young person into the community; and

(h) comply with any other conditions set out in the order that the court considers appropriate, including conditions for securing the young person's good conduct and for preventing the young person from repeating the offence or committing other offences.

TEMPORARY CONDITIONS

(4) When a provincial director is required under subsection (1) to cause a young person to be brought before the youth justice court but cannot do so for reasons beyond the young person's control, the provincial director shall so advise the youth justice court and the court shall, by order, set any temporary conditions for the young person's conditional supervision that are appropriate in the circumstances.

CONDITIONS TO BE SET AT FIRST OPPORTUNITY

(5) When an order is made under subsection (4), the provincial director shall bring the young person before the youth justice court as soon after the order is made as the circumstances permit and the court shall then set the conditions of the young person's conditional supervision.

REPORT

(6) For the purpose of setting conditions under this section, the youth justice court shall require the provincial director to cause to be prepared, and to submit to the youth justice court, a report setting out any information that may be of assistance to the court.

PROVISIONS APPLY

(7) Subsections 99(2) to (7) (provisions respecting reports and notice) and 104(4) (ordering appearance of young person) apply, with any modifications that the circumstances require, in respect of any proceedings held under subsection (1).

PROVISIONS APPLY

(8) Subsections 56(1) to (4) (provisions respecting probation orders), (7) (notice to appear) and (8) (warrant in default) and section 101 (review of youth justice court decision) apply, with any modifications that the circumstances require, in respect of an order made under subsection (1).

SUSPENSION OF CONDITIONAL SUPERVISION

106. If the provincial director has reasonable grounds to believe that a young person has breached or is about to breach a condition of an order made under subsection 105(1), the provincial director may, in writing,

(a) suspend the conditional supervision; and

(b) order that the young person be remanded to any youth custody facility that the provincial director considers appropriate until a review is conducted under section 108 and, if applicable, section 109.

APPREHENSION

107. (1) If the conditional supervision of a young person is suspended under section 106, the provincial director may issue a warrant in writing, authorizing the apprehension of the young person and, until the young person is apprehended, the young person is deemed not to be continuing to serve the youth sentence the young person is then serving.

WARRANTS

(2) A warrant issued under subsection (1) shall be executed by any peace officer to whom it is given at any place in Canada and has the same force and effect in all parts of Canada as if it had been originally issued or subsequently endorsed by a provincial court judge or other lawful authority having jurisdiction in the place where it is executed.

PEACE OFFICER MAY ARREST

(3) If a peace officer believes on reasonable grounds that a warrant issued under subsection (1) is in force in respect of a young person, the peace officer may arrest the young person without the warrant at any place in Canada.

REQUIREMENT TO BRING BEFORE PROVINCIAL DIRECTOR

(4) If a young person is arrested under subsection (3) and detained, the peace officer making the arrest shall cause the young person to be brought before the provincial director or a person designated by the provincial director

(a) if the provincial director or the designated person is available within a period of twenty-four hours after the young person is arrested, without unreasonable delay and in any event within that period; and

(b) if the provincial director or the designated person is not available within that period, as soon as possible.

RELEASE OR REMAND IN CUSTODY

(5) If a young person is brought before the provincial director or a person designated by the provincial director under subsection (4), the provincial director or the designated person

(a) if not satisfied that there are reasonable grounds to believe that the young person is the young person in respect of whom the warrant referred to in subsection (1) was issued, shall release the young person; or

(b) if satisfied that there are reasonable grounds to believe that the young person is the young person in respect of whom the warrant referred to in subsection (1) was issued, may remand the young person in custody to await execution of the warrant, but if no warrant for the young person's arrest is executed within a period of forty-eight hours after the time the young person is remanded in custody, the person in whose custody the young person then is shall release the young person.

REVIEW BY PROVINCIAL DIRECTOR

108. Without delay after the remand to custody of a young person whose conditional supervision has been suspended under section 106, or without delay after being informed of the arrest of such a young person, the provincial director shall review the case and, within forty-eight hours, cancel the suspension of the conditional supervision or refer the case to the youth justice court for a review under section 109.

REVIEW BY YOUTH JUSTICE COURT

109. (1) If the case of a young person is referred to the youth justice court under section 108, the provincial director shall, without delay, cause the young person to be brought before the youth justice court, and the youth justice court shall, after giving the young person an opportunity to be heard,

(a) if the court is not satisfied on reasonable grounds that the young person has breached or was about to breach a condition of the conditional supervision, cancel the suspension of the conditional supervision; or

(b) if the court is satisfied on reasonable grounds that the young person has breached or was about to breach a condition of the conditional supervision, review the decision of the provincial director to suspend the conditional supervision and make an order under subsection (2).

ORDER

(2) On completion of a review under subsection (1), the youth justice court shall order

(a) the cancellation of the suspension of the conditional supervision, and when the court does so, the court may vary the conditions of the conditional supervision or impose new conditions;

(b) in a case other than a deferred custody and supervision order made under paragraph 42(2)(p), the continuation of the suspension of the conditional supervision for any period of time, not to exceed the remainder of the youth sentence the young person is then serving, that the court considers appropriate, and when the court does so, the court shall order that the young person remain in custody; or

(c) in the case of a deferred custody and supervision order made under paragraph 42(2)(p), that the young person serve the remainder of the order as if it were a custody and supervision order under paragraph 42(2)(n).

CUSTODY AND SUPERVISION ORDER

(3) After a court has made a direction under paragraph (2)(c), the provisions of this Act applicable to orders under paragraph 42(2)(n) apply in respect of the deferred custody and supervision order.

FACTORS TO BE CONSIDERED

(4) In making its decision under subsection (2), the court shall consider the length of time the young person has been subject to the order, whether the young person has previously contravened it, and the nature of the contravention, if any.

REASONS

(5) When a youth justice court makes an order under subsection (2), it shall state its reasons for the order in the record of the case and shall give, or cause to be given, to the young person in respect of whom the order was made, the counsel and a parent of the young person, the Attorney General and the provincial director,

(a) a copy of the order; and

(b) on request, a transcript or copy of the reasons for the order.

REPORT

(6) For the purposes of a review under subsection (1), the youth justice court shall require the provincial director to cause to be prepared, and to submit to the youth justice court, a report setting out any information of which the provincial director is aware that may be of assistance to the court.

PROVISIONS APPLY

(7) Subsections 99(2) to (7) (provisions respecting reports and notice) and 105(6) (report for the purpose of setting conditions) apply, with any modifications that the circumstances require, in respect of a review under this section.

PROVISIONS APPLY

(8) Section 101 (review of youth justice court decision) applies, with any modifications that the circumstances require, in respect of an order made under subsection (2).

PART 6
PUBLICATION, RECORDS AND INFORMATION

Protection of Privacy of Young Persons

IDENTITY OF OFFENDER NOT TO BE PUBLISHED

110. (1) Subject to this section, no person shall publish the name of a young person, or any other information related to a young person, if it would identify the young person as a young person dealt with under this Act.

LIMITATION

(2) Subsection (1) does not apply

(a) in a case where the information relates to a young person who has received an adult sentence;

(b) subject to sections 65 (young person not liable to adult sentence) and 75 (youth sentence imposed despite presumptive offence), in a case where the information relates to a young person who has received a youth sentence for an offence set out in paragraph (a) of the definition "presumptive offence" in subsection 2(1), or an offence set out in paragraph (b) of that definition for which the Attorney General has given notice under subsection 64(2) (intention to seek adult sentence); and

(c) in a case where the publication of information is made in the course of the administration of justice, if it is not the purpose of the publication to make the information known in the community.

EXCEPTION

(3) A young person referred to in subsection (1) may, after he or she attains the age of eighteen years, publish or cause to be published information that would identify him or her as having been dealt with under this Act or the *Young Offenders Act*, chapter Y-1 of the Revised Statutes of Canada, 1985, provided that he or she is not in custody pursuant to either Act at the time of the publication.

EX PARTE APPLICATION FOR LEAVE TO PUBLISH

(4) A youth justice court judge shall, on the ex parte application of a peace officer, make an order permitting any person to publish information that identifies a young person as having committed or allegedly committed an indictable offence, if the judge is satisfied that

(a) there is reason to believe that the young person is a danger to others; and

(b) publication of the information is necessary to assist in apprehending the young person.

ORDER CEASES TO HAVE EFFECT

(5) An order made under subsection (4) ceases to have effect five days after it is made.

APPLICATION FOR LEAVE TO PUBLISH

(6) The youth justice court may, on the application of a young person referred to in subsection (1), make an order permitting the young person to publish information that would identify him or her as having been dealt with under this Act or the *Young Offenders Act*, chapter Y-1 of the Revised Statutes of Canada, 1985, if the court is satisfied that the publication would not be contrary to the young person's best interests or the public interest.

IDENTITY OF VICTIM OR WITNESS NOT TO BE PUBLISHED

111. (1) Subject to this section, no person shall publish the name of a child or young person, or any other information related to a child or a young person, if it would identify the child or young person as having been a victim of, or as having appeared as a witness in connection with, an offence committed or alleged to have been committed by a young person.

EXCEPTION

(2) Information that would serve to identify a child or young person referred to in subsection (1) as having been a victim or a witness may be published, or caused to be published, by

(a) that child or young person after he or she attains the age of eighteen years or before that age with the consent of his or her parents; or

(b) the parents of that child or young person if he or she is deceased.

APPLICATION FOR LEAVE TO PUBLISH

(3) The youth justice court may, on the application of a child or a young person referred to in subsection (1), make an order permitting the child or young person to publish information that would identify him or her as having been a victim or a witness if the court is satisfied that the publication would not be contrary to his or her best interests or the public interest.

NON-APPLICATION

112. Once information is published under subsection 110(3) or (6) or 111(2) or (3), subsection 110(1) (identity of offender not to be published) or 111(1) (identity of victim or witness not to be published), as the case may be, no longer applies in respect of the information.

Fingerprints and Photographs

IDENTIFICATION OF CRIMINALS ACT APPLIES

113. (1) The *Identification of Criminals Act* applies in respect of young persons.

LIMITATION

(2) No fingerprint, palmprint or photograph or other measurement, process or operation referred to in the *Identification of Criminals Act* shall be taken of, or applied in respect of, a young person who is charged with having committed an offence except in the circumstances in which an adult may, under that Act, be subjected to the measurements, processes and operations.

Records That May Be Kept

YOUTH JUSTICE COURT, REVIEW BOARD AND OTHER COURTS

114. A youth justice court, review board or any court dealing with matters arising out of proceedings under this Act may keep a record of any case that comes before it arising under this Act.

POLICE RECORDS

115. (1) A record relating to any offence alleged to have been committed by a young person, including the original or a copy of any fingerprints or photographs of the young person, may be kept by any police force responsible for or participating in the investigation of the offence.

POLICE RECORDS

(2) When a young person is charged with having committed an offence in respect of which an adult may be subjected to any measurement, process or operation referred to in the *Identification of Criminals Act*, the police force responsible for the investigation of the offence may provide a record relating to the offence to the Royal Canadian Mounted Police. If the young person is found guilty of the offence, the police force shall provide the record.

RECORDS HELD BY R.C.M.P.

(3) The Royal Canadian Mounted Police shall keep the records provided under subsection (2) in the central repository that the Commissioner of the Royal Canadian Mounted Police may, from time to time, designate for the purpose of keeping criminal history files or records of offenders or keeping records for the identification of offenders.

GOVERNMENT RECORDS

116. (1) A department or an agency of any government in Canada may keep records containing information obtained by the department or agency

(a) for the purposes of an investigation of an offence alleged to have been committed by a young person;

(b) for use in proceedings against a young person under this Act;

(c) for the purpose of administering a youth sentence or an order of the youth justice court;

(d) for the purpose of considering whether to use extrajudicial measures to deal with a young person; or

(e) as a result of the use of extrajudicial measures to deal with a young person.

OTHER RECORDS

(2) A person or organization may keep records containing information obtained by the person or organization

(a) as a result of the use of extrajudicial measures to deal with a young person; or

(b) for the purpose of administering or participating in the administration of a youth sentence.

Access to Records

EXCEPTION—ADULT SENTENCE

117. Sections 118 to 129 do not apply to records kept in respect of an offence for which an adult sentence has been imposed once the time allowed for the taking of an appeal has expired or, if an appeal is taken, all proceedings in respect of the appeal have been completed and the appeal court has upheld an adult sentence. The record shall be dealt with as a record of an adult and, for the purposes of the *Criminal Records Act*, the finding of guilt in respect of the offence for which the record is kept is deemed to be a conviction.

NO ACCESS UNLESS AUTHORIZED

118. (1) Except as authorized or required by this Act, no person shall be given access to a record kept under sections 114 to 116, and no information contained in it may be given to any person, where to do so would identify the young person to whom it relates as a young person dealt with under this Act.

EXCEPTION FOR EMPLOYEES

(2) No person who is employed in keeping or maintaining records referred to in subsection (1) is restricted from doing anything prohibited under subsection (1) with respect to any other person so employed.

PERSONS HAVING ACCESS TO RECORDS

119. (1) Subject to subsections (4) to (6), from the date that a record is created until the end of the applicable period set out in subsection (2), the following persons, on request, shall be given access to a record kept under section 114, and may be given access to a record kept under sections 115 and 116:

(a) the young person to whom the record relates;

(b) the young person's counsel, or any representative of that counsel;

(c) the Attorney General;

(d) the victim of the offence or alleged offence to which the record relates;

(e) the parents of the young person, during the course of any proceedings relating to the offence or alleged offence to which the record relates or during the term of any youth sentence made in respect of the offence;

(f) any adult assisting the young person under subsection 25(7), during the course of any proceedings relating to the offence or alleged offence to which the record relates or during the term of any youth sentence made in respect of the offence;

(g) any peace officer for

(i) law enforcement purposes, or

(ii) any purpose related to the administration of the case to which the record relates, during the course of proceedings against the young person or the term of the youth sentence;

(h) a judge, court or review board, for any purpose relating to proceedings against the young person, or proceedings against the person after he or she becomes an adult, in respect of offences committed or alleged to have been committed by that person;

(i) the provincial director, or the director of the provincial correctional facility for adults or the penitentiary at which the young person is serving a sentence;

(j) a person participating in a conference or in the administration of extrajudicial measures, if required for the administration of the case to which the record relates;

(k) a person acting as ombudsman, privacy commissioner or information commissioner, whatever his or her official designation might be, who in the course of his or her duties under an Act of Parliament or the legislature of a province is investigating a complaint to which the record relates;

(l) a coroner or a person acting as a child advocate, whatever his or her official designation might be, who is acting in the course of his or her duties under an Act of Parliament or the legislature of a province;

(m) a person acting under the *Firearms Act*;

(n) a member of a department or agency of a government in Canada, or of an organization that is an agent of, or under contract with, the department or agency, who is

(i) acting in the exercise of his or her duties under this Act,

(ii) engaged in the supervision or care of the young person, whether as a young person or an adult, or in an investigation related to the young person under an Act of the legislature of a province respecting child welfare,

(iii) considering an application for conditional release or pardon made by the young person, whether as a young person or an adult,

(iv) administering a prohibition order made under an Act of Parliament or the legislature of a province, or

(v) administering a youth sentence, if the young person has been committed to custody and is serving the custody in a provincial correctional facility for adults or a penitentiary;

(o) a person, for the purpose of carrying out a criminal record check required by the Government of Canada or the government of a province or a municipality for purposes of employment or the performance of services, with or without remuneration;

(p) an employee or agent of the Government of Canada, for statistical purposes under the *Statistics Act*;

(q) an accused or his or her counsel who swears an affidavit to the effect that access to the record is necessary to make a full answer and defence;

(r) a person or a member of a class of persons designated by order of the Governor in Council, or the lieutenant governor in council of the appropriate province, for a purpose and to the extent specified in the order; and

(s) any person or member of a class of persons that a youth justice court judge considers has a valid interest in the record, to

the extent directed by the judge, if the judge is satisfied that access to the record is

(i) desirable in the public interest for research or statistical purposes, or

(ii) desirable in the interest of the proper administration of justice.

PERIOD OF ACCESS

(2) The period of access referred to in subsection (1) is

(a) if an extrajudicial sanction is used to deal with the young person, the period ending two years after the young person consents to be subject to the sanction in accordance with paragraph 10(2)(c);

(b) if the young person is acquitted of the offence otherwise than by reason of a verdict of not criminally responsible on account of mental disorder, the period ending two months after the expiry of the time allowed for the taking of an appeal or, if an appeal is taken, the period ending three months after all proceedings in respect of the appeal have been completed;

(c) if the charge against the young person is dismissed for any reason other than acquittal, the charge is withdrawn, or the young person is found guilty of the offence and a reprimand is given, the period ending two months after the dismissal, withdrawal, or finding of guilt;

(d) if the charge against the young person is stayed, with no proceedings being taken against the young person for a period of one year, at the end of that period;

(e) if the young person is found guilty of the offence and the youth sentence is an absolute discharge, the period ending one year after the young person is found guilty;

(f) if the young person is found guilty of the offence and the youth sentence is a conditional discharge, the period ending three years after the young person is found guilty;

(g) subject to paragraphs (i) and (j) and subsection (9), if the young person is found guilty of the offence and it is a summary conviction offence, the period ending three years after the youth sentence imposed in respect of the offence has been completed;

(h) subject to paragraphs (i) and (j) and subsection (9), if the young person is found guilty of the offence and it is an indictable offence, the period ending five years after the youth sentence imposed in respect of the offence has been completed;

(i) subject to subsection (9), if, during the period calculated in accordance with paragraph (g) or (h), the young person is found guilty of an offence punishable on summary conviction committed when he or she was a young person, the latest of

(i) the period calculated in accordance with paragraph (g) or (h), as the case may be, and

(ii) the period ending three years after the youth sentence imposed for that offence has been completed; and

(j) subject to subsection (9), if, during the period calculated in accordance with paragraph (g) or (h), the young person is found guilty of an indictable offence committed when he or she was a young person, the period ending five years after the sentence imposed for that indictable offence has been completed.

PROHIBITION ORDERS NOT INCLUDED

(3) Prohibition orders made under an Act of Parliament or the legislature of a province, including any order made under section 51, shall not be taken into account in determining any period referred to in subsection (2).

EXTRAJUDICIAL MEASURES

(4) Access to a record kept under section 115 or 116 in respect of extrajudicial measures, other than extrajudicial sanctions, used in

respect of a young person shall be given only to the following persons for the following purposes:

(a) a peace officer or the Attorney General, in order to make a decision whether to again use extrajudicial measures in respect of the young person;

(b) a person participating in a conference, in order to decide on the appropriate extrajudicial measure;

(c) a peace officer, the Attorney General or a person participating in a conference, if access is required for the administration of the case to which the record relates; and

(d) a peace officer for the purpose of investigating an offence.

EXCEPTION

(5) When a youth justice court has withheld all or part of a report from any person under subsection 34(9) or (10) (nondisclosure of medical or psychological report) or 40(7) (nondisclosure of pre-sentence report), that person shall not be given access under subsection (1) to that report or part.

RECORDS OF ASSESSMENTS OR FORENSIC DNA ANALYSIS

(6) Access to a report made under section 34 (medical and psychological reports) or a record of the results of forensic DNA analysis of a bodily substance taken from a young person in execution of a warrant issued under section 487.05 of the *Criminal Code* may be given only under paragraphs (1)(a) to (c), (e) to (h) and (q) and subparagraph (1)(s)(ii).

INTRODUCTION INTO EVIDENCE

(7) Nothing in paragraph (1)(h) or (q) authorizes the introduction into evidence of any part of a record that would not otherwise be admissible in evidence.

DISCLOSURES FOR RESEARCH OR STATISTICAL PURPOSES

(8) When access to a record is given to a person under paragraph (1)(p) or subparagraph (1)(s)(i), the person may subsequently disclose information contained in the record, but shall not disclose the information in any form that would reasonably be expected to identify the young person to whom it relates.

APPLICATION OF USUAL RULES

(9) If, during the period of access to a record under any of paragraphs (2)(g) to (j), the young person is convicted of an offence committed when he or she is an adult,

(a) section 82 (effect of absolute discharge or termination of youth sentence) does not apply to the young person in respect of the offence for which the record is kept under sections 114 to 116;

(b) this Part no longer applies to the record and the record shall be dealt with as a record of an adult; and

(c) for the purposes of the *Criminal Records Act*, the finding of guilt in respect of the offence for which the record is kept is deemed to be a conviction.

RECORDS OF OFFENCES THAT RESULT IN A PROHIBITION ORDER

(10) Despite anything in this Act, when a young person is found guilty of an offence that results in a prohibition order being made, and the order is still in force at the end of the applicable period for which access to a record kept in respect of the order may be given under subsection (2),

(a) the record kept by the Royal Canadian Mounted Police pursuant to subsection 115(3) may be disclosed only to establish the existence of the order for purposes of law enforcement; and

(b) the record referred to in section 114 that is kept by the youth justice court may be disclosed only to establish the existence of the order in any offence involving a breach of the order.

ACCESS TO R.C.M.P. RECORDS

120. (1) The following persons may, during the period set out in subsection (3), be given access to a record kept under subsection 115(3) in respect of an offence set out in the schedule:

(a) the young person to whom the record relates;

(b) the young person's counsel, or any representative of that counsel;

(c) an employee or agent of the Government of Canada, for statistical purposes under the *Statistics Act*;

(d) any person or member of a class of persons that a youth justice court judge considers has a valid interest in the record, to the extent directed by the judge, if the judge is satisfied that access is desirable in the public interest for research or statistical purposes;

(e) the Attorney General or a peace officer, when the young person is or has been charged with another offence set out in the schedule or the same offence more than once, for the purpose of investigating any offence that the young person is suspected of having committed, or in respect of which the young person has been arrested or charged, whether as a young person or as an adult;

(f) the Attorney General or a peace officer to establish the existence of an order in any offence involving a breach of the order; and

(g) any person for the purposes of the *Firearms Act*.

ACCESS FOR IDENTIFICATION PURPOSES

(2) During the period set out in subsection (3), access to the portion of a record kept under subsection 115(3) that contains the name, date of birth and last known address of the young person to whom the fingerprints belong, may be given to a person for identification purposes if a fingerprint identified as that of the young person is found during the investigation of an offence or during an attempt to identify a deceased person or a person suffering from amnesia.

PERIOD OF ACCESS

(3) For the purposes of subsections (1) and (2), the period of access to a record kept under subsection 115(3) in respect of an offence is the following:

(a) if the offence is an indictable offence, other than a presumptive offence, the period starting at the end of the applicable period set out in paragraphs 119(2)(h) to (j) and ending five years later; and

(b) if the offence is an offence set out in paragraph (a) of the definition "presumptive offence" in subsection 2(1) or an offence set out in paragraph (b) of that definition for which the Attorney General has given notice under subsection 64(2) (intention to seek adult sentence), the period starting at the end of the applicable period set out in paragraphs 119(2)(h) to (j) and continuing indefinitely.

SUBSEQUENT OFFENCES AS YOUNG PERSON

(4) If a young person was found guilty of an offence set out in the schedule is, during the period of access to a record under subsection (3), found guilty of an additional offence set out in the schedule, committed when he or she was a young person, access to the record may be given to the following additional persons:

(a) a parent of the young person or any adult assisting the young person under subsection 25(7);

(b) a judge, court or review board, for a purpose relating to proceedings against the young person under this Act or any other Act of Parliament in respect of offences committed or alleged to have been committed by the young person, whether as a young person or as an adult; or

(c) a member of a department or agency of a government in Canada, or of an organization that is an agent of, or is under contract with, the department or agency, who is

(i) preparing a report in respect of the young person under this Act or for the purpose of assisting a court in sentencing the young person after the young person becomes an adult,

(ii) engaged in the supervision or care of the young person, whether as a young person or as an adult, or in the administration of a sentence in respect of the young person, whether as a young person or as an adult, or

(iii) considering an application for conditional release or pardon made by the young person after the young person becomes an adult.

DISCLOSURE FOR RESEARCH OR STATISTICAL PURPOSES

(5) A person who is given access to a record under paragraph (1)(c) or (d) may subsequently disclose information contained in the record, but shall not disclose the information in any form that would reasonably be expected to identify the young person to whom it relates.

SUBSEQUENT OFFENCES AS ADULT

(6) If, during the period of access to a record under subsection (3), the young person is convicted of an additional offence set out in the schedule, committed when he or she was an adult,

(a) this Part no longer applies to the record and the record shall be dealt with as a record of an adult and may be included on the automated criminal conviction records retrieval system maintained by the Royal Canadian Mounted Police; and

(b) for the purposes of the *Criminal Records Act*, the finding of guilt in respect of the offence for which the record is kept is deemed to be a conviction.

DEEMED ELECTION

121. For the purposes of sections 119 and 120, if no election is made in respect of an offence that may be prosecuted by indictment or proceeded with by way of summary conviction, the Attorney General is deemed to have elected to proceed with the offence as an offence punishable on summary conviction.

DISCLOSURE OF INFORMATION AND COPIES OF RECORD

122. A person who is required or authorized to be given access to a record under section 119, 120, 123 or 124 may be given any information contained in the record and may be given a copy of any part of the record.

WHERE RECORDS MAY BE MADE AVAILABLE

123. (1) A youth justice court judge may, on application by a person after the end of the applicable period set out in subsection 119(2), order that the person be given access to all or part of a record kept under sections 114 to 116 or that a copy of the record or part be given to that person,

(a) if the youth justice court judge is satisfied that

(i) the person has a valid and substantial interest in the record or part,

(ii) it is necessary for access to be given to the record or part in the interest of the proper administration of justice, and

(iii) disclosure of the record or part or the information in it is not prohibited under any other Act of Parliament or the legislature of a province; or

(b) if the youth court judge is satisfied that access to the record or part is desirable in the public interest for research or statistical purposes.

RESTRICTION FOR PARAGRAPH (1)(A)

(2) Paragraph (1)(a) applies in respect of a record relating to a particular young person or to a record relating to a class of young persons only if the identity of young persons in the class at the time of the making of the application referred to in that paragraph cannot reasonably be ascertained and the disclosure of the record is necessary for the purpose of investigating any offence that a person is suspected on reasonable grounds of having committed against a young person while the young person is, or was, serving a sentence.

NOTICE

(3) Subject to subsection (4), an application for an order under paragraph (1)(a) in respect of a record shall not be heard unless the person who makes the application has given the young person to whom the record relates and the person or body that has possession of the record at least five days notice in writing of the application, and the young person and the person or body that has possession have had a reasonable opportunity to be heard.

WHERE NOTICE NOT REQUIRED

(4) A youth justice court judge may waive the requirement in subsection (3) to give notice to a young person when the judge is of the opinion that

(a) to insist on the giving of the notice would frustrate the application; or

(b) reasonable efforts have not been successful in finding the young person.

USE OF RECORD

(5) In any order under subsection (1), the youth justice court judge shall set out the purposes for which the record may be used.

DISCLOSURE FOR RESEARCH OR STATISTICAL PURPOSES

(6) When access to a record is given to any person under paragraph (1)(b), that person may subsequently disclose information contained in the record, but shall not disclose the information in any form that would reasonably be expected to identify the young person to whom it relates.

ACCESS TO RECORD BY YOUNG PERSON

124. A young person to whom a record relates and his or her counsel may have access to the record at any time.

Disclosure of Information in a Record
DISCLOSURE BY PEACE OFFICER DURING INVESTIGATION

125. (1) A peace officer may disclose to any person any information in a record kept under section 114 (court records) or 115 (police records) that it is necessary to disclose in the conduct of the investigation of an offence.

DISCLOSURE BY ATTORNEY GENERAL

(2) The Attorney General may, in the course of a proceeding under this Act or any other Act of Parliament, disclose the following information in a record kept under section 114 (court reports) or 115 (police records):

(a) to a person who is a co-accused with the young person in respect of the offence for which the record is kept, any information contained in the record; and

(b) to an accused in a proceeding, if the record is in respect of a witness in the proceeding, information that identifies the witness as a young person who has been dealt with under this Act.

INFORMATION THAT MAY BE DISCLOSED TO A FOREIGN STATE

(3) The Attorney General or a peace officer may disclose to the Minister of Justice of Canada information in a record that is kept

under section 114 (court records) or 115 (police records) to the extent that it is necessary to deal with a request to or by a foreign state under the *Mutual Legal Assistance in Criminal Matters Act*, or for the purposes of any extradition matter under the *Extradition Act*. The Minister of Justice of Canada may disclose the information to the foreign state in respect of which the request was made, or to which the extradition matter relates, as the case may be.

DISCLOSURE TO INSURANCE COMPANY

(4) A peace officer may disclose to an insurance company information in a record that is kept under section 114 (court records) or 115 (police records) for the purpose of investigating a claim arising out of an offence committed or alleged to have been committed by the young person to whom the record relates.

PREPARATION OF REPORTS

(5) The provincial director or a youth worker may disclose information contained in a record if the disclosure is necessary for procuring information that relates to the preparation of a report required by this Act.

SCHOOLS AND OTHERS

(6) The provincial director, a youth worker, the Attorney General, a peace officer or any other person engaged in the provision of services to young persons may disclose to any professional or other person engaged in the supervision or care of a young person—including a representative of any school board or school or any other educational or training institution—any information contained in a record kept under sections 114 to 116 if the disclosure is necessary

(a) to ensure compliance by the young person with an authorization under section 91 or an order of the youth justice court;

(b) to ensure the safety of staff, students or other persons; or

(c) to facilitate the rehabilitation of the young person.

INFORMATION TO BE KEPT SEPARATE

(7) A person to whom information is disclosed under subsection (6) shall

(a) keep the information separate from any other record of the young person to whom the information relates;

(b) ensure that no other person has access to the information except if authorized under this Act, or if necessary for the purposes of subsection (6); and

(c) destroy their copy of the record when the information is no longer required for the purpose for which it was disclosed.

TIME LIMIT

(8) No information may be disclosed under this section after the end of the applicable period set out in subsection 119(2) (period of access to records).

RECORDS IN THE CUSTODY, ETC., OF ARCHIVISTS

126. When records originally kept under sections 114 to 116 are under the custody or control of the National Archivist of Canada or the archivist for any province, that person may disclose any information contained in the records to any other person if

(a) a youth justice court judge is satisfied that the disclosure is desirable in the public interest for research or statistical purposes; and

(b) the person to whom the information is disclosed undertakes not to disclose the information in any form that could reasonably be expected to identify the young person to whom it relates.

DISCLOSURE WITH COURT ORDER

127. (1) The youth justice court may, on the application of the provincial director, the Attorney General or a peace officer, make an order permitting the applicant to disclose to the person or persons specified by the court any information about a young person that is specified, if the court is satisfied that the disclosure is necessary, having regard to the following circumstances:

(a) the young person has been found guilty of an offence involving serious personal injury;

(b) the young person poses a risk of serious harm to persons; and

(c) the disclosure of the information is relevant to the avoidance of that risk.

OPPORTUNITY TO BE HEARD

(2) Subject to subsection (3), before making an order under subsection (1), the youth justice court shall give the young person, a parent of the young person and the Attorney General an opportunity to be heard.

EX PARTE APPLICATION

(3) An application under subsection (1) may be made ex parte by the Attorney General where the youth justice court is satisfied that reasonable efforts have been made to locate the young person and that those efforts have not been successful.

TIME LIMIT

(4) No information may be disclosed under subsection (1) after the end of the applicable period set out in subsection 119(2) (period of access to records).

Disposition or Destruction of Records and Prohibition on Use and Disclosure

EFFECT OF END OF ACCESS PERIODS

128. (1) Subject to sections 123, 124 and 126, after the end of the applicable period set out in section 119 or 120 no record kept under sections 114 to 116 may be used for any purpose that would identify the young person to whom the record relates as a young person dealt with under this Act or the *Young Offenders Act*, chapter Y-1 of the Revised Statutes of Canada, 1985.

DISPOSAL OF RECORDS

(2) Subject to paragraph 125(7)(c), any record kept under sections 114 to 116, other than a record kept under subsection 115(3), may, in the discretion of the person or body keeping the record, be destroyed or transmitted to the National Archivist of Canada or the archivist for any province, at any time before or after the end of the applicable period set out in section 119.

DISPOSAL OF R.C.M.P. RECORDS

(3) All records kept under subsection 115(3) shall be destroyed or, if the National Archivist of Canada requires it, transmitted to the National Archivist of Canada, at the end of the applicable period set out in section 119 or 120.

PURGING CPIC

(4) The Commissioner of the Royal Canadian Mounted Police shall remove a record from the automated criminal conviction records retrieval system maintained by the Royal Canadian Mounted Police at the end of the applicable period referred to in section 119; however, information relating to a prohibition order made under an Act of Parliament or the legislature of a province shall be removed only at the end of the period for which the order is in force.

EXCEPTION

(5) Despite subsections (1), (2) and (4), an entry that is contained in a system maintained by the Royal Canadian Mounted Police to match crime scene information and that relates to an offence committed or alleged to have been committed by a young

person shall be dealt with in the same manner as information that relates to an offence committed by an adult for which a pardon granted under the *Criminal Records Act* is in effect.

AUTHORITY TO INSPECT

(6) The National Archivist of Canada may, at any time, inspect records kept under sections 114 to 116 that are under the control of a government institution as defined in section 2 of the *National Archives of Canada Act*, and the archivist for a province may at any time inspect any records kept under those sections that the archivist is authorized to inspect under any Act of the legislature of the province.

DEFINITION OF "DESTROY"

(7) For the purposes of subsections (2) and (3), "destroy," in respect of a record, means

(a) to shred, burn or otherwise physically destroy the record, in the case of a record other than a record in electronic form; and

(b) to delete, write over or otherwise render the record inaccessible, in the case of a record in electronic form.

NO SUBSEQUENT DISCLOSURE

129. No person who is given access to a record or to whom information is disclosed under this Act shall disclose that information to any other person unless the disclosure is authorized under this Act.

PART 7
GENERAL PROVISIONS

Disqualification of Judge
DISQUALIFICATION OF JUDGE

130. (1) Subject to subsection (2), a youth justice court judge who, prior to an adjudication in respect of a young person charged with an offence, examines a pre-sentence report made in respect of the young person in connection with that offence or has, after a guilty plea or a finding of guilt, heard submissions as to sentence and then there has been a change of plea, shall not in any capacity conduct or continue the trial of the young person for the offence and shall transfer the case to another judge to be dealt with according to law.

EXCEPTION

(2) A youth justice court judge may, in the circumstances referred to in subsection (1), with the consent of the young person and the prosecutor, conduct or continue the trial of the young person if the judge is satisfied that he or she has not been predisposed by a guilty plea or finding of guilt, or by information contained in the pre-sentence report or submissions as to sentence.

Substitution of Judge
POWERS OF SUBSTITUTE YOUTH JUSTICE COURT JUDGE

131. (1) A youth justice court judge who acts in the place of another youth justice court judge under subsection 669.2(1) (continuation of proceedings) of the *Criminal Code* shall

(a) if an adjudication has been made, proceed to sentence the young person or make the order that, in the circumstances, is authorized by law; or

(b) if no adjudication has been made, recommence the trial as if no evidence had been taken.

TRANSCRIPT OF EVIDENCE ALREADY GIVEN

(2) A youth justice court judge who recommences a trial under paragraph (1)(b) may, if the parties consent, admit into evidence a transcript of any evidence already given in the case.

Exclusion from Hearing
EXCLUSION FROM HEARING

132. (1) Subject to subsection (2), a court or justice before whom proceedings are carried out under this Act may exclude any person from all or part of the proceedings if the court or justice considers that the person's presence is unnecessary to the conduct of the proceedings and the court or justice is of the opinion that

(a) any evidence or information presented to the court or justice would be seriously injurious or seriously prejudicial to

(i) the young person who is being dealt with in the proceedings,

(ii) a child or young person who is a witness in the proceedings, or

(iii) a child or young person who is aggrieved by or the victim of the offence charged in the proceedings; or

(b) it would be in the interest of public morals, the maintenance of order or the proper administration of justice to exclude any or all members of the public from the court room.

EXCEPTION

(2) Subject to section 650 (accused to be present) of the *Criminal Code* and except if it is necessary for the purposes of subsection 34(9) (nondisclosure of medical or psychological report) of this Act, a court or justice may not, under subsection (1), exclude from proceedings under this Act

(a) the prosecutor;

(b) the young person who is being dealt with in the proceedings, the counsel or a parent of the young person or any adult assisting the young person under subsection 25(7);

(c) the provincial director or his or her agent; or

(d) the youth worker to whom the young person's case has been assigned.

EXCLUSION AFTER ADJUDICATION OR DURING REVIEW

(3) A youth justice court, after it has found a young person guilty of an offence, or a youth justice court or a review board, during a review, may, in its discretion, exclude from the court or from a hearing of the review board any person other than the following, when it is being presented with information the knowledge of which might, in its opinion, be seriously injurious or seriously prejudicial to the young person:

(a) the young person or his or her counsel;

(b) the provincial director or his or her agent;

(c) the youth worker to whom the young person's case has been assigned; and

(d) the Attorney General.

EXCEPTION

(4) The exception set out in paragraph (3)(a) is subject to subsection 34(9) (nondisclosure of medical or psychological report) of this Act and section 650 (accused to be present) of the *Criminal Code*.

Transfer of Charges
TRANSFER OF CHARGES

133. Despite subsections 478(1) and (3) of the *Criminal Code*, a young person charged with an offence that is alleged to have been committed in one province may, if the Attorney General of the province consents, appear before a youth justice court of any other province and

(a) if the young person pleads guilty to that offence and the youth justice court is satisfied that the facts support the charge, the court shall find the young person guilty of the offence alleged in the information or indictment; and

(b) if the young person pleads not guilty to that offence, or pleads guilty but the court is not satisfied that the facts support the charge, the young person shall, if he or she was detained in custody prior to the appearance, be returned to custody and dealt with according to law.

Forfeiture of Recognizances

APPLICATIONS FOR FORFEITURE OF RECOGNIZANCES

134. Applications for the forfeiture of recognizances of young persons shall be made to the youth justice court.

PROCEEDINGS IN CASE OF DEFAULT

135. (1) When a recognizance binding a young person has been endorsed with a certificate under subsection 770(1) of the *Criminal Code*, a youth justice court judge shall

(a) on the request of the Attorney General, fix a time and place for the hearing of an application for the forfeiture of the recognizance; and

(b) after fixing a time and place for the hearing, cause to be sent by confirmed delivery service, not less than ten days before the time so fixed, to each principal and surety named in the recognizance, directed to his or her latest known address, a notice requiring him or her to appear at the time and place fixed by the judge to show cause why the recognizance should not be forfeited.

ORDER FOR FORFEITURE OF RECOGNIZANCE

(2) When subsection (1) is complied with, the youth justice court judge may, after giving the parties an opportunity to be heard, in his or her discretion grant or refuse the application and make any order with respect to the forfeiture of the recognizance that he or she considers proper.

JUDGMENT DEBTORS OF THE CROWN

(3) If, under subsection (2), a youth justice court judge orders forfeiture of a recognizance, the principal and his or her sureties become judgment debtors of the Crown, each in the amount that the judge orders him or her to pay.

ORDER MAY BE FILED

(4) An order made under subsection (2) may be filed with the clerk of the superior court or, in the province of Quebec, the prothonotary and, if an order is filed, the clerk or the prothonotary shall issue a writ of fieri facias in Form 34 set out in the *Criminal Code* and deliver it to the sheriff of each of the territorial divisions in which any of the principal and his or her sureties resides, carries on business or has property.

IF A DEPOSIT HAS BEEN MADE

(5) If a deposit has been made by a person against whom an order for forfeiture of a recognizance has been made, no writ of fieri facias shall issue, but the amount of the deposit shall be transferred by the person who has custody of it to the person who is entitled by law to receive it.

SUBSECTIONS 770(2) AND (4) OF *CRIMINAL CODE* DO NOT APPLY

(6) Subsections 770(2) (transmission of recognizance) and (4) (transmission of deposit) of the *Criminal Code* do not apply in respect of proceedings under this Act.

SECTIONS 772 AND 773 OF *CRIMINAL CODE* APPLY

(7) Sections 772 (levy under writ) and 773 (committal when writ not satisfied) of the *Criminal Code* apply in respect of writs of fieri facias issued under this section as if they were issued under section 771 (proceedings in case of default) of that Act.

Offences and Punishment

INDUCING A YOUNG PERSON, ETC.

136. (1) Every person who

(a) induces or assists a young person to leave unlawfully a place of custody or other place in which the young person has been placed in accordance with a youth sentence or a disposition imposed under the *Young Offenders Act*, chapter Y-1 of the Revised Statutes of Canada, 1985,

(b) unlawfully removes a young person from a place referred to in paragraph (a),

(c) knowingly harbours or conceals a young person who has unlawfully left a place referred to in paragraph (a),

(d) wilfully induces or assists a young person to breach or disobey a term or condition of a youth sentence or other order of the youth justice court, or a term or condition of a disposition or other order under the *Young Offenders Act*, chapter Y-1 of the Revised Statutes of Canada, 1985, or

(e) wilfully prevents or interferes with the performance by a young person of a term or condition of a youth sentence or other order of the youth justice court, or a term or condition of a disposition or other order under the *Young Offenders Act*, chapter Y-1 of the Revised Statutes of Canada, 1985,

is guilty of an indictable offence and liable to imprisonment for a term not exceeding two years or is guilty of an offence punishable on summary conviction.

ABSOLUTE JURISDICTION OF PROVINCIAL COURT JUDGE

(2) The jurisdiction of a provincial court judge to try an adult charged with an indictable offence under this section is absolute and does not depend on the consent of the accused.

FAILURE TO COMPLY WITH SENTENCE OR DISPOSITION

137. Every person who is subject to a youth sentence imposed under any of paragraphs 42(2)(c) to (m) or (s) of this Act, to a victim fine surcharge ordered under subsection 53(2) of this Act or to a disposition made under any of paragraphs 20(1)(a.1) to (g), (j) or (l) of the *Young Offenders Act*, chapter Y-1 of the Revised Statutes of Canada, 1985, and who wilfully fails or refuses to comply with that sentence, surcharge or disposition is guilty of an offence punishable on summary conviction.

OFFENCES

138. (1) Every person who contravenes subsection 110(1) (identity of offender not to be published), 111(1) (identity of victim or witness not to be published), 118(1) (no access to records unless authorized) or 128(3) (disposal of R.C.M.P. records) or section 129 (no subsequent disclosure) of this Act, or subsection 38(1) (identity not to be published), (1.12) (no subsequent disclosure), (1.14) (no subsequent disclosure by school) or (1.15) (information to be kept separate), 45(2) (destruction of records) or 46(1) (prohibition against disclosure) of the *Young Offenders Act*, chapter Y-1 of the Revised Statutes of Canada, 1985,

(a) is guilty of an indictable offence and liable to imprisonment for a term not exceeding two years; or

(b) is guilty of an offence punishable on summary conviction.

PROVINCIAL COURT JUDGE HAS ABSOLUTE JURISDICTION ON INDICTMENT

(2) The jurisdiction of a provincial court judge to try an adult charged with an offence under paragraph (1)(a) is absolute and does not depend on the consent of the accused.

OFFENCE AND PUNISHMENT

139. (1) Every person who wilfully fails to comply with section 30 (designated place of temporary detention), or with an undertaking entered into under subsection 31(3) (condition of placement),

(a) is guilty of an indictable offence and liable to imprisonment for a term not exceeding two years; or

(b) is guilty of an offence punishable on summary conviction.

OFFENCE AND PUNISHMENT

(2) Every person who wilfully fails to comply with section 7 (designated place of temporary detention) of the *Young Offenders Act*, chapter Y-1 of the Revised Statutes of Canada, 1985, or with an undertaking entered into under subsection 7.1(2) (condition of placement) of that Act is guilty of an offence punishable on summary conviction.

PUNISHMENT

(3) Any person who uses or authorizes the use of an application form in contravention of subsection 82(3) (application for employment) is guilty of an offence punishable on summary conviction.

Application of Criminal Code

APPLICATION OF *CRIMINAL CODE*

140. Except to the extent that it is inconsistent with or excluded by this Act, the provisions of the *Criminal Code* apply, with any modifications that the circumstances require, in respect of offences alleged to have been committed by young persons.

SECTIONS OF *CRIMINAL CODE* APPLICABLE

141. (1) Except to the extent that they are inconsistent with or excluded by this Act, section 16 (defence of mental disorder) and Part XX.1 (mental disorder) of the *Criminal Code*, except sections 672.65 (capping of offences) and 672.66 (hearing application procedures), apply, with any modifications that the circumstances require, in respect of proceedings under this Act in relation to offences alleged to have been committed by young persons.

NOTICE AND COPIES TO COUNSEL AND PARENTS

(2) For the purposes of subsection (1),

(a) wherever in Part XX.1 (mental disorder) of the *Criminal Code* a reference is made to a copy to be sent or otherwise given to an accused or a party to the proceedings, the reference shall be read as including a reference to a copy to be sent or otherwise given to

(i) any counsel representing the young person,

(ii) a parent of the young person who is in attendance at the proceedings against the young person, and

(iii) a parent of the young person not in attendance at the proceedings who is, in the opinion of the youth justice court or Review Board, taking an active interest in the proceedings; and

(b) wherever in Part XX.1 (mental disorder) of the *Criminal Code* a reference is made to notice to be given to an accused or a party to proceedings, the reference shall be read as including a reference to notice to be given to a parent of the young person and any counsel representing the young person.

PROCEEDINGS NOT INVALID

(3) Subject to subsection (4), failure to give a notice referred to in paragraph (2)(b) to a parent of a young person does not affect the validity of proceedings under this Act.

EXCEPTION

(4) Failure to give a notice referred to in paragraph (2)(b) to a parent of a young person in any case renders invalid any subsequent proceedings under this Act relating to the case unless

(a) a parent of the young person attends at the court or Review Board with the young person; or

(b) a youth justice court judge or Review Board before whom proceedings are held against the young person

(i) adjourns the proceedings and orders that the notice be given in the manner and to the persons that the judge or Review Board directs, or

(ii) dispenses with the notice if the youth justice court or Review Board is of the opinion that, having regard to the circumstances, the notice may be dispensed with.

NO HOSPITAL ORDER ASSESSMENTS

(5) A youth justice court may not make an order under section 672.11 (assessment order) of the *Criminal Code* in respect of a young person for the purpose of assisting in the determination of a matter mentioned in paragraph (e) of that section.

CONSIDERATIONS OF COURT OR REVIEW BOARD MAKING A DISPOSITION

(6) Before making or reviewing a disposition in respect of a young person under Part XX.1 (mental disorder) of the *Criminal Code*, a youth justice court or Review Board shall consider the age and special needs of the young person and any representations or submissions made by a parent of the young person.

CAP APPLICABLE TO YOUNG PERSONS

(7) Subject to subsection (9), for the purpose of applying subsection 672.64(3) (cap for various offences) of the *Criminal Code* to proceedings under this Act in relation to an offence alleged to have been committed by a young person, the applicable cap shall be the maximum period during which the young person would be subject to a youth sentence by the youth justice court if found guilty of the offence.

APPLICATION TO INCREASE CAP OF UNFIT YOUNG PERSON SUBJECT TO ADULT SENTENCE

(8) If a young person is charged with a presumptive offence or notice has been given under subsection 64(2) (intention to seek adult sentence), and the young person is found unfit to stand trial, the Attorney General may apply to the court to increase the cap that will apply to the young person.

CONSIDERATION OF YOUTH JUSTICE COURT FOR INCREASE IN CAP

(9) The youth justice court, after giving the Attorney General and the counsel and a parent of the young person in respect of whom subsection (8) applies an opportunity to be heard, shall take into consideration

(a) the seriousness and circumstances of the alleged offence,

(b) the age, maturity, character and background of the young person and any previous criminal record,

(c) the likelihood that the young person will cause significant harm to any person if released on expiry of the cap that applies to the young person under subsection (7), and

(d) the respective caps that would apply to the young person under this Act and under the *Criminal Code*.

If the court is satisfied that it would make an order under subsection 64(5) (application for adult sentence unopposed) or 70(2) (no application by young person to avoid adult sentence) or paragraph 72(1)(b) (imposition of adult sentence) if the young person were fit to stand trial, it shall apply to the young person the cap that would apply to an adult for the same offence.

PRIMA FACIE CASE TO BE MADE EVERY YEAR

(10) For the purpose of applying subsection 672.33(1) (fitness to stand trial) of the *Criminal Code* to proceedings under this Act in relation to an offence alleged to have been committed by a young person, wherever in that subsection a reference is made to two years, there shall be substituted a reference to one year.

DESIGNATION OF HOSPITALS FOR YOUNG PERSONS

(11) A reference in Part XX.1 (mental disorder) of the *Criminal Code* to a hospital in a province shall be construed as a reference to a hospital designated by the Minister of Health for the province for the custody, treatment or assessment of young persons.

DEFINITION OF "REVIEW BOARD"

(12) In this section, "Review Board" has the meaning assigned by section 672.1 of the *Criminal Code*.

PART XXVII AND SUMMARY CONVICTION TRIAL PROVISIONS OF *CRIMINAL CODE* TO APPLY

142. (1) Subject to this section and except to the extent that they are inconsistent with this Act, the provisions of Part XXVII (summary conviction offences) of the *Criminal Code*, and any other provisions of that Act that apply in respect of summary conviction offences and relate to trial proceedings, apply to proceedings under this Act

(a) in respect of an order under section 810 (recognizance—fear of injury or damage), 810.01 (recognizance—fear of criminal organization offence) or 810.2 (recognizance—fear of serious personal injury offence) of that Act or an offence under section 811 (breach of recognizance) of that Act;

(b) in respect of a summary conviction offence; and

(c) in respect of an indictable offence as if it were defined in the enactment creating it as a summary conviction offence.

INDICTABLE OFFENCES

(2) For greater certainty and despite subsection (1) or any other provision of this Act, an indictable offence committed by a young person is, for the purposes of this Act or any other Act of Parliament, an indictable offence.

ATTENDANCE OF YOUNG PERSON

(3) Section 650 of the *Criminal Code* applies in respect of proceedings under this Act, whether the proceedings relate to an indictable offence or an offence punishable on summary conviction.

LIMITATION PERIOD

(4) In proceedings under this Act, subsection 786(2) of the *Criminal Code* does not apply in respect of an indictable offence.

COSTS

(5) Section 809 of the *Criminal Code* does not apply in respect of proceedings under this Act.

Procedure

COUNTS CHARGED IN INFORMATION

143. Indictable offences and offences punishable on summary conviction may under this Act be charged in the same information or indictment and tried jointly.

ISSUE OF SUBPOENA

144. (1) If a person is required to attend to give evidence before a youth justice court, the subpoena directed to that person may be issued by a youth justice court judge, whether or not the person whose attendance is required is within the same province as the youth justice court.

SERVICE OF SUBPOENA

(2) A subpoena issued by a youth justice court and directed to a person who is not within the same province as the youth justice court shall be served personally on the person to whom it is directed.

WARRANT

145. A warrant issued by a youth justice court may be executed anywhere in Canada.

Evidence

GENERAL LAW ON ADMISSIBILITY OF STATEMENTS TO APPLY

146. (1) Subject to this section, the law relating to the admissibility of statements made by persons accused of committing offences applies in respect of young persons.

WHEN STATEMENTS ARE ADMISSIBLE

(2) No oral or written statement made by a young person who is less than eighteen years old, to a peace officer or to any other person who is, in law, a person in authority, on the arrest or detention of the young person or in circumstances where the peace officer or other person has reasonable grounds for believing that the young person has committed an offence is admissible against the young person unless

(a) the statement was voluntary;

(b) the person to whom the statement was made has, before the statement was made, clearly explained to the young person, in language appropriate to his or her age and understanding, that

(i) the young person is under no obligation to make a statement,

(ii) any statement made by the young person may be used as evidence in proceedings against him or her,

(iii) the young person has the right to consult counsel and a parent or other person in accordance with paragraph (c), and

(iv) any statement made by the young person is required to be made in the presence of counsel and any other person consulted in accordance with paragraph (c), if any, unless the young person desires otherwise;

(c) the young person has, before the statement was made, been given a reasonable opportunity to consult

(i) with counsel, and

(ii) with a parent or, in the absence of a parent, an adult relative or, in the absence of a parent and an adult relative, any other appropriate adult chosen by the young person, as long as that person is not a co-accused, or under investigation, in respect of the same offence; and

(d) if the young person consults a person in accordance with paragraph (c), the young person has been given a reasonable opportunity to make the statement in the presence of that person.

EXCEPTION IN CERTAIN CASES FOR ORAL STATEMENTS

(3) The requirements set out in paragraphs (2)(b) to (d) do not apply in respect of oral statements if they are made spontaneously by the young person to a peace officer or other person in authority before that person has had a reasonable opportunity to comply with those requirements.

WAIVER OF RIGHT TO CONSULT

(4) A young person may waive the rights under paragraph (2)(c) or (d) but any such waiver

(a) must be recorded on video tape or audio tape; or

(b) must be in writing and contain a statement signed by the young person that he or she has been informed of the right being waived.

WAIVER OF RIGHT TO CONSULT

(5) When a waiver of rights under paragraph (2)(c) or (d) is not made in accordance with subsection (4) owing to a technical irregularity, the youth justice court may determine that the waiver is valid if it is satisfied that the young person was informed of his or her rights, and voluntarily waived them.

ADMISSIBILITY OF STATEMENTS

(6) When there has been a technical irregularity in complying with paragraphs (2)(b) to (d), the youth justice court may admit into

evidence a statement referred to in subsection (2), if satisfied that the admission of the statement would not bring into disrepute the principle that young persons are entitled to enhanced procedural protection to ensure that they are treated fairly and their rights are protected.

STATEMENTS MADE UNDER DURESS ARE INADMISSIBLE

(7) A youth justice court judge may rule inadmissible in any proceedings under this Act a statement made by the young person in respect of whom the proceedings are taken if the young person satisfies the judge that the statement was made under duress imposed by any person who is not, in law, a person in authority.

MISREPRESENTATION OF AGE

(8) A youth justice court judge may in any proceedings under this Act rule admissible any statement or waiver by a young person if, at the time of the making of the statement or waiver,

(a) the young person held himself or herself to be eighteen years old or older;

(b) the person to whom the statement or waiver was made conducted reasonable inquiries as to the age of the young person and had reasonable grounds for believing that the young person was eighteen years old or older; and

(c) in all other circumstances the statement or waiver would otherwise be admissible.

PARENT, ETC., NOT A PERSON IN AUTHORITY

(9) For the purpose of this section, a person consulted under paragraph (2)(c) is, in the absence of evidence to the contrary, deemed not to be a person in authority.

STATEMENTS NOT ADMISSIBLE AGAINST YOUNG PERSON

147. (1) Subject to subsection (2), if a young person is assessed in accordance with an order made under subsection 34(1) (medical or psychological assessment), no statement or reference to a statement made by the young person during the course and for the purposes of the assessment to the person who conducts the assessment or to anyone acting under that person's direction is admissible in evidence, without the consent of the young person, in any proceeding before a court, tribunal, body or person with jurisdiction to compel the production of evidence.

EXCEPTIONS

(2) A statement referred to in subsection (1) is admissible in evidence for the purposes of

(a) making a decision on an application heard under section 71 (hearing—adult sentences);

(b) determining whether the young person is unfit to stand trial;

(c) determining whether the balance of the mind of the young person was disturbed at the time of commission of the alleged offence, if the young person is a female person charged with an offence arising out of the death of her newly-born child;

(d) making or reviewing a sentence in respect of the young person;

(e) determining whether the young person was, at the time of the commission of an alleged offence, suffering from automatism or a mental disorder so as to be exempt from criminal responsibility by virtue of subsection 16(1) of the *Criminal Code*, if the accused puts his or her mental capacity for criminal intent into issue, or if the prosecutor raises the issue after verdict;

(f) challenging the credibility of a young person in any proceeding if the testimony of the young person is inconsistent in a material particular with a statement referred to in subsection (1) that the young person made previously;

(g) establishing the perjury of a young person who is charged with perjury in respect of a statement made in any proceeding;

(h) deciding an application for an order under subsection 104(1) (continuation of custody);

(i) setting the conditions under subsection 105(1) (conditional supervision);

(j) conducting a review under subsection 109(1) (review of decision); or

(k) deciding an application for a disclosure order under subsection 127(1) (information about a young person).

TESTIMONY OF A PARENT

148. (1) In any proceedings under this Act, the testimony of a parent as to the age of a person of whom he or she is a parent is admissible as evidence of the age of that person.

EVIDENCE OF AGE BY CERTIFICATE OR RECORD

(2) In any proceedings under this Act,

(a) a birth or baptismal certificate or a copy of it purporting to be certified under the hand of the person in whose custody those records are held is evidence of the age of the person named in the certificate or copy; and

(b) an entry or record of an incorporated society that has had the control or care of the person alleged to have committed the offence in respect of which the proceedings are taken at or about the time the person came to Canada is evidence of the age of that person, if the entry or record was made before the time when the offence is alleged to have been committed.

OTHER EVIDENCE

(3) In the absence of any certificate, copy, entry or record mentioned in subsection (2), or in corroboration of that certificate, copy, entry or record, the youth justice court may receive and act on any other information relating to age that it considers reliable.

WHEN AGE MAY BE INFERRED

(4) In any proceedings under this Act, the youth justice court may draw inferences as to the age of a person from the person's appearance or from statements made by the person in direct examination or cross-examination.

ADMISSIONS

149. (1) A party to any proceedings under this Act may admit any relevant fact or matter for the purpose of dispensing with proof of it, including any fact or matter the admissibility of which depends on a ruling of law or of mixed law and fact.

OTHER PARTY MAY ADDUCE EVIDENCE

(2) Nothing in this section precludes a party to a proceeding from adducing evidence to prove a fact or matter admitted by another party.

MATERIAL EVIDENCE

150. Any evidence material to proceedings under this Act that would not but for this section be admissible in evidence may, with the consent of the parties to the proceedings and if the young person is represented by counsel, be given in such proceedings.

EVIDENCE OF A CHILD OR YOUNG PERSON

151. The evidence of a child or a young person may be taken in proceedings under this Act only after the youth justice court judge or the justice in the proceedings has

(a) if the witness is a child, instructed the child as to the duty to speak the truth and the consequences of failing to do so; and

(b) if the witness is a young person and the judge or justice considers it necessary, instructed the young person as to the duty to speak the truth and the consequences of failing to do so.

PROOF OF SERVICE

152. (1) For the purposes of this Act, service of any document may be proved by oral evidence given under oath by, or by the affidavit or statutory declaration of, the person claiming to have personally served it or sent it by confirmed delivery service.

PROOF OF SIGNATURE AND OFFICIAL CHARACTER UNNECESSARY

(2) If proof of service of any document is offered by affidavit or statutory declaration, it is not necessary to prove the signature or official character of the person making or taking the affidavit or declaration, if the official character of that person appears on the face of the affidavit or declaration.

SEAL NOT REQUIRED

153. It is not necessary to the validity of any information, indictment, summons, warrant, minute, sentence, conviction, order or other process or document laid, issued, filed or entered in any proceedings under this Act that any seal be attached or affixed to it.

Forms, Regulations and Rules of Court

FORMS

154. (1) The forms prescribed under section 155, varied to suit the case, or forms to the like effect, are valid and sufficient in the circumstances for which they are provided.

IF FORMS NOT PRESCRIBED

(2) In any case for which forms are not prescribed under section 155, the forms set out in Part XXVIII of the *Criminal Code*, with any modifications that the circumstances require, or other appropriate forms, may be used.

REGULATIONS

155. The Governor in Council may make regulations

(a) prescribing forms that may be used for the purposes of this Act;

(b) establishing uniform rules of court for youth justice courts across Canada, including rules regulating the practice and procedure to be followed by youth justice courts; and

(c) generally for carrying out the purposes and provisions of this Act.

Agreements with Provinces

AGREEMENTS WITH PROVINCES

156. Any minister of the Crown may, with the approval of the Governor in Council, enter into an agreement with the government of any province providing for payments by Canada to the province in respect of costs incurred by the province or a municipality in the province for care of and services provided to young persons dealt with under this Act.

Programs

COMMUNITY-BASED PROGRAMS

157. The Attorney General of Canada or a minister designated by the lieutenant governor in council of a province may establish the following types of community-based programs:

(a) programs that are an alternative to judicial proceedings, such as victim-offender reconciliation programs, mediation programs and restitution programs;

(b) programs that are an alternative to detention before sentencing, such as bail supervision programs; and

(c) programs that are an alternative to custody, such as intensive support and supervision programs, and programs to carry out attendance orders.

PART 8
TRANSITIONAL PROVISIONS
. . .

PART 9
CONSEQUENTIAL AMENDMENTS, REPEAL AND COMING INTO FORCE
. . .

Glossary

acculturation
process whereby migrants to a society learn its ways of doing things but do not necessarily give up their ethnic identity

aggravating factor
a circumstance or action during or after the commission of an offence that supports a more onerous sentence—for example, "gay bashing" (a hate-motivated crime)

al-Qaida
international terrorist network that has claimed responsibility for several attacks on western cities; "al-Qaida" means "the base"

alternative dispute resolution (ADR)
a range of processes for dispute resolution that are truly alternative to the existing judicial system, as well as processes that modify or improve upon practices and procedures currently in use within the existing court system (i.e., mediation)

anomie
state of "normlessness" where an individual who has failed to learn the norms and values of society and thus to adapt to society is likely to become a social outsider, living on the margins of society

ascribed ethnicity
characteristics assigned to ethnic group members by the host society, whether or not the ethnic group members actually possess these characteristics

assimilation
process whereby migrants to a society learn its ways of doing things and give up or cease to be seen as having a separate ethnic identity

barrio
Spanish word for "neighbourhood"; used in English to describe a Hispanic neighbourhood or district

caution
formal warning, delivered by police or Crown personnel, under the extrajudicial measures section of the YCJA; in the arrest context, a formal warning, often in a rehearsed or set form, delivered to a person under arrest or being questioned, for the purpose of advising that person of his or her rights

certificate of offence
unsworn, formulaic document (that is, following a set form and requiring set content) for the commencement of certain (less serious) types of proceedings

certificate of parking infraction
parking "ticket" or "tag"

child in need of protection
legal definition/determination, based on an established set of criteria and evidence, that forms the basis of a protective order

classical theory of crime
older theory that assumes that individuals make rational choices about committing crimes and can be deterred from crime by severe punishment, which inflicts a cost that a rational person would choose to avoid

cohort study
study in which the researcher follows a large number of people, or cohort, linked together by some characteristic such as age, profession, or gender to identify and track patterns particular to that cohort

conditional supervision
a portion of a custodial sentence that is served outside custody and during which a youth is subject to strict conditions of behaviour

conflict theory
approach to how societies work that emphasizes conflict, power relations, differences among groups, and social change resulting from group conflict

consensual services
services provided based on the consent of the parties (children and/or their families) and without recourse to a court order

control theory
theory that focuses on different social and environmental factors that shape human behaviour in society

criminogenic needs
unmet needs of an offender—for example, the need for help in controlling anger or in reducing substance abuse—that promote the commission of further crimes

Crown brief
document or package prepared by the police for the benefit of Crown counsel, which sets out the evidence the Crown needs to discharge a burden of proof—for example, the proof required to detain a youth in custody

cybercrime
criminal activity committed on computers over the Internet

disposition
word used in place of "sentence" under the YOA; the YCJA has reverted to the more traditional word "sentence"

diversion
formal or informal process whereby offenders are diverted out of the justice system to have their transgression dealt with in other ways

due process
the administration of justice through the courts in accordance with established rules and principles, especially to enforce and protect private rights

duty counsel
lawyer, either the employee of a court or working under contract for a court, who provides on-the-spot, no-charge (although there may be an eventual charge) advice to unrepresented accused

duty to report
statutorily or legally explicit (as opposed to moral/ethical) requirement to report qualifying incidents or observations

Enlightenment
an intellectual movement characterized by rationalism and scientific inquiry as the basis for understanding the world

environmental theory of crime
theory of crime that assumes that factors in an individual's environment make it more or less likely that the individual will become involved in crime

ethnographic studies
studies that arise from a research approach originally used to describe the social interactions of tribal groups using a variety of observational techniques

extrajudicial measures
in effect, a sort of sentence or remedy imposed under the YCJA, within strict guidelines, by police or Crown personnel, without a finding of guilt or resort to the court system; ways used by police to divert young people who are (precharged) suspected of committing a crime from the criminal justice system

extrajudicial sanctions
in the context of the YCJA, extrajudicial measures that go beyond cautions to impose compliance with a rehabilitative or community service program; post-charge programs designed for young people, when there is sufficient evidence for prosecution, that address a young person's criminal activities without resort to traditional sentences

family group conferencing
an ADR process with Australian origins that brings together the offender, the victim, and their families to promote healing and to develop a plan to prevent reoffending

functionalist theory
approach to how societies work that emphasizes the way various parts of society function and interact to produce social harmony or equilibrium

gender-specific
associated with persons of one gender to the exclusion of the other

globalization
the increasing economic interdependence of countries worldwide through a growing quantity and variety of cross-border transactions in goods and services, free international capital flows, and rapid, widespread distribution of technology

hackers
individuals who, by means of programming skills, gain illegal access to computer files or networks

hate crime
illegal activity motivated by prejudice against an identifiable group

host society
society to which ethnic migrants come and to which they must adapt in some way

incarceration
imprisonment

information
statement sworn, typically before a justice of the peace, for the purpose of laying a more serious charge

intensive rehabilitation and supervision sentence
custody and/or supervision that involves participation in treatment or rehabilitation programs designed to treat the causes of offending in mentally ill youth

interest-based mediation
a type of mediation based on a third-party neutral assisting the parties to understand the needs and desires of each other in order to resolve a dispute

judicial interim release
also know as "bail," the release of an accused from pre-trial custody, often on condition of compliance with court-imposed conditions

jurisdiction
the scope of authority of a court; jurisdiction can be based on a defined territory (Ontario court), a defined age range (youth court), a defined class of offences (small claims court), a defined area of law (family court), and so on.

labelling theory
a subtheory of symbolic interactionism that suggests that individuals will "live up to" stereotypical labels—for example, "juvenile delinquent"—ascribed to them by others

liberal construction
principle of statutory interpretation that requires judges to interpret legislation broadly (liberally) to promote the accomplishment of a general statutory objective

mitigating factor
a circumstance or action during or after the commission of an offence that supports a lighter sentence—for example, sincere and expressed remorse for harm done

motions and applications
mini-hearings, separate from the main trial, to resolve preliminary, usually procedural, issues

neglect
failure of a person responsible for a child to provide necessaries or a minimum standard of care or supervision

organically based
symptoms or behaviours that flow from a disease, defect, or disability of the physical body

parens patriae
legal doctrine based on a concept of the state as parent/protector in relation to its citizens

person in authority
for the purpose of the YCJA, any person that a reasonable young person might perceive as a potential agent of the criminal justice system

piracy
unauthorized use or reproduction of copyrighted or patented software or other creative materials

positivist school of thought
behavioural/criminological theory that places an emphasis on rehabilitation and that attributes criminal behaviour, at least in part, to the influence of social problems on the individual

Potemkin village
place that has a superficial facade that looks pleasant and prosperous but that hides an ugly and unpleasant reality; named after Catherine the Great's prime minister, who erected fake villages along a route Catherine travelled so that she would not have to look at the misery in which her peasants actually lived

preamble
general introductory statement that precedes the actual provisions of a statute and that provides information about the statute's general purposes and objectives

procedural provision
provision that prescribes procedures or rules that govern how justice will be administered rather than regulating a substantive matter

provincial director
for the purpose of the YCJA, a person or "a group or class of persons"—that is, certain members of the provincial corrections administration—designated by a provincial government to perform a wide range of functions under the legislation (for example, assigning the level of custody placements and ensuring that pre-sentence reports are completed)

recidivism
phenomenon of a prisoner re-offending and being sent back to prison for subsequent offences

reintegration leave
a period spent out of custody, with leave of the provincial director, for making arrangements or participating in activities that will facilitate the youth's reintegration into the community

reparation
payment or service provided to make up for a victim's loss or injury

representations
in this context, evidence provided by the offender that is intended to excuse or mitigate guilt, and thus support a lighter penalty

residential services
services provided to children living apart from their families, in foster homes or in other child welfare facilities

restorative justice
an approach to justice that focuses on repairing the harm caused by crime; the intention is to hold the offender responsible for his or her actions by providing an opportunity for the parties directly affected by the crime (i.e., victim(s), offender, and community) to seek a resolution that affords healing and reparation

sanction
in the YCJA context, an extrajudicial measure that goes beyond a caution to impose compliance with a rehabilitative or community service program

secure treatment program
program designed to treat mentally ill children that incorporates restrictions on their liberty, either to ensure completion of the program or for the protection of the public

self-report studies
method of data gathering that relies on self-administered surveys or questionnaires given to a target group in order to obtain a group profile of the identified behaviours in which the researcher is interested

sentencing circle
a group of people, including the accused, the victim, families, justice system players, and members of the community who make recommendations to the court regarding appropriate sentencing

show-cause hearing
also known as a bail hearing; a court appearance by the accused during which the Crown seeks to show cause for the continued detention of the accused pending trial

socialization
process whereby one learns the norms, values, and culture of the society or social group

spontaneous statement
a statement by a youth that is offered without being prompted by police questions or comments and before police have had a chance to advise the youth of his or her s. 146 rights

status offences
offences associated with a personal characteristic such as age or gender

statutory prioritization
organization of a statute in a way that conveys information about legislative priorities, for example, by the use of levels of numbers or headings to give precedence to certain provisions

structural unemployment
persistent and permanent unemployment in a job market that is contracting and thus not providing enough work for the working population

symbolic interactionist theory
approach that holds that individual behaviour is influenced through people's interaction with others and that self-image is constructed by a conscious reading of the symbolic meaning of these social interactions

uniform crime reports
system for classifying reported incidents by type of crime, based on crime detected by police and reported by public; used by virtually all law enforcement agencies in Canada and the United States, it permits comparisons among jurisdictions and comparisons of data in any specific year with data from previous or subsequent years

victim impact statement
a written summary, authored by a victim, of the effects that an offence has had on his or her life, and of any ongoing problems that the incident can be expected to cause for him or her

victimization surveys
crime surveys based on incidents of crime (either reported to police or unreported) as described by self-identified victims

violent offender
under the YCJA, a judicial designation—that is, a judge designates a person a violent offender, and the designation has various implications under the legislation

waiver
the verbal or written giving up or dispensing with the exercise of a legal right

ward/wardship
traditional legal term that implies both clienthood as we understand it today and a fiduciary/protective relationship

xenophobia
fear of strangers or the unknown, especially cultural and racial elements that are considered alien

youth justice court
either a court specifically constituted for the purpose of hearing youth trials, or an existing adult court designated (temporarily or permanently) for that purpose

Index

abuse, 80

acculturation, 38

age-appropriate explanation, 147

aggravating factor, 181

al-Qaida, 9, 221

alternative dispute resolution (ADR), 202, 204, 206

anomie, 42

arrest
    decision to, 136-37
    questioning
        person in authority, 145-46
        preliminary issues, 143-44
        right to consult with counsel and parents, 149-51
        right to information, 147
        right to silence, 148-49
        spontaneous statements, 151
        timing of cautions, 144-45
        voluntariness, 146
    searches and Charter rights, 143
    statements, admissibility of, 141-42

ascribed ethnicity, 37

assimilation, 38

barrio, 38

boot camp, 54-55

break and enter, 31

caution, 121, 136

certificate of offence, 94

certificate of parking infraction, 94

Charter protection, 143

Child and Family Services Act
    abuse or neglect offences, 80
    child protection proceedings, 78-80
    consensual services, 75-76
    delivery of services, 75
    detention of adolescents, 81-82
    duty of report abuse or neglect, 76-78
    economic issue, 84-85
    mental disorders, children and, 83-84
    purposes of, 74-75
    residential service, 76
    rights of children under custody, 82-83

child in need of protection, 78

classical theory of crime, 52

cohort study, 53

community action programs
    community policing, 57-58
    diversion, 56-57
    early intervention, 60
    parenting, 60
    schools, 58-59

community policing, 57-58

conditional supervision, 186

conference
    allowance, 161-62
    types of, 173
    youth committees, and, 172-73

conflict theory, 34

consensual services, 76

control theory, 42

counsel, right to, 149-51, 170-72

criminogenic needs, 62

Crown brief, 160

cybercrime, 218

demographic patterns, 220

detention
    adolescents, and, 81-82
    first police contact
        arrest decision, 136
        extrajudicial measures, 137-41
        suspect's age, relevance of, 134-35
        witness or suspect, determination, 135-36
    pre-trial, 158-61, 163-64
    rights, adolescents, 82

deterrence-based approaches, 53-55

disposition, 124

diversion, 56-57

due process, 105

duty counsel, 172, 174

duty to report, 76

early intervention, 60-61

economic deprivation, 38-39

Education Act, 96-97

Enlightenment, 5

environmental theory of crime, 52

ethnographic studies, 35
extrajudicial measures
    consideration of, 137-38
    referrals, 138-39
    restorative justice, and, 203
    sanctions, 139-41, 173-74
extrajudicial sanctions, 121, 139, 203

family and upbringing, 41, 60
family group conferencing, 205-6
functionalist theory, 34

gangs, 33-34, 214-15
gender roles, 215-17
gender-specific, 217
globalization, 218
gun violence, 33-34, 214-15

hackers, 219
hate crime, 220
Highway Traffic Act, 97
host society, 37

incarceration, 52
Industrial Revolution, 5
information, 94
intensive rehabilitation and supervision sentence, 186
interest-based mediation, 204-5
international tensions, 220-21

judicial interim release, 157, 163-64
jurisdiction, 169
juvenile delinquent, 5, 36
Juvenile Delinquents Act
    background, 104
    criticisms of, 106-7
    passage of, 105

labelling theory, 36
liberal construction, 121

mental disorders, 83-84
mitigating factor, 181
motions and applications, 174
motor vehicle theft, 31
multisystemic therapy, 57

neglect, 76

organically based, 41

parens patriae, 105, 107
parents, *see also* family and upbringing
    right to consult, 149-51
person in authority, 145
piracy, 219

positivist school of thought, 104
Potemkin village, 58
preamble, 120
preliminary motions, 174
pre-trial
    judicial interim release, 157, 162-63
    pre-trial detention
        in practice under YCJA, 163-64
        place of, 160-61
        show-cause hearing, 158-59, 161-62
probation, 55-56
procedural provision
Project Turnaround, 55
provincial director, 183
Provincial Offences Act
    Education Act, and, 96-97
    Highway Traffic Act, and, 97
    intent standards under, 92-93
    Liquor Licence Act, and, 98
    parts of, 94
    procedural provisions, 93
    young persons, and, 94-96

questioning
    person in authority, 145-46
    preliminary issues, 143-44
    right to consult with counsel and parents, 149-51
    right to information, 147
    right to silence, 148-49
    spontaneous statements, 151
    timing of cautions, 144-45
    voluntariness, 146

racial minorities, 37-38
recidivism, 7
reintegration leave, 191
reparation, 120
representations, 94
residential services, 76
restorative justice
    alternative dispute resolution, and, 202, 204
    critical assessment, 206-7
    criticisms of, 206
    defined, 201
    family group conferencing, 205-6
    interest-based mediation, 204-5
    sentencing circles, 205
    YCJA provisions, 203-4
    young offenders, and, 202-3
reverse onus, 110

sanction, 121
scared straight programs, 53-54
schools
    causes of youth crime, 42
    prevention of youth crime, 58
    zero tolerance, 10, 32, 59

secure treatment program, 83
self-report studies, 16, 21
sentencing
    adult sentences, imposition of, 187-91
    assessment, YCJA principles, 192-93
    custodial sentences, limits on, 182
        violent offence, determination, 183
    over-age transfer, 191
    pre-sentence reports, 183
    purpose and principles, 180-81
        common-law principles, 181
        deterrence, role of, 181-82
    reintegration into community, 191-92
    termination of youth sentence, 192
    victim impact statements, 184
    YCJA provisions, 179-80
    youth court sentences, range of, 184-87
sentencing circle, 205
show-cause hearing, 158, 161-62
silence, right to, 148-49
socialization, 5
spontaneous statement, 136, 151
statements
    admissibility, 141-42
    spontaneous statements, 151
status offences, 18
statutory prioritization, 120
strict liability offence, 93
structural unemployment, 40
substance abuse, 32
symbolic interactionist theory, 35

technological change, 218-20

unemployment, 39-41
uniform crime reports, 9, 10, 21
urban life, 42

vandalism, 30-31
victim impact statement, 184
victimization surveys, 18
violent offender, 126, 183
voluntary statement, 146

waiver, 148
war on drugs, 10
war on terror, 9
ward/wardship, 79

xenophobia, 8, 9

young offender, 5
Young Offenders Act
    criticisms of, 109-10
    passage of, 107-8
    purposes of, 108-9

youth, social meaning, 4-6
youth crime
    causes of
        economic deprivation, 38-39
        family and upbringing, 41
        racial minorities, and, 37-38
        schools, 42
        urban life, 42
        youth unemployment, 39-41
    contemporary perceptions, 6-7
    data on, 9-20
        adults charged by type of offence, 13
        crime rate, 11
        total persons charged by type of offence, 17
        total youth court cases, 19
        violent crime rate, 11
        youths charged by type of offence, 15
    emerging factors, 8-9
    historical perceptions, 6
    police perceptions, 20
    prevention
        boot camps, 54-55
        imprisonment, 53-55
        probation, and, 55-56
        scared straight programs, 53-54
    theories of
        conflict theory, 34
        functionalist theory, 34
        labelling theory, 36
        symbolic interactionist theory, 35
    types of
        break and enter, 31
        crimes of violence, 32-33
        gangs and gun violence, 33
        motor vehicle theft, 31
        substance abuse, 32
        vandalism, 30-31
Youth Criminal Justice Act
    criticisms of, 110-11
    preamble, 120
    principles and objectives, 120-21
    structure
        custody and supervision, 125
        extrajudicial measures, 121
        general provisions, 127-28
        judicial measures, 122-24
        organization, youth criminal justice system, 121-22
        publication, records, and information, 125-27
        sentencing, 124
youth criminal justice system
    age jurisdiction, 122
    appeals, 176
    conferences, 172-73
    detention before sentencing, 123
    diversion to extrajudicial measures, 173-74

youth criminal justice system *(cont.)*
    medical and psychological reports, 123
    parental involvement, 123
    pleas, 174
    preliminary motions, 174
    process, 175
    referral to child welfare agency, 123-24
    right to counsel, 122
    sentencing
        adult sentences, imposition of, 187-91
        assessment, YCJA principles, 192-93
        custodial sentences, limits on, 182-83
        over-age transfer, 191
        pre-sentence reports, 183
        purpose and principles, 180-82
        reintegration into community, 191-92
        termination of youth sentence, 192
        victim impact statements, 184
        YCJA provisions, 179-80
        youth court sentences, range of, 184-87
    trial by judge and jury, 122
    youth justice committee, 172-73

youth justice committee, 172-73
youth justice court
    establishment of, 169
    jurisdiction, 169-70
    no transfer to adult court, 170
    pleas, 174
    preliminary motions, 174
    right to counsel, 170-72
    sentences in, 184-87
    trial process, 175
youth unemployment, 39